CONTEMPORARY
REGULATORY
POLICY SECOND EDITION

Marc Allen Eisner
Jeff Worsham
Evan J. Ringquist

LYNNE
RIENNER
PUBLISHERS

BOULDER
LONDON

Published in the United States of America in 2006 by
Lynne Rienner Publishers, Inc.
1800 30th Street, Boulder, Colorado 80301
www.rienner.com

and in the United Kingdom by
Lynne Rienner Publishers, Inc.
3 Henrietta Street, Covent Garden, London WC2E 8LU

Library of Congress Cataloging-in-Publication Data
Eisner, Marc Allen.
   Contemporary regulatory policy / Marc Allen Eisner, Jeff Worsham,
Evan J. Ringquist. —2nd ed.
        p. cm.
   Includes bibliographical references and index.
   ISBN-13: 978-1-58826-411-4 (pbk. : alk. paper)
   ISBN-10: 1-58826-411-4 (pbk. : alk. paper)
   1. Administrative procedure—United States. 2. Administrative agencies—United
States—Decision making. 3. Deregulation—United States. I. Worsham, Jeffrey.
II. Ringquist, Evan J., 1962– III. Title.
KF5411.E58 2006
342.73'066—dc22

                                                                    2006010345

British Cataloguing in Publication Data
A Cataloguing in Publication record for this book
is available from the British Library.

Printed and bound in the United States of America

∞ The paper used in this publication meets the requirements
             of the American National Standard for Permanence of
             Paper for Printed Library Materials Z39.48-1992.

   5   4   3   2   1

CONTEMPORARY REGULATORY POLICY

*To Patricia, Jonathan, and Benjamin, the key actors in the
most important of all subsystems, my family.* —M. A. E.

*As always, to Deb, the source of equilibrium in my policy domain.
And to my parents, who gave up on any attempt at control and
settled for influence long ago. And finally, to Megan, Sean, Daniel,
and Madison, who promised to read this book if I dedicated
it to them. Get cracking, there will be a test.* —J. W.

*To Laurie, who regulates my behavior, and to Rachel and
Hannah, who have taught me volumes about the power of
the agents in principal-agent relationships.* —E. J. R.

Contents

List of Illustrations   xi
Preface   xiii

1   A Primer on Regulation   1

What Is Regulation?   *2*
Why Regulate?   *3*
Policy Choices in Regulatory Politics   *11*
Conclusion   *16*

2   Explaining Regulatory Change   19

The Bureaucratic Politics Perspective   *19*
The Subsystems Perspective   *22*
The Principal-Agent Perspective   *24*
In Search of Common Ground   *27*
Salience, Complexity, and the Politics of
    Regulatory Policy   *28*
A Final Note on Administrative Leadership   *31*
Conclusion   *32*

3   A Brief History of Contemporary Regulatory Politics   33

Regulation Before the Contemporary Era   *33*
The Rise of the New Social Regulation   *37*
Deregulation and Regulatory Reform   *39*
A Reagan-Bush Revolution in Regulation?   *42*
The Clinton Presidency: A Mirror Image?   *45*
The George W. Bush Administration:
    Continuity or Change?   *52*
Conclusion   *55*

4   Regulating Market Competition   57
    Antitrust Policy   *58*
    The Antitrust Agencies   *61*
    The Policy Subsystem   *66*
    The Evolution of Antitrust, 1970–Present   *70*
    Conclusion   *87*

5   Regulating Financial Intermediaries   91
    The Evolution of Financial Regulation   *92*
    Regulating Financial Intermediaries:
        The Banking Subsystem   *95*
    Rethinking Regulation   *100*
    Conclusion   *115*

6   Regulating Telecommunications   119
    A Brief History of Telephony   *119*
    Television and Radio   *122*
    Telecommunications Policy   *123*
    The Federal Communications Commission   *124*
    The Policy Subsystem   *131*
    Conclusion   *146*

7   Environmental Protection Regulation   149
    Environmental Policy   *150*
    The Environmental Protection Agency   *162*
    The Policy Subsystem   *168*
    The Evolution of Environmental Regulation,
        1970–Present   *173*

8   Regulating the Workplace   191
    Occupational Safety and Health Policy   *192*
    The Occupational Safety and
        Health Administration   *194*
    The Policy Subsystem   *199*
    The Evolution of Occupational Safety and
        Health Policy   *202*
    Conclusion   *218*

9   Regulating Consumer Products   221
    Consumer Protection Policy   *222*
    The Consumer Protection Agencies   *224*
    The Policy Subsystem   *233*
    The Evolution of Consumer Protection,
        1970–Present   *235*
    Conclusion   *254*

10   Regulating Energy   257
    A Primer on Energy: Physical and
      Market Characteristics *259*
    A Brief History of the Development of
      Federal Energy Policies *264*
    Energy Policy in a Postembargo World *273*
    Deregulating Electric Utilities *294*
    Conclusion *299*

11   Making Sense of Regulation in a Deregulatory Era   303
    Why Regulate? *303*
    Contemporary Regulatory Politics *308*
    The Lessons *312*

List of Acronyms   317
Bibliography   321
Index   355
About the Book   371

Illustrations

Figures

4.1 Major Antitrust Statutes Enforced by the Antitrust Division
     and the FTC   59
4.2 The Salience of Antitrust   60
4.3 Federal Antitrust Regulation Expenditures   62
4.4 The Antitrust Division   63
4.5 The Federal Trade Commission   65
5.1 The Salience of Financial Regulation   92
6.1 The Salience of Telecommunications   125
6.2 The Federal Communications Commission Budget   126
6.3 The Federal Communications Commission   127
7.1 The Salience of Environmental Protection   152
7.2 Major Environmental Statutes Enforced by the EPA   153
7.3 Goals of the 2003–2008 EPA Strategic Plan   163
7.4 The Environmental Protection Agency Budget   164
7.5 The Environmental Protection Agency   165
8.1 The Salience of Occupational Safety and Health   193
8.2 The Occupational Safety and Health Administration Budget   194
8.3 The Occupational Safety and Health Administration   195
9.1 Major Consumer Protection Statutes Enforced by the FTC   223
9.2 Major Consumer Protection Statutes Enforced by the CPSC   224
9.3 The Salience of Consumer Protection   224
9.4 The Federal Trade Commission Budget, by Division   225
9.5 The Consumer Product Safety Commission Budget   229
9.6 The Consumer Product Safety Commission   230

10.1 The Salience of Energy Policy   258
10.2 The Department of Energy   278
10.3 Federal Energy Subsidies   282
11.1 Regulatory Spending   306
11.2 Regulatory Complexity and Salience   307

Table

4.1 Antitrust Division Workload   85

Preface

IF ONE WERE TO SURVEY the news headlines since George W. Bush assumed the presidency in 2001, one would find an interesting panoply of subjects: arsenic in the drinking water, the abandonment of the ergonomics standard, US withdrawal from the Kyoto Protocol, debates over drilling in the Arctic National Wildlife Refuge, financial disasters at WorldCom and Enron, a retreat from efforts to break up the software colossus Microsoft, new restrictions on spam and telemarketers, Super Bowl wardrobe malfunctions, and Howard Stern testing the limits of obscenity standards. On the surface, there is little to connect greenhouse gas concentrations, repetitive stress injuries, and Janet Jackson's prime-time revelations. Yet each controversy involved regulation. Over the course of the past several decades, the government has extended regulatory controls to a range of activities that would have been unimaginable to those who laid the foundations of the regulatory state in the Progressive Era. There are no longer clear distinctions between "regulated" and "unregulated" sectors of the economy.

Regulatory expansion, in turn, has stimulated ongoing demands for regulatory reform and retrenchment. The focus and vigor of federal regulations is highly contested ground, generating high levels of interest group mobilization, contentious congressional hearings, complex court decisions, and histrionic claims on the part of advocates and opponents alike. Given the central role of regulatory debates in national politics today, knowledge of regulation is indispensable for students of public policy and US politics more generally.

This volume provides an overview of contemporary regulatory policies, focusing on some of the central debates and controversies that have emerged in the past three decades. Although we share a healthy respect for

xiii

economic analysis, we are political scientists by training. As a result, the book approaches the subject matter largely through the lens of policy analysis. Also, we have endeavored to present the material in a fashion that maximizes accessibility—without a single equation—so that the book will offer something of substance to a broader informed audience.

Besides accessibility, the book differs from many of the existing volumes on regulation in two important ways. First, we are committed to a simple proposition: institutions matter. The way in which public authority is organized has a profound impact on political accountability, opportunities for participation, and the ultimate success of public policy. Public policy is a pattern of goal-driven actions. Thus the way in which policy is implemented by regulatory agencies must be of central concern to students of regulation. Yet much scholarship on regulation rests heavily on simplifying assumptions that remove organizations from the picture, essentially transforming regulatory studies into exercises in applied microeconomics.

Second, much work on regulation begins with the explicit or implicit assumption that markets are in and of themselves sufficient and that public policy has little positive role to play. We do not aspire to stake out an ideological argument for or against regulation, but rather to explore the factors that have shaped regulatory policy design and implementation. Although we are critics of bad policy and administration—a point that will become evident in each chapter of this book—we are not critics of regulation per se. We believe there are valid reasons to regulate, and these justifications cannot be reduced to discussions of market failure. It is up to the readers to arrive at their own conclusions regarding the ultimate justification for regulatory policy.

*   *   *

Scholarship is a collective endeavor, and we must acknowledge the role of our colleagues, former mentors, students, friends, and readers of the first edition in contributing to our ongoing collaboration. We will not identify here all those who have deepened our understanding of regulation; the bibliography provides some sense of our intellectual debts. We surrender our right to thank those who have helped us over the years so that members of the larger audience (my, we are presumptuous) do not hold them accountable for our work. But we would like to explicitly thank those who have made the study of regulation so much fun: Thorne Auchter, Paul Rand Dixon, Anne Gorsuch-Burford, Rita Lavelle, Manuel Lujan, Ken "Famous" Meier, James C. Miller III, Gale A. Norton, Daniel Oliver, Terrance Scanlon, M. Danny Wall, and James Watt.

Although this volume is a team effort, there was a division of labor. Chapters 1, 2, and 11 were written (and rewritten) collectively. The remaining chapters were written individually, albeit with some prodding and comments by the other members of the team. Eisner claims primary responsibility for Chapters 3 (regulatory history), 4 (antitrust), 8 (occupational safety and health), and 9 (consumer product safety). Ringquist wrote Chapters 7 (environmental protection) and 10 (energy) and collected a wealth of data on salience and budgets that was integral to the case studies. Worsham wrote Chapters 5 (finance) and 6 (telecommunications). As in the first edition, he remains responsible for 87 percent of the acronyms and all errors of omission or commission committed by his coauthors elsewhere in the book.

1

A Primer on Regulation

GOVERNMENT REGULATION of business has been contested ground in the political contests and rhetorical wars of the past several decades. To critics on the right, regulation describes governmental forays into social engineering designed to undermine markets and encumber corporations with any number of politically defined duties and compliance costs (the so-called regulatory burden). To advocates on the left, regulation describes the positive use of public authority to hold corporate America accountable, a goal that is deemed worthy given the immense power exercised by the modern corporation and the lack of any other direct means of forcing businesses to accept responsibility for workplace injuries, environmental degradation, and potentially hazardous consumer products. The term regulation has become something of a code word for government intervention. Unfortunately, the regulatory debates have often brought more heat than light; there is scant evidence that there has been much of a connection between one's willingness to enter the debates and one's knowledge of regulatory policy. This volume is designed, in large part, to provide a relatively detailed overview of regulatory policy and administration in several issue areas. Readers of this volume should have a clear understanding of the key policies and agencies in a variety of these areas, as well as an appreciation for how (and why) patterns of regulation have changed over the course of the past several decades. We need to preface our discussion with some important preliminary material. Specifically, in this chapter, we develop a definition of regulation, survey the justifications and explanations offered for regulation, examine a host of regulatory tools, and introduce competing explanations typically offered for regulatory policy change.

What Is Regulation?

Regulatory policies are a subset of public policies more generally, so it is useful to begin with a somewhat broader question: What is public policy? James Anderson defines policy as "a purposive course of action followed by an actor or set of actors in dealing with a problem or matter of concern" (1984: 3). Similarly, Clarke Cochran and colleagues define public policy as "an intentional course of action followed by a government institution or official for resolving an issue of public concern" (1990: 2). At first glance, this has much to commend it. The focus turns to patterns of action, as opposed to mere rhetoric or symbolic statements of intent. More important, policy is concerned with goal-oriented behavior rather than random acts. Yet there is a problem, as Thomas Dye reminds us that "we can never be sure whether or not a particular action has a goal, or if it does, what that goal is. . . . All we can really observe is what governments choose to do or not to do" (1992: 3). In the end, Dye's definition is quite minimalist: "public policy is whatever governments choose to do or not to do" (1992: 4). The movement away from intentions is useful. They cannot be observed, and it is difficult to make a connection between statements of intent and patterns of action, given that the former may provide an ex post facto justification of the latter. We depart from Dye, however, on the issue of choice. The patterns of public action that constitute policy are the products of a complex interorganizational system and bureaucratic routines (see Chapter 2). While there are choices, they are often distorted by organizational routines that constrain the opportunity set available to decisionmakers. As a result, it makes sense to adopt an even more minimalist definition of policy as patterns of governmental action and inaction.

This does not mean that we are unconcerned with issues of intentionality and choice. Yet human agency must be understood as being constrained by structure. Decisionmakers operate within a dense organizational context in which a given set of values, methodologies, bodies of expertise, and policy tools are favored over others. When making policy, decisionmakers situate current policies in relation to past initiatives, often seeking to reconcile new initiatives with existing organizational capacities. Nor does this minimalist definition mean that we are unconcerned with policy impacts. We must focus attention not only on what the government does (the patterns of action), but also on whether such actions actually reduce problems, on whether they do so in ways that are cost-effective, and on whether this is accomplished without giving rise to a host of unintended consequences that impose costs that exceed the benefits of government intervention.

What of regulation? One may follow Kenneth Meier, who notes that "regulation is any attempt by the government to control the behavior of citizens, corporations, or subgovernments" (1985: 1). Such a definition may appear too broad at first. All public policy is designed to coerce certain patterns of behavior. If control were unnecessary, the desired results would be forthcoming without governmental coercion. A narrower definition would seem appropriate. In this volume, the term *regulation* will be used to describe an array of public policies explicitly designed to govern economic activity and its consequences at the level of the industry, firm, or individual unit of activity. As this definition suggests, we are not concerned with policies affecting economic activity at the macroeconomic level, but with policies that function directly at a microeconomic level. A useful distinction that we retain is made between traditional economic regulation and the new social regulation. *Economic regulations* govern conditions under which firms may enter and exit the market, competitive practices, the size of economic units, or the prices firms can charge. Economic regulations commonly target a single sector of the economy, and the jurisdiction of the agencies that administer these regulations is generally limited to a single economic sector as well. Most of the regulatory initiatives introduced during the Progressive Era and the New Deal were economic regulatory in nature. The *new social regulations,* in contrast, are designed to force corporations to accept greater responsibility for the safety and health of workers and consumers, as well as for the negative by-products of the production process. They also address various social issues that are not directly economic (e.g., equal opportunity in employment). In clear contrast with economic regulations, social regulations apply across sectors; the associated agencies must regulate on an economy-wide basis. Because they impose large costs on firms, they are bitterly opposed by the regulated parties. Although social regulations have been introduced throughout the history of regulation, they became dominant after the late 1960s, as quality-of-life issues became more salient.

Why Regulate?

Given the diversity of regulatory policies, there is no single explanation of why governments regulate. One can identify several rationales for regulation, each of which is premised on a particular vision of governmental authority and expectations concerning how this authority will be exercised. Each provides some important insights. We restrict our attention to five explanations:

1. Regulations are public policies designed to further the "public interest."
2. Regulations constitute efforts to prevent or compensate for market failure.

3. Regulations are the product of industry demands for wealth transfers.
4. Regulations are the product of agencies captured by regulated industries.
5. Regulations are the product of the competition among regional political economies.

These explanations of why governments regulate are not mutually exclusive. Indeed, several may be simultaneously correct.

Regulation and the Public Interest

The first portrayal of regulation reflects the normative assumption that regulation is the application of public authority to further the "public interest." An early use of this rather amorphous concept in regulation was the Supreme Court decision in *Munn v. Illinois* (1877). In this dispute, state regulators had required that owners of grain elevators be licensed and observe legislatively determined maximum rates. When the regulation was challenged, the Court sided with the state, arguing that the extension of regulatory authority was acceptable given that it was a business "affected with the public interest." The Court continued, arguing that this "affectation could logically be extended to transportation, water supply, telephone, electric and gas manufacturing and transporting companies," opening the door to increased government activity (Sanders 1981: 19). In fact, many of the regulatory agencies created at the national level in the next several decades were directed by statute to regulate in the public interest.

What precisely is the public interest? Presumably, the consuming public has an interest in fair prices, honest dealings, and safety that could be secured effectively through regulation. The problem is, the public interest is often used to legitimize self-interested claims. As Deborah Stone notes: "there is virtually never full agreement on the public interest . . . so much of politics is people fighting over what the public interest is and trying to realize their own definitions of it. Let it be an empty box, no matter" (1988: 15). Be this the case, it is difficult to determine what is gained by adopting a public interest explanation of regulation.

Regulation and Market Failure

Competitive markets allow for a relatively cost-free exchange of property and facilitate an efficient allocation of goods via the price mechanism. Prices signal consumers to make substitutions in their consumption decisions; they signal producers to alter their production levels. Prices also signal producers to adjust the mix of inputs they use, leading them to place a greater emphasis on resources with lower prices. When prices exceed marginal costs, thereby resulting in abnormally high profits, firms are induced to enter the market, expanding supply and eroding monopoly profits. Given the importance of these functions to society, one should not be surprised that market maintenance is an often-cited justification for regulation. There are several conditions deemed essential for perfect markets: (1) there must be a sufficient diffusion of economic power such that all actors are price takers; (2) there must be no public goods; (3) there can be no externalities— that is, all costs must be borne by the parties to an economic transaction; (4) buyers and sellers must have complete information; and (5) there can be no transaction costs (see Stokey and Zeckhauser 1978: 297–317). Of course, this is an idealized state of affairs. If any of these conditions are not met, this ideal is compromised (i.e., market failure occurs). Markets are relatively robust, however, and can continue to function even when some of these conditions are violated. Nevertheless, many argue that regulatory policy is necessary as a means of preventing or compensating for market failure. Let us briefly note how regulatory policies may help address some of the key sources of market failure.

Firms as price takers. A first and most important condition for competitive markets is a decentralization of economic power such that each actor is a price taker (i.e., no buyer or seller should be able to influence the price of a good through independent action). When firms exercise such market power, markets fail. One regulatory response has been antitrust (see Chapter 4), which controls mergers and the use of various nonmarket restraints, such as cartels and price-fixing. There are instances, however, in which promoting competition would impose large costs on society. In certain industries, very large economies of scale may create a situation of *natural monopoly*. A natural monopoly exists when the average cost of producing a good declines over the relevant range of demand for that good. Under these circumstances, a single large producer will be able to manufacture the good at a cost no competitor can match. Monopolies tend to be allocatively inefficient. To maximize profit, they restrict production below the level that would be socially optimal and charge higher prices than those obtainable in a competitive market (i.e., they extract monopoly rents). Promoting competition will not help. A more decentralized economic structure might provide the same level of output, but it would do so at a higher price. Regulators may, as a result, opt for a regulated monopoly and guarantee a certain rate of return in hope of creating incentives to produce at a level that would meet demand (see Averch 1990: 34).

Public goods. All public goods share two characteristics: nonexcludability and nonrivalry. *Nonexcludability* occurs when it is impossible or prohibitively expensive to prevent those who do not purchase the good from consuming it. *Nonrivalry* means that one actor's enjoyment of the good does not reduce or prohibit the enjoyment provided to others. By their very nature, public goods are impossible to provide through the market. No entrepreneur will produce a good for which they can neither restrict access nor charge a price. Take the example of clean air, a classic public good. Because of nonrivalry and nonexcludability, it would be irrational for individuals to voluntarily devote resources to the attainment of clean air by paying to reduce air pollution. The rational individual would free-ride (see Olson 1965). Clean air would thus be characterized by nonprovision or gross underprovision. Environmental Protection Agency (EPA) regulations have dealt with this situation by forcing polluters to employ control technologies. The costs are borne by the firms, but also by consumers via prices and by the population as a whole via taxation.

Externalities. An externality is best understood as the difference between the private costs and benefits of a given product and the costs and benefits absorbed by society. For the price mechanism to function effectively, all costs must be reflected in prices. There are legitimate reasons for wanting prices to internalize all costs of production. Without internalizing the costs, society is essentially subsidizing production, and, as a result, the industry is overproducing. EPA regulations are excellent examples of policies designed to force this internalization of costs by requiring firms to control their release of pollutants (see Chapter 7). Occupational Safety and Health Administration (OSHA) regulations are examples of policies that force corporations to internalize the costs of injury or disease associated with the production process (see Chapter 8). Many critics of social regulation complain that regulations have increased costs and limited production and reinvestment in certain industries. What these critics fail to realize is that this is precisely the point.

Complete information. Although market actors are assumed to rationally pursue their self-interest, it is difficult to make rational decisions concerning whether one will benefit from the purchase of a given product or service at the market price under conditions of *information scarcity* or *information asymmetry.* Producers have more information regarding the cost and quality of a good than do consumers. This is especially true for *experience goods* (i.e., goods for which consumers can judge quality only after purchase) or goods purchased relatively infrequently. Many regulatory policies address problems of information scarcity and asymmetry. Consider truth-in-labeling regulations, which require that firms disclose the ingredients of their products. Certainly, there are cases—such as pharmaceuticals—in which consumers simply lack the expertise to understand the value of the ingredients. The Food and Drug Administration (FDA) approves pharmaceuticals, and this approval certifies that the chemical agent will perform as promised and that known side effects have been disclosed. Consumer protection is examined in some detail in Chapter 9.

Transaction costs. Transaction costs are best defined as "the costs associated with the transfer, capture, and protection of property rights" (Barzel 1989: 2). Stated another way, transaction costs include the costs of determining the price of a good, negotiating the exchange of the good, and monitoring to ensure that both sides live up to the terms of the transaction (Wittman 1995). These costs are not associated with production and thus are not incorporated into the price. Rather, they reflect the uncertainty that may accompany more complex products. If transaction costs are too high, otherwise desirable transactions may not occur. Regulatory policy may provide some means of reducing these costs. As Chapter 5 will reveal, banking regulations have reduced the transaction costs in financial markets by requiring that financial intermediaries meet prespecified capitalization and reserve requirements. The provision of deposit insurance further reduces transaction costs. Consumer protection regulations (Chapter 9) also reduce transaction costs by assigning liability for defective and hazardous products.

*   *   *

Much of what we refer to as *regulation* can be explained analytically as a response to market failure. Yet there are several problems with the market-failure explanation. First, market failure is often introduced ex post as a means of separating "good" from "bad" regulations. Explicit arguments concerning market failure are rare in the debates leading up to new regulatory initiatives; when they occur, they are usually combined with arguments that have distinct social and political dimensions. Yet one routinely discovers arguments concerning market failure in debates over the appropriate limits of governmental authority. As W. Kip Viscusi, John Vernon, and Joseph Harrington note, "Ideally, the purpose of antitrust and regulation policies is to foster improvements judged in efficiency terms. We should move closer to the perfectly competitive ideal than we would have in the absence of this type of intervention" (1995: 10). The underlying assumption is that markets must be assigned a primary role and the state must enter them only when it can facilitate their functioning. "The role of government," in the words of Milton Friedman, "is to do something that the market cannot do for itself" (1962: 27). While there is no reason, on the face of things, to assume that the market will be the institution of choice, market-failure arguments essentially raise the market to the status of a benchmark.

Second, if we are to take the question of market failure seriously, we must recognize that there is probably a good balance between regulatory policies that mitigate market failure and policies that exacerbate it. Occupational regulations commonly impose great barriers to entry in professions characterized by low levels of complexity (e.g., barbers, taxi drivers), thereby allowing established actors to claim monopoly rents. Many economic regulations were designed to circumvent markets by establishing barriers to entry and exit and guaranteeing higher levels of profitability than might exist under a competitive market. Indeed, many critics of regulation have concluded that regulatory policies have been used to aggrandize established industry actors at a high cost to consumers.

Regulation and Cartel Management

Despite the common reference to market failure, regulations have often been used to circumvent market forces. According to George Stigler's classic article "The Theory of Economic Regulation" (1971), regulations are designed and operated for the benefit of the regulated parties. Industries may seek direct subsidies, controls over entry and exit, policies that affect substitutes and complements as a means of protecting or expanding the market for their goods, and authority to engage in some form of price-fixing. Stigler argues that the creation of barriers to entry is the most important form of policy sought by regulated firms, because such barriers can allow a de facto cartel to exist under the authority of the government, particularly when combined with some of the above-mentioned policies. The conclusion that regulations are designed to benefit the regulated parties may appear odd at first blush. Many major pieces of regulatory legislation charge the agencies in question to regulate "in the public interest." How, then, is it possible that behind this justification exists a set of policies that increases the wealth of the regulated and forces the population to absorb deadweight monopoly loss and higher taxes? According to Stigler, because costs are diffuse and information is scarce, uninterested voters lack the incentive to hold their representatives accountable. Moreover, legislators receive political and material rewards from the regulated, who, in essence, purchase the support of the state.

Stigler's economic interpretation was extended through the efforts of Richard Posner (1974) and Sam Peltzman (1976). According to Posner, many regulations did not simply emerge as the products of industry efforts, but reflect the interests of coalitions consisting of the regulated parties and key customer groups. Both have their demands reflected in regulations, with the costs forced on to the unorganized. Peltzman, on the other hand, interprets Stigler's theory as being "ultimately a theory of the optimum size of effective political coalitions" (1976: 212). For Peltzman, there are diminishing returns associated with both group size and wealth transfers in politics. After a point, larger political coalitions are counterproductive (since they reduce the per capita transfer of wealth), and larger wealth transfers provoke public opposition that is difficult to overcome. Regulation concentrates potential benefits among a small group of firms, while the costs are diffuse and borne by an unorganized electorate.

The key methodological assumptions of the economic theory of regulation have been widely adopted among "public choice" scholars. We will examine the difficulties with these methodological and modeling decisions in Chapter 2. For now, it is important to note that, whereas the economic theories of regulation would seem to have some value in explaining key economic regulations, they have little to say about the social regulations that have dominated regulation since the late 1960s. Social regulations impose large costs on the regulated parties and provide diffuse benefits for the public at large. While the public may have few incentives to mobilize on behalf of regulation, the regulated certainly have little to gain and much to lose from the implementation of social regulations. Thus the cartel maintenance so central to the economic theories of regulation may be increasingly irrelevant, particularly following the competitive deregulation of the past two decades (see Derthick and Quirk 1985).

Regulation and Capture Theory

The key insights of the economic theory of regulation were recognized by early analyses of the regulatory state (see, e.g., Herring 1936). Beginning in the 1950s, a number of analysts began arguing that a variety of factors contributed to this state of affairs. In *Regulating Business by Independent Commission,* Marver Bernstein (1955) noted that regulatory commissions tended to move through a life cycle of types. After the energy of gestation and youth is expended, the commission enters a stage of maturity: it "becomes more concerned with the general health of the industry and tries to prevent changes which adversely affect it. Cut off from the mainstream of political life, the commission's standards are determined in light of the desires of the industry affected" (1955: 87). By the time it enters old age, the commission simply strives to maintain the status quo. Samuel Huntington (1952) arrived at similar conclusions with respect to the Interstate Commerce Commission (ICC). Agricultural shipping interests (especially farmers) had been successful in shaping ICC rate making. However, when this core constituency lost political power during the first decades of the twentieth century and railroad regulation declined in salience, the ICC had to turn to the regulated interests themselves for support. The result was the Transportation Act of 1920, which directed the ICC to enforce *minimum* rates designed to guarantee industry profitability. The ICC had been captured and would spend the next half century as a moribund agency guarding railroad profitability.

While regulatory capture was presented by many as resulting from the decline of the original constituency, others argued that this interpretation was far too charitable. Gabriel Kolko (1963, 1965), a revisionist historian, provided a wealth of evidence to support his contention that representatives of the regulated industries commonly played a central role in drafting regulatory legislation. Governmental authority was used to manage industries, thereby reducing the problems of overproduction and "ruinous competition" that might undermine profitability. It also obviated the need for state-level regulations that were often more radical and could have significant negative effects on the regulated industries. The use of regulation to protect industry reflects the contention that advanced capitalism requires a far greater integration of the state and economy than is often supposed by free market advocates (see McConnell 1966; Lindblom 1977).

Of course, the same criticism raised in response to the economic theory of regulation is applicable to capture theory. Although capture may have been commonplace in many economic regulatory agencies, there is little evidence that capture is possible in an age of social regulation (Meier 1988: 21–25; see also Worsham 1997). The new social regulatory agencies enforce economy-wide mandates and impose heavy costs. Moreover, the policy process in these agencies affords advocacy groups multiple veto points and expands access to the courts (see Stewart 1975; Eisner 2000: 118–133). As a result, capture is no longer much of a threat. Instead, the regulated parties have powerful incentives to reduce regulatory autonomy, embroil agencies in lengthy appeals, and force regulators to justify their decisions using market criteria.

Regulation and Sectionalism

The explanations presented above make note of the economic benefits of regulation, either in the abstract (i.e., in relation to their impact on issues of market failure) or as they accrue to individual firms and industries. However, some scholars have sought to discover the extent to which major regulatory initiatives have reflected the competition among regional political economies. Richard Bensel (1984) and Elizabeth Sanders (1986, 1987) have been the primary contributors to this line of inquiry. Sanders (1987) identifies distinct regional trading areas and examines the voting behavior of representatives on key regulatory initiatives. Building on Immanuel Wallerstein's world systems theory, Sanders focuses on competition between an industrial "core" and a "periphery" to reveal that many key initiatives have been attempts to use policies to prevent the shift of economic power across trading areas. For example, early antitrust legislation received a far greater level of support from the representatives of the agrarian periphery than from those of the industrial core of the Northeast (see Sanders 1986).

Given the limited relevance of some of the economic explanations to the new social regulation, the applicability of the regional political economy perspective is particularly noteworthy. The provisions of the 1977 Clean Air Act amendments are especially revealing in this regard. First, a coalition of eastern coal mine operators, coal miners, and environmentalists succeeded in preventing coal-fired power plants from meeting air quality guidelines by shifting from high-sulfur eastern coal to lower-sulfur western coal, even though this would have improved air quality more than the technological pollution control requirements that were eventually adopted. Second, by adopting a "prevention of significant deterioration" standard that allowed little additional air pollution (and thus industrial development) in relatively clean areas, the act reduced the incentives for firms to relocate from the industrial Midwest and Northeast to the relatively less developed South and West (Ackerman and Hassler 1981). In short, both elements of the 1977 legislation protected the interests of the industrial core and handicapped the development of the periphery.

The applicability of the regional political economy approach is not limited to environmental regulation. In explaining the new social regulations of the 1970s, Sanders's analysis of roll-call votes on key amendments to regulatory legislation shows that representatives from the core voted routinely to impose more stringent regulatory standards and impede the diminution of standards, whereas the periphery sought to minimize regulatory burdens. As Sanders explains: "The deindustrializing regions perceived in regulatory law a means of slowing economic decline by raising the costs of capitalization in the periphery, insulating the national economic from international economic forces, undoing the 'artificial' decentralization of the economy promoted by the periphery, and divesting the corporate powerhouses that had emerged out of periphery industries" (1987: 131).

Policy Choices in Regulatory Politics

Regulators have at their disposal a veritable arsenal of policy tools that vary tremendously with respect to the degree to which they replace market mechanisms, impinge on business decisions, and impose costs on regulated industries. In this section, we discuss nine of the most common regulatory policy tools: prohibitions; licensing; price, rate, and quantity restrictions; product standards; technical production standards; performance standards; subsidies; information provision; and assigning property rights and liability.

Perhaps the strongest policy tool available to regulators is the ability to introduce legal *prohibitions*. For example, the EPA has banned the production and use of several pesticides, including DDT and Aldicarb. Other product prohibitions include sales of automobiles without catalytic converters, the sale or purchase of human organs, and the manufacture, sale, or purchase of certain narcotics. In a similar vein, current US regulatory policy prohibits the practice of trading stocks and commodity futures based on insider information and monopolistic practices on the part of businesses.

Regulators may also establish a system of *licensing* or *certification* to control entry and guarantee that all actors meet standards deemed necessary to achieve desired regulatory goals. In banking, for example, regulators have required that financial institutions meet specific capitalization and reserve requirements. Similarly, nuclear power plants must demonstrate a need for additional electric generating capacity and are required to meet certain safety standards before they can receive a government operating license. Licensing systems are not only used in highly technical areas, but are also extended to everything from cosmetology to tree surgery.

Governments have a long history of using *price, rate, and quantity regulation*. They use policy to regulate the prices charged for goods and services, the quantities of these items, and their flow to market. Price controls and rate-setting have been essential components of passenger airline regulation, interstate trucking regulation, long-distance telephone service regulation, banking regulation, and all interstate sales of oil, natural gas, and electricity. Federal regulators set prices and rates on the assumption either that a lack of market competition would result in excessive profits and suboptimal levels of production or that excessive competition could lead the regulated to trade safety for market share. Controls on the quantity of goods produced are common in the area of agricultural products and natural resources. Through marketing orders and production quotas, for example, the US Department of Agriculture (USDA) limits the amount of tobacco, citrus fruit, fresh milk, and other commodities that can be sold in interstate commerce, while the Department of Energy (DOE)—and its precursors—limited for decades the importation and production of various fuels.

Officials may establish and enforce *product quality standards* in hopes of achieving product safety and effectiveness. Food and drug regulation and consumer protection have relied extensively on such standards. For example, the USDA enforces quality standards that ensure a safe food supply, and the FDA requires that all drugs be demonstrated safe and effective before they can be sold in interstate commerce. Product quality standards are also applied to nonconsumable goods, such as the automobile safety standards established by the National Highway Traffic Safety Administration and the home appliance energy efficiency standards promulgated by the DOE.

Whereas product standards establish requirements for the quality and safety of products themselves, *technical production standards* establish requirements for the process by which certain goods are produced. Occupational safety and health policy and environmental protection policy are two areas in which technical standards have been vital to the realization of policy goals. In the former, employers are required to install certain safety devices and provide a certain level of safety training to employees in order to reduce workplace injury and death rates. In the latter, companies are required to install equipment that reduces the pollution released into the environment. In both cases, technical production standards change the process by which goods are produced. These standards are often referred to as *command and control* regulations, since they command firms to meet a certain regulatory goal and control how they reach this goal.

More recently, regulators have begun to experiment with *performance standards* as a tool of regulation. Under performance standards, regulators may establish regulatory goals (e.g., a certain reduction in workplace accidents or pollution emissions) and delegate to regulated parties the task of finding the most cost-effective means of realizing these goals. The assumption here is that firms will be able to meet regulatory goals at a lower cost, because they have the best knowledge of the technologies they apply in the production process and the incentive to minimize costs. Performance standards have been used in recent years in environmental policy as regulators have sought to use incentives rather than command and control policies to reduce air pollution.

Another common regulatory tool is the use of *subsidies*. When employing subsidies, government officials reimburse firms for a portion of their costs or pay these costs themselves. Officials dole out these subsidies to ensure the production of certain goods or services that might not occur under normal market conditions. Subsidies may be direct, as when the USDA pays farmers to leave land fallow or when the DOE pays the costs of enriching uranium fuel for nuclear power plants. Subsidies may also be indirect, as when government regulators allow companies to charge higher prices for long-distance phone service in an effort to keep down the costs of local telephone service (generally referred to as a *cross-subsidy*).

As noted above, information scarcity is a common justification for regulation. One of the least-intrusive tools available to regulators is aimed at remedying this market failure—the *provision of information* to consumers. The government itself may provide information to consumers at little or no cost, as with the Department of Commerce's consumer information pamphlets. More commonly, however, regulators require firms to provide information to consumers directly, through product information statements and through truth-in-labeling laws. Implicit in the decision to rely on information provision rather than product standards is the belief that there is and should be a market for low-price/low-quality goods and services.

The least-intrusive policy tool available to regulators is *assigning property rights and liability* for the harm caused by defective or dangerous products. According to many scholars, most market failures could be remedied by establishing clear property rights and liability standards that would facilitate the use of tort and contract law. For example, if an individual is harmed by the actions of a firm, a defective product, or a faithless contractual partner, he may seek compensation through the courts. In this way, bad corporate actors will be driven from the market, obviating the need for additional regulatory actions by government. While this regulatory tool is seldom used by itself, it is an important component of the regulatory toolbox in areas such as consumer protection, occupational safety and health, environmental protection, and increasingly, financial and securities regulation.

The Relationship Between Regulatory Justifications and Tools

Although it is common to speak of regulatory tools as if they are mutually exclusive, there is in reality much overlap. For instance, a quantity restriction of zero is, for all intents and purposes, a prohibition. Similarly, licensing and certification programs are also a type of indirect information provision, since, for example, USDA inspection and grade certifications provide consumers with information regarding the quality and healthfulness of food. Regulatory tools, in fact, are similar to other tools in that different ones may be used to accomplish the same task. Just as pliers, a crescent wrench, and a pneumatic socket driver can all be used to turn a bolt, a subsidy, a technical production standard, and a performance standard can all be used to protect the health and safety of workers.

Different regulatory tools are best suited to certain tasks. Indeed, there is a close connection between the reasons for regulation and the appropriateness of regulatory tools. Subsidies, for example, are a poor choice for dealing with negative externalities. Paying firms to reduce their pollution may encourage some firms to actually employ *more* polluting production processes. If the subsidies for pollution reduction are high enough, they may provide an incentive for additional firms to enter the market, thereby contributing to overproduction. Similarly, assigning liability and relying on tort law are poor choices for protecting financial investors, since when these investors are entitled to seek compensation for fraud or mismanagement, the financial entity responsible for the damages will often be bankrupt. In fact, assigning property rights and liability is a poor choice of regulatory tools whenever the damages suffered by consumers or other firms cannot be easily reversed (e.g., death or debilitating injury).

Finally, technological and social changes often affect both the justifications given for regulation and the appropriate regulatory tools. Consider the situation of telecommunications. For decades, long-distance telephone service was considered a natural monopoly: the federal government set the rates for American Telephone and Telegraph (AT&T). Improvements in computer and fiber-optic technology, however, opened up the possibility of competition for long-distance service while undermining claims of natural monopoly. In response, in the 1980s, the federal government deregulated long-distance telephone rates (see Chapter 6). We see something very similar occurring today in the area of electricity generation. Improvements in technology have made retail competition for electricity feasible, and soon both wholesale and retail purchasers of electricity will be able to choose their supplier of this commodity, replacing price and rate regulation with competition (see Chapter 10). In a different area, vast improvements in monitoring and remote sensing technology have made measuring levels of pollution much easier and more accurate. These advances have allowed for performance standards in pollution control that require the heretofore unavailable ability to continuously and instantaneously measure pollution emissions.

Deregulation as a Policy Tool

Deregulation—the process of reducing or eliminating government regulations—has been one of the most visible and forcefully articulated elements of the contemporary regulatory debates. Advocates of deregulation provide three general justifications for deregulation. First, even if regulations often stem from honorable motivations (e.g., to protect the public interest or to compensate for market failure), they have unexpected and pernicious effects once put into practice. Second, other observers—on both the right and the left—criticize regulations on political grounds, arguing that they are used to reward political allies and entrenched industrial interests. Finally, other scholars believe that any attempt by government to solve social or economic problems will produce suboptimal results when compared with the free market (see Wittman 1995).

While its most zealous advocates promote deregulation as a cure-all for many economic problems, it is more productive (and more accurate) to view deregulation as simply another regulatory tool, which is better suited to some problems than to others. For example, the deregulation of long-distance telephone rates and airline ticket prices in the 1970s and 1980s was wholly appropriate, given the crumbling natural monopolies in these areas. On the other hand, deregulation (and increased competition) is less appropriate as a remedy for negative externalities. It is important to recognize that deregulation does not always mean moving from regulation to no regulation. Often, deregulation simply involves replacing one tool of regulation with another, less intrusive tool. Consider, for example, recent changes in the regulation of flammability in infant sleepwear. Rather than meeting a government-mandated level of flame resistance, manufacturers now simply provide labels that identify the flame-resistant nature of the garment (i.e., product standards have been replaced with information provision). Even when an industry experiences complete deregulation in one area (e.g., airline ticket prices), regulation continues in other areas (e.g., airline safety and maintenance standards). In thinking about deregulation, then, we have to evaluate it as we would any other policy tool: Is it appropriate for addressing the problem at hand?

Since the mid-1990s, deregulation as a policy tool has been superseded by a related phenomenon: a greater reliance on public-private partnerships and voluntary initiatives. During the Clinton presidency, the creation of partnerships was part of a larger effort to reinvent government (or REGO) by applying lessons gleaned from corporate America. The core idea was to make government more flexible, responsive, and results-oriented (see Osborne and Gaebler 1992). As part of REGO, regulators created a dense network of partnerships designed to promote public-private collaboration and experimentation, with the hope that the lessons learned could be used to future regulatory goals. In some cases, partnerships complemented policy and were effectively integrated into a larger regulatory structure. In other cases, they existed in a tense relationship with existing bureaucratic structures and policy instruments (see Fiorino 1999). However, during the presidency of George W. Bush, there is much to suggest that partnerships and voluntary initiatives have been viewed as a substitute for policy rather than a complement, making them deregulation in new clothing. The case studies in this book will provide several opportunities to explore the growing role of partnerships.

Conclusion

The question "Why regulate?" has multiple answers, some more satisfactory than others. Competing explanations posit that regulation is a response to the demands articulated by elected officials (e.g., public interest theory, sectional political-economic competition), powerful interests (e.g., the economic theory of regulation, capture theory), or the environment (e.g., failing markets). Each explanation has dominated the study of regulation during different periods: the public interest rationale prior to World War II and during the 1960s; the economic theory of regulation and capture theory in the 1960s and 1970s; and the public choice interpretation of regulatory policy as the product of influence and rent-seeking elected officials in the 1980s and 1990s. None of these explanations can account for regulatory policy choices in all areas. The most obvious problem is the fact that the regulatory bureaucracy is de-emphasized or neglected altogether. Regulatory bureaucracies, however, are an important element in the process of regulatory decisionmaking. If public policy is defined as patterns of governmental action, we cannot be content with restricting our focus to exogenous demands for policy, but must also consider factors that are internal to the bureaucracy. Moreover, we must situate regulation in the larger political-institutional network of relationships, seeking to understand how relationships with the president, Congress, the courts, other regulatory and nonregulatory agencies, and state-level implementers shape the patterns of governmental action.

In Chapter 2, we examine in more detail three of the most common theoretical explanations for regulatory policy change: the bureaucratic politics perspective, which posits that most of the forces generating changes stem from forces within the bureaucracy; the subsystems perspective, which focuses on coalitions linking institutional actors and affected interests; and the principal-agent perspective, which emphasizes the relationships between vote-maximizing elected officials and their budget-maximizing bureaucratic agents. We explore the conditions under which each explanation of regulatory policy is likely to be most accurate, grounding this discussion in the concepts of complexity, salience, and bureaucratic leadership. In successive chapters, we discuss recent developments in several regulatory areas, evaluating these developments through each of the three theoretical lenses.

2

Explaining Regulatory Change

HOW DO WE EXPLAIN regulatory change? If "public policy" refers to patterns of public action, we must, of necessity, focus on bureaucracy. Implementation is the primary responsibility of most bureaucratic organizations, their reason for existence, and the source of their power. Three vantages to understanding the role of bureaucracy in the implementation of public policy dominate the field. At the micro level, the bureaucratic politics perspective focuses on the motivation and behavior of bureaucrats and bureaucracy as organizational phenomena. At the meso level, the subsystems perspective views policy as the outcome of bargains struck among a select group of interested actors operating through institutional arrangements normally out of the public eye. At the macro level, the principal-agent perspective is concerned with how elected officials control (or fail to control) their bureaucratic agents.

The Bureaucratic Politics Perspective

Bureaucracy is at the heart of public policy, and implementation in particular. The bureaucratic politics approach models bureaucracy as an organization that shapes the actions of its members and is in turn shaped by them. Understanding the motivation of personnel in an organizational setting, as well as how this shapes the pursuit of particular goals by the organization, is the central preoccupation of the bureaucratic politics approach.

Bureaucrats do not always receive clear signals from elected officials. Legislation quite often incorporates vague or amorphous goals, leaving it to bureaucrats to figure out what it is they are being asked to accomplish. Even when signals are clear, bureaucrats' information advantage over elected officials may allow them to exercise considerable discretion over regulatory policy. Some early formal research suggested that bureaucrats would exercise this discretion in pursuit of material self-interest. This view is most forcefully articulated by William Niskanen (1971) in his portrayal of the "budget-maximizing bureaucrat." According to Niskanen, bureaucrats' self-interest may be satisfied by professional advancement, increased administrative authority, larger salaries, a larger agency, or any number of other rewards, all of which depend on a larger budget. Since bureaucrats know much better than elected officials how much it costs to administer a particular program (the information advantage), they have both motive and opportunity to ask for more money than they really need. Matthew Holden shares Niskanen's assumption of the self-interest motivation of bureaucrats. For Holden (1966), however, this motivation is expressed as a desire to engage in imperialistic behavior, seeking greater policy responsibility and administrative authority.

The Niskanen-Holden perspective on bureaucratic politics reinforces the common perception of increasingly intrusive regulatory agencies with ever larger budgets. Empirical research, however, has not been kind to this perspective. Terry Moe (1989) and Gary Miller and Terry Moe (1983) offer withering theoretical critiques of Niskanen's work; Jonathan Bendor and Terry Moe (1985) demonstrate that budget-maximizing behavior is a destructive strategic choice for agencies; and André Blais and Stéphane Dion (1991) find little empirical support for the budget-maximizing bureaucrat hypothesis (see, additionally, Waterman, Rouse, and Wright 2004). Moreover, Kenneth Meier (1985), Cathy Johnson (1992), and Marc Allen Eisner (2000) discuss numerous instances of agencies fighting to avoid increased policy responsibility (though to be fair, Holden recognizes this possibility).

A slightly different perspective on the importance of bureaucratic politics is offered by Anthony Downs (1967). Downs argues that much of agency action can be explained by the particular type of bureaucratic personality dominant within an agency.[1] Downs creates a typology of five personality types (and, by implication, agency types). The first two groups of bureaucrats are almost purely self-interested: "Climbers" and "conservers" are both interested in personal power, income, and prestige within the organization. The former seek to maximize these, the latter to conserve them. A second collection of bureaucratic types is distinguished by mixed motives, being somewhat less self-interested than climbers and conservers. "Zealots" are loyal to narrow concepts or programs that are an important part of what their organization does. "Advocates" are devoted to a broader set of functions that often take the form of an organization's overarching policy goals. Finally, "statesmen" are motivated by some concept of the public interest and the role their agency has in fulfilling it.

While Downs favors the self-interested portrait of bureaucrats, his typology recognizes motives other than self-interest. In fact, a large body of research concludes that goals other than self-interest do in fact motivate bureaucrats. Programmatic and policy goals play important roles in the bureaucratic calculus. Bureaucrats pursue actions they believe will produce desirable policy outcomes (Marcus 1984; Johnson 1992). Professional values also shape the actions of bureaucrats, and changes in these professional norms often effect significant policy change (Eisner 1991; Khademian 1993). Bureaucrats may even be motivated by abstract notions of the public interest (Kelman 1987). While a mismatch of goals between civil servants and political appointees, personnel in different agencies, and bureaucrats and elected officials may still be a problem, it cannot always be explained by simple assumptions of self-interest. Rather, bureaucrats and the agencies they inhabit possess a hierarchy of goals; identifying this hierarchy offers the interested observer important insight into why they do what they do.

Institutional arrangements also shape and constrain human action. James Wilson (1989) argues that institutional arrangements go a long way in explaining why bureaucrats do what they do. By way of illustration, Wilson draws a parallel between bureaucrats and baseball infielders. No serious student of baseball expects attitudes, values, and beliefs to have much effect on the performance of a second baseman, and students of politics err by expecting these factors to explain the performance of bureaucrats. Agency type is one of the primary factors affecting bureaucratic behavior. Wilson identifies four agency types, focusing on the relationship between *outputs* (what bureaucrats are doing) and *outcomes* (the effect these actions have on attaining the organization's goals). "Production" agencies are those in which outputs and outcomes are readily observable (e.g., the outputs of the Internal Revenue Service [IRS] include audits and claims processing; its outcomes are revenues collected). "Procedural" organizations are those in which managers are able to oversee outputs but have very limited means of determining outcomes (e.g., the EPA can keep track of inspections but finds it difficult to determine if inspections improve environmental quality). "Craft" organizations are those in which outputs are hard to determine but outcomes are readily apparent (e.g., armies during wartime, the Forest Service, and other agencies dominated by autonomous field officers). Finally, "coping" agencies are those in which it is difficult to observe either outputs or outcomes. Universities are often described as coping agencies, since "you can neither describe the product nor explain how it is produced" (1989: 169).

Bureaucrats' behavior is affected not only by the type of organization, but also by their positions within the organization. Wilson identifies three types of personnel operating in any organization: operators, managers, and executives. Operators are "street-level bureaucrats" subject to a variety of stimuli that affect policy implementation. Their actions are shaped by the goals of the organization, the particular situations encountered when implementing policy, prior experiences and beliefs, peer expectations, interest group activity, and "the impetus given to the organization by its founders" (1989: 27). All these give rise to an organizational culture that produces predictable, patterned behavior. Managers constitute an additional stimulus that shapes operators' behavior. A manager's central concern is administering the internal components of the organization—resource allocation, task specification, and maintaining progress toward goal achievement. Wilson suggests that a manager's ability to manage is greatly affected by "the extent to which the goals of the agencies are clear and the work of the agencies' operators is observable" (1989: 28). Executives are top-level agency personnel, careerists, or political appointees whose primary role is organizational maintenance (1989: 181). In its most basic incarnation, maintenance involves securing adequate levels of appropriations, the recruitment and socialization of personnel, and cultivating political support. Since most agencies face no immediate threat to their actual survival, maintenance has evolved into a concern with preserving, or expanding, agency autonomy (1989: 182).

The Subsystems Perspective

Understanding the role of private interests in the formation of public policy is a constant preoccupation of observers of American politics. Subsystem theorists argue that public policy is shaped by well-organized collections of private interests working in concert with a select cast of public actors (Schattschneider 1935, 1960; Bernstein 1955; Maas 1951; Scher 1960; Long 1962; Cater 1964; Freeman 1955, 1965; Lowi 1969, 1979; Balogh 1991; Baumgartner and Jones 1993; Worsham 1997). Instead of focusing on macro-level phenomena involving the president, Congress, or the courts, subsystem theorists argue that interest groups usually operate at the meso level of the polity in subsystems "organized around discrete programs and issues" (Thurber 1991: 319). Interest groups form alliances with interested legislators on congressional (sub)committees and bureaucrats from select agencies to pursue policies that benefit subsystem members.

Subsystems are often viewed as an equilibrium solution to the chaos represented by interest group competition at the macro level of the polity (Baumgartner and Jones 1993). A major problem associated with group politics is the seeming inability to effect closure on decisions that affect large numbers of interests. Subsystems restrict the number of interested parties, greatly simplifying the deal-cutting that occurs during formulation. They do so through the creation of institutional and intellectual barriers to participation in the policy process. Yet such barriers are not impermeable (Riker

1990; Krehbiel 1991). A variety of environmental forces outside the subsystem, as well as internal dynamics within a subsystem, provide a constant set of challenges to subsystem-induced equilibria (see Sabatier and Jenkins-Smith 1993; Baumgartner and Jones 1993; Worsham 1997). Politics bounce back and forth between relatively closed affairs, in which select interests, agency personnel, and legislators from a single committee decide the course of public policy, and more open arrangements, in which several well-organized interest groups, one or more agencies, and congressional committees vie for control of the policy process in a never-ending minuet of bargaining, deal-cutting, and politicking. Thus, while much of policymaking occurs in a subsystem setting, the nature of the setting itself varies over time.

Subsystem politics may assume any of three forms: dominant, transitory, or competing coalitions.[2] Subsystem autonomy in deciding the shape of policy, then, is not uniform and constant through time. Rather, the content of policy is affected by the particular brand of subsystem politics in operation. In order to better understand the shifting nature of subsystem politics, let us consider the three variants of subsystem politics in greater detail.

Dominant coalition politics characterizes the classic "iron triangle" in which legislators from an oversight committee or subcommittee, agency personnel, and special interests get together to decide the course of public policy in a particular policy area. These arrangements were originally christened "iron triangles" because of their autonomy in deciding the course of policy in their field of interest. Outsiders' input is not welcome, and their influence nonexistent. Policy produced in a dominant coalition setting favors select interests over the public interest, expands the budget and responsibilities of agency personnel, and ensures the reelection of legislators on oversight committees. Dominant coalitions specialize in the development and delivery of distributive policy (Thurber 1991: 327–329)—that is, policy that benefits select interests and is paid for, unknowingly, by the public.

A dominant coalition's ability to shape policy to its liking is greatly aided by the decentralized organization of Congress. A committee, or subcommittee, establishes unquestioned jurisdiction in a particular policy area and enters into "mutual noninterference pacts" with other such committees, while members on the floor usually rubber-stamp committee-approved legislation (Lowi 1969). Similarly, bureaucratic agencies avoid turf wars through the establishment of their own policy monopolies or through mutual accommodation among co-implementing agencies. Competition among interests in a dominant coalition subsystem is rare. Indeed, the rationale underlying the formation of a subsystem is to allow interest groups to shun competition for control and predictability. When dominant coalitions have trouble reaching consensus, one is faced with a new variation of subsystem politics: the transitory coalition.

Under the dominant scenario, the various interests that make up the coalition agree on common issues of concern and set aside other interests. *Transitory coalitions* surface when the latent interests of some members of a dominant coalition supersede the common interests. Defectors may try to form a rival coalition, but under the transitory scenario, the challenge is a fleeting phenomenon. Transitory coalitions bargain over the distribution of benefits and costs associated with a particular policy. Such bargaining is usually short-lived and low-key, and ends with a bargain struck among the dominant interests and challengers. With no single coalition able to force closure, the result is a hybrid of distributive and regulatory policy. Transitory coalitions are a subsystem purgatory, with would-be dominant interests waiting for the opportunity to take control or slip into oblivion. If conflict is prolonged, a subsystem characterized by transitory politics may slip into a more competitive mode.

Competitive coalitions are present when traditionally dominant interests are challenged by a new coalition, giving rise to a distinctive form of politics. Transitory coalitions evolve into competitive coalitions, or new coalitions involving outsiders from another subsystem respond to perceived threats to the autonomy of their home base (Ripley and Franklin 1986). Finally, challengers may simply be newcomers to the interest group setting, looking for a subsystem niche of their own (Browne 1988). Competitive coalition politics is reminiscent of what Christopher Bosso refers to as "presence politics" (1987: 246), which finds interest groups fighting to establish, and maintain, their presence in a particular subsystem. Much of the struggle involves establishing the legitimacy of their previously unrecognized claims to a piece of the policy pie.

When subsystem participants change, so do the values and goals of the participants, and perhaps even those of the organization within which the participants operate. Challengers may seek to alter the decisionmaking venue to replace distributive policy with more radically redistributive policy. They may also seek to prevent subsystem players from advancing into new policy territory—either through enforcement of existing prohibitions or by rewriting regulation to create new prohibitions. Even if the dominant coalition does not change, accommodations made with new participants to preserve the subsystem will affect regulatory behavior.

The Principal-Agent Perspective

The principal-agent perspective conveys a hierarchical notion of politico-bureaucratic relations. The dichotomy between politics and administration, first enunciated by Woodrow Wilson (1887), is the logical predecessor of agency theory. Writing four years after the passage of the Pendleton Act,

Wilson was concerned with how Americans could "graft public administration into their Constitution, which [did] not mention the subject" (Stillman 1996: 5). In an attempt to settle fears of an administrative state (literally, government by bureaucracy), Wilson advanced the notion of a dichotomy. This was a rhetorical device that neatly bifurcated governance into two realms—the political and the administrative—and subjected the latter to the will of the former. In so doing, Wilson created new opportunities for introducing administrative models from other contexts while finding a means of deflecting concerns over state expansion.

Administration, for Wilson, was concerned with the "detailed and systematic execution of public law" (1887: 10) created by elected officials who operate in the realm of politics. Political questions were those that decided who got what, and when. Administrative questions addressed how goods were to be delivered. The separation between the realm of politics and that of administration was meant to prevent contamination in either direction. Indeed, Wilson was quite clear that while "politics set the task for administration, it should not be suffered to manipulate its offices" (1887: 10). Administration was simply a separate endeavor that, because it was becoming increasingly complex, required a professional class of administrators. By dividing the political from the administrative, Wilson hoped to put an end to patronage and rest fears of unchecked government power. The dilemma is that government action (administration) requires grants of discretion, is often hard to monitor, and clearly translates into political power. These same concerns are at the heart of principal-agent theory.

Agency theory has long been a component of microeconomic analyses (Arrow 1963; Riker 1962; Goldberg 1976), theories of the firm (Alchian and Demsetz 1972; Jensen and Meckling 1976), and transaction cost economics (Williamson 1975, 1985). In its purest form, it focuses on the relationship between a *principal,* who requires the services of an *agent,* someone with special skills necessary for the fulfillment of the principal's goals (Friedman 1995: 181). Because the principal-agent relationship exists in a context of information asymmetry and uncertainty, agents may act opportunistically to maximize their own wealth. The challenge for the principal is to discover some means of managing this information asymmetry and minimizing the slippage in the relationship with the agent. In business economics, the principal is often a manager or firm, while the agent is a supplier or subcontractor. Applied to regulation, principals are the elected officials who pass legislation and delegate authority to bureaucratic agents who must develop an appropriate pattern of implementation actions.

Barry Mitnick was among the first to suggest that "the roots of the 'bureaucracy problem' lie not so much in bureaucracy as they do in agency" (1984: 2). Agency, "acting for," is at the heart of politics and administration (1984: 3). Agency theory recognizes that "at least some of what the agent does will not be specified or policed, and thus may be contrary to what the principal wants" (1984: 4). Reflecting information scarcity and the difficulties of coalition building, principals often fail to pass detailed legislation. Reflecting the high costs, they often fail to closely monitor their agents. Because the interests and incentives of agents often differ from those of principals, agents can and do pursue goals that may not coincide with those enunciated by principals. Thus, implementation outcomes that do not coincide with a principal's desires are not necessarily the result of bureaucratic incompetence, but are often the product of deliberate agent action (Mitnick 1984: 5).

There may be institutional remedies for institutional failure. One might design institutional arrangements to economize on principal monitoring costs and limit agency discretion (see McCubbins 1985; McCubbins, Noll, and Weingast 1987; Macey 1992; Moe 1985, 1989). For example, Congress might constrain agency discretion by establishing the institutional setting in which regulatory activity is undertaken (e.g., courts, independent commissions, executive agencies); restrict the scope of authority granted regulators by identifying the targets of regulation; specify in detail the policy tools available to implementers; define procedural requirements to limit agency autonomy; or require that certain professional groupings with a bias toward a preferred policy outcome be located within the agency. Alternatively, they may seek to manipulate bureaucratic behavior by altering rewards and sanctions available to the agent (McCubbins 1985: 725–729; see also Huber, Shipan, and Pfahler 2001).

Other variations argue that Congress might economize on monitoring costs by institutionalizing a role for interest groups (Banks and Weingast 1992). Jonathan Macey, distinguishing between single interest group and multiple interest group agencies, suggests that agency design and institutional checks should vary according to the number of interest groups involved. Following Macey (1992: 101–103), agencies may be "hardwired" to favor interest groups with standing (or "repeat players") over groups with a fleeting presence (see also Moe 1985, 1989). Matthew McCubbins and Thomas Schwartz argue that political control has been institutionalized through the creation of incentive-based oversight mechanisms. They contrast traditional "police-patrol" oversight with "fire-alarm oversight," which is exercised through a "system of rules, procedures, and informal practices that enable individual citizens and organized interest groups to examine administrative decisions (sometimes in prospect), to charge executive agencies with violating congressional goals, and to seek remedies from agencies, courts, and Congress itself" (1984: 166). Open rule making, expanded standing, intervenor funding, and the Freedom of Information Act all constitute means by which interests can gain access to agency decisionmaking. Under a fire-alarm oversight system, those with the greatest stakes in and knowledge about decisions are responsible for determining whether they are acceptable. This conserves on principal resources, mitigates information scarcity, and combines the responsibility for oversight with the incentives to monitor agency behavior.

At the heart of agency theory is the assumption that principals must, and quite regularly do, control the discretion of agents.[3] The president reins in runaway bureaucracy, committee chairs bring wayward agencies back into line with congressional or committee desires, and the courts force bureaucrats to follow the letter of the law. In all cases, principals are intent on making agents alter what it is they are doing, either by returning to some previous understanding of what policy responsibilities entail or by renegotiating the agency "contract." As a result, at least in the political science literature, there is usually an equilibrium between principal preferences and agent actions—albeit an equilibrium backed with the threat of coercion.

In Search of Common Ground

The three theoretical perspectives on regulatory policymaking are not mutually exclusive. For example, congressional-bureaucratic relations play a central role in both subsystems theory and principal-agent theory. While subsystems theory posits a larger role for interest groups, variants of principal-agent theory suggest that principals may provide certain groups with preferential access to agents. Moreover, the conflict that characterizes transitory and competitive coalitions may lead elected officials outside of the traditional policy subsystem to try to exert principal authority over an agency. For all of their similarities, however, subsystems and principal-agent approaches differ in two fundamental respects. First, principal-agent relationships are generally perceived as dyadic, while in subsystems, bureaucrats are faced with balancing directions from multiple principals. To complicate matters further, contradictory signals from these principals may allow an agency to play principals against one another while relying upon bureaucratic values to guide agency activity (Woolley 1993). Second, principal-agent theory posits congressional-bureaucratic relationships as conflictual, whereas subsystems theory suggests that these relationships are congenial. From the bureaucratic politics perspective, efforts to protect agency autonomy will inevitably require executives to satisfy constituents, interest groups, political elites, and the like. In short, they must attend to subsystem-like relationships. Bringing this discussion full circle, different types of agencies are more conducive to principal-agent controls. Production agencies, with clearly observable outputs and outcomes, present less uncertainty regarding bureaucratic behavior and are thus less costly to monitor, whereas principal control is less likely to be successful in agencies where monitoring costs are high, where bureaucrats' ability to shirk is high, and where the likelihood of these efforts effecting noticeable change is low (i.e., coping agencies).

One might fruitfully examine a single event from all three perspectives and, as a result, gain a richer understanding. Take the example of bureaucratic professionalization—an important event in many of the agencies examined in the case studies in this book. From a bureaucratic politics perspective, professionalization may be pursued as a means of enhancing agency expertise and thus bureaucratic power (see Meier 1987; Rourke 1984). From the subsystems perspective, one might find that the professionalization reflects a consensus within the subsystem that a given form of expertise is vital for a competent understanding of policy (see Eisner 1991). Professionalization, in this case, serves the additional political function of legitimizing agency actions before dominant coalition members. Finally, from a principal-agent perspective, professionalization might be interpreted as a tool of control. One means of limiting agent discretion is by inculcating a set of values via professionalization that programs an agency to pursue a stable and acceptable enforcement agenda (see Moe 1989).

As this brief discussion suggests, regulatory policy implementation and change may reflect, in many instances, the variables identified by two or more of these perspectives. Rather than asking which theory is "true," we need to ask which is most applicable in a given situation. This said, we believe that instances of outsiders attempting to establish themselves as principals vis-à-vis bureaucratic agents are relatively rare in most regulatory arenas, because subsystems help solve the agency problem. Subsystems allow legislators and interest groups to refine policy mandates, communicate desires and demands, and tinker with policy implementation short of establishing a hierarchical, commandlike relationship envisioned by principal-agent theorists. Indeed, one rationale for establishing a policy monopoly is to improve communications among elected officials, private interests, and agency personnel so as to avoid the need for extensive and costly monitoring and reduce the need to discipline runaway bureaucrats opportunistically exploiting the authority they have been delegated.

Salience, Complexity, and the Politics of Regulatory Policy

Given the imprecision of legislative mandates and the fluidity of political coalitions, members of Congress, the president, interest groups, and other policy participants are often dissatisfied with the policy actions taken by bureaucrats. Elsewhere we have argued that this tendency toward disequilibrium between political preferences and bureaucratic actions is a defining element of policy interactions (Worsham, Eisner, and Ringquist 1997). If this disequilibrium is the normal state of affairs, there would always appear to be ample justification for elected officials and others to attempt to redirect bureaucratic behavior; yet these efforts are not constant across time, nor across regulatory agencies and areas. We are thus left with some puzzles: Under what conditions will elected officials choose to act as political principals? Under what conditions will subsystem relationships be stable or in flux? Under what conditions will bureaucrats act with relative autonomy? In short, when are the explanations outlined above most applicable?

Following William Gormley (1986, 1989), we argue that the regular participants in policymaking can be predicted by the salience and complexity of the issue area. Given that salience and complexity may evade easy definitions (see Gerber and Teske 2000), we should define our terms with some care. By *salience*, we mean the degree of public interest and attention devoted to a particular policy issue. By *complexity*, we mean the technical complexity of the goals faced by an agency and the technical complexity of the tasks required to attain these goals. Salience and complexity vary across agencies, across issue areas, and over time, affecting the stability of policy subsystems, the likelihood of attempts at political influence, and the degree of discretion available to bureaucrats (Gormley 1986). Moreover, salience and complexity affect the predisposition of elected officials to attempt redirection of agency behavior. Due to obvious reelection incentives, high levels of salience attract the president and members of Congress. Complexity, on the other hand, repels or restricts efforts at political control. High levels of complexity pose significant intellectual barriers to entry for members of Congress, particularly for members not part of the relatively closed subsystems that often characterize complex policy areas (Baumgartner and Jones 1993). Highly complex policy areas also promise low expectations of being able to claim credit for policy success in these areas (see Kelman 1987). Even the earliest principal-agent literature recognized that congressional incentives to exercise control vary with levels of uncertainty. According to McCubbins (1985), while high levels of policy uncertainty require Congress to invest agencies with a great deal of substantive discretion, this discretion is subsequently minimized by strong procedural requirements and high levels of monitoring. The net effect of high levels of uncertainty (and political conflict) is to reduce an agency's discretion, because under these conditions, fewer policy options are preferable to the status quo (Calvert, McCubbins, and Weingast 1989; McCubbins 1985).

All other things equal, salience will attract the attention of elected officials, and efforts by these officials to redirect bureaucratic behavior should rise and fall with the public attention paid to an issue or agency. This is true whether we conceive of members of Congress as credit-claiming vote maximizers (Mayhew 1973; Fiorina 1989), as rational actors attempting to conserve resources by relying upon "fire alarms" to identify agencies in need of congressional intervention (McCubbins and Schwartz 1984), or as policy-interested individuals attempting to expand their influence in traditionally closed policy subsystems (Baumgartner and Jones 1993; Sabatier and Jenkins-Smith 1993). The effect of salience, however, is conditioned by complexity. Simply put, elected officials should be less likely to intervene in agencies engaged in complex tasks because such intervention will be less likely to produce electoral rewards, less likely to improve the policy status quo, and less welcomed from participants in the existing policy subsystem.

In each of the case studies in this book, we present data on policy salience. To measure salience, we compiled data on the number of news stories in a given year that focused on each of the policies we examined. Data were compiled through a keyword search of the *Reader's Guide to Periodical Literature*. These data provide a sense of how policy salience has changed over time and of the relative salience of different policies at any given time. While these salience data have certain limitations—for example, they do not account for changing keyword conventions in the *Reader's Guide* or the growing number of media outlets—our methodology for measuring policy salience is the current disciplinary standard (see Baumgartner and Jones 1993).

The interaction of salience and complexity leads to the following expectations regarding the relative merits of our three theories of regulatory policy:

1. The principal-agent theory will be most applicable under conditions of high public salience and low levels of technical complexity. High levels of salience will attract elected officials, while low levels of complexity will not repel them and will limit the ability of dominant subsystem coalitions to prevent the entry of outsiders into the system.

2. Under conditions of high levels of salience and high levels of complexity, elected officials will also attempt to exert principal-agent-like control over regulatory policy, though this propensity for intervention will be lower than in the case of high-salience and low-complexity. Moreover, these efforts will likely be less effective compared with the case of high-salience and low-complexity. This is because of the barriers to entry posed by complexity, but also because of the premium complexity places on bureaucratic expertise. While salience levels are too high to allow an agency free rein in determining regulatory policy, the task of crafting effective policy in these areas is too difficult for elected officials alone. The most likely situation under these circumstances is a situation of two or more coalitions competing within the policy subsystem.

3. Policy areas characterized by low levels of public salience will experience fewer attempts at principal-agent direction of regulatory activity,

though if core agency functions are of a nontechnical nature, elected officials will at least not be discouraged from such actions should they choose to take them. In fact, few policy participants will be attracted to areas with low levels of salience and complexity. We would expect policy to be made in a very limited subsystem where participation is restricted not by technical barriers to entry, but by apathy. Bureaucrats will exercise an extraordinary degree of discretion due to the absence of oversight.

4. The principal-agent explanation for regulatory policy should be least applicable under conditions of low public salience and high technical complexity. The reasons for this should be obvious. Policy in these areas will again be made within relatively closed policy subsystems. The barriers to entry here are technical, and critical policy decisions will be made by upper-level bureaucrats with a high degree of technical expertise, supported by interest groups and a very small number of members of Congress with similar degrees of expertise. Similar to the previous case, these bureaucrats should exercise a significant degree of discretion.

A Final Note on Administrative Leadership

Up to this point, our discussion of rival explanations for regulatory policy has been silent on the importance of administrative leadership. Effective leadership, however, is an indispensable element of bureaucratic power (Rourke 1984). First, effective administrative leaders both possess the technical skills and build technical skills within an agency that are so critical to persuading other political actors of the validity of agency policy positions. Second, effective leaders also possess the professional credentials necessary to command the respect and allegiance of the agency rank and file, and they possess the personal skills necessary for infusing the agency with a high level of morale and sense of mission. They will be capable of building bureaucratic coalitions, uniting potentially conflictive groups behind a common policy agenda. Third, effective leaders possess the political skills to cultivate and maintain external political support from elected officials and interest groups. Fourth, effective leaders use their public relations skills to publicize agency successes and spin agency failures. Effective leadership also has a strong situational component. For example, Caspar Weinberger developed a reputation as a consummate leader during his tenures at the Federal Trade Commission (FTC) and the Office of Management and Budget (OMB). By the end of his stint as Ronald Reagan's defense secretary, however, this reputation had been changed to that of a spendthrift who had lost control of the agency he was directing (Stockman 1986).

Administrative leadership can also play a large role in determining the locus of regulatory decisionmaking. A strong and effective agency head can stave off attempts by elected officials to infringe on agency autonomy, even during periods of high salience. Similarly, a strong and effective agency head will be able to preserve the boundaries of a particular policy subsystem under salience pressure, while directing bureaucratic discretion in such a way as to not draw the ire of elected officials or powerful clientele groups. In short, strong administrative leadership may be able to expand agency autonomy under favorable conditions and preserve a greater degree of agency autonomy under adverse conditions, whereas weak or ineffective leadership will be able to accomplish none of the tasks identified above and will likely be ineffective at extending or preserving agency autonomy. Under conditions of weak leadership, regulatory decisions are more likely to be made in accordance with subsystems theory (particularly the transitory or competitive coalition variety) or principal-agent theory.

Conclusion

As this chapter suggests, there is no single "theory of regulation" that can sufficiently explain regulatory politics. In the field of regulatory studies, blind adherence to theoretical parsimony has far too often resulted in the acceptance of models that rest on highly questionable simplifying assumptions (see Worsham, Eisner, and Ringquist 1997). Occam's razor has been used far too often to surgically remove organizations and politics from the analysis of regulation. Finding that the bureaucratic politics, subsystems, and principal-agent perspectives each have their strengths and their limitations, we choose to work at their theoretical intersection. Not only will this approach allow us to consider a wider variety of variables when examining contemporary regulatory politics, it will also help us clarify our own understanding of the relative merits of the theoretical perspectives and the inclusive strategy we have adopted. We will return to these issues in the concluding chapter. Before stepping into our analysis of contemporary regulation, it is useful to place things in a broader context.

Notes

1. Downs frequently uses the word *bureaucracy* to refer to bureaucrats and the organizational entity.

2. The following is based on the work of Paul Sabatier and Hank Jenkins-Smith (1993) and James Thurber (1991). Thurber would probably add a fourth political variation, disintegrating coalitions.

3. We have argued elsewhere that this effort is better portrayed as an attempt at influence rather than control (Worsham, Eisner, and Ringquist 1997). For ease of presentation and contrast among the three approaches discussed in this chapter, we are choosing to ignore our own advice and speak of such efforts in terms of control.

3

A Brief History of Contemporary Regulatory Politics

THE REGULATORY DEBATES of the past several decades have been intertwined with larger controversies over the role of the state in the economy. Does government have the responsibility to force corporate accountability? Should it promote clean air or worker safety, goods that are systematically neglected by the market? The answers to these questions require trade-offs between the demands for environmental protection, for example, and economic growth. Skepticism over regulation has peaked during downturns in the business cycle, giving rise to debates over how the "regulatory burden" inhibits investment and growth. As these larger debates have evolved, others have focused on regulatory decisionmaking at the agency level. Should agencies promote efficiency by adopting cost-based decision criteria (e.g., cost-benefit and cost-effectiveness analysis), performance indicators, and incentive-based regulatory designs? Should agencies be required to fund the participation of groups that are materially affected by policy but lack the financial wherewithal to make their positions heard? This chapter presents an overview of regulatory history.[1] After a brief examination of regulatory policy before the contemporary era, the chapter explores the rise of the new social regulation in the 1960s and 1970s and the deregulation and reform initiatives of the 1970s through the George W. Bush presidency.

Regulation Before the Contemporary Era

Our overview of regulation begins in the 1880s. It was at this time that a wave of federal regulations began, one that would continue for the remainder of the Progressive Era. In 1887, Congress passed the Interstate Commerce Act, creating the Interstate Commerce Commission to regulate railroads. An 1886 Supreme Court decision invalidating state-level railroad regulation created a vacuum that could be filled only by federal legislation. The act declared that "all charges made for any services rendered . . . shall be reasonable and just." It also prohibited a number of specific practices deemed discriminatory and required that all railroads publish their rate and fare schedules and submit them to the ICC. Although the Court ultimately determined that the act failed to provide the ICC with the authority to set maximum rates, new legislation (the Hepburn Act of 1906) explicitly provided this power.

Three points about the ICC are worth noting. First, although Congress determined that the rates should be "reasonable and just," it failed to provide an operational definition of these vague terms, thereby delegating to the ICC the responsibility of making this determination. Second, although the ICC had no specific information on how to determine rates, it ultimately set rates to reflect costs, thereby creating marketlike outcomes. Any other option would have been quite problematic. Given the high levels of investment and the economies of scale in rail transportation, the industry had many of the characteristics of a *natural monopoly.* Third, the ICC was the first federal agency to take the form of an independent regulatory commission (IRC).

An IRC is formally run by a commission consisting of an odd number of commissioners (usually five or seven), serving staggered terms. The commissions must be formally bipartisan, with no more than a simple majority representing one party. Although the president appoints commissioners, the extent of presidential power is checked by limitations on removal, the staggered nature of appointments, and congressional efforts to protect agency independence. The IRC is an interesting organizational form because it combines quasi-executive, quasi-legislative, and quasi-judicial powers. Vague regulatory mandates (e.g., "reasonable and just" rates) were given substantive meaning through the process of *rule making,* a legislative function. Once an IRC promulgated a rule backed by the force of law, it would identify violators and begin enforcement proceedings, an executive function. Finally, disputes would be resolved through the *adjudication* process conducted within the IRC by administrative law judges. Although this combination of powers violates separation of powers, it was deemed acceptable because this new organizational form was believed to possess the flexibility and concentration of bureaucratic expertise necessary to address some of the more complicated regulatory problems.

In 1890, Congress passed the Sherman Antitrust Act, the legislative foundation of the nation's competition policy (see Chapter 4). By prohibiting monopolization and conspiracies to monopolize, antitrust was designed to preserve markets (see Chapter 1). Although antitrust could be justified on economic grounds, it was understood as having powerful political dimensions as well. Legislators believed that the large business enterprises and trusts that made up the emerging industrial economy constituted so great a concentration of power as to require government to intervene and force accountability. Although the Sherman Act was enforced by the Department of Justice (DOJ), dissatisfaction with the number of prosecutions (and the often convoluted decisions of the Supreme Court) led Congress to pass the Clayton Antitrust Act of 1914, which identified specific practices that were believed to contribute to the creation of monopoly power. The Federal Trade Commission Act (FTCA), passed in the same year, created a new IRC, the Federal Trade Commission. As a result, in antitrust, as in so many other regulatory issue areas, the existence of multiple regulators would become a permanent feature, thereby giving rise to ongoing concerns over redundancy and coordination of enforcement actions.

Although the FTC and the ICC were the flagship regulatory agencies of the Progressive Era, other major regulatory initiatives were introduced during these decades. In 1906, Congress passed the Pure Food and Drug Act, vesting regulatory authority over food additives and pharmaceuticals in an office of the USDA, an entity that would ultimately evolve into the FDA. The same year, consumer protection regulations were extended through the Meat Inspection Act, thereby giving the USDA the responsibility for inspecting meat sold in interstate commerce. The Federal Reserve was created in 1913 to regulate the nation's financial system by establishing reserve requirements and serving as a lender of last resort for member banks. By the eve of World War I, then, a regulatory structure had been put in place that was recognizably modern.

During World War I mobilization, the government had assumed a regulatory posture across the economy through agencies such as the War Industries Board and the Food Administration (see Cuff 1973). In an effort to promote maximum production for the war effort, the mobilization agencies provided assistance in standardizing production and promoting the dissemination of efficiency-promoting innovations. This experience and associationalist doctrines that envisioned a greater role for trade associations working under the supervision of government agencies colored the regulatory record of the 1920s. A number of agencies, including the Departments of Commerce and Interior, the USDA, the FTC, and the ICC, promoted business self-regulation with a minimum of direct government intrusion (see Hawley 1981). In some cases, this was facilitated by new regulatory legislation. The ICC, for example, assumed a very different posture following the passage of the Transportation Act of 1920, which directed the agency to set *minimum* rather than *maximum* rates (Huntington 1952).

As the nation fell into the Great Depression during the 1930s, policymakers searched for some means of promoting economic recovery. Because the potential role of fiscal policy was poorly understood, policymakers sought to introduce economic stability through regulatory initiatives (see Eisner 1995: chap. 6). Thus, the Banking Act of 1933 imposed a number of reforms on the banking industry, mandated the separation of commercial banking (i.e., deposit taking and loan making) and investment banking (underwriting and dealing in corporate stocks and bonds), and created the Federal Deposit Insurance Corporation (FDIC) to insure deposits. Between 1933 and 1935, the National Recovery Administration (NRA) attempted to regulate corporate activity on an economy-wide basis. Through a network of code authorities representing commercial interests by line of business, codes were written to regulate the amount that could be produced, the flow to market, prices, and labor relations. At the same time, the USDA introduced regulations for the farm economy through its Agricultural Adjustment Administration, which sought to elevate farm incomes by introducing voluntary production controls and providing participating farmers with various income supports, such as loans and direct payments. The NRA was declared unconstitutional in 1935; key provisions of the agricultural recovery legislation fell victim to the Supreme Court the next year. Although the agricultural program was retained under new legislation, the NRA ceased to exist. However, the Roosevelt administration promoted a number of new regulatory initiatives designed, once again, to stabilize the economy.

The Securities and Exchange Commission (SEC) was created in 1934 to regulate the stock exchanges and the issuance of corporate securities. That same year, Congress passed the National Housing Act, a mechanism for providing federal charters for savings and loans (S&Ls) and for creating the Federal Savings and Loan Insurance Corporation (FSLIC) to insure deposits in S&Ls. The Federal Communications Act of 1934 established the Federal Communications Commission (FCC) to regulate radio broadcasting, telegraphs, and telephony. The National Labor Relations Board was created in 1935 to regulate industrial relations by guaranteeing the right of workers to organize in unions, prohibiting various devices used in the past to limit unionization, and creating a system of collective bargaining. The Motor Carrier Act of 1935 subjected interstate trucking to the regulation of the ICC. The Civil Aeronautics Act of 1938 extended regulation to air transportation, creating the Civil Aeronautics Authority (renamed the Civil Aeronautics Board [CAB] in 1940).

By the end of the New Deal, the regulatory state had expanded dramatically. Some members of the New Deal were concerned that the new regulatory structures would promote a transfer of wealth to the regulated at the cost of consumers while creating economic bottlenecks that would limit economic dynamism. Expanded antitrust prosecutions were initiated in the late 1930s in hopes of eliminating some of these bottlenecks. However,

World War II quickly drew attention away from these concerns. In the two decades immediately following the war, the regulatory system would look much as it had at the end of the New Deal. However, the critics of regulatory performance would become increasingly vocal, giving voice to some of the capture theories presented in Chapter 1. Increasingly, analysts charged that the agencies that were directed to act in the "public interest" had been captured by powerful economic interests and were using regulations to extract monopoly rents and prevent entry into their industries. The costs to consumers and the impact on the dynamism of the US economy would become increasingly salient once combined with poor economic performance in the late 1970s.

The Rise of the New Social Regulation

A convenient distinction can be drawn between economic and social regulation, as noted in Chapter 1. Although there were social regulations in the Progressive Era (e.g., the Pure Food and Drug Act and the Meat Inspection Act of 1906), they were a minor part of the story. The 1960s and 1970s, in contrast, witnessed the rapid introduction of social regulation and the creation of new agencies such as the Occupational Safety and Health Administration, the Environmental Protection Agency, and the Consumer Product Safety Commission (CPSC). Given the concentrated costs and diffuse benefits associated with social regulatory initiatives, it is a wonder that key pieces of legislation were ever passed. Even if skilled political entrepreneurs might be successful in promoting these kinds of acts on occasion, they do not offer the kinds of electoral returns that attract elected officials.

There are two features of the period that help explain the results. First was the rapid expansion of the interest group universe, particularly with respect to consumer and environmental groups (Schlozman and Tierney 1986). Many activists were drawn to public advocacy as a result of the modern muckraking of Ralph Nader or their experiences in the civil rights and antiwar movements (Berry 1984: 16–45). Second, however, participants were motivated by the New Left's critique of capitalist democracy, which invested their activism with theoretical significance (see Eisner 2000: 118–133; Harris and Milkis 1996). The New Left (see Marcuse 1964; Reich 1970; Domhoff 1970) rejected the domination of large corporate, military, and governmental bureaucracies that promoted conformity and subverted human rights and environmental quality to the demands of capitalism. It called for an affirmation of the individual, the creation of so-called parallel institutions to contest the power of the corporate state and provide the basis for a more participatory democracy. New policies were necessary to increase corporate accountability and protect the environment, workers, and consumers.

As one might imagine, those who accepted the New Left's vision of participatory democracy were attracted to the Nader exposés and the accounts of agency capture by Marver Bernstein (1955), Gabriel Kolko (1963), and Grant McConnell (1966). If existing regulatory institutions were designed or had evolved to protect the regulated by guaranteeing profits and preventing competition, new policies had to be combined with new administrative forms. Certainly, the historical record suggested that the independent regulatory commission was destined for capture and rigidity. But the problems could also be connected to an excessive delegation of authority that diffused accountability and located policymaking authority in the agencies that were more receptive to the demands of regulated interests (see Lowi 1979; Davis 1969). If new regulatory initiatives were to be successful, it was argued, it would be necessary to design institutions to minimize the potential for capture or direct political control, maximize the opportunities for participation, and severely constrain bureaucratic discretion. Thus, Congress placed OSHA in the Department of Labor (DOL); the EPA was established as an independent agency. While the CPSC was created as an independent regulatory commission (a political response to Richard Nixon's efforts to assert control), there were a number of features designed to promote high levels of participation (see Moe 1989).

The rule-making processes at the new agencies were far more complicated than required under the Administrative Procedure Act (see Bryner 1987), including multiple layers of review and ample opportunities for group input. By design, agencies implemented intervenor funding programs to subsidize the participation of interests that lacked the necessary resources (Boyer 1981). At the CPSC, a unique offeror process was put into effect that completely opened the standard-setting process to maximize participation (see Chapter 9). In addition, key regulatory initiatives of the period guaranteed citizens the right to sue agencies to force the execution of nondiscretionary duties. Henceforth, advocacy groups would make frequent recourse to the courts to force compliance with the law (Melnick 1983: 9–13; see also Stewart 1975). The new regulatory legislation also placed severe limits on bureaucratic discretion through detailed legislation. These efforts at programmed implementation led legislators to establish detailed timetables despite the fact that the goals of policy were unachievable under existing technology.

In the end, institutions designed to promote maximum participation and minimal bureaucratic discretion were combined with regulatory mandates that required a heavy reliance on social scientific and scientific expertise. The problems addressed by the new social regulation were highly complex and could not be addressed without detailed analysis. Paradoxically, regulatory mandates consciously designed to minimize delegation addressed such complex issues as to require delegation to scientific and social scientific experts in the agencies. Institutions consciously designed to maximize participation reduced regulatory responsiveness by embroiling agencies in protracted hearings. Although institutions were consciously designed to reduce the influence of regulated parties, the need to muster scientific and social scientific expertise to effectively support one's regulatory recommendations created but another financial barrier to entry that limited the practical impact of the formal procedural guarantees.

Deregulation and Regulatory Reform

The regulatory victories were not the only legacies of the 1970s. Economic *stagflation,* the combination of inflation and low growth, became one of the most salient problems of the decade. Critics of regulation identified stagflation as an important window of opportunity. By drawing an explicit connection between regulatory excess on the one hand, and inflation and low growth on the other, they might be successful in forcing retrenchment, even if the empirical record linking their independent and dependent variables was thin. As one might expect, advocates of free markets drew freely on the older literature of regulatory capture and the economic theory of regulation (Stigler 1971; Posner 1974; Peltzman 1976). If the established regulatory agencies were, in reality, public cartel managers who were conspiring with the regulated to impose monopoly rents, there was reason to withdraw their legal authority and revitalize markets. While this argument was made repeatedly by free market economists, it was also articulated by consumer advocates, who—as noted earlier—saw little justification for extending the lives of such agencies. Deregulation quickly became a central feature of the decade's politics.

This odd alliance of free-marketeers and consumer advocates broke down, however, once attention turned to the new social regulations. Certainly, regulatory critics contended, the correlation of the unprecedented cost of the new social regulations and stagflation was not simply the product of chance. Critics argued that regulatory reform was a necessity: agencies should be required to consider explicitly the economic costs and benefits of their actions. In some cases, it was argued, this should take the form of *cost-benefit analysis.* By forcing policymakers to identify and monetize the costs, benefits, and externalities, they could arrive at a better judgment as to whether their activities were actually contributing to social welfare. In response, advocates of regulation noted that the problems of cost-benefit analysis were legion, particularly in the area of social regulation, where it is impossible to identify and assign monetary value to many benefits because they are expressed in probabilistic terms and occur in a distant future. In contrast, costs are immediate and concentrated, and thus provide clear incentives for mobilization. It was feared that the application of cost-benefit analysis would stack the deck against environmental quality and workplace safety. Some suggested that *cost-effectiveness analysis* was more appropriate in social regulations, since the monetization of benefits was not required. One might argue that the determination of *what* we want to maximize is a political determination; how we pursue these values might be shaped by considerations of cost. Critics were wary, however, and viewed regulatory reform in any of its manifestations as a Trojan horse designed to deliver deregulation instead.

Despite the concerns, regulatory reform became another important feature of the 1970s—one that continues to the present day. Concerns over the costs of the new environmental protection regulations were used by President Nixon to justify the creation of an interagency quality-of-life review process in 1971. Agencies were required to submit significant rules to the OMB thirty days before the announcement of rule making in the *Federal Register,* along with analyses identifying the goals of policy, the alternative regulatory approaches considered, the costs and benefits of each, and the justification for the agency's selection (see Eads and Fix 1984: 48). Gerald Ford built on this legacy when he created the Council on Wage and Price Stability (COWPS) to monitor events that could contribute to inflation. The "inflation impact statement," as established under Executive Order (EO) 11821, became the central document in the review of government activity. Agencies in the executive branch were required to certify that they had considered the potential inflationary impact of new rules and regulations. The OMB instructed agencies to conduct a cost-benefit analysis of rules that would impose costs of $100 million or more, or impact on productivity, employment, the supply of key raw materials, and energy consumption. COWPS reviewed these inflation impact statements, along with the Council of Economic Advisers (CEA) and the OMB (Ball 1984: 51–54; McGarity 1991: 18–19).

President Jimmy Carter contributed to regulatory reform when he created the Regulatory Analysis and Review Group (RARG) in January 1978. Representatives of several executive agencies sat on RARG, which was headed by a committee including a member of the CEA, the OMB, and two additional agency representatives. Although RARG reviewed regulations with an impact of $100 million per year, it concentrated on a small number of rules each year and subjected them to more detailed examination. Under EO 12044, Carter established as administration policy that regulations "shall be as simple and clear as possible. They shall achieve legislative goals effectively and efficiently. They shall not impose unnecessary burdens on the economy, on individuals, or public or private organizations, or on state and local governments." The executive order also required that agencies compile a regulatory analysis for all significant rules, comprising a statement of the problem, a discussion of alternative responses, an economic analysis of these alternatives, and a detailed justification of the agency's final decision. Carter prescribed cost-effectiveness as the proper analytic method. The administration directed agencies to provide maximum opportunities for participation in the regulatory process, mandating advance notice of proposed rule making, open hearings, and a minimum of sixty days for public comment (see Gerston, Fraleigh, and Schwab 1988: 44–48). In hopes of minimizing regulatory redundancy and conflicts, Carter created the Regulatory Council in October 1978. The mission of the council was to compile a regulatory calendar and provide a context in which regulators from the executive branch and independent agencies could discuss their initiatives, explore the potential conflicts with existing regulations, and pool experience (Eads and Fix 1984: 61–62).

The regulatory reform initiatives of the 1970s were limited by some common problems. First, agencies had a great deal of discretion in compliance. Although each administration defined what constituted a *significant* regulation, agencies were responsible for identifying these regulations and initiating the process. Second, although reformers hoped that cost-benefit or cost-effectiveness analysis would provide an analytical framework for decisionmaking, regulatory analyses often occurred after all major decisions had been made. Finally, the review processes failed to provide the OMB or any other body with the tools necessary to prevent the promulgation of a rule that failed to meet the cost-based analyses (see Eisner 1994: 105). Nevertheless, these initiatives elevated economics in status relative to the legal discourse that had for so long dominated the regulatory process. This ascendance of economics in agency decisionmaking would find its ultimate expression in the 1980s (see Tolchin and Tolchin 1983).

Congress supported the regulatory reform efforts of the decade by passing two key pieces of legislation designed to reduce the regulatory burden. The Regulatory Flexibility Act of 1980 amended the Administrative Procedure Act to require that regulators examine alternatives designed to reduce burdens and/or enhance benefits to small entities. It also mandated the review of rules every ten years. The Paperwork Reduction Act of 1980 required agencies to justify their collection of information by establishing the need and intended use of the information, estimating the burden that the collection would impose, and showing that they had adopted the least burdensome way to gather the information. It provided the OMB with the broad power to review requests made by government agencies for information and reports from businesses and individuals (Weiss 1981; GAO 1996a).

In addition to regulatory reform, the 1970s also brought waves of deregulation. Economic regulations were, in many cases, phased out.

Alternatively, market-based reforms were introduced to reorient regulation. Deregulation was not completely separate from regulatory reform. Regulators who encountered economic arguments from the OMB and other executive review organs (and, increasingly, the courts!) searched for ways to internalize the debates within their agencies. A host of agencies (including the Justice Department's Antitrust Division, the FTC, the SEC, the ICC, the FCC, the EPA, and CAB) established or enlarged economics and policy staffs or offices. Economists and policy analysts often became important internal advocates for deregulation (see Eisner 1994: 107–109). As a result, in some cases, deregulation found its origins in agency actions that were subsequently affirmed and extended by legislation (e.g., the Airline Deregulation Act of 1978, the Motor Carrier Act of 1980, the Depository Institutions Deregulation and Monetary Control Act of 1980). While the detailed history in each case is complicated, as a generalization the results reflected the intersection of academic debates on the economics of regulation, bureaucratic activism, and congressional action (see Derthick and Quirk 1985). Deregulation affected virtually every sector of the economy that had come under economic regulation. Commercial aviation, commercial banking, natural gas, railroads, securities underwriting and brokering, telecommunications, and trucking would never be the same.

A Reagan-Bush Revolution in Regulation?

Ronald Reagan made the battle against regulation a central plank of his economic recovery program, explicitly linking the regulatory sprawl of the 1970s with stagflation. The Reagan agenda in regulation had clear goals: to prevent the introduction of new regulations that could not be justified by cost-benefit analysis and to revoke or revise existing regulations that circumvented the market. The means of accomplishing these goals were also clearly defined. First, regulators would be subjected to intensified regulatory oversight centralized in the OMB—a continuation and culmination of earlier reform efforts. Second, regulatory agencies would be forced to endure new and often crippling budget constraints. Third, loyalists would be placed in management positions within the agencies to further the president's regulatory goals.

One of Reagan's first acts on assuming office was to create the President's Task Force on Regulatory Relief under the chairmanship of the then vice president, George H. W. Bush. The task force was given a large mandate: to take a broad view of existing and proposed regulations to determine whether they contributed net social benefits. In the process, it was to identify the regulations that imposed the greatest regulatory burden. One month after the creation of the task force, Reagan issued EO 12291, which imposed a sixty-day freeze on pending regulations and final rules so that the task force could examine their economic impact. By August 1983 the task force had identified 119 regulations deemed ripe for review. In the end, 76 were revised or struck from the books altogether (Andrews 1984: 73–74; Clark 1981).

Executive Order 12291 not only imposed a freeze, but also imposed a new process for regulatory review. The order clearly stated the administration's commitment that "regulatory action shall not be taken unless the potential benefits to society for the regulation outweigh the potential costs." To this end, all executive branch regulators were required to compile a regulatory impact analysis (RIA) for all major significant rules. The RIAs were to be based in cost-benefit analysis (recall that Carter's EO 12044 had directed agencies to conduct cost-effectiveness analysis). Under EO 12291, the OMB was empowered to flag any regulation as requiring review. At the same time, it could wave the RIA requirements. Agencies that failed to file RIAs or failed to incorporate the OMB's comments into the rule-making package were prohibited from proceeding toward rule making. Appeals to the OMB's decisions could be made to the Task Force on Regulatory Relief, an entity with a clear antiregulatory bias.

Three impacts of the Reagan regulatory reform activities are worth noting. First, as a result of OMB regulatory clearance, the pace of regulation fell dramatically. The OMB was serving quite consciously as a bottleneck in the regulatory process. Second, the new internal review requirements were imposed in an environment of shrinking budgets, thereby diverting funds from enforcement. Finally, agencies commonly reacted to the enhanced status of economic analysis in the regulatory process by creating or further expanding internal policy offices and explicitly integrating economics into the policy process.

In addition to intensified regulatory oversight, agencies were forced to weather budgetary retrenchment, particularly during Reagan's first term of office. Here, the budgetary figures paint an unambiguous picture. In real inflation-adjusted terms, the reductions in budgets between 1980 and 1988 were 44.8 percent for the CPSC, 39.4 percent for the EPA, 8.7 percent for the FCC, 25.6 percent for the FTC, 34.1 percent for the Antitrust Division, and 12.0 percent for OSHA. In each of these cases, dramatic budget reductions forced staffing cuts. In some cases, such as the EPA and the CPSC, the loss of personnel and the poor morale it inspired were close to disabling.

The final element in the Reagan regulatory strategy was to place loyalists into management positions where they might exercise greater control over the pace of regulatory growth at the agency level. They also commonly implemented reorganization plans that placed greater power in the hands of administration appointees and consolidated offices following the staff reductions forced by the budget cuts (see Eads and Fix 1984: 140–148). In many cases, the new regulatory managers shared an expertise in economic analysis and applied this expertise to make certain that the agencies would bring their actions into line with economic theory. In these cases, the new executives often promoted economic professionalization of their agencies and the integration of economic analysis in each stage of regulatory decisionmaking. In other cases, the executives simply shared a strong antiregulatory posture that would allow them to prevent a continuation of old enforcement patterns (e.g., Anne Gorsuch-Burford at the EPA; Thorne Auchter at OSHA). In some cases, obstructionism often attracted the attention of Congress and the media, embroiling the agencies in controversy.

A Kinder, Gentler Regulation

Given his tenure as head of the President's Task Force on Regulatory Relief, many expected George H. W. Bush to continue the war against regulation once he assumed the presidency. Yet, on the campaign trail, he promised *more* environmental protection in the areas of acid rain, toxic wastes, and wetlands preservation. Critics of regulation were relieved when one of Bush's first presidential acts was to take the functions that had been assigned to the Task Force on Regulatory Relief and give them to a new President's Council on Competitiveness, headed by Vice President Dan Quayle. The elation disappeared, however, when there were clear indications that regulatory reform was not going to receive the emphasis many had expected. The council languished without internal structures or a full-time staff until July 1990. Moreover, Bush's choice to head the OMB's Office of Information and Regulatory Affairs (OIRA) remained stalled in the Senate as Democrats extracted payment for the role OIRA had played during the Reagan years. When late in 1989 and into 1990 administration critics began writing articles about "re-regulation" under Bush, the council received staffing support and became far more active. Functioning under the authority of Reagan's EO 12291, the council forced executive branch agencies to subject their proposed regulations to cost-benefit analysis at an early stage in the process—with results that were particularly disturbing for the EPA (Victor 1991).

Late in 1991, more coverage on the Bush record in regulation was released, including a *National Journal* cover story that labeled Bush the "regulatory president." As Jonathan Rauch (1991) has detailed, the *Federal Register* had grown almost 14,000 pages longer than it had been in the final year of the Reagan presidency. Adjusted for inflation, regulation was costing 22 percent more than it had during the final year of the Carter presidency. In an effort to reverse this trend, Bush introduced a ninety-day moratorium on new regulations in his 1992 State of the Union speech. During the ninety days, regulations deemed pro-growth were to be accelerated, whereas those that were deemed to impose a "substantial cost on the economy" were to be examined to determine whether they were cost-beneficial, whether they were sufficiently flexible, whether they adopted market mechanisms, and whether they were clear enough to avoid litigation. The moratorium was coordinated by White House counsel C. Boyden Gray and CEA chairman Michael Boskin, with the "Quayle Council" reviewing regulations with the support of OIRA. To critics, the moratorium seemed to be little more than a political ploy designed to appeal to conservative Republicans who questioned Bush's conservative credentials. After all, a moratorium had made more sense after the Carter presidency than at a point when the Republicans had controlled the executive branch for eleven years. Moreover, the review mandated by Bush could have been conducted under the Reagan executive orders (Victor 1992; Kolb 1993: 73–78).

In the end, Bush can be best described as having a "regulatory schizophrenia," as one of his former advisers notes (Kolb 1993: 70). The same president that created the President's Council on Competitiveness and imposed a regulatory moratorium was an active participant in shaping two of the most expensive regulatory statutes in the nation's history: the Americans with Disabilities Act of 1990 and the Clean Air Act (CAA) of 1990. This latter piece of legislation, which earned the scorn of regulatory critics, was described by Bush as "the most significant air pollution legislation in our nation's history" and by White House counsel Gray as "the most sweeping environmental statute in the history of the world" (Mervin 1996: 96). In fact, many regulatory agencies (including the EPA, OSHA, and the FTC) entered a period of mild revitalization and budgetary growth under the leadership of Bush appointees who were far more committed to active regulation than one would have imagined, given Bush's role in the Reagan deregulation efforts.

The Clinton Presidency: A Mirror Image?

One might easily attempt to portray the Clinton presidency as the mirror image of the second Reagan term. The presidency was controlled by a Democrat sympathetic to the mandates of key regulatory agencies, and after the 1994 midterm elections, Congress was under unified Republican control. As one might expect, this made the political environment conflictive. Yet many of the conservative assumptions concerning regulatory policymaking and analysis introduced in the late 1970s and 1980s had been accepted by Democrats and advocated by the Clinton administration as part of the larger effort to "reinvent government."

During the 1992 presidential campaign, Bill Clinton proclaimed his support for regulatory agencies addressing environmental protection, consumer protection, and workplace safety and health. On the twenty-second anniversary of Earth Day, candidate Clinton promised his audience "a new covenant for environmental progress" with "three priorities: exerting new American leadership to protect the global environment; preserving the quality of our environment here at home; and finding ways to promote innovation and growth consistent with firm environmental goals" (Clinton 1996: 138). His vice presidential selection of Al Gore, a noted environmental advocate, gave an additional indication of his support for vigorous environmental protection. Similarly, he called for a "new energy policy" premised on "renewable resources and natural gas and energy efficiency" (Clinton 1996: 404). The Democratic Party's platform echoed these themes, noting its commitment to environmental quality and a safe workplace.

On assuming office, Clinton moved quickly to eliminate the Reagan-era regulatory review system. Executive Order 12866 of September 30, 1993, revoked Reagan's EO 12291 and expunged the Council on Competitiveness. While these revocations might have offered hope to regulatory advocates, EO 12866 established a regulatory review process that was not markedly dissimilar from that which existed under EO 12291. Under the new review system, agencies were responsible for conducting analyses justifying all significant regulations (once again, defined as those with an impact of $100 million or more) and submitting them for review to the OMB. The analyses had to identify the problem; determine whether the problem was the result of existing regulations; identify alternatives, "including providing economic incentives to encourage the desired behavior, such as user fees or marketable permits, or providing information upon which choices can be made by the public" and the option of no regulation at all; and "assess the costs and the benefits of the intended regulation and, recognizing that some costs and benefits are difficult to quantify, propose or adopt a regulation only upon a reasoned determination that the benefits of the intended regulation justify the costs." As under EO 12291, OIRA was given the responsibility of analyzing agency submissions and requesting revisions. Agencies were prohibited from publishing in the *Federal Register* until OIRA had waived its review or completed its review and no corrective actions were required on the part of the agency (§ 1).

In an effort to coordinate regulatory actions and minimize duplication, EO 12866 required annual policy meetings in which agency heads would identify their regulatory priorities for the upcoming year. All regulatory agencies (including independent agencies) were to submit regulatory agendas to OIRA, which would be combined as a "unified regulatory agenda." In addition, beginning in 1994, each agency was required to submit regulatory plans stating objectives, each planned significant regulatory action, the legal basis for the actions, the need for the action, and a schedule. These plans would then be circulated to all affected agencies, which in turn were directed to submit their comments or concerns to OIRA, which would then seek to eliminate conflicts. Finally, EO 12866 established the Regulatory Working Group, consisting of agency heads, which would meet quarterly "as a forum to assist agencies in identifying and analyzing important regulatory issues (including, among others [1] the development of innovative regulatory techniques, [2] the methods, efficacy, and utility of comparative risk assessment in regulatory decision-making, and [3] the development of short forms and other streamlined regulatory approaches for small businesses and other entities)" (§ 4[d]). Thus, EO 12866 emphasized the need for regulatory review to reduce redundancies and burdens where possible, although there were questions as to whether the Clinton appointees were complying with its provisions (see Weidenbaum 1997).

The same themes were articulated as part of the "reinventing government," or REGO, activities during the Clinton administration. The idea of reinventing government had been hotly debated during the previous administration, as Bush and his advisers sought to introduce the so-called New Paradigm, whereby government would incorporate insights from the private sector to enhance agency performance and responsiveness. Influenced by David Osborne and Ted Gaebler's book *Reinventing Government* and the communitarianism of Amitai Etzioni, advisers to Bush saw the New Paradigm as a way to counter the claims that the president lacked the "vision thing" (see Kolb 1993: 284, 330). The Clinton administration was far more committed to the venture. On assuming office, Gore and a staff of 260 began working on the REGO project. At a press conference on the south lawn of the White House, Gore announced the basic findings of his staff against the backdrop of two large forklifts loaded with government regulations. He noted that the goal was to produce rules that work—rules that are results- and customer-oriented, free of duplication, and empower workers. This would require a simplification of process, a reduction in middle management, and an increase in government responsiveness. Gore linked REGO to deficit reduction, noting that it would allow government to eliminate 252,000 bureaucrats and cut spending by $108 billion—a soft figure that the OMB refused to endorse (Drew 1994: 294–295).

Congress joined in with the administration's efforts. The Government Performance and Results Act of 1993 (Public Law [PL] 103-62) required executive agency heads to prepare a strategic plan for their agencies, identifying goals for all major activities. These plans, submitted jointly to the director of the OMB and Congress, had to adopt a time frame of at least five years, with three-year updates. Agencies were required to prepare annual performance plans and to report annually to the president and Congress on the success in achieving the goals presented for the previous year, including "performance indicators, actual program performance, and a comparison with plan goals for that fiscal year." In hopes of stimulating public-sector innovations, the act required the OMB director to "designate: (1) no fewer than ten agencies (representing a range of Government functions) as pilot projects in performance measurement; (2) no fewer than five agencies (selected from agencies in performance measurement pilot projects) as pilot projects in managerial accountability and flexibility; and (3) no fewer than five agencies (selected from agencies in performance measurement pilot projects) as pilot projects in performance budgeting" (PL 103-62, "Summary"). Critics expressed concerns that agencies would emphasize goals that could be expressed in simple indicators that would, in the end, become more important than the broader public interest (see *OMB Watch*, December 19, 1997).

To be certain, President Clinton made a number of appointments to regulatory agencies that reflected his sympathy for the goals that had been under fire for the previous twelve years. Given the attention paid to the efforts of these appointees in subsequent chapters, we will not summarize their activities or qualifications here. Yet the level of regulatory activity was, in many cases, *less* than that which had existed under Bush. William Niskanen, chair of the Council of Economic Advisers during the Reagan presidency and a staunch critic of regulation, noted: "Clinton's regulatory record (so far) is better than Bush's. This is the good news. You already know the bad news: the Bush record was *awful*. The Bush administration imposed more costly, new regulatory legislation than that of any administration since Nixon" (Niskanen 1996: 25). Writing four years into the Clinton presidency, Niskanen noted that the number of pages in the *Federal Register* (a painfully imprecise indicator of regulatory sprawl) had grown at a 3.2 percent annual rate under Clinton—slightly above the Bush administration, which had restricted growth to 3.0 percent (compared with a 4.5 percent annual decline under Reagan). Real budgetary outlays had grown by 2.0 percent per year, less than half the 4.6 percent annual growth during Bush (but well above the 1.1 percent growth of Reagan). Regulatory staff had grown by 1.2 percent per year under Clinton, almost one-quarter the 4.7 percent growth rate of Bush. The Reagan administration had realized a 1.9 percent annual reduction in regulatory staff. Finally, the real regulatory costs imposed per household had grown 0.4 percent per year during the Clinton presidency, compared with a 2.8 percent growth rate during Bush and a 2.7 percent annual *reduction* under Reagan (Niskanen 1996).

One might attribute some of the disparity between regulatory promise and performance to Clinton's Democratic Leadership Council centrism. Clinton clearly identified himself as a "New Democrat," a label claimed by politicians who believe that some core Democratic values may be best pursued through private-sector activities and market forces. Yet Clinton's regulatory record may be a product of three additional factors. First, the Reagan-Bush years may have effectively changed the terms of the regulatory debate, giving rise to a new consensus that recognized the importance of considering economic impacts. Second, the dramatic cuts in regulatory budgets during the Reagan presidency and the deprofessionalization of many agencies may have made them less capable of returning to an activist posture. Both of these issues will be examined in more detail in the case studies in this book. Third, the president does not act in a political vacuum. In regulation, as in so many other domestic policy arenas, he must operate as part of the system of separate institutions sharing power (Neustadt 1980). Even if Clinton had sought to return to a high level of regulatory activism, the new Republican majority in Congress would have made that impossible.

Regulation After the "Contract with America"

The 1994 midterm elections were devastating for anyone who believed that the Clinton victory two years earlier had marked a return to unified Democratic Party rule. The 1994 elections placed both chambers under Republican control, albeit by relatively slim margins of 230 to 204 in the House and 53 to 47 in the Senate. Two Democratic incumbents in the Senate and thirty-five Democratic incumbents in the House were defeated, whereas no Republican incumbents suffered this fate. The House Republicans ran on the basis of the Contract with America, a platform that promised to alter dramatically public-sector governance and the role of the state in the economy and society. The contract promised the passage of the Job Creation and Wage Enhancement Act, consisting of "small business incentives, capital gains cut and indexation, neutral cost recovery, risk assessment/cost-benefit analysis, strengthening the Regulatory Flexibility Act and unfunded mandate reform to create jobs and raise worker wages." While voters may have had scant knowledge of the contract's provisions, public sentiment clearly supported any platform devoted largely (seven of the ten planks) to reducing the role of government. Data from polls taken on the eve of the election are presented in the Roper Center's publication *America at the Polls, 1994* (Ladd 1995: 26–27). Some 66 percent of those polled identified government as the problem, not the solution. Another 80 percent saw the government as being run for the benefit of special interests, not the people. Only 22 percent believed they could trust the government to do what is right most or all of the time. To the extent that the Contract with America promised to scale back on government and increase its efficiency, accountability, and responsiveness, it found a ready constituency.

The Job Creation and Wage Enhancement Act of 1995 quickly passed the House of Representatives on March 3, 1995, sending a shock wave through the regulatory community. The detailed risk-assessment and cost-benefit requirements, the extension of the rule-making process, and the multiple venues for review and appeal promised to mire regulatory agencies in a procedural quagmire (Benenson 1995a, 1995b). In the end, HR 9 was reported to the Senate, where it quickly became the victim of presidential politics. Bob Dole, the Senate majority leader, who would subsequently claim the Republican presidential nomination in 1996, embraced the legislation to shore up conservative support. Democrats, in turn, used parliamentary maneuvers to kill the legislation. Other bills also languished in the Senate when it became clear that the narrow Republican majority was incapable of preventing filibuster (Freedman 1995a, 1995b, 1995c, 1995d, 1995e; Gruenwald 1995). Despite the failure of many key provisions of the Contract with America legislation, what is surprising is how many of the regulatory reform proposals actually emerged from the legislative process and were signed into law.

In March 1995, Clinton signed the Unfunded Mandates Reform Act (PL 104-4), designed to prevent Congress from passing laws that impose mandates on private-sector actors or other levels of government without appropriating the funds for their implementation. Many social regulatory policies have, in the past, required state governments to bear implementation duties without providing funds. Under the act, the Congressional Budget Office (CBO) has to analyze bills that would impose a significant burden (defined as $50 million or more to state, local, and tribal governments; $100 million to the private sector). Analyses would have to include "a qualitative, and if practicable, a quantitative, assessment of costs and benefits anticipated from the Federal mandates (including the effects on health and safety and the protection of the natural environment)" (§ 423[c]). If the analysis is not conducted or if the bill exceeds the above-mentioned thresholds and Congress fails to provide funding, the bill is automatically subject to a point of order on the floor of the chamber (§ 425[a]).

Congress also passed a reauthorization of the Paperwork Reduction Act (PL 104-13), which was signed into law in May 1995 (see Ponessa 1995). This act, originally passed in 1980, was designed to reduce the paperwork burdens placed on the private sector. Since paperwork requirements are some of the greatest costs associated with regulation, critics of regulation who wanted to increase government accountability deemed the reauthorization of this act important. The act expanded electronic information dissemination and required agencies to reduce the hours required to comply with paperwork by 40 percent by 2001, under the direction of the OMB's OIRA (see Shanahan 1997).

Congress passed the Small Business Regulatory Enforcement Fairness Act of 1996 (PL 104-121), which was signed by the president in March 1996. The act established a number of protections for small businesses that might be adversely affected by regulation. Subtitle A, "Regulatory Compliance Simplification," requires agencies to publish compliance guides for small businesses for rules that require a regulatory flexibility analysis. The act also requires agencies to answer inquiries regarding compliance through the creation of a program explicitly for this purpose. Section 413 amended the Small Business Act to require that small business development centers provide information regarding regulatory requirements. Subtitle B, "Regulatory Enforcement Reforms," requires the Small Business Administration to create a position of ombudsman for small business and agriculture regulatory enforcement, as well as, in each regional office, a regulatory fairness board for small business, to comprise "owners, operators, or officers of small entities." The boards will meet annually with the ombudsmen and report "on instances of excessive enforcement actions taken against small businesses." The act also requires all agencies regulating small entities to create, within one year, a program "for the reduction and possible waiver of civil penalties for violations of a statutory or regulatory requirement by a small entity." Subtitle C, "Equal Access to Justice Act Amendments," requires the award of defense fees and adjudication costs "in which the demand of a regulatory agency against a small entity is found to be substantially excessive and unreasonable."

PL 104-121 also amended the Regulatory Flexibility Act by requiring that proposed and final interpretive rules involving the internal revenue laws be accompanied with initial and final regulatory analyses. It also required that the final analyses explicitly identify the number of small businesses affected, the compliance requirements imposed, and the steps taken to minimize the economic impact. The amendments also increased the demands on agencies by requiring that their determinations of impact be backed with analysis. The law requires that the EPA and OSHA provide small businesses (through the Small Business Administration) with information regarding the impact of a proposed rule on small businesses prior to the publication of an initial regulatory flexibility analysis. It also requires the agencies to use a review panel consisting of small business representatives to collect information on the impact of a proposed rule and solicit recommendations, all of which would become part of the rule-making record.

Subtitle E of PL 104-121 also included new provisions for congressional review. The act subjected rules to congressional review by establishing that, before a rule can take effect as a final rule, the agency must submit to both chambers (and the Office of the Comptroller General) a report containing, among other things, the agency's determination of whether the rule is a major rule and a cost-benefit analysis for all such rules. The act explicitly prohibits a rule from taking effect "if the Congress passes a joint resolution of disapproval." It also prohibits agencies from reissuing a disapproved rule in substantially the same form. Of course, the president can veto the joint resolution, and a rule can be exempted if the president notifies Congress in writing that it is "(1) necessary because of an imminent threat to health or safety or other emergency; (2) necessary for the enforcement of criminal laws; (3) necessary for national security; or (4) issued pursuant to any statute implementing an international trade agreement." Additionally, the act prohibits judicial review of determinations made under this title (PL 104-121, "Summary").

The Omnibus Appropriations Act of 1997 (PL 104-208) required the OMB to establish a regulatory accounting system to track the costs and benefits of significant regulations (once again, those with an annual impact of $100 million or more). More important, the act required the OMB, no later than September 30, 1997, to submit to Congress a report providing estimates of the total annual costs and benefits of federal regulatory programs. The analysis had to include an assessment of the direct and indirect impacts of federal rules on the private sector, state and local government, and the federal government. The OMB director had to make recommendations (reflecting public comments) "to reform or eliminate any Federal regulatory program or program element that is inefficient, ineffective, or is not a sound use of the Nation's resources."

Critics of the Contract with America created the impression that the Republican juggernaut was effectively defeated following Clinton's "E-squared, M-squared" strategy of summer and fall 1995, whereby the administration mobilized interests and used the media to question what would occur to the environment, education, Medicare, and Medicaid under the contract (Walker 1996: 338; Weisman 1996c). However, this impression was not entirely correct. While most of the successful initiatives were less extreme than those initially proposed, they were nonetheless consequential. Through the measures listed above, Congress sought to impose ever tighter control over regulatory agencies by requiring a more thoroughgoing application of cost-benefit analysis, heightening agency accountability to Congress through greater reporting requirements and congressional review, and increasing agency consideration for the impact of their decisions on key constituents who have traditionally borne a large share of regulatory compliance costs.

The George W. Bush Administration: Continuity or Change?

In the late 1970s and early 1980s, critics characterized regulatory agencies as rigid bureaucracies that exhibited a perverse fascination with command and control instruments and an arrogant disregard for compliance costs and economic impacts. There were few, if any, means of forcing accountability for performance. Two decades later, the standard critiques of regulation seemed shopworn at best. Consider the issue of accountability for performance and economic impacts. Cost-benefit analysis-based regulatory review had survived multiple presidencies. Although Vice President Gore had denounced the regulatory review process of the Reagan-Bush years, the system enacted during the Clinton presidency retained both a central role for the OMB-OIRA in regulatory clearance and for cost-benefit analysis as the methodology of choice. Under the Government Performance and Results Act, agencies were now required to submit strategic plans with clear performance indicators and report on their performance on an annual basis. Consider the issue of bureaucratic rigidity. While standard bureaucratic organizations continued to flourish following a decade-long experiment with REGO, regulators routinely employed public-private partnerships, worked to build alliances with "stakeholders," emphasized compliance assistance over traditional enforcement, and disseminated voluminous information to the public via agency websites.

Following the first two-term Democratic presidency in decades, many wondered if the presidency of George W. Bush would be characterized by continuity with Clinton-era regulations or a return to the antiregulatory rhetoric and practices of the early 1980s. On the face of things, one could easily make the case for continuity. Perhaps the nation's first president with a Harvard MBA would prove to be a strong supporter of regulatory reinvention, with the newfound emphasis on public-private partnerships, voluntarism, and regulatory flexibility. Yet members of the public interest community were highly suspicious. Both President Bush and Vice President Dick Cheney had well-established ties to corporate America, the vice president having left the helm at Halliburton to assume his new position. On the campaign trail they made frequent references to the need for tort reform, which members of the consumer movement viewed as anathema to consumer protection. With respect to energy policy, they called for further electricity deregulation and new incentives for the petroleum industry (including permitting oil and gas exploration in the Alaskan National Wildlife Refuge). This latter position, when combined with opposition to the Kyoto Protocol on Climate Change, raised profound concerns for environmentalists. While Bush promised to bring "compassionate conservatism" to the White House, critics feared that there would be a return to Reagan's "morning in America."

As noted earlier, the Reagan presidency began with a regulatory freeze, the imposition of a new system of regulatory review, deep budget cuts, and the appointment of loyalists throughout the regulatory bureaucracy. When viewed in this context, the new Bush presidency bore only a distant resemblance to its predecessor. Like the Reagan administration, one of the Bush administration's first actions was to issue a sixty-day freeze on final regulatory rules that had not yet gone into effect. Some of these rules, like the EPA's new arsenic standard, raised immediate objections on the part of environmentalists. Although the Bush administration decided to retain the

regulatory review process put into place by the Clinton administration—
clear evidence of the extent to which cost-benefit analysis-based review had
become part of a new consensus—the Bush OMB-OIRA would assume a
far more activist stance with respect to scrutinizing new regulations (see
Goldstein and Cohen 2004). On the budgetary front, although several agencies faced reduced appropriations in the early years of the Bush presidency,
they were nothing comparable to the severe reductions encountered in the
first years of the Reagan presidency. Moreover, most major agencies realized budget increases thereafter; in many cases, these increases were substantial. As one might expect, ongoing budgetary support often translated
into continued enforcement, although the vigor and focus on enforcement
varied by agency.

The new president made some appointments that raised distinct concerns (see Labaton 2001a). Mary Sheila Gall, for example, was appointed to
serve as chair of the Consumer Product Safety Commission, despite (or
because of) her record of citing consumer negligence as a leading source of
product-related injuries and deaths and her opposition to the "federal nanny
state" that the CPSC had allegedly promoted through its policies. The
appointment failed to clear Senate confirmation following vigorous lobbying by consumer advocates (Javitt and DeFrancesco 2001). In contrast,
other appointments were viewed more or less positively, either because of
their acknowledged regulatory expertise (e.g., Timothy Muris at the Federal
Trade Commission) or because of the high profile they might bring to the
policy area in question (e.g., Christine Todd Whitman at the Environmental
Protection Agency). As the following chapters will reveal, it is difficult to
arrive at any simple characterization of such a diverse cast of actors.

In many agencies, there was, as one might expect, a continuation of
Clinton-style public-private partnerships and voluntary initiatives. Yet there
was a distinct difference compared with earlier REGO experiments. During
the Clinton administration, REGO initiatives were used to complement regulations; in contrast, there is reason to believe that during the Bush administration they have been viewed as substitutes. Consider two of the more
striking examples. The Bush administration stopped development of
OSHA's mandatory ergonomics rule in 2001. Rather than revising the rule,
it moved forward with a set of industry-specific advisory guidelines and a
series of "strategic partnerships" designed to promote voluntary reductions
of repetitive stress injuries (see Chapter 8). Similarly in 2001, President
Bush officially announced the US withdrawal from the Kyoto Protocol.
Although the outcry from environmental groups was deafening, there was
no reason to believe that the protocol would have received Senate ratification. Yet rather than moving forward with mandatory domestic regulations
for carbon dioxide, the administration focused on promoting reductions in
"greenhouse gas intensity" and developed a new voluntary initiative called

Climate Partners, whereby corporations could pledge to achieve reductions in greenhouse gas emissions through whatever means they found most attractive (see Chapter 7). While one might celebrate voluntary initiatives and partnerships as a means of achieving gains greater than those mandated by regulation, in the absence of regulatory requirements they may well be viewed as insufficient substitutes.

Thus, in regulatory policy as in so many other policy areas (e.g., education, social welfare), the presidency of George W. Bush is not easy to characterize. Strands of continuity and change were interwoven such that there may be little in the way of a coherent Bush regulatory legacy. In part, this may reflect the lower salience of regulation more generally in an age dominated by events like the terrorist attacks of September 11, 2001, the collapse of the booming stock market of the 1990s, successive wars in Afghanistan and Iraq, natural disasters like Hurricane Katrina, and the looming deficit and debt. In part, this may reflect the growing consensus over many of the issues that were at the heart of previous regulatory conflicts.

Conclusion

The contemporary history of regulatory politics is in many ways paradoxical. The wave of new social regulatory initiatives in the 1970s expanded the regulatory state to dimensions previously unimaginable. As consumer, environmental, and labor advocates celebrated their victories, critics of regulation successfully used the window of opportunity opened by stagflation to introduce regulatory reform and deregulatory initiatives, efforts that accelerated during the 1980s, as one would have expected, given the Reagan administration's antipathy for government. Yet the greatest achievements of the Reagan and George H. W. Bush presidencies resulted from efforts to use the bureaucracy to control regulatory sprawl. The OMB, armed with executive orders, forced agencies to adhere to cost-benefit analysis in regulatory decisionmaking. For good or ill, the result was a dramatic reduction in regulatory activism.

The 1990s witnessed a continuation of OMB control under Clinton's EO 12866. The continuation of regulatory review is a testament to the changing contours of the policy debates. What had once been a serious point of contention—that cost-benefit analysis had a role in regulatory review—was now part of a consensus that cut across parties. Moreover, as this chapter has revealed, the Republican majority in Congress made substantial progress in providing a statutory foundation for the kinds of reforms that had previously been a product of presidential control. The presidency of George W. Bush, while a departure from that of Clinton, has been characterized by sufficient continuity to suggest that many of the conflicts that have punctuated the contemporary history of regulation have lost their salience. Yet as we turn to the regulation case studies in the remainder of this book, we will discover that beneath the apparent consensus, there were significant departures during the Clinton presidency—and that, indeed, there have been significant departures during the Bush presidency. While presidential and congressional politics are an important part of the story, it is virtually impossible to understand the evolution of regulation in the contemporary period without focusing on the activities within the individual agencies.

Note

1. For a more detailed examination of regulatory history, see Eisner 2000.

4

Regulating Market Competition

MARKET POWER IS COMMONLY cited as a source of market failure. Antitrust policy regulates corporate organization and conduct to prevent or stop forms of behavior that could create market power, thereby undermining the price mechanism. Beyond the economic rationale, antitrust has strong political dimensions as an expression of American political values (Pitofsky 1979; Adams and Brock 1986). As Walter Adams notes, the antitrust laws "are founded on a theory of hostility to the concentration of power in private hands so great that even a government of the people can be trusted to have it only in exceptional circumstances" (1982: 487).

Antitrust policy at the national level finds its origins in the Sherman Antitrust Act of 1890, the Clayton and Federal Trade Commission Acts of 1914, and several key amendments. The Sherman Act prohibits "conspiracies in restraint of trade" (§ 1) and monopolization or attempts to monopolize (§ 2). At present, Sherman Act violations are deemed felonies and are punishable by prison terms of up to three years and fines of up to $350,000 for individual defendants and $10 million for corporate defendants. The courts may alternatively impose a fine of up to twice the gain or loss associated with the activity if it is greater than $10 million. Given the criminal provisions, Sherman Act enforcement is assigned to the DOJ. In addition, provisions for private antitrust suits under the promise of treble damages have given rise to ongoing waves of private antitrust litigation. In 1914, Congress passed the Clayton Act to prohibit forms of behavior that contributed to the creation of monopoly power, thereby moving the government from a prosecutorial to a regulatory posture. The act declared illegal price discrimination (§ 2), exclusive dealing and tying (§ 3), the acquisition of "the stock or other share capital of another corporation" (§ 7), and corporate

57

interlocks (§ 8) where the effects "may be to substantially lessen competition or tend to create a monopoly in any line of commerce." Section 4 provided once again for the recovery of treble damages and legal fees in private litigation. The Clayton Act's key provisions have been refined through a few major amendments. The Robinson-Patman Act of 1936 amended Section 2 to prohibit the provision or acceptance of price discounts when unjustified by cost differentials or when they undermined competition or contributed to monopoly. The Clayton Act's Section 7 was amended by the Celler-Kefauver Act of 1950, strengthening the prohibitions against anti-competitive mergers. This amendment was reinforced by the Hart-Scott-Rodino Antitrust Improvements Act of 1976, which created a premerger notification system that allowed regulators to assess the competitive impact and legality of mergers and guide parties in restructuring the merger in advance rather than seeking legal remedies after the fact.

In addition to the Clayton Act, Congress passed the Federal Trade Commission Act of 1914, which created the FTC. The organization and powers of the FTC will be discussed in greater detail below, but it is important to note here that Section 5 of the FTCA, as amended by the Wheeler-Lea Act of 1938, provided the commission with a broad grant of authority by establishing an economy-wide prohibition of "unfair methods of competition in commerce and unfair or deceptive acts or practices in commerce." The commission was given the authority to bring civil proceedings against business practices that were not explicitly declared illegal by the Sherman and Clayton Acts. In addition to the broad Section 5 prohibition, the FTC enforces the civil provisions in the Clayton Act and its amendments. The FTC thus shares enforcement responsibilities with the Antitrust Division in several areas, including the important merger regulations and the premerger notification system established in 1976. The major antitrust statutes enforced by the DOJ and the FTC are presented in Figure 4.1.

Antitrust Policy

Although the values that antitrust promotes are relatively straightforward, statutory imprecision has guaranteed a substantial role for the courts, which have given the laws substantive content, albeit through a complicated series of decisions that have often proved difficult to reconcile. The courts have been forced to determine what kinds of practices are illegal under the provisions of the law and whether they should be viewed as being *illegal per se* or addressed under a *rule of reason*. If a given practice (e.g., price-fixing) is per se illegal, then prosecutors need only prove a matter of fact to prevail in court. In contrast, under the rule of reason, the courts must address issues of

**Figure 4.1   Major Antitrust Statutes
Enforced by the Antitrust Division and the FTC**

Sherman Antitrust Act (15 U.S.C. §§ 1–7, as amended)
Wilson Tariff Act (15 U.S.C. §§ 8–11)
Clayton Act (15 U.S.C. §§ 12–27; 29 U.S.C. §§ 52–53, as amended)
Antitrust Civil Process Act (15 U.S.C. §§ 1311–1314, as amended)
International Antitrust Enforcement Assistance Act of 1994 (15 U.S.C. §§ 46,
    57b-1, 1311–1312, 6201–6212)
Racketeering Influenced and Corrupt Organizations Act (18 U.S.C. §§
    1961–1968)
Hart-Scott-Rodino Antitrust Improvements Act of 1976 (15 U.S.C. § 18a, as
    amended)
Webb-Pomerene Act (15 U.S.C. §§ 61–66, as amended)
Deepwater Port Act of 1974 (33 U.S.C. §§ 1501–1524, as amended)
Defense Production Act of 1950 (50 U.S.C. §§ 2061–2169, as amended)
Outer Continental Shelf Lands Act Amendments of 1978 (43 U.S.C. § 1337)
Conservation Service Reform Act of 1986 (42 U.S.C. §§ 8201 et seq.)
Deep Seabed Hard Minerals Act (30 U.S.C. §§ 1401–1473, as amended)
National Cooperative Research and Production Act of 1993 (15 U.S.C. §§
    4301–4306)
Interstate Commerce Commission Termination Act of 1995 (49 U.S.C. §§
    10101–11917)

reasonableness, effect, and intent. The kind of evidence deemed necessary to address these issues has varied by type of violation and over time.

The greatest source of complexity in recent decades has been the growing role of economics. Since the 1960s, economists have become central players at both agencies. As economics has come to play an ever greater role, the models applied in antitrust decisionmaking have changed, reflecting changes within the economics discipline and the subsystem debates. When economics first entered the policy process, the field of industrial organization was dominated by the structure-conduct-performance (SCP) paradigm (Weiss 1979). Under this framework, market structure was considered determinant of various forms of conduct. In highly concentrated markets with barriers to entry, firms were far more likely to engage in collusive behavior. The overall impact on economic performance was deemed to be negative, undermining consumer welfare, economic efficiency, and technological dynamism. This paradigm supported economic deconcentration and the elimination of vertical and horizontal restraints through enforcement that drew on all the provisions of the antitrust laws. The SCP paradigm reinforced the political goals traditionally associated with antitrust.

Over the course of the 1970s, the SCP paradigm lost influence in the antitrust debates. The key difficulty was tied to the assumption that structure was determinate. Critics from the Chicago school of economics made the case that firm size and concentration levels in a particular industry reflected the interplay of market forces and the technology of production (see Reder 1982; Posner 1979; Bork 1978). Applying George Stigler's survival test (1968: 72–74), the best single guide to what *should* exist is what has survived the competitive process. If large firms characterized an industry, it was because this scale of production provided superior efficiencies to alternative industrial structures. Absent government intervention, competitive forces would force firms to adopt the most efficient practices and scale of production. As one might conclude, the Chicago school supports a more limited range of enforcement actions. There is support for prosecution of horizontal restraints due to the sizable short-term welfare losses. There remains skepticism regarding the economic justification of efforts to prevent concentration and vertical restraints (see Eisner 1990, 1991: 90–118).

Complexity is only one of the two dimensions shaping regulatory politics: we should also expect official attention to be a product of issue salience. As the salience data on antitrust reveal (see Figure 4.2), coverage of the policy area varied wildly over the last decades of the twentieth century. Not surprisingly, salience increases during periods of negative economic performance, when attention turns to whether corporate practices impede

Figure 4.2 The Salience of Antitrust

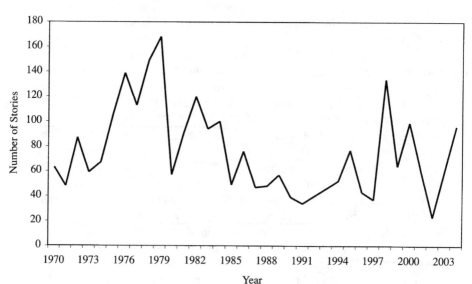

Year

growth or create inflationary biases (e.g., the stagflation of the 1970s, the deep recession of 1982–1983). During such periods, attention turns to the role of policy in returning the economy to a high-growth profile. What is surprising is that the high level of salience is not combined with high levels of negative coverage. Coverage remains largely neutral; negative stories are a fraction of the total stories in any given year.

The Antitrust Agencies

Two agencies enforce the antitrust laws: the Antitrust Division of the DOJ and the FTC. A dual regulatory authority is not unique to antitrust (see, e.g., Chapters 5 and 9). Problems of duplication have been minimized over the years with liaison arrangements and greater consultation and cooperation (see Higgins, Shughart, and Tollison 1987). Yet the overlapping jurisdiction has given rise to ongoing calls for the consolidation of antitrust activities in the Antitrust Division, leaving the FTC free to concentrate on consumer protection (see Chapter 9). Let us examine the two agencies separately.

The Antitrust Division

The Antitrust Division is part of the Department of Justice and is under the leadership of an assistant attorney general (AAG), a presidential appointee. For fiscal year 2005, the Antitrust Division had a budget of $139 million, $101 million of which was collected from filing fees paid by firms undergoing premerger review. As Figure 4.3 reveals, the budget of the division has increased steadily since 1970. In nominal terms, the budget has more that doubled since 1993.

The Antitrust Division is hierarchical in organization (see Figure 4.4). Priorities are formally established and cases are approved by the AAG, working closely with the deputy assistant attorneys general. The division's five deputy assistant attorneys general cover economic analysis, international enforcement, criminal enforcement, civil enforcement, and regulatory affairs. The division is organized into thirteen sections: appeals, competition policy, economic litigation, economic regulation, foreign commerce, legal policy, national criminal enforcement, networks and technology, telecommunications and media, transportation, energy, and agriculture, as well as three litigation sections. Although the division is a large litigation shop, there is close interaction between the lawyers and economists at the staff level, especially on the task forces and in investigation and case-selection processes, where they develop the legal and economic dimensions of a case simultaneously. The division operates seven regional field offices.

Although the division once relied heavily on private complaints as a

Figure 4.3 Federal Antitrust Regulation Expenditures

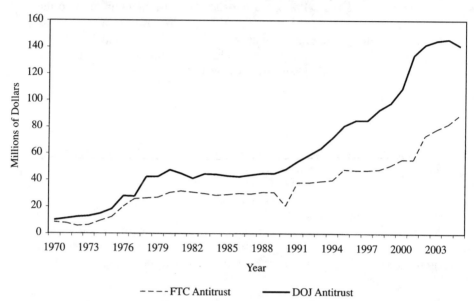

source for its prosecutions (see Weaver 1977), over the past several decades it has assumed a <u>proactive posture</u>, basing its decision to proceed on independent analysis and data from business publications, private antitrust cases, SEC filings, premerger notifications, complaints from other agencies, and economic analyses. As the division increased its emphasis on planning, evaluation, and proactive case selection, economists were elevated within the policy processes. Division attorneys, working with staff economists, determine whether a potential case has sufficient legal *and* economic merits to warrant a formal investigation.

The Antitrust Division has <u>significant investigative powers</u>. If there appears to be economic and legal grounds for filing a case after a preliminary examination, it initiates a formal investigation. In civil cases, the division can issue civil investigative demands, a form of administrative subpoena. Civil proceedings are also often filed to achieve regulatory remedies. The court may issue injunctions placing restrictions on future corporate behavior. However, civil proceedings are rarely brought in response to per se violations, because an injunction could only restate what was already fixed in law. Civil cases may be settled via consent decrees that provide relief without the expense, delays, negative publicity, and disclosures of a trial. Since they are inadmissible as prima facie evidence of guilt, the defendant's vulnerability to private action is not altered. For these reasons, the

Figure 4.4 The Antitrust Division

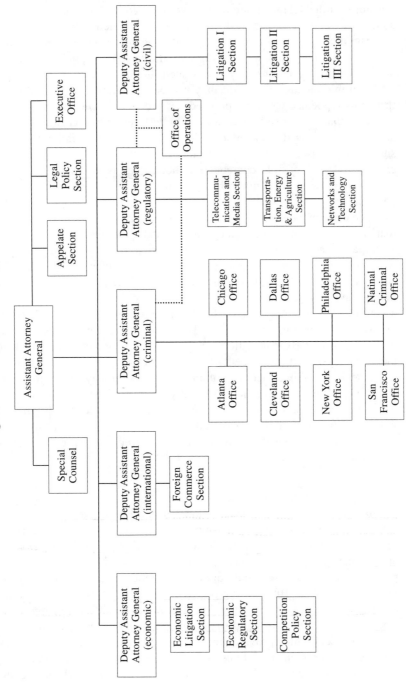

division and the defendant are often eager to negotiate consent decrees, and a majority of civil cases are resolved through negotiated settlement.

The division may employ the grand jury system in criminal matters. These investigations are a serious threat: the scope of inquiry is unlimited, and undetected violations may be revealed through discovery. Private parties in treble-damage litigation may use documentary evidence obtained through subpoenas. Criminal proceedings are usually filed in response to activities that are per se illegal, such as price-fixing. Once criminal charges are filed, the accused often enters a plea of nolo contendere rather than marshaling a defense, in the hopes of minimizing the litigation expenses and exposure. A plea of nolo contendere is not an admission of guilt and thus does not increase the vulnerability to private litigation (Eisner 1991: 25–29).

The division was given the task of premerger screening in 1976, a duty that came to dominate the agency during subsequent merger waves. Firms anticipating a merger with combined assets above a size threshold are required to provide information to the two antitrust agencies (the threshold is indexed to growth in gross domestic product). The agencies have sixty to ninety days to rule on the merger or request additional information, thus extending the waiting period. To facilitate enforcement, the Antitrust Division (in cooperation with the FTC) issues merger guidelines that are updated periodically. The guidelines provide an economic framework for merger analysis and a statement of the conditions under which the division might seek to enjoin a merger. Although the division may seek injunctions, a statement of agency intentions is usually sufficient. The division routinely works with corporations to restructure mergers in advance (the "fix it first" policy). When time constraints make this impossible, the division may approve the merger subject to a consent decree requiring subsequent divestiture.

The Federal Trade Commission

As an independent regulatory commission, the FTC is headed by a five-member, bipartisan commission. An organizational chart for the FTC is presented in Figure 4.5. The Bureau of Competition is the FTC's antitrust enforcement arm. It investigates alleged violations of the antitrust laws, prepares and litigates cases, and conducts ongoing research on competition policy issues. The Bureau of Consumer Protection protects consumers against unfair, deceptive, and fraudulent practices by enforcing a number of consumer protection laws and trade regulation rules (see Chapter 9). The Bureau of Economics provides technical support in the development and selection of enforcement actions and compiles information and reports on American industry. The FTC also makes use of a network of regional offices. The FTC's budget for 2005 was $204 million, $89 million of which

Figure 4.5 The Federal Trade Commission

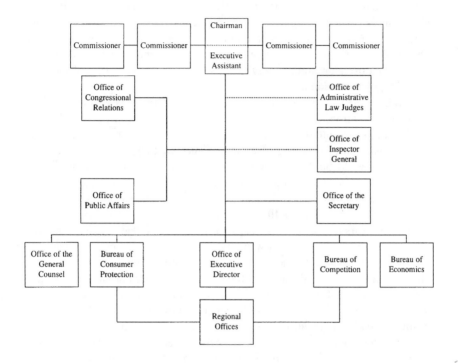

was devoted to antitrust. As Figure 4.3 shows, the agency experienced steady budgetary expansion during the early 1970s, followed by periods of sharp decline and, more recently, renewed growth.

The FTCA provided unprecedented investigative powers. Under FTCA Section 6(a), the FTC has the power "to gather and compile information concerning, and investigate from time to time, the organization, business conduct, practices and management of any corporation engaged in commerce." The act provided the FTC with the power to demand of corporations "reports or answers in writing to specific questions, furnishing the Commission such information as it may require" on a host of issues regarding corporate organization and performance. The exercise of these powers is not contingent on evidence of a crime. The FTC can demand information "merely on suspicion that the law is being violated, or even just because it wants assurance that it is not." This power is used regularly, particularly by the Bureau of Economics.

The FTC's cases may originate from a number of sources, including private complaints, referrals from the Antitrust Division, business publications, premerger notification filings, and economic market studies. Although a majority of cases historically originated from private complaints, since the early 1970s the FTC has developed a greater capacity to generate cases through economic analysis (see Katzmann 1980a). Prior to initiating formal investigations, potential cases are assessed in screening and evaluation committees. Although these committees are centralized in the Bureau of Competition, Bureau of Economics economists form part of the evaluation team and actively consider the economic merits of the proposed regulatory action.

When the Bureau of Competition believes there is evidence of an antitrust violation, it requests that the FTC file a formal complaint. The decision to prosecute requires a majority vote of the commission and is generally based on a weighing of evidence and whether (as required by the FTCA) it would be "to the interest of the public." Once a complaint is issued, attorneys and economists work as a team to prepare a case. Bureau attorneys and the lawyers representing the accused appear before an administrative law judge, who defines the limits of discovery, approves depositions, and hears the case. After hearing the case, the judge prepares findings of fact, findings of law, and a written decision. If the commission does not act on a decision and it is not appealed within thirty days of receipt, it automatically becomes the decision of the commission. The commission usually issues a cease and desist order on the basis of the adjudicative decision. Violation of a cease and desist order may result in a fine of $11,000 per day, insofar as each day is defined as a separate violation. Appeals are commonly made to the FTC, which has the power to reject, accept, or modify decisions. Decisions may also be appealed to the US Court of Appeals. The majority of cases are settled through consent orders following the issuance of a complaint. This option has become so routine that an order is often drafted along with the complaint.

The Policy Subsystem

In recent decades, the antitrust agencies have converged in their enforcement priorities largely as a result of common understandings of policy and administration that have evolved within the policy community and subsystem. As noted above, over the past three decades a consensus that emphasizes the centrality of economic analysis in antitrust decisionmaking has emerged. While many actors in the antitrust policy subsystem may echo the shift toward economics and the more conservative enforcement agenda it entails, the political dimensions of antitrust periodically rise to the surface.

Congress and the Executive
Congress and the president are responsive to shifts in public opinion and interest group demands. We should expect greater attention to a policy area

when salience is high, particularly if the coverage is strongly negative. Although the salience of antitrust has fluctuated wildly over time, stories that can be coded as negative constitute a fraction of the universe of cases. There have been few calls for the revocation of antitrust, and both parties regularly pledge vigorous enforcement. In part, this affirmation is a product of antitrust's support of open markets, private property, individualism, and equal opportunity—all expressions of American liberalism (see Hofstadter 1966). Since antitrust enforcement budgets are small when compared with other government functions, support for the policy carries few costs. Despite the economy-wide coverage of the antitrust laws, enforcement does not stimulate the mobilization of political opposition or support, due to the combination of diffuse benefits and concentrated costs. The lack of mobilization has been a mixed blessing for the agencies: on those rare occasions when the agencies come under sustained attack, they have been unable to depend on the support of a committed coalition. Consumer groups and small business associations have periodically supported antitrust, but their interest has been peripheral.

Business associations occasionally attempt to redirect enforcement by seeking individual or sectoral exemptions, and Congress has often been responsive. Although corporations have also worked to manipulate the outcome of individual cases, there is little evidence of success. The Nader Study Group's report on antitrust (Green, Moore, and Wasserstein 1972) could identify only thirty-two cases in a twenty-five-year period in which members of the executive branch or Congress attempted to influence outcomes, most of which were unsuccessful. That said, the antitrust agencies could identify a number of interests external to the agency that might be considered stakeholders and thus actors in the policy subsystem. This group would include state attorneys general and antitrust agencies, the Business Roundtable, the Consumer Federation of America, the Consumers Union, the Federal Bar Association, the National Association of Attorneys General, the National Association of Consumer Affairs, the National Association of Manufacturers, the National Consumer League, the National Federation of Independent Businesses, and the US Chamber of Commerce. In addition to this group, special attention must focus on the Antitrust Section of the American Bar Association (ABA) (see FTC 1997: iv). The ABA has been regularly involved in overseeing enforcement, agency organization, and policy. ABA task forces, which routinely include influential members of the antitrust bar and former agency officials, provide for peer review (see, e.g., ABA 1969, 1989). Officials from both agencies regularly appear before the ABA's Antitrust Section to discuss enforcement priorities or challenges, and members of the ABA Antitrust Section often testify before Congress to comment on appointees, budgets, or the need for new legislation.

To what extent are the antitrust enforcement agendas determined externally by the president and Congress? Let us begin with the president. The most powerful tool the president possesses to influence enforcement priorities is the power of appointment. If an AAG attempts to bring cases that contradict an administration's policies, presidents may intervene through their attorneys general. Although all potential cases and policy statements require AG clearance, there is little evidence that presidents have used this mechanism to shape enforcement. Although presidents also appoint FTC commissioners, FTC independence limits presidential authority (see Wellborn 1977). Presidents who have sought to use appointments to manipulate formal bipartisanship for partisan ends have met with congressional resistance.

Presidential control is further limited by the inability to remove commissioners over questions of policy: commissioners do not serve at the pleasure of the president (see *Humphrey's Executor v. United States* 1935). Be this the case, a president's control over the chairmanship has been, at times, a source of substantial power. President Nixon used this power to revitalize the FTC when he appointed Caspar Weinberger and Miles Kirkpatrick as successive chairmen. President Reagan used the appointment of James C. Miller III to force the agency to adopt a more market-oriented approach (see Pertschuk 1982; Miller 1989). The Senate may influence the president's power of appointment through its power of confirmation. In the case of the Antitrust Division, confirmation has usually been pro forma. Senate influence has been far greater in the FTC because of its independence and its multiheaded executive. Past chairmen Paul Rand Dixon and Michael Pertschuk held top staff positions in important Senate subcommittees at the time of their selection, a testament to the Senate's power in this area.

Although presidents might use the power of the purse, the OMB has not exerted much influence over agency priorities. Antitrust has been rather uncontroversial, and the agency budgets are relatively small. Moreover, presidential appointees screen their budget requests in advance, making policy-related alterations before they reach the OMB. In the end, one might question whether Congress would sustain large budget cuts. In the 1980s, for example, Congress rejected the OMB-recommended budget cuts, even when the Reagan administration supported reductions. House and Senate appropriations subcommittees review the agencies' budget requests. Typically, Congress does not undertake a detailed evaluation, but focuses instead on levels of enforcement or specific investigations and enforcement programs. Although Congress often expresses dissatisfaction with some aspect of agency performance, this rarely translates into budget revisions. As with the OMB, this may reflect the broad support for antitrust and the small size of agency budgets, relative to other agencies that fall under the jurisdiction of the same committees.

While Congress does not monitor agency effectiveness as part of the budgetary process, the same cannot be said for its oversight activities. The committees that regularly interact with the antitrust agencies include the House and Senate judiciary committees (especially the Senate Subcommittee on Antitrust, Competition Policy, and Consumer Rights), the House and Senate small business committees, and the House and Senate commerce committees. Oversight has addressed major problems in particular sectors of the economy and the agencies' efforts to eliminate the problems under consideration. While senators have occasionally expressed dissatisfaction with enforcement priorities or levels, the relationship has been quite cordial. Historically, the Senate Commerce Committee has been most active in overseeing the FTC. Although it usually has been supportive, there have been heated conflicts from time to time. Because the FTC is independent, it is more closely connected with Congress. In addition, whereas the division is viewed primarily as a law enforcement agency, the FTC's flexible administrative procedures, broad grants of discretionary authority (FTCA § 5), and consumer protection duties clearly mark it as a regulatory agency. With its industry-wide rule-making authority, each decision creates its own constituency. Given the problematic status of regulation in recent decades, this has only accentuated its vulnerability to Congress. Indeed, one can detect a distinct dynamic: congressional support appears to be the greatest when the FTC adopts a moderate enforcement agenda. As agency activism increases, the mobilization of business interests increases, placing ever greater pressure on Congress to rein in this "runaway regulator" (see Kovacic 1987).

The Courts

The authority that Congress delegated to the antitrust agencies can be exercised only within the discretionary field established by the courts. The courts determine whether to view a given form of conduct as being per se illegal or requiring the application of the rule of reason. Second, court decisions send important cues as to what kinds of evidence will prove most persuasive, a point that is particularly important when applying a rule of reason. As a generalization, the courts have embraced a rule of reason approach for most matters and have recognized the role of economic analysis in weighing competitive effects. In keeping with this economic emphasis, a majority of the bench has received formal training in price theory; most law schools now train attorneys in law *and* economics (see Fox 1988).

As a law enforcement agency, the Antitrust Division must file cases in district court and marshal the resources to bring cases to a successful conclusion. Even if a majority of cases are settled early, precedent must provide the division with the authority to bring a particular kind of case. Moreover, the accused must have reason to believe that nothing would be gained (and much might be lost) should the case be tried to a conclusion. The likelihood of success in court will be determined through an examination of past judicial behavior in similar cases and a calculation of the costs and benefits of protracted litigation. Since all consent decrees are subject to court approval, the Antitrust Division must be able to collect the necessary data and conduct the analyses to design and justify the desired relief. As an independent regulatory commission, the FTC is marginally less vulnerable to courts that are hesitant to accept an appeal over findings of fact. Rather, they will usually view the factual record as closed and focus on issues of process or law. In all other respects, the FTC's dependence on the courts mirrors that of the division.

One might incorrectly assume that the agencies could shape court doctrine through the careful case selection. However, the promise of treble damages in private suits generates a flood of private cases. Private cases have at times provided a context for significant shifts in judicial policy. The agencies regularly file briefs amici curiae in cases that they believe are important. But the courts are under no compulsion to consider the agency positions in deciding a case. The agencies remain subject to judicial decisions over which they exercise little control.

The Evolution of Antitrust, 1970–Present

Three basic perspectives may be helpful in untangling the complexities of regulatory politics (see Chapter 2). The principal-agent perspective directs attention to elected officials and their efforts to control regulatory bureaucracies. If this perspective correctly describes events in antitrust, one would expect to see frequent interventions by presidents and Congress seeking to use the policy to maximize political support. The bureaucratic politics perspective, in contrast, locates the source of policy change within the bureaucracy and interprets policy change as a product of changes within the organization. Here, one would focus on changes in organization, staffing, and internal policy processes and their impact (intentional or unintentional) on regulatory actions. Finally, the subsystems perspective seeks to understand the evolution of regulatory policy as being a product of changing coalitions and shifts in the dominant policy image. The coalitions in the policy subsystem may well include elected officials and bureaucrats, as well as members of the policy community and mobilized interests. The line of demarcation separating the perspectives is less than concrete. Changes in subsystem debates have a profound effect on the evolution of the regulatory bureaucracies and the enforcement priorities. The biases established in the bureaucracies place limits, thereafter, on the discretion exercised by presidential appointees. The extent to which they can redefine the missions of their agencies will depend on the degree to which they can reconcile these missions with the biases already established in the bureaucracy.

Antitrust in the 1970s

The dominant trend in antitrust regulation during the 1970s involved a greater reliance on economic analysis. The FTC had economists on staff since its creation, and the Antitrust Division had relied on a small economic support staff for several years. However, in both cases, economics provided technical support for what was essentially law enforcement. Even though the courts had given explicit consideration to economics and there were clear economic dimensions to prevailing enforcement guidelines, the dominant SCP framework relied on rudimentary measures of concentration that could be applied without a great deal of economic expertise. As noted above, this framework legitimized a broad enforcement agenda against high levels of concentration and a wide variety of vertical and horizontal restraints, thereby winning the allegiance of litigation-minded economists (see Baker and Blumenthal 1984). During the 1970s, both agencies expanded their economics staffs and created new mechanisms for integrating economic analysis into the selection of cases. As economics became more prominent, significant changes began occurring in the economic debates. As noted earlier, the Chicago school was far more successful in making the case that existing forms of organization and conduct are often the products of market competition. For both agencies, the consequences of the new economics would be profound.

In 1973, Assistant Attorney General for Antitrust Thomas Kauper began his efforts to enhance the status of economic expertise in the Antitrust Division by creating the Economic Policy Office (EPO). He hoped that an economist could be routinely assigned to every case at an early stage in the process as an independent analyst. Even after the EPO had gained a sufficiently large staff to make this possible, the role envisaged for economists conflicted with the division's legal culture. Attorneys, hoping to build a litigation record, were reluctant to be constrained by economic analysis. At first, the EPO economists worked with the attorneys in developing the economic dimensions of investigation and enforcement recommendations. Within a few years, they had revealed that economic analysis could also provide a tool for identifying enforcement opportunities (see Kauper 1984; Eisner 1990).

Although the courts had long applied economics in forming their decisions, they drew largely on the SCP framework. Economic efficiencies were seen as largely irrelevant (Bork 1978: 287). Things would change dramatically as a result of the 1977 decision *Continental T.V. v. GTE Sylvania*. The

Supreme Court overturned the per se illegality of territorial and customer restraints, arguing instead for an application of the rule of reason. Justice Lewis Powell's decision noted that "vertical restrictions promote inter-brand competition" by allowing manufacturers to "achieve certain efficiencies." He noted that "economists have identified a number of ways in which manufacturers can use such restrictions to compete more effectively" and went on to explore these factors in greater detail. Attention was directed to the importance of economics and, more significantly, to the growing importance of the efficiency considerations.

The decision in *Sylvania* created pressure for the attorneys to give greater attention to complicated economic issues and to accept a greater role for economists in the case-selection process. The Antitrust Division was already well on its way, however, as a result of two other events: the Antitrust Improvements Act of 1976 and the wave of competitive deregulation that was sweeping the nation. Because premerger clearance was largely an economic task, it forced a greater integration of lawyers and attorneys in the agencies (see Brunner et al. 1985). In addition, the status of economics in the division's activities was enhanced by competition advocacy. When intervening before other regulatory agencies, the division sought to prevent private restraints from replacing those erected by policy. To this end, it often testified and filed analyses with other agencies—tasks that both placed a great premium on economic expertise (see DOJ 1979: 26–27; DOJ 1978: 117).

By the end of the 1970s, the division's EPO had been expanded, professionalized, and integrated into virtually every stage of the antitrust enforcement process. Economists came to play the role of equal partners; their professional values played an ever greater role in defining the antitrust caseload. As a generalization, the division was no longer committed to enforcing anything more than the Sherman Act provisions against horizontal restraints and the occasional horizontal merger that was too big to ignore. As these changes were occurring in the caseload, President Carter's AAG, John Shenefield, argued for a structuralist enforcement agenda and discounted the purely economic interpretation of antitrust. Nevertheless, the priorities established at the executive level had little impact on the enforcement record. The primary decisions had already been made.

A similar set of events occurred at the FTC. Following the trenchant critiques of the ABA (1969) and "Nader's Raiders" (Cox, Fellmeth, and Schultz 1969), the agency was quickly reorganized under the direction of Caspar Weinberger and his successor, Miles Kirkpatrick, the head of the ABA task force. The reorganization eliminated eighteen of the top thirty-one staff members and nearly one-third of the agency's 600 lawyers. Vacancies were filled with recruits from the nation's best law schools. Prominent industrial organization scholars took charge at the Bureau of

Economics and new positions were filled with economics doctorates from the best graduate programs in the country (see Katzmann 1980a; Eisner 1991: 163–167). Congress supported the FTC with budget increases (from $19.9 million to $62 million in a decade) and broad new powers (see Chapter 9).

As with the Antitrust Division, the FTC created new mechanisms for planning enforcement efforts and integrating economic analysis into its efforts. To this end, the Office of Policy Planning and Evaluation was created to set long-term regulatory objectives (Gardner 1972; Singer 1975a; Clarkson and Muris 1981). For present purposes, the most important factor was the creation of evaluation committees in 1973. Traditionally, economists had been isolated by the FTC's legal culture (Auerbach 1964). With the new evaluation committees, economic and legal analysis would be integrated in the initiation of formal antitrust investigations and the process of selecting cases for prosecution. Much the same can be said of the merger screening committees that were created following Hart-Scott-Rodino. As with the division, what constituted "economic merits" would change rapidly as the SCP framework fell from grace, with an effect on regulatory outputs.

Thus far, the story of antitrust in the 1970s would appear to be best told through a combination of the subsystems and bureaucratic politics perspectives. Changes in the debates within the subsystem and the rising status of economics and economists within these debates had a direct impact on bureaucratic change. Furthermore, policy change—the increasing emphasis placed on horizontal restraints relative to all other antitrust violations— reflected the changes that had occurred within the agency and the growing status of Chicago-school influence in the subsystem (see Eisner and Meier 1990). However, there is some evidence to support the principal-agent perspective, particularly in the case of the FTC.

The agency entered a period of unprecedented regulatory activism under the leadership of Carter's chairman, Michael Pertschuk. A dramatic expansion of resources, vast new legal powers, and rule-making authority led the FTC to press the limits of its regulatory mandate. An agency that had been described as the "Little Old Lady on Pennsylvania Avenue" in the 1960s was suddenly described as the second most powerful legislature in Washington, D.C. Some of this newfound activism focused on antitrust enforcement, as the FTC attacked professional association rules (e.g., bans on advertising) that were believed to support price-fixing, and initiated antitrust proceedings to explore such new areas as joint monopolization (the cereal industry). Since FTC activism was most pronounced in consumer protection, a more detailed account will be reserved for Chapter 9. High levels of commission activism stimulated high levels of interest group mobilization, contentious oversight hearings, and media coverage of "the national nanny." Congress, in turn, passed the ill-named Federal Trade

Commission Improvements Act of 1980, which established a legislative veto over commission rules, undermined a number of existing investigations, and placed new and onerous restrictions on this agency (see Singer 1979; Weingast and Moran 1982, 1983; Katzmann 1980a, 1984). Much as one might expect under the principal-agent perspective, Congress responded to organized interests and forcefully intervened in FTC enforcement.

Antitrust and the Reagan-Bush Presidencies

The reaction against the FTC in 1979–1980 was a harbinger of things to come. Following the regulatory zealotry of the 1970s, the 1980s marked a genuine sea change in regulatory politics. The Reagan administration expressed severe skepticism concerning the economic justification for an expansive antitrust agenda, much of which was viewed as an effort to substitute the judgment of politicians and bureaucrats for market outcomes. To be fair, the Antitrust Division remained highly active throughout the period, filing an unprecedented number of cases in many years. Yet these cases were primarily against horizontal restraints—a perfect expression of the underlying economic arguments. The FTC, in contrast, fell almost completely from view in the area of antitrust.

The Reagan transition team examined the FTC and made a number of recommendations to hobble the runaway regulator. The transition report called for a 25 percent reduction in the FTC's budget and the elimination of the field offices. In addressing the focus of antitrust prosecutions, the report rejected any more actions in pursuit of shared monopoly. It dismissed merger enforcement as being based on misguided doctrines regarding the causal importance of concentration. It similarly eschewed vertical restraint proceedings. All of these activities were seen as being forays into social engineering. Increased enforcement was justified only in the area of horizontal restraints. To facilitate this transformation, the transition team recommended that the Bureau of Economics be elevated to a gatekeeping function, with the requirement that it sign off on the economic merits of all new actions (*Antitrust and Trade Regulation Report* 999 [January 29, 1981]: G1–G3). A coalition consisting of members of Congress, the Small Business Legislative Council, the National Federation of Independent Businesses, state attorneys general, the ABA, and consumer groups was successful in preserving the field offices and limiting the severity of the budget cuts. However, other changes were quick to come.

James C. Miller III, head of the FTC transition team and a veteran of regulatory reform in the Ford administration, was appointed as chairman (see Miller 1989). As the first PhD economist to assume a position on the commission, he used his powers as chairman to reorient the agency in keeping with the transition team recommendations. Miller's appointees were characterized by their unparalleled academic credentials, expertise, and allegiance to the "new" economics. Miller also reorganized the FTC to centralize control in the chairmanship and enhance the coordination between the Bureau of Economics and the litigation shops. In-house training in economics was instituted so that those attorneys who remained would be better able to integrate economic analysis into their enforcement activities. Increasingly, the universe of potential enforcement actions was determined in evaluation committees that were dominated by economists and Miller loyalists. The task force recommendations had been implemented through administrative means (see Eisner 1991: 212–220).

The enforcement record of the Reagan FTC was in some ways the polar opposite of that of the Carter FTC, and in other ways a continuation. The economic doctrines that had gained prominence during the 1970s were now entrenched within the bureaucracy, shaping the caseload at a very early stage—much as one would expect, given the bureaucratic politics perspective (Eisner 1993). Moreover, these economic doctrines were being applied in some innovative ways. The FTC made a number of attempts to extend the reach of Section 5 of the FTCA by filing test cases against the kinds of horizontal restraints that were previously reachable only under the Sherman Act. Continuing the efforts of the 1970s, proceedings were initiated against professional association codes of ethics. Continuity was combined with change. Levels of enforcement fell dramatically, and mergers—including some of the largest in the nation's history—were routinely accepted without revision. Rule modifications of existing orders often outnumbered new case filings.

As the FTC had given up its activist orientation in regulation, it had become highly active in competition advocacy. A minor reorganization of the FTC in 1982 resulted in the creation of the Division of Regulatory Analysis within the Bureau of Economics. It became the center of competition advocacy, presenting analyses before regulatory agencies at the state and federal levels, testifying before various congressional committees, and filing briefs amici curiae in state courts. By 1987, these regulatory interventions numbered over 100 per year. While the economists in the FTC took great pride in these regulatory interventions, the former chairman, Pertschuk, argued that the interventions "were often ideological in tone and analytically shallow and simply restated what the economists within the agency receiving the comments were saying already" (Pertschuk 1982: 26; but see also Eisner 1991: 224–225). In the end, the FTC had become primarily a deregulatory agency, devoting substantial resources to regulatory reversal and reform. Miller left the FTC in 1985 and became OMB director. His replacement, Daniel Oliver, a former editor of *National Review,* did not exert the same leadership in the agency as had Miller. With enforcement at historically low levels and little room left for reorientation, such leadership was no longer important. Nonetheless, Oliver's reign at the FTC was characterized by heated conflicts both within the agency and in its relationship with a Congress that, paradoxically, objected to the impotence of an agency it had stripped of power but a few years before.

Events at the Antitrust Division bore a striking resemblance to those at the FTC. Large staffing cuts (the Washington, D.C.–based professional staff fell from 352 to 166 between 1980 and 1986, with cuts falling disproportionately on attorneys rather than economists) were combined with a stronger commitment to apply price theory. Under the direction of AAG William Baxter, a strong Chicago-school proponent, economists were given de facto veto power over cases. This forced the attorneys who remained to focus even more on the economic merits of their activities (see DOJ 1982). To facilitate this transformation, the EPO conducted mandatory courses in price theory at "EPO-U." As a final expression of the heightened status of economics in the division, the head of the EPO (soon to be renamed the Economic Analysis Group) was elevated in title to deputy assistant attorney general for economic analysis (see Gorinson 1985).

As one might expect, the agency adopted an enforcement agenda that focused on horizontal restraints, de-emphasizing (or ignoring completely) other provisions of the antitrust laws. As with the FTC, the Antitrust Division devoted substantial resources to rescinding old decisions and promoting the market wherever possible. With respect to the former activity, Baxter initiated the "Decree Project" to review some 1,200 existing consent decrees. This activity, which placed a heavy demand on division economists, entailed modifying or vacating decrees that had a negative impact on competition or prohibited activities that were now considered benign or even efficiency promoting (*Antitrust and Trade Regulation Report* 1032 [September 24, 1984]: A16–A17). With respect to the latter activity, the division drafted regulatory briefs and submitted them to Congress and regulatory agencies on literally hundreds of occasions. The division identified competition advocacy as one of its top priorities, second only to the prevention and termination of private cartel behavior (see Eisner 1990: 283). Baxter's successors—Douglas Ginsberg, J. Paul McGrath, and Richard Rule—maintained the course established in the first Reagan term.

The Reagan administration's enforcement priorities and economic interpretation of antitrust were presented in a series of guidelines, including new merger guidelines in 1982 and 1984 and vertical restraint guidelines in 1985. In each case, the guidelines identified numerous efficiency gains that one might expect to capture from the activities, thereby providing a clear defense of practices that would have been prosecuted but a decade earlier. Understanding that the guidelines could be easily replaced by a new presidential administration, the Reagan antitrust enforcers promoted amendments to the existing antitrust statutes. The legislative agenda was stalled, however, as the administration faced a hostile Democratic majority in Congress. Senator Howard Metzenbaum (D-OH), chair of the Senate Antitrust, Monopoly, and Business Rights Subcommittee, worked diligently to preserve the antitrust laws. He and other antitrust advocates were successful in ensuring that the Reagan legislative package never emerged from committee.

In antitrust, as in so many other policy areas, the George H. W. Bush presidency constituted a consolidation of the Reagan agenda, albeit one that moderated its more extreme points. As one might guess, there remained a strong bias in support of horizontal cases at the FTC and a presumption that mergers were efficiency promoting. President Bush named Janet Steiger, a moderate who had occupied executive positions in both the Carter and Reagan administrations, as commission chair. Steiger worked diligently to repair some of the damaged relationships with key constituents in Congress and the larger policy community that she had inherited from the Miller-Oliver years. Under her direction, there were modest budget increases and a minor revitalization of antitrust enforcement. However, a commission deeply divided between moderates and Reagan loyalists limited the extent to which the course set in the early 1980s could be altered (see Harris and Milkis 1996: 302–331).

Comparable changes occurred at the Antitrust Division, where Bush's AAG for antitrust, James F. Rill, proved more moderate than his predecessors. Under his direction, the division challenged a larger number of mergers in 1990 than in any single year since 1973 (Moore 1993). However, the efficiency presumption and the horizontal bias remained secure within the agency. Indeed, given the clear evidence that changes in policy were in many ways a product of bureaucratic changes, one would have predicted that the changes were now so firmly established that another reorientation of antitrust would be difficult if not impossible to achieve (see Eisner and Meier 1990; Eisner 1993; but see also Wood and Anderson 1993).

The Clinton Administration and Antitrust

When Bill Clinton assumed the presidency, he inherited antitrust agencies that were remarkably different from those that had existed in the last Democratic administration. The agencies had weathered significant reductions in resources. Moreover, the economic professionalization, which began in the 1970s, had been completed; entire portions of the antitrust laws that were now deemed to be of questionable economic merit had not been enforced for over a decade. Beyond changes in the bureaucracy, any effort to reorient antitrust was complicated by two additional factors. First, the courts had become more sympathetic to efficiency claims, as revealed by a series of court decisions, including the above-mentioned *Sylvania* decision and *Montsanto v. Spray-Rite Services* (1984). Second, there was a fundamental conflict within Congress with respect to the role of antitrust. While populists continued to make structuralist arguments on behalf of deconcentration, champions of industrial policy argued that antitrust must be altered fundamentally given the challenges of competing in a global economy. Following the 1994 midterm elections, many in the new Republican majority saw active antitrust enforcement as simply another expression of regulatory zealotry. In this environment, any effort to revitalize antitrust could prove politically challenging.

President Clinton appointed Anne K. Bingaman as AAG for antitrust. A former Washington antitrust litigator, Bingaman brought to the position a publicly articulated commitment to reverse the trend of the last several years and prove the relevance of antitrust policy in an increasingly global economy. Given the staffing cuts of the previous decade, one of Bingaman's first moves was to secure an additional $4.7 million in appropriations for 1994 and introduce a request for an extra $11.5 million in the Justice Department's 1995 fiscal year budget request. In addition, the new AAG initiated a reorganization of the Antitrust Division, which entailed creating a new civil litigation task force to concentrate on new cases deemed to be of national or international importance and a unit to identify, review, and assess new cases. Bingaman secured top talent to fill senior management positions. Routine price-fixing cases, the bread and butter of Reagan enforcement efforts, were delegated to the regional offices, thereby freeing the Washington, D.C., attorneys to focus on more complicated matters. The results were new levels of activism in enforcement and a handful of major cases, including a 1996 criminal price-fixing fine of $100 million against Archer Daniels Midland (Moore 1993) and *United States v. Microsoft* (see below). Bingaman resigned abruptly in November 1996 and was replaced by Joel Klein, a former deputy assistant attorney general (1995–1996) and deputy council to President Clinton (1993–1995).

Clinton failed to send any clear signals concerning his support for the FTC until well into 1994. Finally, in April 1995, his appointee for the chairmanship, Robert Pitofsky, was sworn in. Pitofsky had impressive credentials as a legal scholar, director of the Bureau of Consumer Protection (1970–1973), and an FTC commissioner during the Carter administration. Pitofsky's agenda was one of moderation. In his words: "The Commission of the 1990s has tried to strike a middle ground between what many people believe was an excessively active enforcement in the 1960s and the minimalist enforcement of the 1980s." This entailed restoring "much of the antitrust agenda that was abandoned during the period 1980 through 1988." He promised that the FTC was "prepared to enforce the law against resale price maintenance agreements, some carefully selected non-price vertical restrictions, attempts to monopolize, boycotts and vertical and conglomerate mergers—all areas of antitrust that were left completely or largely unenforced during much of the 1980s" (Pitofsky 1996: 2).

Reducing the regulatory burden. As stated previously, one of the key objectives during the Clinton presidency was to "reinvent government" in hopes of making regulatory agencies more responsive and results-oriented. The reinvention of government impacted on the antitrust agencies quite early. The Antitrust Division's 1994 annual report noted the importance of providing "more guidance to the business community than ever before" in an effort to reduce compliance costs and uncertainty (DOJ 1994: 1) and prevent delays and litigation. The division also adopted a number of measures to enhance internal efficiency. Cross-functional teams were employed at an early stage in investigations to reduce miscommunication and facilitate a rapid resolution of investigations. In-house, case-oriented training was adopted to build litigation skills, and paralegals were hired to execute some functions previously assigned to attorneys. Finally, the division worked with the FTC to streamline clearance procedures and handle matters electronically. In each case, the goal was to do more with fewer resources (DOJ 1994: 26–27).

At the FTC, reinvention involved streamlining administrative trial procedures, reducing the demands placed on business, and identifying and eliminating potentially negative impacts of past consent orders. In 1994 the FTC established a "sunset" on all competition orders older than twenty years upon petition by the parties involved. As of 1995 this sunset became automatic (Pitofsky 1996: 8–9). As part of this reinvention process, the FTC developed a strategic plan in 1996–1997 that presented a clear mission statement, goals, indicators, and a timetable for meeting its goals. The strategic plan was framed in the language of business consultants, with frequent appeals to cost-effectiveness and the need to develop "partnerships" with "stakeholders" in the private sector. The document claimed that the FTC was now oriented toward achieving the traditional enforcement while observing the need to "constantly review its law enforcement policies, eliminate orders and regulations that place unwarranted burdens [on] business, and ensure law enforcement activities are effective" (FTC 1997: 4). One might, on the face of things, assume that the agencies had fully embraced the probusiness orientation of the previous administrations. However, the talk of reinvention was combined with the rejection of many of the doctrines of the 1980s.

Antitrust in a global market. During the Clinton presidency, international antitrust became a major focus of the agencies, a shift that provided an expanded role for a policy that appeared to be of declining relevance in the 1980s. The two agencies began to emphasize the need to preserve international markets, protecting domestic consumers from international conspiracies while providing a level playing field for US firms.

In 1994, Attorney General Janet Reno obtained congressional approval to appoint the first deputy assistant attorney general for international affairs. In pursuit of a larger international role, the Antitrust Division doubled the number of cases deemed to have significant international aspects. It worked to develop or extend cooperative relationships with foreign antitrust agencies, particularly in Canada, Japan, and the European Union. These arrangements facilitated the rapid conclusion of major investigations and the breaking up of international price-fixing conspiracies (see Ordover 1997). Reflecting the new orientation, the division initiated new legislation, the International Antitrust Enforcement Assistance Act of 1994, which won the overwhelming support of Congress. The new law authorized the agencies to negotiate reciprocal assistance agreements with antitrust enforcers abroad (see DOJ 1994: 2). In April 1997 the agencies announced an antitrust assistance agreement with Australia, the first formal agreement under the provisions of the 1994 act. The antitrust agencies also started working with other Organization for Economic Cooperation and Development countries, members of the North American Free Trade Agreement (NAFTA), and the proposed Free Trade Area of the Americas to promote a harmonization of competition policies and enforcement practices. With the financial support of the Agency for International Development, the Clinton FTC began providing expanded technical assistance to new antitrust agencies in the former Soviet-bloc nations and Latin America.

In 1994 the agencies jointly issued new "Antitrust Enforcement Guidelines for International Operations." The guidelines noted: "Although the federal antitrust laws have always applied to foreign commerce, that application is particularly important today. Throughout the world, the importance of antitrust law as a means to ensure open and free markets, protect consumers, and prevent conduct that impedes competition is becoming more apparent" (DOJ 1994: 2). As a result, the agencies made enforcement of the antitrust laws with respect to international operations a top priority. Drawing on the Supreme Court decision in *Hartford Fire Insurance v. California* (1993), the guidelines assumed that various kinds of anticompetitive acts may actually be violations of the US antitrust laws even if the conduct involved foreign firms and occured outside of US borders. The guidelines presented a detailed discussion of the factors that would be considered when determining whether to prosecute, the limits of foreign sovereign immunity, and the various channels that exist for cooperation with foreign antitrust agencies.

The record in international antitrust enforcement was impressive, as reflected in a growing number of successful prosecutions against international price-fixing conspiracies resulting in tens of millions of dollars in fines and prison sentences (see DOJ 1996). To be certain, the application of antitrust to the international arena is fraught with difficulties ranging from the lack of international standards for competition to the plethora of industrial policies that promote activities questionable under US laws. Moreover, there are concerns about protecting confidential company information in a highly competitive global economy. Although this revitalization of policy was significant, it occurred within the opportunity set established by the earlier changes in the bureaucracy. The new international cases focused on international price-fixing conspiracies. Under the new economics, restraints of this type stood alone in their ability to attract the attention of antitrust enforcers.

Revitalizing enforcement.   During the Reagan-Bush era, horizontal restraints became the focus of enforcement. Vertical restraints fell from favor, as exhibited by the DOJ's 1985 vertical restraints guidelines. The Antitrust Division and the FTC announced, in 1994, the revocation of the Reagan-Bush version of these guidelines. Bingaman announced that, henceforth, vertical price-fixing would be treated as a per se violation of the Sherman Act and vertical restraints that did not involve price-fixing would be considered under a "meaningful" rule of reason analysis (i.e., one that did not contain so many contingencies as to make prosecution impossible). Indeed, in 1994 the Department of Justice filed the first resale price maintenance case since the late 1970s (see Ordover 1997).

There were also significant changes in the treatment of mergers. The agencies jointly introduced a revision of the horizontal merger guidelines that forced partners to provide stronger evidence in support of the kinds of efficiency claims that were routinely accepted in the 1980s. Assuming at the outset that "competition usually spurs firms to achieve efficiencies internally," the revisions noted that there are cases when mergers can in fact result in efficiency gains. Yet the guidelines clearly stated that the agencies would consider efficiency claims *only* when they were "unlikely to be accomplished in the absence of either the proposed merger or another means having comparable anticompetitive effects." Moreover, the guidelines warned parties to "substantiate efficiency claims so that the Agency can verify by reasonable means the likelihood and magnitude of each asserted efficiency" (DOJ 1997; FTC 1997).

In addition to the more skeptical treatment of efficiency claims, the agencies broadened the issues deemed important in determining the competitive impact of mergers to include competition in research and development. This constituted a fundamental "realignment of merger review from static structural models toward an examination of the effect of a transaction on future competition." The goal of the new policy was to consider explicitly "dynamic efficiency considerations" and view innovation as a form of nonprice competition that can directly contribute to social welfare. As a result, even if a merger would not affect the price of goods, it might be challenged if its effect was to lessen competition in innovation or research and development (Chin 1997).

A reconsideration of merger policy was an important task. The 1990s witnessed a merger wave that was far greater than earlier waves, as reflected by the growing number of premerger filings (1,589 premerger notifications in 1992, compared with 4,926 in 2000). The high level of merger activity was a drain on agency resources (Ota 1998), requiring a reallocation of staff to merger review. To the extent that the merger wave was a response to increases in global competition, the logic of merger review needed to be connected to larger concerns of international antitrust (Pitofsky 1996).

In addition to its merger wave, the 1990s will be remembered for the case against Microsoft. The history of antitrust is punctuated by a handful of cases that were filed against the greatest economic behemoths of the times. During the Clinton administration, the Justice Department decided to add Microsoft to this list, initiating a civil suit that had the potential to rival the 1911 breakup of Standard Oil. The stakes were stunning for Microsoft and the economy as a whole. If successful, the Justice Department could force Microsoft to divest certain businesses or dissolve itself into separate companies, thereby permanently altering the structure of one of the nation's most dynamic industries (Ota 1998). This could have massive ramifications. In the 1990s, rapid advances in information technology were "driving the simultaneous consolidation, deregulation and globalization seen in the retail, banking, health care, transportation, entertainment and telecommunications sectors" (Munro 1998: 2768). Microsoft Windows—the global standard in computer operating systems—was at the heart of these changes.

The case in question, *United States v. Microsoft,* found its origins in the early 1990s. In 1993 the Antitrust Division assumed responsibility for an FTC investigation regarding potential collusion between Microsoft and IBM. By 1994 the investigation had resulted in a consent decree between the Justice Department and Microsoft barring the latter from requiring original equipment manufacturers (OEMs) who license the Windows operating system to also obtain license to other software. The consent decree was accepted by US District Court judge Thomas Penfield Jackson in 1995. Although the original consent decree focused on "tying," Microsoft accomplished the same end by integrating its web browser (Explorer) with the Windows 95 operating system. This posed the concern that Microsoft was using its monopoly position in operating systems to foreclose competition in web browsers. The Antitrust Division began investigating these activities in late 1996 and in October 1997 it filed a petition with Jackson alleging that Microsoft had violated the terms of the consent decree. Jackson, in turn, issued a preliminary injunction barring Microsoft from requiring

OEMs from installing Internet Explorer as part of the Windows bundle. By January 1998 the Justice Department and Microsoft had negotiated an agreement by which Microsoft would give OEMs the option to install Windows without Explorer. Although things might have appeared settled by this point, the battle against Microsoft was only starting.

In May 1998, twenty states and the District of Columbia filed a civil complaint alleging antitrust violations by Microsoft in *State of New York v. Microsoft.* The federal government subsequently filed charges in *United States v. Microsoft,* in 2000. The two cases were consolidated. The case quickly assumed center stage at the Antitrust Division, claiming some $5–6 million, upward of 10 percent of the Antitrust Division's budget (Klein 2000). Following a bench trial that lasted from October 1998 to June 1999, Jackson issued his finding of fact: Microsoft had maintained an illegal monopoly, attempted to monopolize, and engaged in unlawful tying in violation of Sections 1 and 2 of the Sherman Act and analogous state antitrust laws. The case was referred to chief judge of the US 7th Circuit Court of Appeals, Richard Posner, for voluntary mediation. As these efforts proved unsuccessful, Judge Jackson ruled in June 2000 that Microsoft be divided into two separate corporations, thereby separating the Windows operating system from the applications business. Jackson characterized Microsoft as an "untrustworthy monopolist" and claimed that the decision to break up the company into two separate businesses was the "least drastic" remedy he considered, one that was far superior to creating an onerous regulatory scheme (Grimaldi 2000: 1).

United States v. Microsoft held the potential to be the most significant antitrust action in nearly a century. As one might expect, Attorney General Janet Reno heralded the decision as a "strong, effective remedy to address the serious antitrust violations that Microsoft has committed." AAG Joel Klein predicted: "When the remedy is implemented—and this is the key point—customers, consumers, in a free and competitive marketplace, will decide for themselves what software they want to purchase. Neither a monopolist nor the government will dictate that choice" (Grimaldi 2000: 1). Although the decision would be appealed under a new presidential administration, Klein minimized the impact given the "continuity and commitment to law enforcement in the Department of Justice" (Klein 2000: 1694). Whether Klein's optimism would be borne out would be determined in the early days of the Bush presidency.

George W. Bush and Antitrust

There was little in George W. Bush's 2000 campaign that suggested that there would be a shift in antitrust. Yet for his key appointments at the FTC and the Antitrust Division, he reached back into the history of the two agencies to draw on individuals who had been center stage during the Reagan presidency. Bush appointed Timothy Muris to serve as chairman of the FTC (Balto 2001). Muris had served as director of the FTC's Bureau of Consumer Protection (1981–1983) and Bureau of Competition (1983–1985), and director of the Office of Management and Budget (1985–1988). A prolific author of books and articles on regulation, Muris argued that "a freely functioning market, subject to the rules of antitrust, provides maximum benefits to consumers." With respect to antitrust policy, "we must have solid economic analysis that is firmly grounded in facts and real-world institutions" (Frater and Steel 2001: 2024).

At the Justice Department, Bush appointed Charles A. James as AAG for antitrust. James was a veteran of the FTC (1979–1985), where he served in a number of capacities, including assistant to the director of the Bureau of Competition—Timothy Muris. After a stint in private practice, he returned to public service in 1989 as deputy AAG under George H. W. Bush (and briefly as acting AAG in 1992). Given the close connections between James and Muris, many wondered if these appointments would herald a new era of interagency cooperation. Indeed, in 2002 the two agencies attempted to reduce overlap in merger review, with the Antitrust Division assuming responsibility for the communications, entertainment, and software industries and the FTC assuming jurisdiction over the health care, biotechnology, and computer hardware industries. This effort attracted the ire of some members of Congress intent on protecting the jurisdiction of the independent FTC; it was abandoned after Senate Commerce Committee chairman Ernest Hollings (D-SC) threatened to withhold agency funding (Ota 2002). James's appointment as AAG was short-lived; in October of 2002 he resigned his position to become vice president and general counsel of Chevron Texaco Corporation. R. Hewitt Pate, formerly a deputy AAG in the Antitrust Division, was confirmed to serve as AAG in June 2003.

During the George W. Bush presidency, the two antitrust agencies have experienced significant growth in resources. The Antitrust Division had a budget of $110 million in 2000. By 2005 its budget reached an unprecedented $139 million. In nominal terms, the budget had more than doubled since the first year of the Clinton presidency (DOJ 2005b). Even greater budgetary growth occurred at the FTC. Its budget grew from $125 million in 2000 to $205 million in 2005. In nominal terms, it had doubled since 1997 (FTC 2005b). Between 2001 and 2005 the FTC's antitrust budget increased from $59.2 million to $89.2 million (FTC 2001a, 2005b). While this record of growth is impressive, three caveats are in order. First, much of the growth in revenue was driven by filing-fee revenues derived from the premerger notification program. Large mergers must comply with the premerger notification process, paying fees of between $45,000 and $280,000.[1] From 2000 to 2003 these revenues were so great as to cover the Antitrust Division's entire budget. Second, the merger wave of the late 1990s dramatically increased the resources required for premerger notification, essentially claiming the lion's share of the budgetary increases. Reforms in 2001, which increased the program's threshold from $15 million to $50 million, combined with a reduction in merger activity in the early years of the Bush presidency, partially reduced the demands of merger analysis.

Third, and most important, increased resources were not translated into higher levels of enforcement. Consider the case of the Antitrust Division. A comparison of Clinton's second term and Bush's first term is quite revealing (see Table 4.1). The most striking difference between the two administrations is the level of merger activity. The period 1997–2000 witnessed an unprecedented level of merger activity, with premerger notifications peaking at 4,926 in 2000. The annual average during Bush's first term was one-third that of Clinton's second term, due both to the reduction in merger activity and increases in the thresholds for merger review. Another important difference comes in nonmerger activity. Although there were few differences in the investigations initiated (outside of the area of grand jury investigations), the Bush Antitrust Division filed far fewer civil and criminal cases than did its predecessor. Moreover, total fines imposed fell from an annual average of $432 million under Clinton to approximately one-third that level under Bush (DOJ 2005a).

In contrast to the Antitrust Division, there was far greater activism at the FTC under Bush. The annual number of nonmerger investigations opened per year (forty-five) was more than double the level achieved in 2000 (twenty-five), largely what one would expect given the end of the merger wave and the changes in the premerger notification thresholds. By

Table 4.1   Antitrust Division Workload

Enforcement Activities	1997–2000 Annual Average	2001–2004 Annual Average
Premerger notifications received	4,499.50	1,507.75
Investigations initiated, by primary type of conduct		
Sherman § 1—Restraint of trade	90.5	97.5
Sherman § 2—Monopoly	10.5	10.0
Clayton § 7—Mergers	283.00	135.75
Merger civil actions filed in district court	17.5	16.5
Nonmerger civil actions filed in district court	8.5	2.5
Criminal grand jury investigations	25.75	30.25
Criminal cases filed in district court	55	40
Sherman § 1 cases filed in district court	48.50	27.75
Total fines imposed (in millions)	$432	$145

Source: DOJ 2005a. Calculations by author.

2004, 63 percent of these investigations resulted in enforcement actions. Where the FTC made a second request for information on mergers, enforcement actions resulted in an average of 65 percent of the cases per year. Finally, the FTC's success rate when it initiated cases due to anticompetitive violations reached an astounding 100 percent by 2002–2004 (FTC 2001b, 2002b, 2003a, 2004, 2005a). While some observers may have hoped that the Bush administration would be far more accommodating to business, many were struck by the growing vigor of enforcement at the FTC, attributing much to the leadership provided by Muris (Seiberg 2002). Muris was the only individual ever to serve as head of both the Bureau of Competition and the Bureau of Consumer Protection and proved far more willing than his predecessor to employ complicated consent decrees, particularly in the area of mergers (Seiberg 2001; for an alternative view, see Stoll and Goldfein 2002).

Outside of the enforcement figures, there is remarkably little to differentiate the Clinton and Bush administrations with respect to policy. Indeed, the guidelines for mergers, international operations, enforcement in the health care industry, and intellectual property have been in place since the mid-1990s. As a generalization, the nation's antitrust policy has exhibited great continuity since the late 1980s, leading many to suggest that the policy was no longer ripe for partisan shifts in enforcement (see ABA 2005; McDavid and Leibenluft 2001). Of course, when the Bush administration's antitrust record is held up to scrutiny, the vigor of enforcement efforts may be less memorable than the conclusion reached to the most important case filed by the Antitrust Division during the 1990s: *United States v. Microsoft.*

On June 28, 2001, the US Court of Appeals for the District of Columbia Circuit ruled on the appeal to *United States v. Microsoft.* Although the Court of Appeals accepted the factual findings, it threw out two of the three charges against Microsoft (the attempt to monopolize the market for web browsers and the improper tying of Explorer to Windows). At the same time, the court affirmed only limited violations of Section 2 of the Sherman Act (i.e., the finding that Microsoft was illegally maintaining a monopoly with its Windows operating system). It vacated the order to break up Microsoft and ordered the Justice Department and Microsoft to negotiate a consent decree proposing remedies for the "commingling of browser and operating system code," which constituted "exclusionary conduct, in violation of Section 2" of the Sherman Act. US District Court judge Thomas Penfield Jackson who had ordered the breakup was removed from the case for bias (Clark 2001; Munro 2001a).

Pursuant to the appellate decision, in September 2001 the Bush Justice Department formally abandoned the effort to break up Microsoft, focusing instead on remedies that addressed the company's conduct. AAG Charles

James negotiated a consent decree with Microsoft, one that gained the support of half of the state attorneys general who had been involved in *State of New York v. Microsoft*. The Justice Department assumed that the issue of "commingling" had been largely resolved by requiring Microsoft to include an effective add/remove utility to its system. Under the agreement, the government would monitor Microsoft's practices for five years to prevent efforts to abuse its monopoly on its operating system. Microsoft would be required to divulge some of its software application programming interfaces and server protocols to software developers who produce "middleware" (e.g., web browsers, e-mail programs, media players, instant messaging) so their products can be fully compatible with the Windows operating system. Computer manufacturers (and consumers) would be free to substitute competing middleware software on Microsoft's operating system without facing retaliation. The implementation of the technical aspects of the judgment would be overseen by an on-site panel of three independent computer experts with full access to all of Microsoft's books, records, systems, and personnel, including source code (Clark 2001; DOJ 2001; Munro 2001b).

Microsoft accepted the provisions of the judgment and moved quickly to convince the holdout states to join the settlement in exchange for reimbursement for all litigation costs, including attorney fees (Krim 2001). California, Connecticut, Florida, Iowa, Kansas, Massachusetts, Minnesota, Utah, West Virginia, and the District of Columbia rejected this and subsequent offers, proposing a settlement that would have imposed a host of sanctions on Microsoft. Nevertheless, in November 2002 the US District Court approved with minor modifications the settlement between Microsoft and the Department of Justice. Although reactions were mixed, there was something of a consensus that Microsoft had been fortunate to avoid far more serious sanctions, because the Bush Justice Department had been overly conciliatory in negotiating the consent decree. Although several of the state attorneys general vowed to continue the fight against Microsoft in the state courts, the Bush Justice Department considered the matter closed (Opatrny 2002).

Conclusion

More than a century ago, antitrust emerged as a regulatory response to the emerging corporate order and an effort to preserve decentralized markets and traditional American political values in an industrial economy. Although the modern industrial economy has been replaced by a postindustrial service economy, antitrust continues to exert an impact on economic organization and decisionmaking. Antitrust has undergone significant changes in the past several decades. Patterns of enforcement were increasingly informed by economic analysis. As the antitrust bureaucracies were professionalized to reflect the importance of economics, new norms were introduced into the regulatory process. A primary lesson one can draw from the case of antitrust is that professionalization can create an important, if subtle, source of policy change, particularly in regulatory areas that place a premium on expert knowledge. A second lesson is equally important: the analytical models presented in Chapter 2 need not work in exclusion. In antitrust, changes in the subsystem resulted in changes in the bureaucracy, which both increased the responsiveness of the agency to subsequent subsystem shifts, and directly affected the priorities established in enforcement. Subsequently, biases established within the bureaucracy limited the discretion of new political executives. They could successfully redefine priorities, but only to the extent that this redefinition could be reconciled with the norms established within the agencies. With these changes in place, it appears that antitrust has entered a period of stability reinforced by a broad bipartisan consensus.

In 2005 the American Bar Association's Section on Antitrust released its report on antitrust enforcement during the first term of the George W. Bush administration. The bipartisan committee, cochaired by former FTC chairman Robert Pitofsky and former AAG James F. Rill, offered little in the way of criticism: "given what appears to be a balanced, moderate, and bipartisan enforcement program, major changes in antitrust enforcement do not appear to be in order" (ABA 2005: 3). Indeed, the report noted that the earlier partisan battles surrounding antitrust—so evident in the 1960s, 1970s, and 1980s—were but a distant memory:

> During the last third of the 20th century, the U.S. witnessed profound changes in the nature of antitrust enforcement and, in the past 16 years, a remarkable bipartisan convergence of enforcement policy to incorporate tools of industrial organization economics. Modifications and improvements can certainly be introduced . . . but the extraordinary differences of views that raged in the 1960s and later in the 1980s have almost disappeared. . . . In the past 16 years, there has been a remarkable convergence of thinking about antitrust principles in the U.S. A bipartisan consensus formed during the administrations of Presidents George H.W. Bush, William J. Clinton, and George W. Bush so that enforcement priorities in many areas of antitrust are roughly the same whether the U.S. enforcement agencies—the DOJ and the FTC—are led by Democrats or Republicans. (ABA 2005: 7, 8)

According to the report, the consistency in enforcement reflects a broad acceptance of several key points. First, "in establishing priorities and goals, the primary concern should be the welfare of consumers—not shareholders of corporations or competitors." Second, enforcement should "devote primary attention to horizontal cartel activity and to horizontal restraints in merger and nonmerger cases." Third, there is broad "agency recognition of an essential role for economic analysis to inform the design and application of legal rules." Fourth, there should be "continued enforcement against practices, not horizontal in themselves, that can facilitate horizontal restraints." Fifth, there should be "increased sensitivity and concern about private restraints achieved through state action. Finally, there should be "a far more modest role for challenges to price and service discrimination under the Robinson-Patman Act; to conglomerate mergers based on theories of raising barriers to entry; and to vertical distribution arrangements that have no significant horizontal effect" (ABA 2005: 8–9).

As readers will note, the consensus recognized by the American Bar Association—what others refer to as the "antitrust mainstream" (Manson 2005)—was largely a product of the changes that occurred during the late 1970s and 1980s. What once appeared to be a radical departure from the historical legacy of antitrust now constitutes the consensus position occupied by both Democrats and Republicans. One may question whether this consensus will prove durable (Bobelian 2004). The forces of globalization, the dearth of international regulatory institutions, and the complexities of intellectual property rights in a digital age open new challenges that may force policymakers to reconsider the nature of market competition and the efficacy of the Sherman and Clayton Acts. These considerations, in turn, may test the strength of the new consensus in antitrust.

Note

1. Reforms to Hart-Scott-Rodino (Section 630 of Public Law 106-553, 114 Stat. 2762), effective February 1, 2001, raised the threshold for mergers from $15 million to $50 million, and replaced the flat fee of $45,000 with a three-tiered fee structure ranging from $45,000 to a high of $280,000.

5

Regulating Financial Intermediaries

WHENEVER SAVING and investing are carried out as separate activities, or when investors use the funds of savers, one has a financial services industry (which, for convenience, we refer to as banking). Banks take savers' funds and invest them through loans to borrowers, assuming responsibility for both the risk of investment as well as the major portion of the proceeds that come out of such activity (Litan 1987: 8–9). Because they collect a large pool of funds, financial intermediaries (banks, thrifts, and credit unions) are able to diversify the risk of investing by spreading loans among long-term and short-term borrowers and between high-risk and low-risk endeavors, greatly increasing the probability of a positive return on their investment. Because the business of banking involves investing "other people's money," financial institutions have always been subject to some form of regulation.

The regulation of financial intermediaries brings together a complicated network of regulators and regulated. Given the unusual institutional decentralization, this chapter departs somewhat from the organization adopted in other chapters in this volume. Rather than focusing on the actions of a single agency, it provides a broader overview of events within this regulatory arena. While the extreme decentralization in finance makes bank regulation[1] complex, it is not normally salient. Instead, interest in banking is restricted to those intimately involved in the business—financial intermediaries, state and national regulators, and select members of congressional banking committees (Worsham 1997). Still, as the following brief historical overview makes clear, periodic crises have raised the salience of financial regulation, shaking up the normally staid subsystem and producing change in financial regulation. As Figure 5.1 suggests, the salience of financial regulation

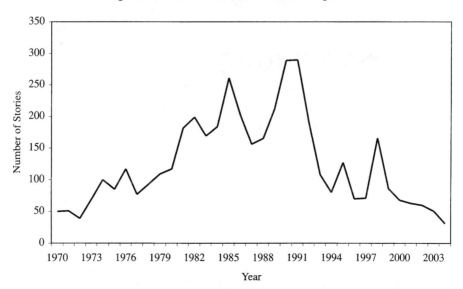

Figure 5.1 The Salience of Financial Regulaion

increased from 1977 through 1985, coinciding with the stagflation of the 1970s, the recession of 1982, and the tremendous instability introduced into the nation's financial system. It peaked again in the late 1980s as the savings and loan crisis took hold.

The Evolution of Financial Regulation

Financial regulation has its origins in legislation passed during three periods of US history. Born during the Civil War, national bank regulation was a fairly haphazard affair up through the New Deal, despite the passage of the Federal Reserve Act early in the twentieth century. The New Deal banking regulation created the system of distinct financial intermediaries—commercial banks, thrifts, investment banks—that still exists, in some form, today. Changes in financial regulation originating in the larger deregulatory wave of the 1980s have resulted in major alterations in the New Deal system; whether they have buried it is still a question for inquiry. In this section, we offer a short history of the evolution of financial regulation to provide the background necessary to understand the events that unfolded after 1980.

The Birth of Financial Regulation
The origin of financial regulation can be dated to the Civil War and the passage of the Currency Act of 1863 and the National Bank Act of 1863. The

Currency Act was intended to create a single, uniform, government-backed currency. Seen as essential to the war effort, the issuance of "bond-backed" currency (essentially small-denomination Treasury notes) was meant to introduce a safe and sound currency into an economy that was too often plagued by a flood of overvalued, if not worthless, private banknotes (Hammond 1957; Trescott 1963; Robertson 1968). At the time, banks issued their own notes based on deposits of "hard" currency—gold and silver (referred to as *specie*). Unscrupulous "wildcat" banks were known to print notes almost at will, creating panics when those who held the notes discovered their true worth and sought to withdraw their deposits from both honest and dishonest institutions. Federal government issuance of notes, through government-chartered national banks, was presented as the solution to the problem of wildcat banking and the periodic bank failures that plagued the economy. Federal government control of note issue also allowed the government to levy a small tax on the notes, creating much needed revenue to fight the Civil War.

The National Bank Act laid the groundwork for a national banking system through the creation of the Office of the Comptroller of the Currency (OCC). The OCC was given responsibility for approving charter applications of individuals who wanted to run a national bank, as well as oversight of capital and reserve requirements. Capital requirements simply mandate that anyone who wants to form a bank must first put up a set sum of capital, to be held by the comptroller, as backing for the venture. Reserve requirements force a bank to hold currency or specie in reserve as security for outstanding loans and as a safeguard to avoid shortfalls when depositors seek to withdraw funds.[2]

While the two Civil War–era acts set the stage for federal government regulation of banking, they fell short of creating a purely national banking system. States had long chartered banks, subject to varying reserve, capital, and other regulatory requirements. While it was believed that the two acts would eventually eliminate state banks, because of a tax feature designed to put an end to the issuance of state banknotes, this never came to pass. The result is that the United States has a dual banking system in which state-chartered and regulated institutions operate alongside national banks. This competition was not conducive to monetary or economic stability and contributed, in part, to a series of economic downturns and bank panics between 1870 and the first decade of the twentieth century (West 1977; White 1983).

The Federal Reserve Act
Congress passed the Federal Reserve Act in 1913 to put an end to the recurrent bank failures of the previous decades.[3] The act was intended to create a banking system managed by a unique combination of government

regulation and private industry cooperation. Control of the system is divided between the Federal Reserve Board of Governors and regionally based reserve banks. The board, selected by the president and confirmed by the Senate, looks much like a prototypical independent commission. Unlike the systemwide responsibilities of the board, the reserve banks serve geographically delimited districts. A board of directors chosen by the various national banks in the district runs each bank. The sum total of the various reserve banks' responsibilities gives them a claim to managing the system (see Livingston 1986; Worsham 1997). The struggle over control of the system, between the reserve banks with their privately controlled boards and the Federal Reserve Board of Governors and its executive branch backer, dominated the first twenty years of the Federal Reserve's existence. Nationally chartered banks had to join the new system and maintain reserves at regional reserve banks. Membership allowed banks to take advantage of a variety of services to promote currency stability and bank profitability.

Unlike the OCC, the Federal Reserve ("the Fed") is not a bureau within the Treasury Department, although the secretary of the Treasury was originally included on the Board of Governors. The Fed is set up as a hybrid independent commission cum public corporation. That is, the board looks much like the typical independent commission with a bipartisan, staggered-term, presidential-nominated, and Senate-confirmed membership. The reserve banks enjoy a more corporate form of organization and actually turn a profit on their operations. The result is that the Fed does not depend on Congress for its budget, but rather earns its own way through its day-to-day operations. The Federal Reserve Act attempted to create a system that would promote economic stability via regulation by the Board of Governors and management by the reserve banks. The problem was that the act did not clearly establish who was in charge of the new system—the board or the banks—greatly hindering operations, as became abundantly clear during the Great Depression of the 1930s (Livingston 1986; Worsham 1997). The relatively late and limited actions by the Fed during the depression convinced critics that the system needed further tinkering if it was to run smoothly.

New Deal Regulation

Four pieces of legislation passed between 1933 and 1935, in response to the crisis of the Great Depression, rewrote financial regulation.[4] The first piece of legislation, the Banking Act of 1933, also called the Glass-Steagall Banking Act, established a deposit insurance fund managed by the newly created Federal Deposit Insurance Corporation. The act separated investment banking from commercial banking, laying the groundwork for the creation of separate financial intermediaries, each serving a particular niche in the banking world.

The move toward creating unique institutional niches in the financial services market was furthered by the passage of legislation in 1934 that created a separate savings and loan insurance fund run by the Federal Savings and Loan Insurance Corporation. Linked to this was a 1935 act offering a national charter to thrifts that had previously been exclusively state chartered. The new chartering authority, the Federal Home Loan Bank Board (FHLBB), was charged with additional oversight responsibilities, which made it resemble a combination OCC–Federal Reserve for thrifts. The final piece of New Deal legislation, the 1935 Banking Act, settled the question of where authority lay in the Federal Reserve System. The Board of Governors, reduced to seven members with the OCC and Treasury secretary removed, was given ultimate power. The act also created the position of a president to head the Federal Reserve banks and established the Open Market Committee to oversee monetary policy. The New Deal banking legislation gave rise to a system of financial intermediaries and government regulation that remained in place, untouched, for nearly half a century.

The New Deal system was intended to promote stability in banking and, by doing so, economic stability. The separation, through regulation, of banking from other forms of commerce was recognition of banks' unique and important role in economic growth. The separation of commercial lending, home loans, and investment banking allowed the government to practice a uniquely American form of macroeconomic management. The pace of the US postwar economic growth is, at least in part, testimony to the success of the New Deal system. The changes in financial regulation that occurred in the 1980s, as well as the ongoing debate over financial regulation today, involve these New Deal institutions.

Regulating Financial Intermediaries:
The Banking Subsystem

The New Deal separation of financial intermediaries into commercial banks, thrifts, investment banks, insurance firms, and a host of related services slowly came undone in the 1980s. Still, because some of these distinctions survive in regulation and practice today, and because the politics of financial institution regulation involves efforts to alter or preserve these distinctions, a brief review of the regulatory system created by the New Deal is essential. Because so much of regulation is institution-specific, we start each section below with a discussion of the primary target of regulation, followed by a discussion of the regulatory agencies.

Commercial Banks

Commercial banks are the most common form of financial intermediary, numbering 7,527 at the end of 2005, with nearly 70,000 branches controlling $9,039,674 in assets (FDIC 2006b: III-A). This number can be further delimited according to the chartering source—state or national. Of the preceding total number of commercial banks, 1,818 were national banks, controlling $6,003,169. An additional 5,709 were state banks, with $3,036,506 in assets (FDIC 2006a).

Not only does the dual banking system offer financial intermediaries a choice of regulatory authority, national regulatory authority is divided among three agencies—the OCC, the Fed, and the FDIC. The OCC, an agency within the Treasury Department, was expressly developed to regulate the banking industry. The comptroller is responsible for the chartering of national banks, as well as the conduct of examinations and the enforcement of select consumer protection provisions. Bank supervision responsibilities are separated according to the size and nature of the institution. Large-bank supervision targets the thirty-two largest banking companies and is carried out under the supervision of a deputy comptroller located in the District of Columbia. Midsize or credit card banks include banks that present unique supervisory challenges based on size, complexity, or product line, and are also subject to DC-based supervision. The remaining banks, which tend to operate in smaller geographic markets and are involved in less sophisticated kinds of banking activities, are subject to regionally based supervision. The OCC breaks the country down into four such markets, with a district office headed by a deputy comptroller in each and bank examiners operating out of field offices located in areas with a large concentration of national banks.

The Federal Reserve System is concerned with control of the money supply and how it affects the economic health of the nation, as well as the regulation of member banks. Following the passage of the Federal Reserve Act, all national banks were required to subscribe to the stock of individual reserve banks and to keep a set amount of reserves on deposit at the reserve bank in their district (there are twelve such districts). In return for these obligations, they were able to use their reserve bank to clear checks, borrow funds, and take advantage of a variety of additional services that aid them in the conduct of their business. State-chartered banks are given the option of joining the Federal Reserve System, a move that was not very popular until the series of state bank failures in the 1980s.

Each reserve bank has a nine-member board of directors. Six of these, the Class A directors (representing the member banks) and the Class B directors (representing the public), are elected by the member banks. The final three Class C directors (representing the public) are chosen by the Board of Governors. The Board of Governors manages the system, engaging in both the formulation of monetary policy and the regulation of member banks. The seven members of the Board of Governors are appointed to staggered fourteen-year terms by the president, subject to Senate confirmation, and can be removed only through impeachment.[5] The primary regulatory responsibilities of the Fed include the approval of mergers, the supervision of multiple-bank holding companies (nonbank companies that hold an interest in two or more banks), and the enforcement of a variety of consumer protection statutes.

The FDIC is a government corporation that insures the deposits of national banks. In addition to national banks, the vast majority of state-chartered banks (with over 96 percent of deposits) are insured by the FDIC. The principal regulatory role of the FDIC is aimed at ensuring the soundness of state-chartered banks that receive insurance, and the issuance of cease and desist orders in the case of improper management by insured banks (national and state). The FDIC is governed by a five-member board, which includes the comptroller, three members appointed for six-year terms by the president (one of whom serves as the chair), and the director of the Office of Thrift Supervision.

Banks are well organized, with two national-level trade associations representing their interests. The largest and oldest is the American Bankers Association. Originally formed by midwestern banks to advocate the creation of the Federal Reserve, this association now represents the industry as a whole. Given the proclivity of the association to weight the interests of larger institutions over those of smaller ones, the Independent Bankers Association of America (IBAA) was formed specifically to represent the interests of small banks. Together, these two organizations form a ubiquitous presence at congressional hearings dealing with financial regulation, often functioning as agenda setters and formulators of banking policy.

Savings and Loans

Savings and loans, or thrifts, were originally formed to aid those interested in purchasing a home. Like commercial banks, thrifts accept deposits and make loans. Historically, they can be distinguished from banks, at least before 1980, by the longer period borrowers had to pay back loans—which were principally long-term mortgages for the purchase of homes—and the higher rate of interest thrifts could offer savers before the demise of Regulation Q in the 1980s. Regulation Q was legislation permitting thrifts to offer a higher rate of return on deposits than that offered by commercial banks, in effect carving out a market for thrift deposits through regulation. At the end of 2005 there were 1,305 thrifts with assets of $1,837,400. Of these, 772 were nationally chartered, with the remaining 533 state chartered (FDIC 2006b: IV-A).

Until 1992 the primary trade association for thrifts was the US League of Savings Institutions (USLSI), with a variety of state-level groups representing particular regions and factions of the industry. The USLSI merged with the National Council of Community Bankers to form the Savings & Community Bankers of America in 1992, changing its name to America's Community Bankers in 1995. In addition to the preceding, thrifts often join forces with housing-industry trade associations, contractors, retirees, insurance firms, or anybody with any interest in homeownership in their attempt to shape financial regulation.

Until 1989 the FHLBB was the thrift-industry equivalent of the Federal Reserve. All nationally chartered thrifts and mutual savings banks were members; state membership was optional. The FHLBB offered deposit insurance through the FSLIC, the stock of which was subscribed to by member institutions. The FHLBB also chartered thrifts, regulated all insured institutions, conducted examinations of members, and operated the Federal Home Loan Mortgage Corporation, which bought and sold home mortgages (Rom 1996). Like the FDIC, the FHLBB was governed by a three-person board, nominated by the president and confirmed by the Senate. Following the massive failure of thrifts in the 1980s and the bankrupting of the deposit insurance fund, the FHLBB was reformed as the Office of Thrift Supervision (OTS).

The newly reorganized OTS stresses supervision of thrift investments and economic forecasting to aid in understanding the ever-changing economic context in which thrifts operate. A director appointed by the president and confirmed by the Senate heads the OTS. In 2004 the Office of Examinations, Supervision, and Consumer Protection was reorganized into three subunits to allow the OTS to focus on three interrelated tasks. The first entity oversees savings and loan holding companies with substantial international operations, as well as those with the most complex portfolios and operations. A second entity oversees examinations and supervision of the rest of the industry. The final subunit focuses on evolving policy developments affecting the industry, making suggestions for regulatory change necessary to promote a healthy industry. The OTS divides the country into four supervisory regions—northeast, southeast, midwest, and west—with a director for each who oversees divisions concerned with corporate activity, compliance, supervision policy, and accounting policy.

Credit Unions

Credit unions are depository institutions that serve a select group of individuals based on a common bond of employment, association, or residence. Members purchase shares in the operation in the form of deposits, while credit union officers act as intermediaries in making loans to other members. Compared to commercial banks and thrifts, credit unions are small-time operations; there are approximately 9,500 federally insured credit unions, with some $520 billion in deposits. The National Credit Union Association (NCUA) is the most prominent trade group representing the interests of credit unions.

The NCUA was established in 1970 to charter federal credit unions, operate an insurance fund (the National Credit Union Share Insurance Fund), and regulate all those institutions subscribing to the insurance fund. A three-person board appointed by the president and approved by the Senate governs the NCUA. Board members serve staggered six-year terms, the president designates a chair, and no more than two members may be from the same party. The board holds monthly meetings, open to the public, in every month except August. The executive director, who answers directly to the chairman, oversees the day-to-day operations of the NCUA and those of ten central offices, which deal with matters ranging from examinations and insurance to public and congressional affairs. The director also directs the five regional offices charged with oversight of examination and supervision activities for credit unions in their region.

Financial regulation, then, involves a wide array of regulatory authorities attempting to control the activities of an equally diverse selection of financial intermediaries. Factor in the complex nature of what banks do—a task that became increasingly complicated because of a variety of economic and technological changes in the world of banking beginning in the 1970s—and the enterprise is nothing short of mind-boggling for the uninitiated.

In an effort to coordinate the regulatory activities of the various regulators, Congress created the Federal Financial Institutions Examination Council (FFIEC) in 1979. The council is empowered to prescribe uniform principles, standards, and report forms for the federal examination of financial institutions. Membership on the council consists of a representative from the Federal Reserve Board of Governors, the comptroller of the currency, the director of OTS, and the chairs of the FDIC and NCUA. The FFIEC was created in an effort to promote uniformity in the supervision of financial institutions by federal regulators. It works with the State Liaison Committee, an advisory body composed of five representatives of state supervisory agencies, to better coordinate state and federal regulatory efforts.

Due to the complexity, and the usually low salience, of financial regulation, the banking policy subsystem often resembles a dominant coalition. That said, no subsystem equilibrium is static, and the financial services subsystem is no exception. During periods of heightened salience the financial subsystem is transformed into one in which competition is the norm. While the New Deal regulatory arrangements were an effort to partition this competition into subcommittee-based fiefdoms organized around the various types of financial intermediaries, the new system was not always able to keep conflict in check. In addition to this intramural competition, the contemporary period begins with a period in financial regulation that, at first blush, appears unusual. Beginning in the 1970s, financial regulation was subject to scrutiny from people not normally interested in banking. This interest peaked in the 1980s, when the subsystem was subject to the punctuating effects of the deregulatory wave washing over the American polity. In the late 1980s and early 1990s, a rash of thrift and bank failures pushed the subsystem further into the public limelight.

Rethinking Regulation

Financial deregulation has been occurring in a piecemeal fashion since the creation of the New Deal system in the 1930s. That said, it was in the 1970s that changes in technology, along with inflationary pressures and a corresponding rise in interest rates, opened the door to an organized challenge to the thinking behind New Deal (Glass-Steagall) regulatory firewalls. Initiated by economists, the call for a change in financial regulation was eventually voiced by the president, regulators, and most parts of the financial industry.

The first concerted effort at altering New Deal regulatory restrictions on banking was the product of a presidentially sponsored commission staffed by economists, the Hunt Commission. Sparked by a slowdown in credit for housing and a general economic downturn, the Hunt Commission recommended an end to the regulation that separated commercial banking, investment banking, and thrifts from one another, arguing that they were an outmoded artifact of the New Deal. The rationale offered was simple: Glass-Steagall regulation artificially separated and restricted the variety of activities that would normally be engaged in by financial intermediaries. Rethinking the proposition that competition greatly increases the likelihood of bank failure, the Hunt Commission argued that competition is essential for maximizing credit availability for a housing-hungry public.

In response to the Hunt Commission's recommendations, which were viewed by most members of the financial subsystem as a presidential intrusion, the House Banking Committee commissioned its own study, *Financial Institutions and the Nation's Economy (FINE)*, in 1975. The *FINE* study was intended to wrest control of the banking agenda from President Nixon, as well as provide information to committee members on the rapidly changing financial services policy arena. *FINE* was also a reaction to several high-profile bank failures that caught regulators, and members of the Banking Committee, by surprise. The study identified poor interdepartmental communications among Federal Reserve, OCC, and FDIC examiners as a factor that exacerbated the situation caused by the failures. *FINE* also discussed how increasingly high rates of inflation were causing problems for thrifts, devaluing their portfolios of fixed-rate mortgages and hampering their ability to make new mortgages. *FINE* suggested that the existing regulation limited the ability of thrifts, and thrift regulators, to raise the rate of interest to keep pace with inflation. Similarly, *FINE* identified *disintermediation* as a growing problem plaguing both thrifts and banks. Disintermediation involves the loss of savers. Neither thrifts nor banks were having success attracting new savers, and were actually losing savers at an increasing rate. Savers were switching their money to new forms of financial instruments that promised a better rate of return in the inflationary 1970s.

FINE contained several reform recommendations, all of which were opposed by various factions of regulators and regulated. A suggestion to consolidate regulatory responsibilities into a single agency was criticized by both the agencies targeted for downsizing—primarily the OCC, but later the Fed—and the banking industry. Calls for doing away with New Deal investment restrictions, the so-called regulatory firewalls, were opposed by smaller banks, the thrift industry, and select regulators (see Worsham 1997). In the end, the slowdown in inflation, the resurrection of housing starts, and the stalemate among financial intermediaries put an end to the reform discussion.

Deregulation?

The debate over altering financial regulation was taken up in 1976, when a series of technological changes and regulator-initiated policy change made much of the existing regulation a moot point. The advent of electronic banking ushered in new computer and data transmission technology that allowed banks to circumvent branching restrictions, minimize their working balances, and free up more assets for investment purposes. At the same time, the rise in inflation meant that traditional investment outlets, especially for thrifts, no longer promised a competitive rate of return. Savers and financial intermediaries were increasingly attracted to the stock market and commercial real estate, two areas that were producing high rates of return for investors. While many savers were able to move their funds into these new investments, banks and thrifts were prohibited from doing so by Glass-Steagall restrictions. The result was increased disintermediation when savers switched funds to brokerage and insurance firms, christened "nonbank banks" because they were able to offer customers a higher rate through a new investment opportunity, money market funds (MMFs).

Initially developed as a means to allow small investors to pool their funds and purchase instruments normally restricted to large investors, security firms, most notably Merrill Lynch, used MMFs to set up banklike accounts not subject to bank regulation. Individuals placed a minimum balance with a brokerage firm, to be invested in various stock and bond offerings, in return for which they were able to write drafts (checks) on the account, receive cash advances through a VISA card drawn on the account, and borrow money, all while receiving market rates of interest. MMFs were a serious competitor to thrift and bank savings accounts, because of the artificially low, regulatory enforced rate of interest these financial intermediaries could offer to customers (Frank 1981; Meier 1985). Institutions that offered MMFs were not subject to reserve requirements, did not carry deposit insurance (nor pay insurance premiums), and were able to use depositor funds to invest in avenues closed to banks and thrifts. When the Fed attempted to extend reserve requirements to MMFs, brokerage houses simply "moved" the funds offshore to nonregulated foreign offices. Because of the development of electronic transfers, in which credits and debits were recorded instantly via phone lines, such a move was easily accomplished.

While competition from the nonbank banks was bad enough, a variety of smaller financial intermediaries—credit unions and mutual savings banks—were making a dent of their own in the customer base of banks. They did so by offering interest on checking. Glass-Steagall regulation restricted checking accounts (demand deposits) to commercial banks, and prohibited the payment of interest on them—something MMFs had found a way around. Still, not all customers could meet the minimum balance requirements of MMFs. Enter the negotiated order of withdrawal (NOW) account. First developed by state-regulated mutual savings banks, NOW accounts allowed savers to use what were technically savings withdrawal slips to pay debts directly (Mayer 1974; Meier 1985). NOW accounts soon spread to all banks, state and national, operating in New England and New York. Credit unions offered a similar instrument in the mid-1970s: share drafts. Following suit, the FHLBB allowed thrifts a similar privilege vis-à-vis automated teller machines (ATMs) a year later. ATMs, in allowing depositors to withdraw cash from savings, were in effect checking accounts that paid interest. The result was that, by the mid-1970s, banks no longer enjoyed the exclusive privilege of offering checking to their customers. What was once a cheap source of investment funds was drying up at the very time that technological change was making deposits an even more lucrative source of investment capital.

By 1979, thrifts and mutual savings banks were offering checking that paid interest. With the blessing of state regulators and the FHLBB, banks were allowing instant transfer of funds from savings to checking via wire transfers approved by the Fed, and credit unions were offering checking, while the NCUA turned a blind eye to the infraction of existing regulation. Meanwhile, brokerage firms were busily creating banklike operations not subject to bank regulation. Quite simply, something had to give. And give it did when the financial subsystem broke out into a series of pitched battles fought in the courts. The USLSI sued the Fed, the American Bankers Association filed suit against the NCUA, and the Independent Bankers Association of America went after the FHLBB (Conte 1979). The Washington, D.C., Circuit Court of Appeals consolidated the cases into a single action, *American Bankers Association v. Connell* (1980), and promptly vacated the earlier court decisions that upheld the various agency actions. Rather than force the agencies to rescind their decisions, the court gave Congress until the end of the year to settle the dispute. In returning the question to the Senate Banking Committee and the House Banking Committee, the court was giving the subsystem one last chance to get its house in order.

The court decision coincided with an announcement by the White House that it would include banking as part of its larger deregulatory agenda. Despite the prodding of the court, and the turf threat from the president, the banking committees could not reach agreement on a course of action. Instead, they agreed to extend the practices for ninety days, after which they enshrined the impasse into law as the Depository Institutions Deregulation and Monetary Control Act (DIDMCA) of 1980. In ratifying regulator-authored deregulation, the DIDMCA was a stopgap at best. Still, the act is important for several reasons. First, it did manage to extend regulation, ever so slightly, to the nonbank banks. It did so by requiring that any intermediary accepting deposits be subject to Federal Reserve regulations, including reserve requirements. The act phased out interest-rate ceilings, eliminated the interest-rate differential between thrifts and banks (Regulation Q), authorized NOW accounts for all intermediaries, approved ATMs, loosened loan restrictions affecting thrifts, and raised deposit insurance from $40,000 per account to $100,000 (Cargill and Garcia 1985; Worsham 1997). The DIDMCA illustrates a central feature of subsystems characterized by competing coalition politics: their tendency to eke out temporary compromises that simply set the stage for future rounds of negotiation. Although the DIDMCA managed to ease the court out of its role of financial-industry umpire, and although it short-circuited the presidential attempt to assume the role of agenda setter, it did not end the competition among financial-industry players, nor did it eliminate the challenge from outsiders (securities firms).

Indeed, following the 1982 congressional elections, and the subsequent change in party control of the Senate, the fault lines grew sharper. On the one side was a deregulatory coalition led by the new chair of the Senate Banking Committee, Jake Garn (R-UT). The American Bankers Association, bank regulators, and a sizable contingent of constituents who wanted a higher return on their savings backed Garn. On the other side, the antideregulatory coalition, ostensibly led by Fernand St. Germain (D-RI), the chair of the House Banking Committee, consisted of small banks, most of the thrift industry, homebuilders, the FHLBB, securities firms, and the insurance industry. St. Germain's position as committee chair made him the natural leader of the forces that favored the maintenance of Glass-Steagall restrictions (Ehrenhalf 1983; Whittle 1983). Still, he was not the only committee chair laying a claim to the role. John Dingell (D-MI), chair of the House Energy and Commerce Committee, was invited by St. Germain to join the antideregulatory coalition. The problem was that once Dingell got his foot in the door, it was increasingly difficult to get rid of him.

The House Commerce Committee has been described as a committee in search of turf (King 1997). Dingell was intent on both protecting his committee's turf, which included the insurance and securities industries, and influencing the shape of financial regulation. More to the point, Dingell did not want financial regulators' authority extended any further into the business of securities firms offering MMFs. He also resisted the request by banks and thrifts to be allowed into securities brokerage or insurance underwriting. Inviting Dingell in as an ally institutionalized competition in the financial subsystem, further complicating the task of cutting a deal that would please the deregulatory and New Deal coalitions.

Once again, events forced a compromise solution, dubbed "Garn–St. Germain," when a rash of thrift failures threatened the FSLIC with insolvency. The act gave regulators increased power to deal with failing thrifts, permitting mergers across state lines and across industry boundaries (between thrifts and commercial banks). It institutionalized interest-bearing checking for banks and thrifts and widened the investment opportunities and individual loan limit for thrifts (Worsham 1997). While thrifts were given wider latitude in making investments, a feature that proved disastrous, both thrifts and banks were kept out of insurance underwriting and the securities field. Once again, deregulatory forces were facing a glass that appeared half empty rather than half full.

Regulator-Led Deregulation

The reaction to the stalemate engineered by the DIDMCA and Garn–St. Germain was a new round of regulator-led deregulation. The OCC used the nonbank-bank loophole to open the door to national bank activity prohibited by law. By shedding their commercial loan portfolios while holding on to deposits and deposit insurance, banks were able to reconstitute themselves as nonbanks, without any change in their charters. As nonbanks, they were able to engage in a wide variety of forbidden activities, all with the backing of the OCC. Banks were also using the nonbank-bank loophole to engage in interstate branching, a subject that struck a populist nerve in Congress and irritated the IBAA and its small-bank clientele to no end. When the Fed joined in on the side of expansion, approving a charter by a New York–based bank to open a Florida office, St. Germain declared that it was time for Congress to reassert its authority over the direction of banking policy (Calmes 1984a). St. Germain and Garn reached an agreement with the OCC to extend a moratorium on any further branching activity until Congress could consider the issue.

The problem was that St. Germain refused to consider any legislation that allowed banks to expand into business not directly linked to banking as defined by New Deal regulation. The House Banking Committee held weekly hearings critical of any further deregulation, meetings that found fewer and fewer committee members in attendance. St. Germain's intransigence alienated the American Bankers Association, bank regulators, and much of the House Banking Committee as well. When the Senate passed a deregulatory piece of legislation in September 1984, St. Germain announced that his committee had no time to consider it, further irritating his fellow committee members. Upon hearing St. Germain's pronouncement, the OCC announced its intention to begin approving branching applications again (Calmes 1984b).

Meanwhile, state bank regulators, most notably those in South Dakota, were allowing banks to purchase a state-chartered bank and use it to sell insurance out of state, set up credit card operations, and engage in activity normally prohibited to banks. Banks were also entering into state-backed regional banking compacts that allowed them to circumvent prohibitions against interstate branching and a variety of economic activities not directly related to banking. When the Supreme Court upheld regional compacts (in an 8–0 decision), it was clear that deregulation would continue with or without congressional guidance (Calmes 1985).

Unable to pass legislation reinstituting the prohibitions, the coalition led by St. Germain became increasingly reliant on Dingell's Energy and Commerce Committee to stem financial regulators bent on opening new markets for their charges. The increasing conflict among regulators, financial-industry factions, and the banking and commerce committees produced a legislative stalemate that could only slow, but not stop, the course of bank expansion into new economic activities. Abandoning any hope for legislative deregulation, the American Bankers Association turned to the OCC, and increasingly to the Fed, to approve its entry into new economic ventures.

Failure as the Norm: The Savings and Loan Crisis

It took a major disaster to cement Dingell's role as watchdog of financial regulation. Bank and thrift failures continued to increase in the mid-1980s, setting a postdepression record in 1987. Overnight, the estimates of the cost of rescuing the FSLIC, the thrift deposit insurance fund, increased by a factor of six. The conference committee called to patch together the bailout was unusual for both its size, 102 members, and its composition, which, while including predominantly members of the banking committees, also included representatives from the two chambers' tax committees, as well as members from Energy and Commerce and other House committees.

In addition to bailing out the insurance fund, the Competitive Equality Banking Act of 1987 dismantled both the FHLBB and the FSLIC, replacing them with the Office of Thrift Supervision. The act created the Resolution Trust Corporation, operating under FDIC auspices, to oversee the liquidation of assets seized from failed thrifts. It included new universal capital requirements for all financial intermediaries, required institutions to devote a set fraction of funds to home mortgages in order to qualify for tax breaks, banned investments in junk bonds by thrifts unless they set up a separately capitalized affiliate to do so, and contained more rigorous disclosure requirements. Most important, at least from the standpoint of Dingell and his insurance and securities clientele, the bill prohibited the entry of banks into securities brokerage, insurance underwriting, and commercial real estate (Elving 1987).

And the Walls Come Tumbling Down: The End of Glass-Steagall

Just prior to the bailout of the FSLIC in 1989, an important critic of deregulation, Senator William Proxmire (D-WI), reversed himself, introducing legislation that would repeal much of what remained of Glass-Steagall regulation. The Financial Modernization Act of 1988 was the first of many that tried to tear down the firewalls separating commercial banking, thrifts, securities firms, and the insurance industry. The bill, and all those that followed, recognized that deregulation was occurring whether Congress mandated it or not. Proxmire realized that if Congress wanted to maintain some semblance of influence in the realm of financial services, it needed to get on top of the changes under way or cede control to state regulators and market forces (Cranford 1988a). St. Germain, fighting one last holding action against deregulation, attempted to force a vote on a bill of his own that maintained most Glass-Steagall prohibitions. The House Banking Committee, kept in the dark on the contents of the bill until the markup, split into two opposing factions. One group, consisting of all the Republicans and several Democrats, introduced the Senate bill as a substitute for St. Germain's offering. Seeing trouble brewing, Dingell weighed in, staking a claim to any bill that allowed banks into the securities or the insurance field. This three-ring-circus format of conflicting coalitions—consisting of much of the thrift industry, small banks, and consumer advocates versus the American Bankers Association, and some of the larger thrifts versus the House Energy and Commerce Committee, along with securities and insurance firms—became the dominant motif of the 1990s. Congressional players in the financial subsystem were too fractured to exercise much influence on the course of policy.

The split between the Senate Banking Committee and House Banking Committee, not to mention the division of the House Banking Committee itself, coupled with Dingell's aggressive turf-grabbing strategy, was a recipe for congressional inaction—or more accurately, congressional reaction, since the only signs of legislative activity were the halfhearted responses to the recurrent crisis involving thrift and bank failures, and the insolvency of the Savings Association Insurance Fund and the threatened insolvency of the FDIC.

With the financial subsystem mired in the conflict associated with competing coalitions, the George H. W. Bush administration tried its hand at settling the impasse with a proposal for dismantling the remaining provisions of Glass-Steagall. The Bush proposal phased in interstate branching, allowed "well-capitalized" banks to establish separate affiliates dealing in insurance and securities, and streamlined regulation by combining the OTS and the OCC into a single agency (Cranford 1991b). Eventually whittled down into a narrowly focused bailout of the FDIC, the Bush proposal suffered the same fate as Proxmire's earlier attempt to phase out Glass-Steagall provisions separating banking, insurance, and the securities industries. The interindustry squabbling paralyzed the congressional players in the financial subsystem. Not that policy innovation ceased. Rather, congressional inaction left it to regulators to determine just what the law permitted. The 1990s were characterized by regulator-engineered deregulation. Regulators allowed the industry to engage in new endeavors that invariably involved a court challenge and a ruling on what was permissible and what was forbidden. In this fashion, regulated and regulators explored the boundaries of Glass-Steagall, all the while pushing the envelope of New Deal regulation.

The most common result of the regulator-backed redefinition of Glass-Steagall was eventual congressional ratification of what had become common practice. Take the issue of interstate branching, first broached by Proxmire in 1988 and pushed by the Bush administration in 1991. Although never passed as law, banks had engaged in a variety of activities that, in effect, gave them such powers. Using holding companies and regional pacts, banks were able to establish branchlike operations long before interstate branching was actually approved in 1994. Not that the passage of legislation permitting branching was unimportant. Indeed, the overwhelming support in both congressional banking committees for the legislation, along with the agreement of Senator Christopher J. Dodd not to attach an amendment limiting bank activities in the insurance field to the bill, marked a return of some semblance of order to the financial subsystem (Taylor 1994b). Dodd had sunk similar legislation in 1991 because of the objections of the insurance industry to banks' inroads into its turf (Taylor 1994a).

Just when it appeared that the financial subsystem was back to something resembling a dominant coalition, fissures reappeared. The age-old splits between large and small banks, banks and thrifts, the insurance industry and banks came to the surface when the discussion to remove remaining Glass-Steagall provisions was taken up by the new Republican Party chair of the House Banking Committee, Jim Leach of Iowa. Leach's attempt to keep the deregulatory ball rolling suffered from several missteps. While Leach was no newcomer to the committee—he had served on it since 1976—he did seem to misread the feelings of the various industry factions when it came to dismantling what remained of New Deal regulation. To be sure, his proposals were not as far-reaching as those of his Senate counterpart, Alfonse D'Amato (R-NY), who advocated allowing banks to affiliate with any commercial endeavor. Nor were they as radical as the stance of one of his subcommittee chairs, Richard A. Baker (R-LA), who argued that banking should be treated like any other business and allowed to engage in whatever endeavors proved profitable. Leach instead sought a middle road, which would allow banks into securities and insurance underwriting, under the supervision of regulatory authorities (Hager 1995a). With thirty-one members having joined the House Banking Committee after the 1991 dogfight over deregulation, the committee could be forgiven for its misreading of the lessons of passing branching legislation in the previous Congress. Adding to the perception that the time was ripe for change was the advocacy of both the OCC, which was nothing new, and Alan Greenspan, the Federal Reserve chair. Greenspan, originally appointed by President Reagan and reappointed by President Clinton, was nearly an icon in banking policy. His backing of changes in Glass-Steagall was seen by Leach as an indicator that the time had come to do what Congress had been unable to do for nearly two decades: rewrite banking regulation.

What Leach did not count on was the manner in which all matters in the 104th Congress were to take on larger political meaning in light of the Republican takeover of the chamber. Leach's proposal was soon tied to an attempt to repeal community reinvestment requirements passed at the president's request in the last (Democratic-controlled) Congress and eliminate truth-in-lending and truth-in-savings regulation that lay at the heart of consumer protection provisions favored by Democrats. The preceding were pushed by the new Republican leadership, and if the regulations were not enough to complicate Leach's task, the involvement of D'Amato, the Senate Banking Committee's new chair, in the Whitewater investigation being conducted by the Republican-controlled Congress was the straw that broke the camel's back. The question of presidential involvement in the S&L failures of the 1980s was not new. The Bush administration had been tangentially linked to the scandal through the involvement of the president's son. Now President Clinton was associated with the debacle through his involvement in a failed real estate venture in Arkansas. Democrats viewed the hearings as a Republican-orchestrated witch hunt, and the role of the banking committees in the investigation strained bipartisanship on the panels.

It was not simply party politics that complicated Leach's task. The insurance industry was in strong form during 1995 and 1996, rounding up a wide variety of opposition to banking entry into insurance. The Political Action Committee of the Independent Insurance Agents of America (IIAA), having donated $539,000 in the 1993–1994 election cycle, did not have to look far for allies in either chamber. Using the Commerce Committee as its home base, it insisted on, and got, a provision in the legislation that put a "permanent moratorium" on OCC approval of insurance sales by banks. The OCC had been using an obscure World War I vintage provision in regulation that allowed small-town banks to sell insurance, in order to open up insurance sales to most banks that applied for the privilege. After the Supreme Court upheld the OCC's interpretation of the act in *Barnett Bank v. Nelson* (1996), the IIAA had no choice but to try to limit such practice through regulation (Taylor 1996a, 1996b). With the addition of the insurance provision, the American Bankers Association pulled its support of the act, preferring to rely on regulator-sponsored deregulation to open new markets to banking. In the end, the Leach effort died in committee, after initially being reported out favorably, when Leach realized the bill would not likely pass in the House and would never garner support in the Senate.

The Clinton administration returned to the subject of deregulation in 1997 when Secretary of the Treasury Robert Rubin, a former investment banker, suggested that "the old lines that separated the insurance, securities and banking industries have increasingly blurred as new financial products and services have appeared. And regulatory and judicial rulings continue to erode many of the barriers that were put in place to restrain competition among financial services firms" (Taylor 1997b: 1190). Rubin, and the administration, called for revamping regulation to allow banks and securities firms to merge, although Rubin did back off from his earlier proposal to dismantle all barriers between commercial firms and banks. Short on specifics, the administration had clearly placed the ball in the congressional court with an endorsement to pursue a deregulatory agenda.

Leach responded with a bill (HR 10) that relaxed many of the barriers between insurance, securities, and commercial banking. Reported out of committee by a 28–26 vote, it was clear that the House Banking Committee was still split on the issue of deregulation. This was captured best in a statement by Leach, who had supported the bill in committee, suggesting he might vote against it when it came to the floor (Hosansky 1997a: 1431). The bill was sent to the Commerce Committee, where it was amended and reported out on a 33–11 vote. Passed by a one-vote margin, 214–213, the bill was referred to the Senate, where it eventually died. In the end, subsystem competition resulted in a legislative stalemate. Banks did not like the bill because it extended regulatory authority to state regulators for insurance and to the SEC for securities. Thrifts were opposed to the elimination of national charters. Insurance firms, obviously, did not like the portion that allowed banks onto their turf. The securities industry opposed the legislation for the same reason, as well as because it provided for Fed oversight of financial services holding companies. Finally, consumer advocates worried about the creation of megabanks, privacy issues, and similar concerns (Hosansky 1997c).

If legislative efforts to deregulate financial services came to naught, it was due in part to the regulator-led deregulation that was actually occurring in the market for financial services. Increased merger activity between financial service providers was accomplishing even more than what the legislation proposed. So, for example, a merger between Salomon Inc. and Travelers Insurance Group resulted in a $9 billion monster-corporation that dealt in both securities and insurance. Similarly, the efforts by State Farm Insurance to open a chain of thrifts in Illinois, Missouri, and Arizona blurred the line between banking and insurance. With Congress unable to act, due principally to well-entrenched subsystems locked in a stalemate, policy was being made by regulators and the courts (Hosansky 1997b: 2292). In a scene reminiscent of the 1980s and DIDMCA/Garn–St. Germain, the OCC was deregulating via regulation, as were securities and insurance regulators. Banks who might otherwise push more forcefully for legislation were ambivalent, given the willingness of the OCC to meet their deregulatory needs in the short term. So, for example, in 1986 the OCC reinterpreted the National Bank Act provisions that permitted banks located in towns of 5,000 or fewer to sell insurance, as applying to more than just the local communities as the market for such sales. Similarly, a 1996 Supreme Court ruling prohibited states from excluding national banks from selling insurance if state banks were allowed to do so (Hosansky 1997b: 2295). In an earlier 1995 ruling the Court had backed the OCC interpretation of annuities as a "banking product," further expanding the field of economic activity open to banks.

And the OCC was not alone in reinterpreting existing regulation in this fashion. In 1987, interpreting Glass-Steagall provisions that forbade banks from affiliation with an organization "engaged principally" in activities that were prohibited to banks, such as securities underwriting, the Fed allowed bank holding companies to engage in some securities activities. Initially setting the limit at no more than 5 percent of their gross revenue, the Fed raised it to 10 percent in 1989, and 25 percent in 1996. It also allowed bank officers to serve on the board of a securities subsidiary, as long as they did not constitute a majority of the board (Hosansky 1997b: 2295).

The problem, according to former Fed chair Paul Volcker, was that "every new ruling has a way of exposing fresh inequities and creating new uncertainties. In the absence of clear and up-to-date congressional mandates, there is seemingly endless squabbling in the courts" (Hosansky 1997b: 2293). Congress, or more accurately the House Banking Committee and the Senate Banking Committee, along with the House Commerce Committee, finally reached such an accord in 1999. The Financial Services Act of 1999 (HR 10) was again a product of the House Banking chair, Jim Leach. Joined by twelve cosponsors, the bill was reported out of the House Banking Committee on a 51–8 vote, suggesting Leach had been able to overcome most of the objections that had scuttled his previous efforts. The legislation then went to the House Commerce Committee, indicative of the competing coalitions involved in rewriting financial services regulation. After some tinkering, the Commerce Committee sent the bill to the floor on a voice vote, an indication that there was near unanimous support for the legislation on committee. When the bill reached the Senate, the Banking Committee substituted a measure of its own (S 900) that easily passed in the Senate. A conference committee was assembled to iron out the differences, and the bill became law in November (PL 106-102). The bill repealed those portions of Glass-Steagall and the 1956 Bank Holding Company Act that prohibited affiliation between banking and securities and banking and insurance, respectively. Regulators had already altered many of the provisions, but the passage of the act backed what was increasingly common practice with the force of law.

The 1999 act was in essence the same bill that Leach had attempted to shepherd through the House in 1997 and 1998, failing both times because he could not get the industry and consumers behind the effort. Phil Gramm, the Senate Banking Committee chair, derailed the 1998 bill when he failed to remove provisions that required banks to invest in poor and minority communities as part of the Community Reinvestment Act of 1977. The 1999 act relaxed reinvestment reviews for banks with under $250 million in assets, unless they were involved in a merger, attempted to establish a new branch, or sought to relocate their home office. It also added a provision requiring that any banks that sought to expand the operations of the act into insurance or securities had to demonstrate that they had been involved in community reinvestment. The compromise was an effort to bridge the gap between financial industry opponents and their allies (led by Gramm) and supporters and their allies (Leach and most Democrats). Having spent millions on congressional campaigns—some $6.6 million in 1999, with $1.2 million going to members of the House Banking Committee and $480,000 to their Senate counterparts—the banks were clearly a force to be dealt with. After a closed-door meeting of GOP committee leaders only, in which Leach (House Banking chair), Gramm (Senate Banking chair), and Bliley (Senate Commerce chair) hammered out their differences, the bulk of banks lined up behind the bill (Parks 1999a: 2375).

A second obstacle to previous efforts involved privacy issues. The 1999 act required banks to develop a written policy regarding the sharing of consumer information and to make it available to consumers. Consumers were given the option to opt out of information sharing with unaffiliated third parties, although a Democrat-backed proposal that would have allowed consumers to opt out of any information-sharing arrangement was defeated. The bill also required ATMs to give notice of any transaction fees, and allowed consumers to cancel a transaction before any fee was imposed.

In addition to redlining and privacy, the major obstacle to previous efforts at deregulation involved the objectives of the various financial intermediaries—notably securities, insurance, and banking firms. The act allowed federal bank subsidiaries to sell title insurance, and overrode state prohibitions against such sales if state banks were allowed to engage in such sales. Insurance underwriting and real estate development could only be offered as part of a holding-company operation subject to Fed oversight. The use of subsidiaries was limited to those cases in which the total assets of a bank's subsidiaries did not exceed $50 billion or 45 percent of the bank's assets, whichever was less. In a concession to the insurance industry and state regulators, insurance and real estate were subject to state and federal regulation, even when such operations were part of a bank subsidiary, thus preserving the state role in regulating insurance.

In a compromise between the Treasury and the Fed, banking conglomerates were allowed to operate most financial services, except for insurance underwriting and real estate development, as subsidiaries subject to Treasury oversight and regulation. Banks wanting to engage in securities underwriting could only do so if the parent bank met debt-rating requirements established by federal regulators (Parks and Conlon 1999: 2797). In addition to banking, insurance, and securities activities, banks were allowed to engage in activities considered "financial in nature, incidental to activities that are financial in nature, or complementary to such activities" (Parks and Conlon 1999: 2797). The act specifically mentioned investment advisory activities, merchant banking, and insurance-company portfolio investments as being financial in nature, and left the door open to a wide variety of additional activities, subject to Treasury approval. All securities operations were subject to SEC oversight, thus preserving SEC turf.

Finally, the bill created a new type of bank, designated "wholesale financial institutions," or "woofies." Woofies could accept only large deposits, $100,000 at a minimum, and were to be geared toward the needs of institutional and large individual investors. They would not be subject to the same level of regulation as commercial banks, and would operate without deposit insurance (Parks 1999b: 2500–2501).

Most of the financial industry was united behind the act. The lone exception was the thrifty industry, which took two major hits. The first, originating in the Senate version of the act, prohibited thrift mergers with commercial enterprises. Wal-Mart, which had been working on acquiring an Oklahoma-based thrift so that it could enter the realm of banking, was now prohibited from doing so (Nitschke and Parks 1999: 2506). In prohibiting such associations, the act seemed to end the efforts to eliminate the distinction between banking and business enshrined in the Civil War bank acts. Nevertheless, Wal-Mart continued its attempts to enter banking with a 2005 application to acquire an industrial bank charter in the state of Utah, which has yet to be approved by the FDIC. The second prohibition was the death knell for thrifts. The act prohibited the creation of thrifts after March 4, 1999. In ending the national chartering of thrifts, the act recognized thrifts as causing more problems than they were worth. No doubt the expense of the thrift bailout in the 1980s, the continuing run of thrift failures, and the political fallout associated with the industry were enough to convince most members of Congress that thrifts were simply not worth the trouble. In ending their national chartering, and prohibiting their merger with commercial enterprises, Congress signaled its reluctance to abandon the regulation of financial intermediaries as a distinct class of economic actors. That said, it was willing to allow the various types of financial intermediaries to cross over previously established boundaries within the financial services sector.

What did not change as a result of the 1999 act was the fragmentation of regulatory authority that necessitated cooperation among various regulators. The Fed and the OCC still shared oversight authority with respect to banks. Similarly, the act partitioned regulation of subsidiaries to their "functional" regulator. So, for example, securities subsidiaries are still subject to SEC oversight, and state regulators still oversee insurance subsidiaries. The new wrinkle is that national bank regulators are authorized to police relationships between banks and subsidiaries to safeguard the system and ensure financial stability. Even so, the Fed is expressly prohibited from examining functionally regulated nonbanks unless it suspects their actions pose a material threat to an insured bank. Nor can the Fed impose capital requirements or other such regulations on such entities (Parks and Conlon 1999: 2797). Thus, while dismantling a large portion of Glass-Steagall prohibitions on particular types of activities by specific intermediaries, the act still preserved the mix of regulatory authorities created by the New Deal.

Following the passage of the 1999 Financial Services Act, policymaking settled back into a subsystem-induced equilibrium, with only minor perturbations related to privacy issues and the newly emerging field of Internet commerce. The privacy issue, which had not been settled to the complete satisfaction of consumer advocates in the act, resurfaced when several states acted on provisions allowing them to establish tighter privacy requirements for financial intermediaries doing business in their states. Twenty states, led by California, Massachusetts, and Iowa, had enacted or were in the process of enacting provisions that required banks to secure written permission from customers before they could share personal information with other businesses (Ota 2000: 638). The banking industry was busily working the banking committees in both chambers in an effort to get them to revisit the 1999 act and remove the option. When several legislators, along with the Clinton administration, responded with proposals for even stricter national standards, the banks backed off.

Privacy resurfaced as an issue in 2003 when one of those legislators, Richard C. Shelby (R-AL), took over the chairmanship on the Senate Banking Committee. As a cofounder of the Congressional Privacy Caucus, Senator Shelby was particularly critical of the provisions of the 1999 act that allowed financial intermediaries to share customers' financial information with other companies, suggesting that such sharing led to unwanted commercial solicitations and identity theft (Hughes 2003a: 207). Shelby backed a bundle of proposals, including provisions that would simplify the policy notices sent out by banks, require banks to seek customers' approval before sharing financial information, and restrict the companies with which banks could share personal information (Hughes 2003a: 207). Banks fought the proposals, forcing Shelby to give in and back the renewal of the 1970 Fair Credit Reporting Act with only minor changes. On the plus side, consumers were allowed a free copy of their credit report, and provisions intended to protect against identity theft were included in the renewal. But in the end, banks were the major victors, securing a prohibition against state enactment of more restrictive privacy regulations (Hughes 2003b: 2359).

Privacy issues had become salient, at least in part, due to the technological changes that were affecting the financial services industry and business in general. The development of e-commerce threatened to spark turf wars among committees claiming it as their responsibility. In an effort to head off open warfare, the GOP-controlled House rewrote the policy responsibilities of the Commerce Committee and replaced the Banking Committee with a newly created Financial Services Committee. The latter now included jurisdiction that was more in keeping with the industry created by the 1999 act, somewhat broadening its turf in an effort to head off a power struggle between W. J. "Billy" Tauzin (R-LA), the new Commerce chair, and Michael G. Oxley (R-OH), who had sought the post but settled for chair of Financial Services. Tauzin was intent on returning Commerce to the stature it enjoyed under John Dingell (D-MI), who once claimed the world as Commerce turf (King 1997). His efforts to do so would place the Commerce

Committee in competition with the Financial Services Committee and the Judiciary Committee, thereby institutionalizing low-level conflicts over the regulation of e-commerce (Bettelheim 2002a).

In 2004 the House Banking Committee engaged in a further effort to eliminate what was left of New Deal regulations. The Financial Service Regulatory Relief Act sought to relax restrictions on banks opening branches across state lines, permit savings associations to offer more business loans, and allow credit unions to expand their membership. It also sought to contain the expansion of a new type of financial intermediary, known as the "industrial loan company." Industrial loan companies are owned by commercial enterprises that are typically banned from banking, but are allowed to engage in credit card services and auto loans as a result of a 1987 loophole in financial industry regulation. Overseen by the FDIC, these companies are exempted from normal banking regulation and are major employers in Utah and California, where the bulk of them are headquartered. The chair of the House Financial Services Committee, Jim Leach, wanted to bring them under the banking regulatory umbrella. The provision of the Financial Service Regulatory Relief Act that applied to banks would also allow industrial loan companies to expand their services across state lines without having to receive a new charter. Leach attempted to make chartering mandatory, arguing that without such regulatory requirements, industrial loan companies would be an ideal entry point for major retailers looking for a back door into the financial services industry. Despite his efforts, the legislation passed the House without the prohibitions he sought. The legislation eventually died in the Senate, because the chair of the Banking Committee, Robert F. Bennett (R-UT), saw it as too restrictive despite the lack of outright prohibitions with regard to the operations of industrial loan companies (Hughes 2004: 702).

Conclusion

The failure to pass the Financial Service Regulatory Relief Act in 2004 appears to signal a return to the recent past, in which regulators and their industry charges will test the policy waters through policy innovations that stretch, but stop short of breaking, the current law. The fragmented nature of the financial services subsystem, and the multiple venues in which policy is made and discussed, provide ample opportunity to derail radical legislative change, as was the case with previous efforts to dismantle Glass-Steagall prohibitions. Competing coalitions, both within the financial subsystem and across subsystems, produce stalemate by threatening to raise the salience of financial regulation. Although similar occurrences in the past provided an opportunity for the temporary intervention of the White House in the role of principal, this has not occurred with the presidency of George W. Bush.

The long-standing rift between the House Banking Committee and the Senate Banking Committee concerning deregulation still works against complete abandonment of the belief that banking is distinct from other forms of commerce. While the Senate seems more sympathetic to complete deregulation, and is often joined by the administration in advocating change, the House Banking Committee and the House Commerce Committee continue to resist such wholesale change.

The rift between the House and the Senate is a reflection of the conflict among the various industry factions that constitute the financial services industry. Removing the barriers to competition that are an important basis of the New Deal system, and that are seen as vital to their survival by many of the industries created by the New Deal divisions, is no small task. While many of these restrictions were loosened in the 1990s, they were altered in such a way as to ensure that the primary regulator from each subsystem— banking, securities, and insurance—still policed players engaged in business affecting their turf. Regulation is still preoccupied with the safety and soundness of depositor funds, but has been modified to allow industry players to do more with those funds to combat disintermediation. The deregulatory efforts of the 1990s will no doubt continue the trend toward consolidation and the creation of financial services conglomerates. Still, as long as those who see themselves as potential losers in such a scenario have congressional allies, such action will proceed in a piecemeal fashion. What this means is that policy change will continue to unfold as a product of deals orchestrated and managed by regulators, who all too often are themselves reacting to innovations by large institutions intent on bending the envelope of financial regulation.

Notes

1. Historically, the regulation of financial intermediaries involves several distinct classes of institutions: commercial banks, thrifts, credit unions, state chartered, nationally chartered, and so forth. We shall refer to the process using the generic term *bank regulation*.

2. The concept of *reserve requirements* came from the private sector. It was developed by large banks, primarily operating in New York City, that acted as clearinghouses for the currency issued by the variety of small banks in operation throughout the country. In order to guarantee the value of a bank's notes, the bank was required to maintain with the clearinghouse a fraction of the total value, in gold or silver, of the notes in circulation.

3. For a more detailed treatment of the origins of the Federal Reserve, see Livingston 1986; Mints 1945; West 1974; and White 1983.

4. This section draws on the excellent accounts in Kennedy 1973 and Burns 1974.

5. We do not include a discussion of the Federal Reserve's Open Market

Committee in our synopsis, because it is not really involved in the regulation of financial intermediaries per se. The committee comprises the seven members of the Board of Governors, the president of the New York reserve bank, and four of the remaining eleven reserve bank presidents who rotate onto the committee on a yearly basis. The committee makes decisions regarding open market operations—the purchase or sale of government securities—as well as reserve requirements, which in turn affect the cost and availability of money and credit.

6

Regulating Telecommunications

ORIGINALLY A PART OF the Interstate Commerce Commission's regulatory responsibilities, communications regulation became the responsibility of the Federal Communications Commission as part of the Communications Act of 1934. The FCC was created following the recommendations of an interdepartmental commission set up to study the problem of regulating the newly emerging field of electronic communications. The act charged the FCC with doling out the electromagnetic spectrum and regulating both foreign and interstate communications services "so as to make available, so far as possible, to all the people of the United States a rapid, efficient, Nation-wide, and world-wide . . . communications service with adequate facilities at reasonable charges" (Hilliard 1991: 1). These responsibilities involve a wide variety of telecommunications technologies—most notably radio, television, and telephony. Because telecommunications regulation itself was focused on telephony for the first century or so of telecommunications policy, the chapter adopts a similar focus. We open with a discussion of telephony and the central place it played in the evolution of telecommunications policy, introducing television regulation as it becomes salient in the latter part of the twentieth century.

A Brief History of Telephony

One cannot understand telecommunications regulation without studying the role of AT&T in the development and evolution of telecommunications technology. Formed in 1877, a year after the invention of the telephone, the Bell Company embarked on the process of vertical integration from its inception. Following the acquisition of Western Electric in 1882, at the time the largest producer of electrical equipment in the United States, the Bell Company perfected the use of switched networks. Switched networks consist of connections organized into local switchboard exchanges. Coupled with improved transmission, Bell created a thriving market for telecommunications. In 1885, AT&T, specializing in long-distance telephone service, was spun off from the Bell Company. AT&T embarked on an aggressive campaign of acquiring competitors and, failing that, refusing connection to local networks, prohibiting the use of Bell equipment by non-Bell companies, and a host of other policies designed to perfect the Bell monopoly on telecommunications.

The first attempt at telecommunications regulation, in 1887, involved a congressional effort to promote wider service by telegraph operators, an early precursor of the *universal service* theme that runs throughout the history of telecommunications regulation. Universal service, quite simply, involves extending affordable communications services to all citizens. The maintenance of communications among citizens throughout the country has been a central preoccupation of the national government. The creation of the US Postal Service at the inception of the Republic and the system of postal roads, canals, and transportation infrastructure that grew out of it were all attempts to maintain communications among the various parts of the nation. The efforts by Congress to create a national telegraph network constituted simply one more step in this direction.

The next push for regulation, in 1910, was a response to charges that AT&T was engaged in monopolistic practices when it denied independent phone companies access to its long-distance lines (Crandall and Waverman 1995: 40). The solution, enshrined in the Mann-Elkins Act, was to define telephone and telegraph companies as *common carriers* and place them under the supervision of the Interstate Commerce Commission. In addition to making sure that AT&T granted access to local companies, the ICC was entrusted with making sure that the phone rates charged to customers were "just and reasonable" (Vietor 1994: 171). Congress, then, was careful to define universal service as affordable service. Shortly after the passage of Mann-Elkins, the Department of Justice, reacting to widespread complaints, opened an investigation of AT&T's business practices. The Department of Justice reached an agreement with AT&T in 1913, requiring AT&T to sell Western Union, ease up its aggressive acquisition strategy, and agree to connect all qualified phone lines to the Bell System (which provided for competition in long-distance service, at least in theory).

The first efforts at telecommunications regulation illustrate the one constant throughout the development and evolution of telecommunications policy: the intervention of Congress usually centers on defining, or redefining, what constitutes universal service. While these interventions are important, much of the evolution of telecommunications is, in effect, a seminar on how the Bell Company came to monopolize telephone service. Born in the heyday of corporate capital, the Bell System pursued a strategy of vertical integration not unlike that practiced by Standard Oil. Several factors aided the Bell Company in its monopoly-building endeavor. Primary among the contributing factors was the belief among state-level and federal regulators that phone service was a natural monopoly. This belief was greatly strengthened by the advent of World War I and the concurrent federal effort to consolidate phone service so as to aid the war effort. Following the end of the war, the monopoly enjoyed by the Bell System was furthered by congressional passage of the Willis-Graham Act (1921), which permitted mergers between competing phone companies. By 1930, AT&T's market share of local service was 79 percent, Western Electric sold 92 percent of all telephone equipment, and AT&T was the exclusive provider of long-distance service. If that were not enough, a congressional study of telecommunications, the "Splawn Study" (1931), concluded that the "telephone business is a monopoly—it is supposed to be regulated" (Vietor 1994: 176). The result of the belief that phone service was a natural monopoly and the Bell System's aggressive efforts to make it so was that, by midcentury, the Bell System had developed into *the* telephone company.

If Congress and state regulators were not the actual architects of the Bell monopoly, they were willing accomplices through the first half of the twentieth century. It came as a shock to some, then, when the government filed an antitrust suit against the Bell System in 1949. *United States v. Western Electric Company* charged that AT&T's exclusive purchase agreement with Western Electric was a monopoly that practiced price discrimination, delayed the introduction of new technology, and artificially raised the costs of phone service. Settled in 1956, AT&T agreed to license its technology and restrict its business to common carrier communications services in return for preservation of its vertical integration. The agreement, therefore, laid the groundwork for competition in the provision of equipment. Although it did not alter Bell System control of local and long-distance service, the settlement did open the door to competition in the telecommunications field by successfully challenging the monopoly on equipment.

AT&T's monopoly in phone service was made possible, in no small part, by the FCC's rulings on matters of entry, equipment, and rate-setting. Between 1948 and 1982, the FCC tended to rule in favor of the Bell System more often than not. The *Hush-a-Phone* case (1948–1956), the *First Computer Inquiry* case (1966–1971), and the *Execunet I* and *II* cases (1974 and 1978) all found the FCC ruling in favor of barriers to entry that served to preserve AT&T's monopoly in phone service and equipment.[1] Still, the FCC was not simply captured by Bell. It did allow increased competition in microwave systems in the *Above 890* case (1959), opened the door for competition in the provision of phone equipment in the *Carterfone* case (1965–1968), and promoted competition in both microwave and local services in the *Specialized Common Carrier Services* case (1971).[2]

By the 1970s, the FCC's rulings were subject to increased scrutiny by the courts and Congress—not that the FCC ever operated without some guidance from other interested actors. As early as 1956, the US Court of Appeals overturned the *Hush-a-Phone* ruling by the FCC. But the penultimate move to influence telecommunications regulation occurred when the attorney general filed an antitrust suit, *United States v. AT&T,* in 1974. The suit accused AT&T of violating the Sherman Antitrust Act through the creation of a telecommunications monopoly in local, long-distance, and manufacturing services. The suit was settled in 1982, and the Bell System agreed to the divestiture of its twenty-two local phone companies, transforming them into seven regional companies—the "Baby Bells"—restricted to offering local service. AT&T was limited to long-distance and equipment manufacture. The consent decree, policed by Judge Harold H. Greene, put an end to the "natural monopoly" that had dominated for nearly 100 years.

Television and Radio

Radio and television regulation find their roots in the Radio Act of 1927 and the Communications Act of 1934. The acts were intent on organizing the fledgling radio broadcast industry, and as such were preoccupied with doling out portions of the radio spectrum in a way that fit with a public service mission like that underlying telephony. While this initially involved licensing all comers in the fledgling industry, by 1922 it was clear that applications would soon overwhelm the Department of Commerce, the original regulatory authority, as well as the airwaves. Secretary of Commerce Herbert Hoover organized a series of yearly radio conferences in the 1920s that brought together broadcasters and regulators to help manage the development and expansion of broadcasting. Hoover's associational impulse gave rise to the Radio Act of 1927 and the creation of the Federal Radio Commission (FRC), charged with managing and coordinating the new policy field (Shipan 1998: 480). A clear predecessor of the FCC, the FRC was a five-member independent commission charged with licensing radio broadcasters. By 1931 broadcasting was a major industry whose interests were represented by a peak organization, the National Association of Broadcasters (NAB), that worked hand in hand with the FRC in the call for federal regulation of broadcasting. The goal of the NAB was to control entry into the field and protect the market share of existing firms (Shipan 1998: 481). In an argument similar to that being made in telephony, broadcasters suggested that limited airwaves made broadcasting a natural monopoly in need of government management (on

NAB terms). Their demands were enshrined in the Communications Act of 1934, which empowered the newly created FCC with licensing authority; made renewal of existing licenses pro forma, as long as broadcasters met loosely defined public service requirements; and left the evolution of broadcasting, for the most part, up to the industry to decide.

Telecommunications Policy

Telecommunications regulation, then, evolved in response to changes in technology, customer demand, the economics of information processing, and politics. Several points are worth noting when it comes to regulating telecommunications. First, as the brief historical introduction made clear, in telephony a single player, the Bell Company and its offshoots, has dominated the field since the development of the first phone in 1876. Much of this dominance can be explained by the fact that telephone service was deemed a natural monopoly early on. This meant it was subject to regulation that sought to eliminate "wasteful" competition, set reasonable prices, and guarantee universal service. In radio, and later television, broadcasters influenced policy through a peak association, the NAB. Regulation of telecommunications, therefore, often took the form of managing the enterprise rather than policing the market. Telephone service has always been considered an essential public good; that is, providers, customers, politicians, and regulators all believe in universal service as a primary policy goal. Thus, telecommunications is regulated as if it were a public utility because it is considered a public necessity.

Second, telephone regulation is a joint enterprise involving both national and state-level regulators. This serves to complicate the regulatory task, because state-level public utility commissions and the FCC do not always move in sync. For example, state-level public utility commissions were the first to adopt value-of-service pricing. Value-of-service pricing allows phone companies to charge business users more than residential customers. The professed logic is that the benefit of service is greater for business customers than for residential users (Vietor 1994: 173–174). A similar logic applies to large exchanges, urban markets in which there are more users versus small ones. Since the former involves more potential service connections than the latter, even though costs are higher in the latter, companies are allowed to charge higher prices in urban markets. In reality, value-of-service pricing stresses universal service and allows cross-subsidization of costs to achieve it. State regulators allow cross-subsidization to ensure the availability of local phone service at an affordable price. The irony is that state regulators encourage the type of activity that federal regulators prosecute in other markets.

Further complicating the regulatory task is its multifaceted nature. Regulating telephone service involves policing rate-setting in both local and long-distance markets, as well as overseeing the development and control of telecommunications equipment. The difficulty of accomplishing the preceding is compounded by the fact that the telecommunications market is dominated by a single player. This means regulators are forced to guess, or accept the word of the Bell System, on matters involving costs, rates of return for service, and the meaning of technological breakthroughs in telecommunications. Regulating broadcasting was simpler, licensing spectrum appeared straightforward, renewals were almost automatic, and for the next half century broadcasting was subject to benign neglect.

Telecommunications policy involves fairly complex and ever-evolving technology. While the technology is in a constant state of flux, a series of technological changes beginning in the 1950s dramatically altered the nature of telecommunications. The use of coaxial cable, multiplexing (multiple simultaneous circuits on a single wire), electromechanical switches (which replace human operators), and microwave transmission, as well as the development of computers and high-speed data transmission, complicated and expanded the role of telecommunications in the market and polity. When telecommunications went from simply moving information to actually shaping the content and format of information, a whole host of new policy questions became relevant.

Quite simply, new technology often acts as a spark for change in existing regulation, usually involves the entry of new players, and almost invariably raises interest in the policy realm on the part of those involved in similar endeavors or among those who see new applications for new technologies. All this further complicates the job of regulators. Moreover, there is reason to believe that these changes also impact on issue salience. As Figure 6.1 reveals, telecommunications became highly salient in the early 1980s and again in the mid-1990s—two periods of intense debate over deregulation and the introduction of market mechanisms in what had long functioned like a stable public utility.

The Federal Communications Commission

Created by the Communications Act of 1934, the FCC is the archetypal independent commission. It is directed by five commissioners appointed by the president for five-year terms and confirmed by the Senate. Headed by a chairman selected by the president, the commission is bipartisan; only three commissioners may be members of the same political party. Reflecting the growing importance of telecommunications and the ongoing communication revolution, the FCC has been blessed with constant budgetary growth:

Figure 6.1 The Salience of Telecommunications

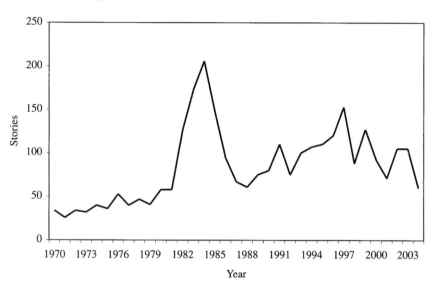

since 1970, its budget has grown from some $25 million to $223 million, a rate of growth that has greatly outpaced inflation. The budgetary history of the FCC is presented in Figure 6.2.

The chairman delegates administrative and management responsibilities to the Managing Director. The FCC staff is organized along functional lines, with six bureaus and ten staff offices (see Figure 6.3). The Media Bureau licenses operators of radio and television broadcast services, as well as offering advice to the commission on a wide variety of matters affecting the broadcasting industry. The Consumer and Governmental Affairs Bureau serves as both a point of contact between the FCC and consumers, as well as between the telecommunications industry and other government agencies. The Enforcement Bureau has oversight responsibilities for the Communications Act, as well as enforcing FCC rules, orders, and authorizations. The Wireless Telecommunications Bureau conducts the FCC's spectrum actions and manages domestic wireless communications (cellular phones, personal communications services phones, pagers, and two-way radios). The International Bureau represents the FCC in international affairs, advising the commission with regard to international telecommunications rate structures, satellite technology, treaty obligations, bilateral discussions, and relations with international organizations. Finally, the Wireline Competition Bureau continues the responsibilities of the old Common Carrier Bureau, regulating wire-based telephone service and working with state-level public utility commissions in an effort to ensure

Figure 6.2 The Federal Communications Commission Budget

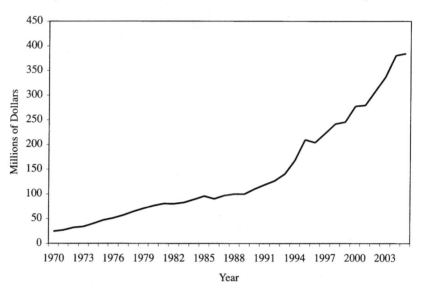

Year

that phone service is provided in an efficient manner at reasonable rates. These six bureaus, then, are the policy arms of the FCC.

The ten staff offices offer a variety of technical support and information services to both the FCC and its customers. The Office of Administrative Law Judges presides over hearings and issues initial decisions regarding interpretation of agency actions and rule-making responsibilities. The Office of Communications Business Opportunities serves as a liaison with small business and minorities interested in entering the telecommunications realm. The Office of Engineering and Technology serves as a technical adviser on engineering matters, keeps the commissioners and bureaus abreast of any breakthrough in telecommunications technology, and allocates spectrum for nongovernmental use. The Office of General Counsel offers advice on legal issues involved in implementing policy mandates, helps draft FCC decisions, represents the agency in court, and handles any legal questions dealing with internal operations. The Office of Inspector General conducts and supervises audits and investigations of the FCC and its programs. The Office of Legislative Affairs serves as a liaison with Congress. The Office of the Managing Director works under the FCC chairman and serves as the manager of the various bureaus and offices. The Office of Strategic Planning and Policy Analysis serves as an economic and technical adviser to the commission, developing long-range forecasts to aid the commission in setting broad policy goals. The Office of Media

Figure 6.3 The Federal Communications Commission

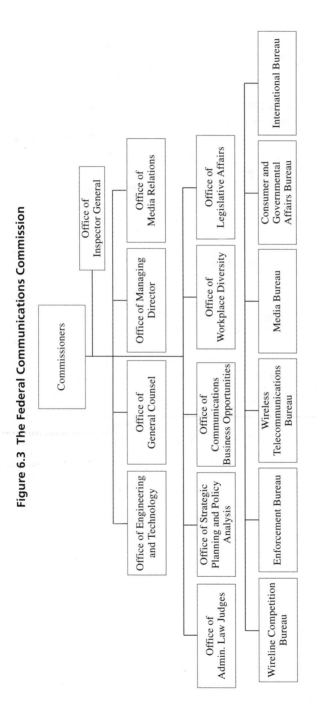

Relations is the principal point of contact between the FCC and the media. Finally, the Office of Work Place Diversity advises the FCC on work force diversity, equal employment opportunity, and affirmative recruitment.

In addition to the six bureaus and ten offices that constitute the FCC, there are currently seven advisory committees that deal with telecommunications matters. These committees are congressional creations intended to serve as additional sources of advice to agencies when they engage in rule making. Historically, advisory committees served as an additional access point for industry players, and as such made sure the telecommunications industry interest was not forgotten by the FCC. Following the passage of the Federal Advisory Committee Act (FACA) in 1972, there was an effort to make the committees more balanced and to bring in viewpoints that might otherwise be excluded during rule making (Rosenbloom 2000: 42–44). The current mix of advisory committees reflects this effort to include diverse viewpoints, although the membership of most committees is a testimony to the staying power of the telecommunications industry.

Some advisory committees deal with the mundane. The North American Numbering Council exists to advise the FCC on numbering issues and the administration of phone numbers. Similarly, the Network Reliability and Interoperability Council offers advice regarding technology, connecting networks, and the "best practices" available in the ever-changing telecommunications industry. Both are filled predominantly with industry interests, guaranteeing industry input on any proposed changes in telecommunications regulation. Other committees are temporary sounding boards: the Advisory Committee for WRC-07 was created to solicit public comment regarding the 2007 meeting of the World Radiocommunication Conference, which will deal with regulating and distributing access to the radio-frequency spectrum.

Some advisory committees tread on more unsettled turf, the Technological Advisory Council (TAC) is charged with keeping the FCC abreast of technological changes that are making traditional distinctions between telephony, cable television, and data services increasingly blurred. As such, the TAC provides technical advice to the FCC, but advice that has political and policy ramifications that often pits one industry faction against another. The council is heavily loaded with industry representatives, with all but three of the thirty-three members having clear industry ties.

Two committees are a direct result of the passage of FACA. The Advisory Committee on Diversity for Communications in the Digital Age focuses on increasing the participation of minorities and women in the telecommunications industry, both as employees and as owners of media outlets. And the Consumer Advisory Committee serves as a watchdog on consumer issues and facilitates the participation of consumers in FCC proceedings.

Finally, the Media Security and Reliability Council is a clear response to more recent events. It is charged with planning a strategy for maintaining and sustaining telecommunications facilities in the event of terrorist attacks, natural disasters, and other nationwide threats or attacks.

Doing the Telecommunications Shuffle: Policymaking by the FCC

An individual of the president's choosing chairs the FCC.[3] The chair presides over all meetings, coordinates the work of the commission, and serves as the FCC representative in dealing with Congress and other government actors. In the absence of the chair, the commissioners can designate one of themselves as acting chair. The FCC chair relies on its managing director to handle day-to-day management and administrative responsibilities of the FCC, while delegating other functions to the various bureaus, offices, or committees composed of the commissioners. The commission meets regularly (usually weekly), in open and closed sessions, to consider questions prepared by the staff. Commissioners often add items of their own choosing to the weekly agenda. Meetings may also be conducted using "circulation." This involves the circulation of an item among the commissioners for their approval or rejection without holding an actual meeting of the commissioners (Hilliard 1991: 11).

The commissioners are dependent on their own staffs for keeping abreast of matters before the FCC. Each commissioner is provided a budget for personal staff. Most commissioners hire a legal assistant versed in telecommunications law and an engineering assistant who specializes in telecommunications technology, in addition to the usual secretarial staff (Hilliard 1991: 13). The commissioners' assistants serve as the eyes and ears of the commissioners, writing briefs on upcoming agenda items and suggesting items for consideration by the commission.

Suggestions for new regulations, or changes in existing rules and regulations, come from a variety of sources. Anyone may petition the commission with such suggestions. Petitions, stating the reasons for the change and the specific language to be used in the rule, are sent to the FCC secretary, who forwards them to the appropriate office or bureau for consideration (Hilliard 1991: 71). In addition to the petition route, suggestions for policy change may originate in any of the advisory committees created by Congress. Probably the most authoritative call for change takes the form of congressional requests. Such requests may be enshrined in legislation, but they often take the form of suggestions made in hearings or through other communications with the commission. Presidents also suggest changes in existing rules, using speeches, direct communications, or White House personnel to make suggestions to the commission. Finally, suggestions for change may come from within the FCC itself, from the various bureaus or subject matter offices or via commissioners and their staffs.

The review of petitions, discussion of suggestions for change, and consideration of new regulations occur during weekly commission meetings. These are similar to judicial proceedings. The commission, sitting en banc, listens to briefs by bureau chiefs and other professional staff, questions the speakers on items of interest, discusses the issue, and then votes to reject, accept, or remand an item for further work. Before petitions for rule making reach the commission, they must make their way through the various bureaus or offices under the jurisdiction of which the proposed rule falls. The office studies the proposal, formulates a recommendation, and, if it decides the proposal has merit, requests that a rule-making number be assigned to it. Before making this recommendation, the office normally clears the decision further up the chain of command, being sure to include one or more of the commissioners in the decision. In this fashion, the commissioners are rarely surprised by any item on the docket.

All proposed rules are listed in a weekly public notice, with a thirty-day "comments" period that allows interested parties to offer their assessment of the proposed rule. After the first comments period, the FCC observes a "reply comments" period, providing a chance for a dialogue of sorts among the various parties who participated during the first period. After processing the comments, the proposal is further refined by the appropriate bureaus and offices, with recommendations attached. The recommendations normally suggest one of four courses of action: a memorandum opinion and order, to deny the petition or discontinue action on the petition; a notice of inquiry, which describes the problem and asks for further public comment regarding possible solutions; a notice of proposed rule making, which describes in detail a proposed course of action; or a report and order adopting change, involving editorial, not substantive, change in an existing rule.

If the FCC issues a notice of inquiry or notice of proposed rule making, it must assign a docket number to the item to allow interested parties to track its progress and provide comments on the proposed changes. A notice of inquiry must be followed by a notice of proposed rule making or a memorandum opinion and order concluding the inquiry. If the commission is not satisfied with the input during the comments stage, it may issue additional notices of inquiry or notices of proposed rule making in an effort to elicit more interest or participation in an issue area. If a new rule is reported vis-à-vis a notice of proposed rule making or denied with a memorandum opinion and order, the commission concludes by issuing a report and order clearly stating the new rule or its rationale for ending the inquiry (Hilliard 1991: 72–73). While theoretically the end of the line, the report and order is itself subject to a thirty-day period in which an interested party may file a petition for reconsideration, which, if successful, may begin the process anew.

From this brief description of FCC policymaking, it is clear that when it comes to regulation, the commission does not function in a way similar to the other agencies discussed throughout this book. The FCC does not engage in regular inspection of the regulated, as do OSHA, the OCC, the FDIC, or the EPA. It does not initiate major lawsuits in an attempt to curb violations of law, as does the Antitrust Division of the Justice Department. Nor is it on constant lookout for violation of consumer protection provisions, as is the Consumer Product Safety Commission. While there is a nominal regulatory role in telephony when overseeing rate changes, depreciation of equipment, and the auditing of accounts, this role does not compare to the inspection and auditing activities of the FDIC, the OCC, and the Federal Reserve. And while the FCC does have an investigative office, the Enforcement Division of the Common Carrier Bureau, it is quite limited. Indeed, one commissioner complained that three field inspectors were hardly enough to handle vigorous enforcement, especially in light of the agency rule that requires the inspectors to work in pairs (Hilliard 1991: 103). Rather, the FCC seeks to manage the telecommunications industry in a fashion that is compatible with the universal service goals enunciated in the 1934 Communications Act. The ability of the FCC to carry out this mission is shaped by a variety of forces.

The Policy Subsystem

Sam Rayburn (D-TX) once gave clear advice to FCC chair Newton Minow: "Just remember one thing, son. You belong to us. Remember that, and you'll be all right" (Starobin 1988: 484). While most FCC chairs have traditionally kept this advice in mind, relations between the FCC and its congressional overseers, the House Commerce Committee and the Senate Commerce Committee, became increasingly rocky in the 1980s.[4] A number of factors—technological changes, politics, and the entry of competitors in telephone service—worked to transform the usually consensual telecommunications subsystem into a nightmare of competing coalitions allied with multiple would-be principals.

From Calm to Chaos:
Explaining Telecommunications Policy Change
Foremost among the factors that explain the change in telecommunications policymaking are the rapid changes in technology that date to the late 1960s and continue to this day. The development of computers and their role in data analysis and telecommunications, the invention of fiber-optic cable, and the increasing use of microwave and satellites in the transmission of

communications signals all revolutionized telecommunications. In telephony the revolution in technology presented the Bell System, which was at the forefront of many of the technological breakthroughs, with not only more effective means of transmitting telephone signals, but also a variety of potentially lucrative new business opportunities in endeavors only tangentially related to telephony. It also attracted a new host of people interested in becoming telecommunications service providers. In television the changes ushered in similar opportunities, as well as a major challenge in the form of cable television as a rival of traditional broadcasting.

Technological change did not come quietly. What had been a fairly consensual policy arena characterized by a dominant coalition began to show signs of stress. The increasingly conflictual style of policymaking was exacerbated by the success of the Reagan administration in establishing a principal-agent-like relationship with the FCC in the 1980s. Reagan administration FCC appointees were such ardent supporters of telephone deregulation, despite the objections of the Democrat-controlled commerce committees, that the Senate Commerce Committee chair, Ernest "Fritz" Hollings (D-SC), characterized the FCC as "a runaway animal" in 1988 (Starobin 1988: 479). Hollings's House counterpart, John Dingell (D-MI), declared that the FCC was "not trusted" to follow congressional mandates after FCC chair Dennis Patrick, a deregulation advocate, argued that Congress "invested in this commission a great deal of discretion to resolve public policy issues [as they saw fit]" (Starobin 1988: 480).

The problem was not so much one of unbridled bureaucratic discretion. Rather, it involved whose lead the FCC was following. In the Senate Commerce Committee's eyes, the commission seemed a bit too eager to do the president's bidding, even when it directly contradicted committee desires. Patrick answered the Democrats' charges that the commission was not following congressional mandates by noting: "There is a lot of loose talk about the will of Congress. What does that mean? . . . Am I supposed to take a poll of the majority of a particular committee? . . . If Congress passes a statute, I'll be the first to stand up and salute" (Starobin 1988: 480).

In insisting on legislation to guide his actions, FCC chair Patrick was abandoning the collegial norm of policymaking via subsystem, challenging the oversight committees to assume the role of principal. The debate between Patrick and the committees involved both the application of a revised version of the "Fairness Doctrine" passed by Congress but vetoed by President Reagan and "rate of return" pricing used in telephony. To be fair, both the president and the courts had come out against the former, leaving Patrick with the unenviable task of trying to please contradictory demands from multiple principals. Like many regulatory agencies at the time, the FCC found itself caught between the demands of an administration that was enthusiastically pursuing economic deregulation and a Congress with mixed feelings about the wisdom of systemwide deregulation. On the issue of telephone rates, Patrick wanted to introduce price caps indexed to inflation in an attempt to put an end to suspected cost-padding by the Baby Bells. When both commerce committees introduced legislation to scrap the FCC proposal, Patrick backed off and announced that the FCC would reconsider its price cap initiative.

Much of the tension between the FCC and the commerce committees, as well as Patrick's challenge to the committees to assert their authority, can be explained by yet another factor: the role of the court in telecommunications regulation following the breakup of AT&T. The consent decree that ended the government antitrust action against AT&T placed US District Court judge Harold H. Greene in an oversight role, institutionalizing outsider intervention in the formulation and implementation of telephone regulation. In separating long-distance service and manufacturing from local service, the consent decree introduced a fault line in the telephone subsystem. AT&T became preoccupied with local service, cable, and data processing, while the Baby Bells perseverated on all these, as well as on long-distance service and manufacturing. The consent decree gave Judge Greene the power to limit the expansion of both players into these potentially lucrative markets and in the newly developing markets of electronic publishing, data transmission, and the like. Greene made it increasingly difficult for the FCC, the commerce committees, the Baby Bells, and AT&T to reach mutually beneficial compromises. Greene demonstrated a tendency to interpret regulatory prohibitions conservatively, ruling against Bell and AT&T involvement in the rapidly changing data analysis, cable, and electronic publishing fields without some legislative backing for such expansion. He also sided with the up-and-coming rival phone companies—MCI, Sprint, and others—on questions of entry. Greene's active role in deciding policy questions worked to further the transformation of the telephone subsystem from a dominant coalition into competing coalitions.

Given the rapid technological changes, the Reagan revolution, and the involvement of Judge Greene in policymaking, it is little wonder that telephone policymaking became increasingly conflictual in the 1980s. Relations between the FCC and the commerce committees became so rocky after Reagan's inauguration that the FCC lost its permanent funding and was placed on a two-year authorization to allow more congressional scrutiny (Starobin 1988: 484). In effect, the commerce committees were forced to reassert themselves in the process, something they did in earnest during the 1980s and 1990s.

The 1996 Telecommunications Act

Arguably the most important congressional players in the telecommunications drama that culminated in the passage of the 1996 Telecommunications

Act were the chairs and subcommittee chairs of the various congressional committees claiming jurisdiction over telecommunications. This pitted the chair of the House Energy and Commerce Committee, the chair of the Senate Energy and Commerce Committee, and their subcommittee chairs against one another, as well as against the House Judiciary Committee chair, who claimed jurisdiction due to oversight entrusted to the courts as a result of Bell System antitrust settlement. The House Commerce Committee pursued both substantive changes in telecommunications policy, as well as regaining its control over the telecommunications policy arena. This meant that on one front it considered changes in existing policy, attempting to iron out differences among the various telecommunications providers. On another front it sought to ease Judge Greene out of the process of monitoring the breakup of the Bell system, while also cutting the FCC's ties to the president. While there may have been little early consensus on the former, the latter found the committee united in an effort to return the subsystem to a dominant coalition equilibrium. The Senate Commerce Committee also moved aggressively on the deregulation front, prompting the FCC to pursue deregulation via rule making.

While there was growing deregulatory sentiment among many members of the telecommunications subsystem, a central stumbling block involved the universal service provision of the 1934 Communications Act. The task before deregulatory advocates was to demonstrate how deregulation did not mean abandonment of the goal of low-cost communications services. Vice President Al Gore took the lead in this regard when he suggested it was the obligation of telecommunications firms to "connect all classrooms, libraries, hospitals and clinics to networks by 2000" (Mills 1994a: 68). In emphasizing and redefining the universal service obligation of those involved in telecommunications, Gore clearly established a link among the latest technological advances, deregulation, and any firm interested in offering services on the rapidly evolving information superhighway.

Building on work begun when he was a senator, Gore argued that the lessons learned from opening the university leg of the information superhighway—which linked high-performance supercomputers at universities through existing phone lines—should be applied elsewhere. In demonstrating the superiority of fiber-optic networks for moving information, the project verified that the means used by the cable industry to provide video services to its customers was equally well suited to moving other forms of information, if not essential to such operations (Mills 1993: 830–831). Thus the question was not so much one of eliminating regulatory protection as it was one of promoting the most effective means of providing universal service to the American public. The Clinton administration effectively redefined universal service to include new advances in telecommunications technology. It also made the case that the players best equipped to make such services widely available through existing technology, the Baby Bells, were being unreasonably prevented from doing so.

Still, turf wars among the Baby Bells, AT&T, the cable companies, and other long-distance providers for a piece of the information superhighway slowed progress on deregulation. Vice President Gore, in a January 1994 address, sought to quell the infighting among the would-be information providers by proposing sweeping deregulation of the telecommunications industry that promised something for everybody and still preserved universal service. In proposing the removal of the "regulatory firewalls" separating local phone providers, long-distance carriers, cable operators, and broadcasters, the administration was advocating fairly radical change in telecommunications regulation. Yet it was not as radical as earlier deregulatory movements in other policy areas, since it did not pit different congressional committees or regulators against one another. Rather, the commerce committees and the FCC could rightfully claim primary jurisdiction, with only minor complaints from the House Judiciary Committee. The administration's effort to broker a deal fizzled out when congressional attention became fixated on the upcoming congressional elections.

Following the 1994 midterm elections, when the Republican Party gained control of both the House and the Senate, the push for telecommunications deregulation took on a heated pace. The new Speaker of the House, Newt Gingrich, with Bell South headquartered in his Georgia district, needed little convincing when it came to arguments for opening long-distance and cable markets to the Baby Bells (Healey 1995b). Despite the calls from various quarters for a change in the regulatory structure, or perhaps because none were asking for exactly the same thing, the deregulatory drama took another two years to unfold.

The 1996 Telecommunications Act was first and foremost a compromise between those pursuing near-complete deregulation (the Republican House and Senate leadership, and some Republican Party members of the commerce committees) and those interested in maintaining a regulatory floor to ensure that the universal service criteria contained in the original 1934 act would not be abandoned (the Clinton administration and most of the Democratic and Republican members of the commerce committees). The relevant portions of the act dealt with everything from preconditions for the Baby Bells' entry into previously prohibited activities to new regulatory mandates to guide the FCC in implementing telecommunications policy.[5]

First, the act required all telecommunications carriers to link with one another their facilities and equipment. The intention, similar to congressional mandates dealing with telegraph lines nearly a hundred years earlier, was to create a seamless communications network. Second, the act removed all state and local barriers to entry in telecommunications, with the exception of those that promote or safeguard universal service, quality of service, or public safety and welfare. Third, the act opened the door to phone service by power companies and cable operators as long as they established separate subsidiaries for those purposes. Both federal and state regulators were given authority to prevent cross-subsidization, direct and indirect, between such holding companies and their telecommunications subsidiaries (Healey 1996: 410). Fourth, any Bell organization that wanted to enter into cable services, long-distance service, equipment manufacturing, electronic publishing, or data storage and retrieval had to establish a separate subsidiary to do so (Healey 1996: 411–413). The Bells were also prohibited from offering services across their local boundaries until they faced competition in their home market. What this means in practice is that a Bell organization has to enter into at least one interconnection agreement with a company that provides local service with the company's own equipment before it can venture outside its home market (Healey 1996: 411). The interconnection agreement has to satisfy a fourteen-point "competitive checklist" designed to measure the openness of the home market.[6] Finally, established long-distance carriers—AT&T, MCI, and Sprint—were temporarily barred from entering local markets until a Bell was permitted to offer long-distance services or until February 1999 (Healey 1996: 411).

While the realm of broadcasting received little attention in the act, several changes were made in broadcast regulation policy. First, the time period of licenses was lengthened from five years for radio and seven for television to eight years for both. Second, the act relaxed ownership rules so that radio broadcasters were no longer limited in the number of outlets they could own nationally. The limit on the number of stations owned in a single market was also increased. Similarly, national ownership limits were removed for television broadcasters, although they could not operate stations that reached more than 35 percent of the population. The act also loosened restrictions on owning both radio and television outlets, and provided guidelines for merging radio and television units. Finally, the act rewrote the license renewal procedure in favor of existing stations, rewriting the comparative hearing process in which the FCC was required to hear from challengers and render a renewal decision based in part on how well the licensee had met public service obligations. The act now mandates that "the Commission shall not consider whether the public interest, convenience, and necessity might be served by the grant of a license to a person other than the renewal applicant" (Shipan 1998: 487). Applicants for renewal no longer have to prove they have served the public interest; rather the FCC certifies this, along with checking to make sure the station did not engage in any serious violations of law or regulation during it previous tenure, nor abuse the terms of its license. If a station appears to have committed any of the preceding sins, it is still not automatically denied renewal. Rather the FCC is instructed to look for mitigating circumstances before it denies a renewal (Shipan 1998: 487–488).

While the preceding changes suggest that broadcasters came out major winners, in effect creating larger barriers to entry into the field of broadcasting, there is a potential downside. While the burden is now on the FCC to certify that public interest criteria have been met, or not met, this could provide opportunities for more detailed FCC oversight (Shipan 1998: 488). Of course, for this to occur the FCC would need the backing of both Congress and the executive, something rarely if ever achieved in any regulatory field, let alone one as potentially volatile as broadcasting.

The 1996 Telecommunications Act was an effort to restore calm to the telecommunications subsystem. Removing the federal district court from its oversight role was obviously the first step in returning policymaking to its pre–consent decree equilibrium. Still, the tug-of-war between the president and Congress for control of the FCC did not disappear with the passage of the act. During the October 1997 confirmation hearing for four new commissioners, the nominee for chairman, William E. Kennard, received many questions (and much instruction) regarding the direction in which he should move the agency regarding competition in phone and cable services.

Members of the Senate Commerce Committee took the opportunity during the confirmation hearings to express their displeasure with the manner in which the 1996 act had been implemented. While all could agree that the act was supposed to produce increased competition, which would in turn produce lower prices and encourage the development of cutting-edge technology, the new commissioners could be excused if they were not entirely certain how to go about achieving these goals, since the committee members themselves often suggested contradictory routes. Senate Commerce chair John McCain (R-AZ), who voted against the 1996 act, advocated complete deregulation. Commerce Telecommunications Subcommittee chair W. J. "Billy" Tauzin (R-LA) asked that the FCC simply follow the law as written—despite the conclusion of most observers that the law was vague and purposely left much discretion to the FCC. Ranking Democrat Ernest Hollings, who failed in his effort to have a former staff member placed on the commission, wanted the FCC to force the Bells to open their markets to competition, while Tauzin fought just as hard to help the Bells maintain their local monopoly. Perhaps only Edward Markey (D-MA) recognized the irony and impossibility of what the FCC was often asked to do by Congress: "to remain tough on companies that want the best of both worlds, that is to retain monopolies in their own market places while competing in other areas of telecommunications" (Gruenwald 1997: 2391).

Markey's remarks were a not-so-veiled criticism of the stance of some of the congressional Republicans on the Commerce Committee, who argued that the 1996 act accomplished little in the way of opening the doors to competition in phone and cable service, due to FCC reluctance to approve new Bell ventures. Senate Commerce chair McCain led the charge, accusing the FCC of impeding, instead of implementing, deregulation (Schiesel 1997). McCain's complaint focused on the requirements in the act that prohibited the Bells' entry into long-distance services and other ventures until they opened their local markets to competition. The Bells proved reluctant to do the latter, enlisting state regulators, GOP members of the commerce committees in both chambers, and the court in their efforts to maintain barriers to entry by would-be competitors (Victor 1997a).

Indeed, far from impeding the deregulation of local phone service, the FCC may have appeared too enthusiastic a promoter of competition for some. In one of his last acts as FCC chair, Reed Hundt overturned state prohibitions against MCI's entry into local service in Texas and voided state requirements that companies wishing to engage in local service build their own local networks. These rulings raised the ire of committee members whose districts were home to the Bells. Decrying the enforcement of existing regulation as "bureaucratic," Tauzin, chair of the House Telecommunications Subcommittee, argued that the FCC was "setting the bar for Bell entry into long distance unnecessarily high." Tauzin was joined by Democratic senator Ernest Hollings, who suggested Congress had to work to "break that lawyer approach" that dominated FCC decisionmaking (Schiesel 1997: C10).

The Clinton administration's choice of Kennard, who as general counsel had defended FCC actions regarding MCI, was a signal that the FCC would continue on this front. The problems associated with implementing the 1996 act were especially prickly from the vantage of the FCC, since some of the major differences over interpretation of the requirements of the act involved a split between a Democrat administration and a GOP Congress. If this were not enough of a problem, the party-based split was reflected on the commerce committees on at least some issues, while on others the House and Senate appeared to take opposite sides. Further complicating FCC-Senate relations was the rift between John McCain, the chair of the Senate Commerce Committee, and Conrad Burns (R-MT), chair of the Commerce Subcommittee on Telecommunications, which produced mixed signals on broadcasting issues in particular (Browning 1997a: 1130). Finally, changes in technology unanticipated by the 1996 act meant the FCC was dealing with a situation that was in a near-constant state of flux. In combination, the preceding made the effort to restore the calm of a dominant coalition especially difficult.

An immediate result of the 1996 act that no elected official seemed to have anticipated was the move toward increasing concentration in the industry. What began as industry-specific mergers in television soon spread to telephony, and then took off across industries, producing increasingly large telecommunications behemoths. The FCC found itself with its hands full when AT&T proposed a merger with SBC Communications, one of the largest of the regional Bell companies created by the AT&T breakup. The proposed company would have controlled some $50 billion in assets, hardly the head-to-head competition envisioned by backers of deregulation. Calling the proposed merger "unthinkable" in a 1997 speech, outgoing FCC chair Hundt sent a strong signal that ended the initial merger talks (Browning 1997b: 1553).

Aside from FCC signals to telephone companies, such mergers had been occurring for some time in television and radio. Jack Fields (R-TX), chair of the House Commerce Subcommittee on Telecommunications and Finance and credited as the architect of the deregulation of telecommunications in the House, was an advocate for allowing concentration of ownership in media markets. While he was unable to secure a provision that would have allowed a single company to own multiple television stations, newspapers, and a cable network in the same community/market, what critics refer to as "concentrated media," he continued to back such efforts from his House perch (Victor 1996: 480–481).

The arguments against such concentration reference the danger of quashing editorial diversity, along with the usual arguments regarding market share and economic returns. Advocates answer back that the proliferation of cable outlets and the Web promote competing ideas and competition in the market. Regulators seemed sympathetic to the latter view, allowing the Disney-ABC merger, the creation of the Fox news empire, and offering few objections to a proposed TBS–Time Warner merger (Victor 1996: 482). Not everyone was complacent regarding the competition that would derive from multiple information streams. The *New York Times* featured an editorial suggesting that the danger was not so much in the pricing of services, which antitrust regulation could still handle, but rather in controlling the flow of information. Using as an example CNN's refusal to run an ad against the 1996 act, on the grounds that the ad did not meet CNN standards for accuracy, not to mention that it ran counter to the interests of TBS (CNN's parent company) in deregulation, the *Times* suggested that industry mergers posed First Amendment problems (Victor 1996: 483). These problems aside, 1997 saw a continuation of the trend of increased concentration. US West acquired Continental Cablevision Incorporated, the third largest cable firm, while Westinghouse Electric Corporation, the largest radio station owner, joined with Infinity Broadcasting, the second largest (Victor 1997a: 1132, 1997b).

By the end of 1997, some began to question the growing concentration in the industry, along with the rise in local phone and cable rates and the failure of long-distance prices to drop (Browning 1997b). Further complicating the efforts at promoting competition in phone service, a decision by the US 8th Circuit Court of Appeals, on July 18, recognized the right of state utility commissions to set rate standards for local service, even if by doing so the end result would be variation from state to state that would make it harder for the long-distance carriers to enter those markets (Browning 1997b: 1552). The dispute between the Bells and the long-distance carriers pitted the chair of the House Commerce Committee, Thomas J. Bliley Jr. (R-VA), against those members allied with the Bells. In addition, it found Senate Commerce Committee chair McCain disagreeing with his House counterpart over what the 1996 act had wrought. Bliley argued that the changes envisioned in the act would take more time to unfold, while McCain retorted that change had occurred, but it involved higher rates, more concentrated ownership, and too much regulation (Victor 1997c: 2311).

By 1999, the original seven Baby Bells—Ameritech Corporation, Bell Atlantic Group, Bellsouth Corporation, NYNEX Corporation, Pacific Telesis Group, SBC Communications Incorporated, and US West Incorporated—had merged to create four companies. Pacific Telesis merged with SBC in 1997, as did Bell Atlantic with NYNEX; Ameritech merged with SBC in 1999, as did Bell Atlantic with GTE. While GTE was not one of the Baby Bells, it was one of the largest providers of local phone service (Victor 1999: 1883). On the long-distance side, AT&T merged with the cable firm Tele-Communications Incorporated in 1998, and then with the cable firm MediaOne Group in 1999. The result was a market dominated by increasingly larger firms, a situation spurred by the initial approval of the Bell Atlantic–NYNEX merger, which triggered similar consolidations by firms seeking to remain competitive (Victor 1999: 1881). Consumer groups blamed the chief of the Antitrust Division, Joel Klein, for the merger mania. While there were reports that at least some of the staff attorneys wanted to challenge the mergers, Klein overruled them claiming there were no grounds for such action. Recall from Chapter 4 that the 1914 Clayton Antitrust Act requires the department to show that the proposed merger "may substantially lessen competition" (Victor 1999: 1882), a standard which most acknowledge is difficult to prove. Indeed, Philip L. Verveer, a former Justice Department lawyer, could not recall a successful such case in the last twenty-five years (Victor 1999: 1882).

Interestingly enough, the FCC operates under less demanding standards, needing only to demonstrate that a merger would not be in the "public interest" (Victor 1999: 1882). This standard is usually met during hearings in which testimony from any interested party—state regulators, consumers, competitors, employees, and the like—is solicited, after which the FCC writes an order based on their interpretation of the comments. The FCC tends to be much more skeptical of proposed mergers and imposes conditions intended to ensure that future competitors are able to enter the market. In the case of the Bells, the FCC suggested it would not look favorably on continued mergers among them, raising the ire of the Baby Bells and some members of Congress—McCain in particular (Victor 1999: 1883). McCain and Orin Hatch (R-UT) cosponsored legislation (S 1125) reducing FCC authority to use "public interest" standards, requiring it to abide by Justice Department or FTC approval of mergers. Even more drastic, if neither agency acts regarding a merger, the FCC is to treat such inaction as tacit approval (Victor 1999: 1884). The legislation also reduced the time the FCC had to consider merger proposals from twelve months to eight. For mergers that involved more than $15 million in assets, the time frame was 180 days, with a onetime sixty-day extension. Smaller deals were given a ninety-day deadline with a thirty-day extension (Ota 1999b). Despite gaining the endorsement of Tauzin, chair of the House Telecommunications Subcommittee, who agreed that mergers were a necessity if firms were to be competitive in the global marketplace, the bill died in the Senate.

While mergers may have seemed necessary to some for survival in the global marketplace, decisions on regulatory policy were fought and made in the domestic political arena. The Bells in particular were opposed to AT&T's moves to further consolidate its place in telecommunications via a merger with Telecommunications Incorporated, one of the largest cable television providers in the US market. AT&T had made no secret of its intention to provide local phone service via cable, and if that were not enough, it announced the same intentions with regard to the Internet, rankling the nation's top Internet service provider, AOL. Both AOL and the Bells sought a ruling from the FCC to allow them access to AT&T's cable network if the deal went through. Chairman Kennard showed little interest in granting the request, arguing that "because the Internet is still in its infancy, it is not appropriate today to write such rules" (Ota 1999a: 331).

When the Supreme Court upheld the FCC authority to certify whether the Bells had opened their markets to competition as a precondition to their entry into other ventures, the Bells began exploration of the legislative route to regulatory relaxation. Senate Communications Subcommittee chair Conrad Burns suggested that "Chairman Kennard basically gets a little overenthusiastic in some areas in promoting the policies of the administration. They tend to forget at the FCC that they are an arm of Congress, not an arm of the administration" (Ota 1999a: 333). The upcoming presidential election would offer a new opportunity for Congress to reestablish that relationship.

The return of the Republican Party to the White House in 2001 at least temporarily removed what some members of Congress saw as unwarranted presidential intrusions on telecommunications turf. What the 2000 election did not do was to eliminate the dispute among congressional allies of the

Bells and AT&T regarding the regulation of telecommunications. The new bone of contention was broadband service. Broadband encompasses a wide range of constantly evolving high-speed digital technologies, including voice, high-speed data, video, and interactive delivery services.

In 2000, Congress considered several proposals aimed at extending broadband service. Rural members, led by Byron Dorgan (D-ND), favored policy along the lines of rural electrification efforts, with a revolving loan fund to bankroll expanded service to rural areas at below-market loans. Others, such as John Kerry (D-MA) and Daniel Patrick Moynihan (D-NY), pushed efforts to entice companies to offer next-generation high-speed connections to urban and suburban domestic markets, using a universal service rationale. Finally, legislators operating from the House Commerce Committee and led by W. J. Tauzin and John Dingell backed an effort that would allow the Bells into the data transmission game. Tauzin and Dingell argued that the result of the Bells' entry would be a "natural expansion" of service to underserved areas, rapid development and deployment of next-generation technology, and competition that would lower prices (Bettelheim 2000a: 766). The major hurdle for this "free market" approach was Thomas Bliley, chair of the House Commerce Committee. Bliley used his position to prevent the consideration of any legislation that sought to allow the Bells into broadband service before they opened their own markets to competition. Due to Bliley's success in creating a hostile environment, those interested in opening broadband service to the Bells engaged in venue switching. Efforts to rewrite regulation moved from the Commerce Committee to the Judiciary Committee. Two such attempts, one to allow the Bells into the broadband market without opening their markets to competition, and another that would force cable firms to open their lines to any competitor interested in providing broadband services (read, the Bells), were referred to the Judiciary Committee in 2000. Judiciary chair Henry Hyde (R-IL) was unable to act on either proposal, due in no small part to the opposition of the FCC, AT&T, and the bulk of Internet providers (Bettelheim 2000b: 1810).

By 2001 there was a new chair of the FCC. Michael Powell, son of Secretary of State Colin Powell and a protégé of Senate Commerce chair John McCain, advocated a hands-off approach to broadband. Powell described telecommunications as being "in the midst of revolution." He suggested that rather than regulation, the telecommunications industry (and those interested in broadband technology in particular) required incentives to encourage expansion and innovation (Bettelheim 2001a: 723). Under the 1996 act the Bells could offer digital subscriber lines (DSLs) over their existing copper phone lines within geographic zones known as local access and transport areas (LATAs). Cable companies offered hookups over their coaxial cable networks, which are unregulated and not subject to competition requirements. For the Bells to offer service between LATAs (there are

164 such areas), they had to open their systems to local competition, which involves meeting the requirements of the fourteen-point checklist enshrined in the 1996 Telecommunications Act. Tauzin and Dingell sought to relax the competition criteria for data transmission, while long-distance carriers, which have a regulatory-established monopoly on such transmissions, resisted the effort (Bettelheim 2002a: 456).

At the same time that Powell was advocating a "wait and see" approach toward broadband, he was also advocating the relaxation of ownership limits that barred media companies from owning television and newspaper outlets in the same market. Powell recommended elimination of the 1996 regulations that restricted broadcast and cable companies from owning stations that collectively reached 35 percent of the national market. Powell received backing for his initiatives from the new chair of the reorganized Energy and Commerce Committee, Tauzin, who suggested that "Chairman Powell inherited an agency that has drifted. It has drifted from its designated mission, and it has drifted from the law" (Bettelheim 2001a: 723).

With Tauzin as chair, and the ranking minority member, Dingell, on board, the Energy and Commerce Committee again took up the entry of the Bells into broadband. As was the case before, the Tauzin-Dingell proposal would allow the Bells into the broadband market without having to share their networks with competitors. Tauzin reasoned that the regulations governing the Bells only applied to voice traffic, not digital signals. Reported from the subcommittee by a 19–14 vote, the bill was not an overwhelming favorite of the Commerce Committee. Among those opposed were members allied with the FCC, AT&T, and cable operators. In addition, they were joined by a new ally, the Judiciary Committee (Bettelheim 2001b: 922).

Both Tauzin of Commerce and James Sensenbrenner (R-WI) of Judiciary claimed jurisdiction over the Internet and broadband communications (Bettelheim 2001c: 1012). The split on the subcommittee was reflected in the 32–23 vote in the full committee to send the legislation to the floor. In an effort to enlarge support, the legislation contained a provision allowing competitors to use the Bells' copper-based lines to send broadband signals. Opponents characterized the addition as halfhearted: copper lines are a much slower route than the fiber-optic networks the Bells were planning on using. An amendment that would have forced the Bells to allow competitors to use their fiber-optic lines produced a tie, while a proposal requiring service to underserved regions was scaled back (Bettelheim 2001d: 1083).

Sensenbrenner asked the Speaker for a sequential referral of the Tauzin-Dingell bill, arguing that it had been rushed through committee, dealt with Judiciary turf, and appeared to favor the regional Bells. Opening a second front in the battle over broadband, Sensenbrenner introduced legislation that would require the Bells to reduce their share of local phone markets to a maximum of 85 percent before they could carry Internet traffic. The legislation also created a loan program to aid independents in deploying broadband technology, marking Judiciary as a venue friendly to Internet start-ups and new entrants into the market (Bettelheim 2001c: 1012). The Judiciary Committee amended and reported Tauzin-Dingell unfavorably by voice vote, sending mixed signals to both the Rules Committee and the floor. Judiciary's failure to record a vote was a strong indication that the panel was split or near deadlocked on the bill and more than likely on Sensenbrenner's amendment to the bill (Bettelheim 2001e: 1434). Sensenbrenner's amendment required Justice Department certification that the Bells had opened their markets to competition before the Bells could move into broadband. Justice would also be given the power to pursue antitrust actions against any Bell that refused to allow competitors to connect to its lines, negating an Appeals Court ruling that such a refusal was not subject to antitrust action (Bettelheim 2001e: 1435).

Sensenbrenner was clearly attempting to establish the role of both his committee, as well as his bureaucratic counterpart, in the realm of broadband telecommunications. As such, his efforts were an attempt to transform a dominant coalition into a competitive mode. The earlier efforts by President George W. Bush, characteristic of transitory coalitions, had opened the door for such an effort. Sensenbrenner's efforts were aided by the economic downturn that hit the high-tech portion of the telecommunications industry especially hard, as well as the technological innovations and changes that made old-style regulation appear dated. In the end, it was Tauzin's inability to broker a deal within the subsystem that left the bill in limbo for the remainder of the session.

Tauzin-Dingell was taken up again in 2002, during the second session of the 107th Congress. Energy and Commerce appeared to have won the battle in the House, where Tauzin-Dingell passed without the Sensenbrenner amendments. But the legislation went nowhere in the Senate, where Ernest Hollings, the new chair of the Commerce Committee, called it "blasphemy" (Bettelheim 2002b: 581). Hollings had taken over the chairmanship following a Senate GOP defection to the Democrats, and when the bill came before his committee he took the opportunity to engage in a heated exchange with the House authors of the bill during a two-hour hearing (Bettelheim 2002c: 1303). Hollings introduced legislation of his own, extending loan guarantees to those who offered broadband to underserved areas, and proposed splitting the Bells into wholesale and retail units. Hollings slammed the FCC for its failure to regulate the Bells and open their markets to competition, declaring: "If we had a Federal Communications Commission, we wouldn't need a law" (Bettelheim 2002b: 583).

Not that the entire Senate panel was hostile to the House effort. One of the top GOP members of the committee, John Breaux (R-LA), introduced a bill that looked much like Tauzin-Dingell. It called for the FCC to come up with rules within 120 days that would promote "regulatory parity" between all broadband providers, leaving voice service rules in place (Bettelheim 2002c: 1304). Breaux's bill was an effort to see if a majority of the panel, and the Senate, would back some form of deregulation. Breaux himself favored allowing the FCC to decide how best to proceed, to avoid the bitter fight that took place in the House: "We say look, we're not going to let politicians make the decisions about what the rules are to level the playing field, but let the independent agency do it" (Bettelheim 2002c: 1305). The problem, from the Bells' perspective, was that Hollings was not alone in his opposition. John McCain, now the ranking minority member on the panel, was complicating the discussion by linking telecommunications regulation to his efforts to reform the conduct of political campaigns.

When the GOP returned to power in the Senate following the off-year elections in 2002, it appeared that the time was ripe for a move on broadband. Rather than focus their efforts on the congressional venue, the Bells decided to concentrate on the Federal Communications Commission. FCC chair Powell was clearly sympathetic to the Bells, and just as important, the White House signaled its intention to allow regulatory-backed deregulation, or at least Bell expansion into broadband sans regulation (Cohn 2003a). Because nothing had changed in the House, the chamber was assumed to still be in favor of Bell entry into broadband. Given these green lights, the FCC issued a rule in February 2003 that adopted the Bells' "new wires, new rules" argument. In essence, the rules exempted any new broadband equipment added by the Bells from the 1996 requirement that they open their networks before competing in long distance.

Despite this regulatory victory, the Bells still pursued a court challenge to those parts of the 1996 act that required them to open access to local networks for three years for voice and data transmission, and to offer indefinite access to switching equipment used for other voice services (Cohn 2003b: 513). In this fashion the Bells pursued regulatory-authored deregulation via the FCC, while attempting to switch the discussion of regulatory requirements to the venue of the courts. Clearly the telecommunications subsystem was suffering from internalized competition, which once again threatened to upset the policy equilibrium.

While Congress appeared to be willing to see if the FCC could deal with the broadband issue in 2003, by 2004 it was pulled back into the debate by yet another technological innovation. Internet phone technology, know as Voice-over-Internet Protocol (VoIP), was fast blurring the distinction between the data transmission and telephony.[7] By 2004, several states were already stepping into the fray, with California and Minnesota defining VoIP as a telecommunications service and subject to regulation, while

Florida enacted a statute that exempted such service from regulation (Sharma 2004: 492). The 1996 act also allowed VoIP providers to escape access fees, the Universal Service Fund, and other arrangements intended to meet public service requirements. Tied to this was the issue of emergency services such as 911 connections. The question was whether VoIP providers should be required to make their systems accessible to such service. Further complicating the issue, the Federal Bureau of Investigation insisted that the FCC guarantee that such communications were subject to wiretaps by authorities armed with the proper warrants (Sharma 2004: 494).

The FCC decided not to regulate computer-to-computer communications, and was leaning toward not regulating computer-to-phone, or phone-to-phone via computer, both of which were available technologies (Sharma 2004: 492). The dilemma was that the 1996 act appeared outdated in its distinction between voice and data transmission. The trick, from the view of most subsystem players, involved allowing firms to engage in and improve data transmission services while not upsetting the competitive balance enshrined in the 1996 Telecommunications Act. The problem was that the 1996 act had created monopolies for particular kinds of service, many of which were becoming obsolete. Those protected by the system abhor the thought of competition, yet technology is changing so rapidly that regulatory-established cartels are proving nonprofitable. All this is compounded by the fact that no one is quite sure how the new technology fits into the old system (Bettelheim 2002a: 456).

Conclusion

Mike Mills (2002: 584) suggested that, when they penned a law that dealt with twentieth-century means of communication, failing to recognize that they were on the cusp of the twenty-first century, the authors of the 1996 Telecommunications Act were wearing "technology blinders." On the telephony end, because it was based on a series of assumptions that by 2004 appeared false—competition was the norm, the Bells wanted into long-distance, competition would produce lower prices—the law left it to the FCC, the courts, and industry to manage policy change in the fast-changing field of telephony. Rather than arguing that legislators wore blinders, it is probably more accurate to say that various factions, legislative- as well as administrative-based, answered to different industry segments in writing the legislation. The legislation, far from setting the agenda, simply ratified much of what regulators had already been experimenting with. As such, Congress was again ratifying piecemeal change authored by bureaucratic entrepreneurs, much as it had done in the realm of banking.

That said, the 1996 Telecommunications Act restored some semblance of calm to the telecommunications subsystem. Removing the federal district court from its oversight role in telephony was an important step in returning policymaking to its subsystem-based equilibrium. On a related note, the tug-of-war between the president and Congress for control of the FCC appeared to end with the election of George W. Bush, who showed little initial interest in telecommunications. By the same token, the infighting between the House and Senate communications committees was still very much alive, as were turf wars within the House. The problem, from the view of many congressional Republicans, was that telecommunications was still overregulated. While united in this belief, the GOP fractured when it came to the question of which industry faction's view of deregulation should prevail. While the split between AT&T and the Bells was the most obvious, one could find fissures along other lines as well.

As always, it falls to the FCC to find a compromise that pleases the various industry factions and their congressional allies. In this regard, telecommunications regulation asks the FCC to balance the goals of industry management, consumer protection, and technological retooling under the rubric of *regulation,* while dancing to the often disparate tunes piped by the House and Senate commerce committees, with an occasional chorus from Judiciary. If that were not enough, the potential for a recurrence of a situation in which a president advocates one course of action while oversight committees back another is quite possible if off-year elections usher in a Democratic Party majority in either chamber. Indeed, nothing seems to pique presidential interest and principal-like behavior more than having the other party in charge of oversight. Whether or not the current equilibrium will remain long-lasting depends on how effectively the FCC navigates the shoals of telecommunications policy. As always, the split among industry factions has a tendency to produce competing coalitions, which, if they spin out of control, create a situation ripe for outsider intervention.

Notes

1. The hush-a-phone was a cuplike device attached to a phone receiver that muffled background noise. AT&T argued that the device violated tariff restrictions and sought to remove it from the market, which the FCC did in 1956. When the removal decision was overturned by the US Court of Appeals in 1956, the FCC altered its enforcement of tariff restrictions and considered the validity of any nonelectronic attachment on a case-by-case basis.

In the *First Computer Inquiry* decision, the FCC rules that data processing is not subject to FCC regulation. The decision allows common carriers to engage in data processing so long as they establish a separate corporate entity to do so. The ruling opened the data-processing market to AT&T.

MCI introduced Execunet, which allowed MCI customers to dial a local MCI number, connect to MCI's long-distance circuits, and connect to any telephone in another city where MCI offered Execunet. This rendered the paper difference between local and long-distance service moot. The FCC ordered MCI to stop the service. MCI successfully challenged the order in court. Following the court decision, the FCC tried to rein in MCI and other would-be long-distance providers, only to have the ruling in *Execunet II* overturned in court. A compromise was reached by which the new long-distance carriers paid a reduced fee (around 35 percent of what the Bell System paid) to cover the costs of local services.

2. In the *Above 890* decision, the FCC ruled to invite competition in the licensing of microwave systems, despite arguments by the Bell System that this would detract from Bell's goals of universal service. In the *Carterfone* decision, the FCC ruled, after three years of deliberation, that the AT&T policy prohibiting electronic attachments on phones was "unreasonable, discriminatory, and unlawful," opening the equipment market to competition. In the *Specialized Common Carrier Services* decision, the FCC forced Bell to allow competition in specialized communications—microwave transmissions, data transmissions, and satellite relays—by providing access to local Bell lines at reasonable rates. The FCC also refused a Bell request to alter its pricing arrangements to provide lower prices in markets subject to competition.

3. Much of this section comes from Hilliard 1991, an excellent policy primer on the FCC.

4. While we refer to the principal oversight committees as "Commerce," their formal titles are the House Committee on Energy and Commerce, with the Subcommittee on Telecommunications, Consumer Protection, and Finance assuming direct oversight responsibility; and the Senate Committee on Commerce, Science, and Transportation, with the Subcommittee on Communications involved in day-to-day oversight. Appropriations questions are handled in the House by the Appropriations Subcommittee on Commerce, Justice, State, and Judiciary; while the Senate refers such questions to the Subcommittee on Commerce, Justice, State, the Judiciary, and Related Agencies.

5. The act also contains sections dealing with broadcasting, cable services, indecency, and privacy, which are not the subjects of this chapter.

6. The Bells are prohibited from entering into manufacturing agreements with other Bells or their affiliates, and are required to give the FCC complete information on technical requirements for making connections. The act also contains a variety of restrictions on the manufacture of equipment by so-called standard-setting organizations (Healey 1996: 412).

7. The major player in the market is Vonage Holding Corporation, which in 2004 served 100,000 of the 135,000 Internet phone subscribers. For $34.99 a month users could make unlimited local and long-distance calls to both digital and analog users. Time-Warner launched a similar service in several test cities in 2004, while traditional phone companies initially held back for fear of making their traditional service options obsolete. The problem by 2004 was that many of these companies missed out on the wireless revolution, hence both Qwest (of the Baby Bells) and AT&T are exploring VoIP options (Sharma 2004: 494).

7

Environmental Protection Regulation

ENVIRONMENTAL POLICY is an extraordinarily broad term that encompasses several distinct (though obviously related) sets of policy activities and goals. For many observers, environmental policy is concerned with species protection, habitat preservation, and land use. Protecting species almost inevitably requires the federal government to limit development activities on public and private lands, raising the ire of private property owners and entrepreneurs who depend on federal lands for their livelihoods. One of the most contentious debates in environmental policy during recent years has surrounded revising the Endangered Species Act to provide less protection for the rights of plants and animals and more protection for the rights of property owners. A second element of environmental policy is addressing the environmental consequences of energy production. The federal government ensures the safety of nuclear power plants (the responsibility of the Nuclear Regulatory Commission [NRC]) and the safe disposal of the radioactive wastes from these power plants (a joint responsibility of the Environmental Protection Agency and the Department of Energy). In a similar vein, coal mining—especially strip mining—produces large-scale environmental consequences. The federal government began regulating these consequences with the passage of the Surface Mining Control and Reclamation Act of 1977, currently administered by the Interior Department's Office of Surface Mining Reclamation and Enforcement.

When most citizens think about environmental policy, however, they think of federal efforts at controlling pollution. Most federal regulatory efforts in the area of environmental protection, in fact, address the problems of air pollution, water pollution, pesticide contamination, and the proper management of hazardous wastes and toxic substances. Legislation aims to reduce current levels of these pollutants, prevent future pollution, and clean up areas polluted in the past. It is this aspect of environmental policy that we will focus on in this chapter, as well as on the EPA, the lead agency for administering pollution control regulations.

Environmental Policy

Federal environmental policies deal with air pollution, water pollution, land pollution and refuse disposal, noise pollution, the use and disposal of pesticides and other toxic chemicals, cleaning up contaminated neighborhoods and ecosystems—in general, what economists often refer to as *residuals.* Many of these regulations provide and protect a particular public good: environmental quality. The public-good nature of protecting and preserving environmental quality leads many observers to advance "public interest" justifications for environmental regulation. (What could be more in the public's interest than protecting environmental quality?) Moreover, because environmental quality is a public good, it is susceptible to overconsumption and contamination by externalities (i.e., pollutants or residuals).

Market failure and protecting the public interest are the most common rationales offered for environmental regulation. In fact, most of the other reasons for regulation offered in Chapter 1 have little face validity when it comes to explaining environmental regulation; it is difficult to envision what economic advantages accrue to industrial or sectional interests when moving from a situation of no environmental regulation to life under an environmental regulatory regime. Once the decision has been made to regulate environmental quality, however, industrial and sectional interests do have much to gain by structuring regulation in a particular fashion. Thus, while cartel management, capture, and sectionalism may not explain the existence of regulation in this area, they may help us to understand the form these regulations take.

Complexity and Salience in Environmental Regulation

Environmental regulation may be the most technically complex area of regulatory policy. Consider a brief list of typical regulatory tasks faced by the EPA: setting safe exposure levels for air pollutants; evaluating ecosystem effects of various water pollutants; assessing the human health effects of pesticide exposure; designing techniques to safely treat and dispose of hazardous chemicals; monitoring emissions from hundreds of thousands of pollution sources; and projecting the global atmospheric consequences of increased emissions of chlorofluorocarbons, carbon dioxide, methane, and other gases. Each of these tasks requires knowledge at the forefront of the fields of chemistry, physics, epidemiology, endocrinology, and remote sensing, to name only a few. Furthermore, these environmental problems must be addressed without seriously disrupting the existing system of private property rights or compromising economic performance, which requires considerable legal and economic skill. Finally, the reliance of environmental regulation on scientific knowledge and technical expertise is increasing as targeted environmental problems themselves become more complex (e.g., banning DDT is a much simpler task than halting global warming).

Observed in isolation, the technical complexity of environmental protection might be seen as a barrier to any policy activity taking place. As mentioned above, however, environmental regulation is an excellent example of issue salience overcoming the obstacles to action posed by complexity. Prior to the late 1960s, environmental protection was a nonissue with the American public. This changed dramatically in a short period of time. Due in large part to focusing events like the publication of Rachel Carson's *Silent Spring* in 1962, the wreck of the oil tanker *Torrey Canyon* off the coast of California in 1967, and Ohio's Cuyahoga River catching fire in 1969, public concern regarding the environment skyrocketed by the 1970s. For example, in 1965 only 17 percent of respondents in a Gallup poll identified air and water pollution as a top national problem worthy of governmental attention. By 1970 this figure stood at 53 percent (Dunlap 1995).

Scholars observing the explosive growth in the salience of environmental protection believed this phenomenon would soon fall victim to the "issue-attention cycle," whereby public attention and support for addressing environmental problems would quickly wane (Downs 1972). The history of environmental regulation since 1970 has proved these observers wrong. With the exception of a brief dip in the middle to late 1970s, public support for environmental protection has remained at high levels for nearly thirty years. Moreover, as Figure 7.1 shows, media attention to the issue of environmental regulation has remained high as well. Thus, environmental regulation is a policy area characterized by enduring and uniformly high levels of both complexity and salience.

The Statutory Basis for Environmental Regulation

There is no single or "organic" statute empowering the federal government to regulate pollution. Rather, different environmental problems are addressed in separate pieces of legislation. These statutes were adopted at different times, under different circumstances, with little or no attention paid to regulatory coordination. Indeed, the statutes sometimes work at cross-purposes. A relatively comprehensive list of federal environmental legislation is provided in Figure 7.2. Below, we examine in greater detail the most important of these environmental statutes.

Figure 7.1 The Salience of Environmental Protection

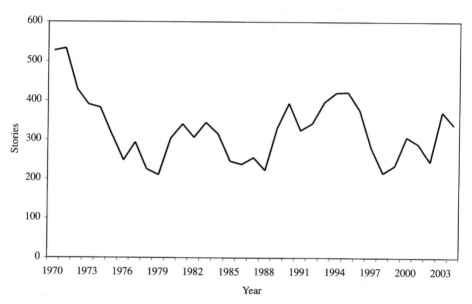

The National Environmental Policy Act. Among the major threats to the environment in the 1960s was the federal government. The government operated power plants, built thousands of miles of highways, managed millions of acres of public lands, and sponsored research on pesticides, among other related activities. The National Environmental Policy Act (NEPA), enacted in 1969, established the prevention and reduction of environmental damage as a goal of all federal agencies when carrying out the routine business of government. The main tool of NEPA is the requirement that all federal agencies prepare an environmental impact statement (EIS) anytime their activities might damage the environment. Requiring an EIS guaranteed that federal agencies would at least consider the environmental ramifications of their actions and allow citizens and other federal agencies to comment on the environmental impact of federal activities and sue to enforce compliance with NEPA. While environmental impact statements provide environmentalists with a short-term tactic for delaying federal construction projects, NEPA forces agencies to change their decisionmaking procedures, not the substance of their actions. Yet in altering these procedures, federal agencies give greater consideration to environmental factors than they did before (Caldwell 1982; Mazmanian and Nienaber 1979).

Air quality regulation. With the 1970 Clean Air Act, the federal government embarked on an ambitious and aggressive campaign of national leg-

Figure 7.2   Major Environmental Statutes Enforced by the EPA

National Environmental Policy Act of 1969 (42 U.S.C. §§ 4321–4347)
Clean Air Act (42 U.S.C. §§ 7401 et seq.)
Clean Air Act Amendments of 1990 (42 U.S.C. §§ 7401 et seq.)
Clean Water Act (33 U.S.C. §§ 121 et seq.)
Comprehensive Environmental Response, Compensation, and Liability Act
    (42 U.S.C. §§ 9601 et seq.)
Endangered Species Act (7 U.S.C. § 136; 16 U.S.C. §§ 460 et seq.)
Federal Insecticide, Fungicide, and Rodenticide Act (7 U.S.C. §§ 135 et seq.)
Federal Food, Drug, and Cosmetic Act (21 U.S.C. §§ 301 et seq.)
Food Quality Protection Act (PL 104-170)
Occupational Safety and Health Act (29 U.S.C. §§ 61 et seq.)
Oil Pollution Act of 1990 (33 U.S.C. §§ 2702–2761)
Pollution Prevention Act (42 U.S.C. §§ 13101–13102 et seq.)
Resource Conservation and Recovery Act (42 U.S.C. §§ 321 et seq.)
Safe Drinking Water Act (43 U.S.C. §§ 300f. et seq.)
Superfund Amendments and Reauthorization Act (42 U.S.C. §§ 9601 et seq.)
Toxic Substances Control Act (15 U.S.C. §§ 2601 et seq.)
Water Quality Act (33 U.S.C. §§ 1251 et seq.)

islative leadership in pollution control. To meet the goal of improving air quality, the CAA empowered the EPA to set national ambient air quality standards (NAAQS), which are limits on the allowable atmospheric concentrations of certain key or "criteria" pollutants (nitrogen dioxide, sulfur dioxide, total suspended particulates, carbon monoxide, hydrocarbons, ozone, and lead [added in 1978]). The CAA also empowered the EPA to study the effects of toxic air pollutants (e.g., benzene, vinyl chloride) and set standards for these pollutants as necessary. Agency discretion in setting the standards was virtually unlimited, because the scientific study of pollutants was just beginning. Congress explicitly recognized that this scientific uncertainty might pose problems, and thus it directed the EPA to reconsider these standards every five years.

Responsibility for meeting NAAQS was shared among the federal government, state governments, and polluters. For its part, the federal government established specific reductions for automobile emissions and set performance standards for new stationary sources of pollution. The federal government often mandated what types of equipment polluters should use to meet these pollution reduction standards (e.g., the "best available pollution control technology," or BAT). States are ultimately responsible for meeting NAAQS through state implementation plans, in which states outline how they will enforce federal regulatory requirements, establish their own performance standards for existing stationary sources of pollution, and highlight what additional actions, if any, the state will take to meet NAAQS. Interestingly, new federal source performance standards were almost always more strict than existing state source performance standards for the same industry. One consequence of this policy is that older and dirtier plants have been kept in operation longer than they would have been without the policy (Crandall 1983).

The CAA was amended and reauthorized in 1977, and several of the 1977 amendments either relaxed the stringency of air quality regulations or rolled back the dates for attaining clean air goals. In addition, the 1977 amendments extended regulation into new areas. First, Congress required all new coal-fired power plants to install expensive smokestack scrubbers to reduce their sulfur dioxide pollution. Second, since the 1970 CAA required strong pollution controls only in areas not currently meeting NAAQS, environmental groups feared that this would induce polluting industries to locate in areas with exceptionally clean air. To prevent this, the Sierra Club sued the EPA and forced the agency to develop a set of prevention of significant deterioration (PSD) regulations. Congress formalized the EPA's guidelines as a set of legislative PSD requirements in the 1977 CAA. Under PSD, air quality in all regions of the country is protected from becoming significantly more polluted, even if this additional pollution does not violate NAAQS.

The CAAs of 1970 and 1977 were criticized from a number of perspectives. Environmentalists felt that several of the pollution control provisions in the acts were not strong enough, pointing to relaxed emission standards, a lack of progress in meeting NAAQS, and the absence of pollution controls aimed at acid rain and toxic air pollutants. Alternatively, industrialists and many economists argued that the pollution control requirements of the act were too expensive. Disagreements over how a new CAA should address these criticisms led to intense political debates throughout the 1980s, but the act remained unchanged. The deadlock over clean air policy was broken in 1990, when Congress and the George H. W. Bush administration were able to agree on reauthorization of the CAA. The 1990 CAA amendments significantly strengthened the act, and it is clear that the architects of the law listened carefully to critics of the earlier legislation.

To begin, the 1990 amendments strengthened automobile pollution reduction requirements, doubled the required life-span of automobile pollution control equipment (to 100,000 miles), and required the use of reformulated automotive fuels in those cities with the worst smog problems. Second, the act instituted a toxic air pollution control program, the goal of which was a 75 percent reduction in the emission of over 180 toxic chemicals. Third, the 1990 amendments addressed the acid rain problem by requiring a 50 percent reduction in sulfur dioxide emissions and significant reductions in nitrogen dioxide emissions. These last goals will be met by using marketable emission permits that allow electric utilities (and others) to buy and sell the right to emit sulfur and nitrogen dioxides. Over time, the number of permits (and thus the level of allowable pollution) will be reduced. Finally, the 1990 CAA placed all metropolitan areas on strict compliance schedules for the atmospheric pollutant ozone.

Water quality regulation.   Surface water quality regulations are firmly rooted in the watershed Clean Water Act (CWA) of 1972 (also called the Federal Water Pollution Control Act). The CWA may be the most ambitious piece of environmental legislation ever passed at the federal level. In its zeal to satisfy the rising tide of environmentalism, Congress passed a law with the goal of zero discharge of pollution into the nation's waters by 1985. As an interim standard, the act set a goal of all waters being "fishable and swimable" by 1983.

While there are no national water quality standards comparable to NAAQS, states are required to devise their own standards for what constitutes "fishable and swimable" water. Under the CWA, states are also responsible for establishing and implementing plans to meet water quality goals. The act provided two major tools states may use to carry out this responsibility: the Municipal Wastewater Treatment Grant Program (MWTGP) and the National Pollutant Discharge Elimination System (NPDES). With the MWTGP, municipalities were required to treat their sewage, but the federal government contributed 75 percent of the cost of constructing municipal wastewater treatment plants. Under the NPDES, state and federal regulators provided permits to all facilities that discharged wastes into public waterways. The permits, which must be renewed on the average of every five years, also imposed a strict set of reporting requirements on each facility. Moreover, the NPDES permits required industrial sources of pollution to install the "best practicable pollution control technology" (BPT) by 1977 and the aforementioned BAT by 1983, while municipal treatment plants were required to install BPT by 1983. Subsequent CWA reauthorizations in 1977 and 1981 rolled back deadlines for attaining national water quality goals and reduced to 55 percent the federal share of constructing municipal wastewater treatment plants.

Experience with controlling industrial pollutants under the CWA was generally positive. Nevertheless, the structure and implementation of this act left several water quality problems unaddressed. The Water Quality Act (WQA) of 1987, passed almost unanimously over the veto of President Reagan, sought to address these problems. First, the WQA addressed nonpoint water pollution (e.g., pollution from farmland and urban runoff) by directing the states to assess the seriousness of nonpoint source pollution and minimize the impact of these pollutants on the environment. States and localities must devise implementation plans incorporating "best management practices" that will control nonpoint pollution sources (Hansen, Babcock, and Clark 1988). Second, prior to the mid-1980s, surface water regulation emphasized the traditional pollutants of bacteria, sediments, and oxygen-demanding wastes. The 1987 WQA, however, focused more attention on trace toxic elements in water, such as pesticides and heavy metals. The WQA required states to develop impact control strategies for sources contributing to toxic pollution, and it required municipalities to adopt industrial pretreatment programs (in pretreatment, industries must treat their toxic pollutants before releasing them into municipal sewage systems) (EPA 1990). Finally, the 1987 WQA replaced the increasingly expensive MWTGP with a series of onetime grants to the states for municipal wastewater treatment. States use these grants to set up revolving loan funds, and municipalities that want to build or upgrade wastewater treatment facilities receive loans out of these funds.

Regulating hazardous wastes. Environmental regulation distinguishes between contemporary hazardous wastes and preexisting hazardous wastes. Currently the United States produces about 30 million tons of hazardous waste each year, and the storage, treatment, and disposal of these wastes are regulated under the Resource Conservation and Recovery Act (RCRA) of 1976. In regulating hazardous wastes, the EPA and empowered state agencies employ three tools. First, the EPA is to identify and classify all types of hazardous waste. Second, the RCRA requires a "cradle-to-grave" manifest tracking system for hazardous wastes. Any person engaged in the production and storage, transport, treatment, or disposal of hazardous wastes must file a manifest that identifies the source of the waste, the type and amount of the waste, and the final destination of the waste. Although an important tool, the manifest system affects only a small portion of hazardous wastes, since no more than 10 percent of all hazardous wastes produced are disposed of off-site (Dower 1990). Finally, the EPA requires all facilities that treat or dispose of hazardous wastes to meet strict construction and performance standards. For example, hazardous waste landfills must have two synthetic impermeable liners separated by a thick layer of clay, a leachate collection system, and monitoring wells to detect leakage.

The RCRA was reauthorized as the Hazardous and Solid Waste Amendments (HSWA) of 1984. The HSWA has been described as "among the most detailed and restrictive environmental requirements ever legislated" (Dower 1990: 165). More than any other piece of environmental regulation, the HSWA is a product of the conflict between Congress and the president over the direction of environmental policy. Dissatisfied with the EPA's slow progress in promulgating regulations and issuing permits, Congress required the agency to develop treatment and disposal standards for all hazardous wastes by 1991. Congress was also extremely distrustful of the regulatory direction of the EPA under President Reagan, and consequently, legislators took on the role of regulators. Congress placed within the HSWA standards for everything from the permeability of landfill liners to allowable pollutant concentrations in hazardous waste incinerator stack gases. If the EPA did not develop approved treatment and disposal standards by the deadlines, "hammer clauses" within the HSWA meant that these congressionally designed standards would take effect (Rosenbaum 1989). The EPA met most of the regulatory guidelines within the HSWA, and by 2003 there were nearly 500 commercial and over 1,700 on-site facilities for treatment, storage, and disposal across the country with RCRA permits (EPA 2003a).

While the RCRA and the HSWA regulate the treatment and disposal of hazardous wastes currently produced, neither addresses the problem of environmental contamination from hazardous wastes produced before the laws were enacted. These wastes, most of them concentrated in abandoned hazardous waste sites, have become a significant environmental and political issue. Energized by the discovery of an abandoned hazardous waste dump at Love Canal in Niagara Falls, New York, Congress passed the Comprehensive Environmental Response, Compensation, and Liability Act (CERCLA) of 1980, better known as the "superfund." The goals of CERCLA are to evaluate all abandoned hazardous waste sites across the country, place the worst of these sites on the National Priorities List (NPL), clean up these sites, and assess liability for the costs of these cleanups. There are currently about 1,600 sites on the NPL.

CERCLA contains two powerful tools to assist the EPA in remediating abandoned hazardous waste sites. First, the law imposes a condition of strict, joint, and several liability based on the "polluter pays" principle. *Strict liability* means that parties can be held responsible for cleanup costs even if they complied with all applicable regulations when they disposed of their wastes. *Joint liability* means that several parties may be held responsible for cleanup costs, while *several liability* means that a single responsible party may be held liable for all site cleanup costs, regardless of how much waste that party actually disposed of at the site. Second, the law created a $1.6 billion fund (thus the name "superfund") financed by a feedstock tax on the petroleum and chemical industries (86 percent) and by general revenues (14 percent) that the agency uses to cover cleanup costs when potentially responsible parties cannot be found or refuse to pay these costs. In practice, the agency has had little success recovering costs from responsible parties (Dower 1990).

The cleanup of abandoned hazardous waste sites progressed slowly, and soon it became clear that the problem was larger and more expensive than was envisioned in 1980. One respected estimate pegged the total cost of cleaning up the most dangerous hazardous waste sites in the country at $68 billion (GAO 1987). The Superfund Amendments and Reauthorization

Act (SARA) of 1986 extended and replenished the superfund to the tune of $8.5 billion. In passing SARA, Congress prohibited companies from filing for bankruptcy to avoid liability under the superfund. The legislature also directed the EPA to increase the use of out-of-court settlements to entice responsible parties to share cleanup costs. Finally, Title III of SARA, the Emergency Planning and Community Right-to-Know Act (EPCRTKA), required industries to inform communities about potentially dangerous chemicals used in day-to-day operations. These industries are also required to report yearly emissions of toxic chemicals in the Toxics Release Inventory (TRI). The EPCRTKA does not require industries to control the production or release of these chemicals—only to report this information. Still, the production and release of TRI chemicals has dropped precipitously since 1987, and several observers have pointed to the TRI as an example of the effectiveness of information provision as a regulatory tool (Hamilton 2005).

While superfund-authorizing legislation has not changed since SARA, the program itself underwent far-reaching changes in the 1990s. First, the Clinton administration placed a high priority on removing contaminated sites from the NPL. While the pace of superfund cleanups has slowed in recent years, by 2004 remediation efforts were completed at 966 NPL sites, with work progressing at another 422 (EPA 2004). Second, the chemical feedstock tax that funds the superfund was allowed to expire in 1995. The expiration of this tax has significantly limited EPA's ability to take remediation actions unilaterally. The Republican leadership in Congress has refused to consider reauthorizing the tax unless CERCLA undergoes major revisions, including abolishing the strict liability standard (Kriz 1996b; Freedman 1997c).

Regulating pesticides.   Pesticide regulation is far different from other types of environmental regulation. First, where traditional environmental regulations regulate the externalities from the production of products, pesticide legislation regulates the products themselves. Second, unlike the CAA, CWA, and RCRA, pesticide statutes require the EPA, before issuing regulations, to weigh the benefits of these products with the risks posed by their use. The goal of pesticide regulation, then, is to ensure the safe and effective use of these chemicals. The EPA's authority to regulate pesticides comes from the Federal Insecticide, Fungicide, and Rodenticide Act (FIFRA) of 1947. The purpose of the act was to protect farmers from ineffective or excessively dangerous pesticides. FIFRA was reauthorized and amended in 1972 to emphasize environmental protection. The EPA regulates pesticides much as the Food and Drug Administration regulates drugs; in order for any pesticide to be sold, it must be registered by the EPA. The FIFRA amendments of 1972 required the EPA to produce, by 1974, registration standards that ensured pesticides were safe, environmentally benign, and effective.

FIFRA provides three strategies for pesticide regulation: testing pesticides for safety and effectiveness, registration requirements, and use restrictions and prohibitions. Testing and registering new pesticides is a manageable task, given that the EPA receives fewer than fifty requests for new pesticide registrations each year. In addition to registering new pesticides, however, FIFRA required the EPA to evaluate and register the roughly 50,000 existing pesticides on the market. According to Christopher Bosso (1987), the reaction among EPA careerists to these requirements was "disbelief." Pesticides supported by adequate industry data were presumed safe without formal toxicity testing. The agency also conserved resources by relying on private laboratories to assess the safety and effectiveness of pesticides. This magnified the difficulties surrounding pesticide regulation when, in the late 1970s, the country's largest private chemical testing firm was discovered to have falsified data for over 200 EPA-registered pesticides (Bosso 1987). After evaluating all relevant data, the EPA could place restrictions on the production, use, or distribution of a pesticide, or refuse to register it. The EPA could also cancel a pesticide's registration and remove it from the market, and the agency has banned over fifty pesticides. For every pesticide banned, however, the agency had to compensate the manufacturer for product costs and lost sales revenue. These costs were significant: in fiscal year 1989 the EPA's budget for pesticide testing and registration was $45 million; its budget for compensation was $53 million (Kriz 1988).

Congress has been trying since the mid-1970s to overhaul FIFRA, though only a few minor changes have been made. Amendments to FIFRA in 1978 relaxed data reporting requirements on industry and required the EPA to compensate manufacturers when trade secrets were required in the pesticide registration process. During the Reagan administration, pesticide regulations were relaxed administratively when the EPA abandoned the genotoxic theory and adopted the epigenetic theory of pesticide toxicity. In the former theory, genotoxic chemicals are more dangerous, because these chemicals alter the genetic makeup of cells (Wines 1983a). By the late 1980s, however, congressional agricultural committees were in danger of losing jurisdiction over FIFRA, because of their inability to craft a reform proposal. To avoid this possibility, the committees decided to reform the legislation piece-by-piece rather than attempt a comprehensive overhaul, as had been done with SARA in 1986 and the WQA in 1987.

The resulting reforms, enacted in 1988, eliminate the indemnification provisions of FIFRA. Now if the EPA bans a pesticide, compensation is made to a limited number of applicators (e.g., farmers) instead of the chemical manufacturer. Second, the 1988 amendments required the EPA to review all active pesticide ingredients and make registration decisions on the more than 19,000 existing pesticides on the market by 1997 (Kriz 1988). But by the end of 1992 the agency had completed reviews of only two pesticide ingredients. Pressure for comprehensive reform of FIFRA is again building in response to a National Academy of Sciences report that found children are much more susceptible to pesticides than previously thought, and in response to a 1991 Supreme Court decision that allows localities to enact stricter pesticide limits than the EPA (Kriz 1992a).

Limited changes to pesticide legislation were also made in 1996. The Food Quality Protection Act (FQPA) relaxed pesticide tolerance standards for processed foods, extended the period between pesticide license reviews from five to fifteen years, and made it easier to sell existing inventories of suspended or canceled pesticides. The FQPA also expedited the approval process for "public health" pesticides (i.e., pesticides used by professional exterminators), and required the EPA to re-register a large number of existing pesticides by 2006.

Regulatory Tools in Environmental Protection

Contrary to popular belief, environmental protection legislation employs more than the tools of "command and control" regulation. During the 1970s, it is true that environmental legislation displayed a penchant for technical production standards and other tools associated with the command and control approach. Consider the new source performance standards, existing source performance standards, and automobile emission reduction mandates under the CAA; the BAT requirements under the CWA; the incinerator and hazardous waste landfill construction standards under the RCRA; and so forth. As the very first example of environmental regulation in the modern era, however, NEPA employed information provision in the form of an environmental impact statement as its only tool. Other examples of federal environmental regulation impose prohibitions (e.g., banning certain pesticides), licensing requirements (e.g., all enterprises engaged in the storage, treatment, or disposal of hazardous wastes must obtain an operating license), product quality standards (e.g., requiring that all pesticides be proven effective), and performance standards (e.g., the sulfur dioxide trading system under the 1990 CAA), and they assign property rights and liability (e.g., the sulfur dioxide trading system and the strict, joint, and several liability provision of CERCLA), as well as provide subsidies (e.g., paying the majority of construction costs for municipal wastewater treatment facilities).

In addition to this wide variety of regulatory tools, "voluntary" tools are also used in environmental protection. Voluntary environmental programs generally take one of three forms (Brouhle, Griffiths, and Wolverton

2004). First, public voluntary programs are designed by governmental enti-ties, typically to address environmental problems not currently addressed by other formal regulations. Industry is then invited to participate in these pro-grams. Most voluntary environmental programs in the United States are of this type, including Green Lights (which sought voluntary improvements in lighting energy efficiency) and 33/50 (which sought voluntary reductions in the use of toxic chemicals). Second, bilateral negotiated agreements are environmental improvement projects agreed to by government agencies and individual firms. Common in countries like the Netherlands and Japan, bilateral negotiated agreements are relatively rare in the United States, largely because the EPA does not have the discretion to customize regulato-ry requirements for individual firms or the authority to enforce such agree-ments on industry. Project XL, described later in this chapter, is an example of a bilateral negotiated agreement in the United States. Finally, unilateral commitments are industry-led initiatives to improve environmental per-formance with no governmental involvement. Examples of unilateral com-mitments are the adoption of ISO 14001 standards and the Responsible Care program of the American Chemical Council.

The EPA enacted its first public voluntary program in 1991 (Green Lights), and by 2005 the agency was managing sixty-two voluntary envi-ronmental programs (Coglianese and Nash 2005). Thomas Lyon and John Maxwell (2004) explain this rapid growth of voluntary programs during the 1990s as a function of the increasing complexity and cost of traditional reg-ulation, improvements in technology that make possible both environmental improvements in industrial production and accurate monitoring of environ-mental performance, and political opposition to the adoption of traditional regulations in these areas. Whatever the reason for their growth, voluntary environmental programs can serve as complements or substitutes for tradi-tional environmental regulations, though most research indicates that they will be most effective in a complementary role (e.g., Alberini and Segerson 2002). The overwhelming majority of these programs were created by the Clinton administration (Brouhle, Griffiths, and Wolverton 2004), and Clinton appointees generally viewed voluntary programs as complements to traditional regulatory efforts. By contrast, the George W. Bush administra-tion has created a relatively small number of voluntary environmental pro-grams (Coglianese and Nash 2005), but these programs are much more like-ly to be used as substitutes for traditional regulatory efforts. For example, the President's Climate Leaders program took the place of promised regula-tions on carbonyl sulfide emissions, while voluntary programs have been used in place of traditional regulations in controlling air pollution from con-centrated animal-feeding operations.

There have not been any significant changes to environmental statutes since the 1990 CAA amendments, and no statutory changes at all since

1996. Congress and the president have been unable to agree upon changes to the major pieces of environmental legislation, even though much of this legislation is overdue for reauthorization. Recently, the National Research Council (NRC) issued a report concluding that major environmental legislation in the United States is outdated and in need of significant revision. In particular, the NRC pointed out the need to (1) expand the use of cap-and-trade tools like those found in the 1990 CAAA, (2) integrate environmental permits and standards for large sources of pollution, (3) address the interstate transfer of pollution, and (4) control the emission of carbon dioxide and other greenhouse gasses (Revkin 2004). Given the current gridlock between advocacy coalitions in the environmental policy subsystem, however, it is unlikely that Congress will act on these NRC recommendations anytime soon.

The Environmental Protection Agency

Unlike most regulatory agencies, the EPA was neither established nor empowered by an organic act. This fact has had important consequences for agency performance. First, rather than being designed from the ground up, the EPA was pieced together in 1970 from several different offices and bureaus previously scattered across nearly a dozen different agencies. While this Frankenstein approach to administrative creation did produce a functioning agency in very short order, it also guaranteed that the agency would have problems with coordination and intra-agency conflict. For example, the original Office of Pesticide Policy was routinely criticized by other elements inside the EPA for a lack of scientific expertise and a pro-pesticide orientation that clashed with the agency's environmental mission, largely because the staff of this office were imported from their former home, the USDA. Second, because the EPA's legislative authority comes from several equally important statutes rather than a single organic act, the agency must operate without any legislative mission statement to set regulatory priorities. This is problematic because the various acts discussed above often force the agency to work at cross-purposes (e.g., using smokestack scrubbers to reduce air pollution from power plants produces thousands of tons of toxic sludge, which must be disposed of on land or in the water), or force agency personnel to compromise the goal of environmental risk reduction in pursuit of statutory obligations (e.g., CERCLA requires the EPA to spend billions of dollars cleaning up abandoned hazardous waste sites, even though many of these sites pose little threat to public health). Whereas the EPA has devised an administrative mission statement and routinely engages in strategic planning (see Figure 7.3), these actions have not resolved the difficulties and contradictions posed by the lack of an organic act.

The EPA is the nation's largest regulatory agency. For fiscal year 2006 the EPA was allotted 17,631 full-time employee positions (two-thirds of which are in the agency's ten regional offices) and a budget of $7.6 billion (EPA 2005). Both of these figures are reductions from 1998 (see Figure 7.4). The EPA is unique structurally, as it is the only regulatory agency (i.e., headed by a single person rather than a commission) that is not located in an executive branch department. The agency's structure reflects both its origin and its enabling legislation. The EPA's architects originally contemplated an agency organized into functional units (e.g., monitoring, enforcement, research). Practical considerations, however, meant that the new EPA maintained the structural division of program responsibilities as they were inherited from other agencies (e.g., an office of air pollution, water pollution, pesticides). Congress quickly passed separate environmental acts that reinforced this division, as mentioned above.

The current structure of the EPA still reflects this emphasis on media-specific program organization, with administrations for air and radiation; water; solid waste and emergency response; and prevention, pesticides, and toxic substances (see Figure 7.5). While this organizational scheme initially allowed the agency to "hit the ground running," it does not facilitate integrated environmental management. Over the past twenty years, the agency has slowly been moving toward a more integrated or functional organizational structure, as evidenced by the administrations for policy, planning, and evaluation; research and development; administration and resources management; and enforcement and compliance assurance. In addition, the agency has been working hard to improve coordination among the media-specific offices. In most cases, this coordination has been relatively informal, consisting of interoffice memoranda of understanding regarding regulatory priorities and a multioffice team-oriented approach to regulatory

---

Figure 7.3   Goals of the 2003–2008 EPA Strategic Plan

The mission of the US Environmental Protection Agency is to protect human health and the environment. To fulfill this mission, the EPA's strategic plan emphasizes the following goals:

1. Clean air and global climate change.
2. Clean and safe water.
3. Land preservation and restoration.
4. Healthy communities and ecosystems.
5. Compliance and environmental stewardship.

Source: Adapted from EPA 2003b.

Figure 7.4 The Environmental Protection Agency Budget

innovation. In a few instances, however, this interoffice coordination has been given a formal structure, as in the Office of Pollution Prevention and the Office of Environmental Justice, which are part of the Office of Enforcement and Compliance Assurance. Until and unless Congress rewrites the enabling legislation, it is unlikely that the EPA will ever abandon the media-specific offices and evolve an organizational structure completely along functional lines.

Without oversimplifying, we can organize most of the EPA's statutory responsibilities into two categories. First, the agency is responsible for developing standards and regulations to protect and improve environmental quality. Second, the agency is responsible for issuing environmental permits, inspecting facilities for compliance with these permits, and sanctioning facilities for permit noncompliance. These two responsibilities require different types of expertise. In carrying out its first policy responsibility, the EPA relies heavily on leading-edge research in the natural sciences, engineering, and epidemiology. In carrying out its second policy responsibility, the agency requires substantial engineering expertise, as well as legal expertise. Thus the EPA follows a dual-track system of personnel recruitment: the agency aggressively recruits scientists, engineers, and economists to fulfill its first policy responsibility, while it employs attorneys and engineers to carry out the second set of responsibilities. Faithful execution of program responsibilities in these two areas requires different regulatory

Figure 7.5 The Environmental Protection Agency

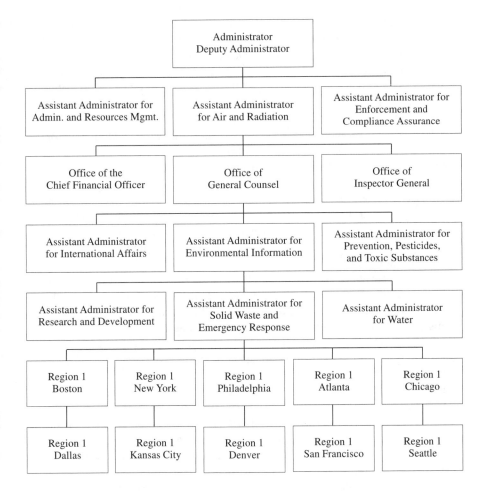

emphases and professional criteria and values. These differences inevitably have led to some tensions between personnel carrying out the scientific missions of the agency, and those carrying out the legal missions (see Marcus 1980b).

On the surface, the professional friction among EPA personnel may look very similar to the disagreements between economists and attorneys observed in Chapter 4. Closer examination, however, reveals that the professional schisms within the EPA are not nearly as severe as those within the Antitrust Division of the Department of Justice. First, the scientists at the EPA do not decide which violations of environmental law will be prosecuted. Second, civil and criminal violations of environmental statutes are rarely prosecuted by EPA attorneys, but are instead prosecuted by attorneys in the DOJ's Environment and Natural Resources Division. Thus, in enforcement and litigation, environmental scientists are typically limited to technical support to EPA and Justice Department attorneys. Third, attorneys and scientists within the EPA do not bicker over regulatory priorities, since these priorities, such as they are, are set into legislation by Congress (often to the chagrin of both scientists and attorneys). Finally, unlike the antitrust case, the EPA has faced no political pressure to elevate one group to preeminence or relegate another to oblivion. In short, although scientists, attorneys, and economists within the EPA may not always agree, they have not been forced to compete for policy influence, nor has any group been threatened with obsolescence.

Early in the EPA's history, the agency's personnel—scientists and attorneys alike—had a reputation for being environmental zealots. Over time, however, the "character" of EPA personnel has changed from zealotry to a position more akin to advocacy (a transformation common in many new agencies; see Downs 1967). While such a position is at odds with the norm of the "neutral bureaucrat," it is not inconsistent with the position of the EPA's founders that the agency itself was to take a strong advocacy position vis-à-vis the environment. Two factors have helped the agency to preserve this sense of mission among its personnel. First, as much as for any agency in the federal government, for the EPA the pool of potential personnel is shaped by self-selection. Professionals with strong environmental sensibilities are attracted to the advocacy stance of the agency, while others without such sensibilities rarely consider the agency as a potential career option. This self-selection process hardly deprives the EPA of high-quality applicants, since the environmental goals of the agency mesh easily with the training and professional values of the scientific disciplines from which the agency is seeking to recruit. Second, the EPA has a well-developed system of staff education whereby agency personnel are required to attend classes and seminars emphasizing the EPA's approach to environmental protection. Recently, these educational efforts have emphasized integrated environmental management, pollution prevention, environmental justice, and collaboration with industry in seeking "beyond compliance" corporate behavior (i.e., practices that accomplish more than what would have been accomplished under traditional regulation).

Agency Implementation Structure

Personnel at EPA headquarters in Washington, D.C., focus most of their attention on research and development (though the agency does have research centers in Massachusetts, Minnesota, North Carolina, and elsewhere), regulatory development and rule making, representing the agency in court proceedings, and policy coordination. Headquarters personnel are responsible for almost none of the day-to-day implementation of existing environmental regulation. Instead, this work is carried out by the EPA's ten regional offices and by the states.

State governments in general and state environmental agencies in particular are arguably the most important actors in administering environmental regulations, because of two provisions of environmental statutes. First, many environmental statutes include partial preemption provisions. Under partial preemption, states can take over responsibility for administering environmental programs simply by demonstrating to the EPA that the state programs meet federal minimum requirements. If state performance under primacy ever falls below these minimum requirements, the EPA is authorized to take back policy responsibility from the state. In practice, however, this rarely happens, since the agency does not have the resources to replace even a substandard state effort (e.g., state agencies complete anywhere from three to ten times the number of inspection and enforcement actions as does the EPA). Second, almost all environmental statutes allow states to substitute stronger state environmental standards for federal standards. States are then responsible for meeting these standards.

At first blush, one may wonder why any state would voluntarily spend more money and accept more regulatory responsibility in the area of environmental protection. After all, aggressive regulatory efforts may deter businesses from locating to or expanding within the state, much of the benefits of pollution control regulation accrue to states that are downwind or downstream, and the federal government will regulate polluters if the state does not act. Once a state accepts primacy, however, the EPA pays a significant portion of the costs of administering these programs ($1.2 billion in fiscal year 2006). Moreover, increased state responsibility translates into increased state authority and control over how the law is administered in any particular state. Primacy does not guarantee complete autonomy; state actions are overseen by the relevant EPA regional office. And while most states would like more regulatory autonomy under primacy (Scheberle 1998), most are willing to accept this trade-off.

Even those states that accept primacy often seek help for the largest and most difficult regulatory violations. This is where the EPA's regional offices excel. In addition to monitoring state actions, the regional offices issue permits, inspect facilities, and sanction facilities for noncompliance. Furthermore, all cases in which the EPA seeks civil or criminal penalties against violators must travel through the regional offices. In a typical case, attorneys at the EPA's regional offices begin civil proceedings against a violator only after informal negotiations and an escalating series of administrative remedies have failed to produce compliance. Traditionally, all civil case referrals had to be forwarded from the regional offices to EPA headquarters. Beginning in 1983, however, procedures were changed so that now most case referrals bypass EPA headquarters (EPA 1988). The EPA rarely brings suit to force compliance with environmental protection statutes, and once a suit is filed the EPA faces powerful incentives to avoid taking the suit to trial. As a result of these pressures, roughly 90 percent of all civil penalty cases have been settled through consent decrees between the EPA and the violators (Ringquist and Emmert 1999). Finally, EPA regional offices are encouraged to develop innovative regulatory programs designed to address environmental problems that are especially severe in their area of the country.

The Policy Subsystem

The complexity of the policy tasks in environmental protection would seem to pose substantial barriers to entry for most policymakers, leading to a relatively closed and insular policy subsystem. But as noted at the outset of this chapter, the salience of the policy area, coupled with the economic impact of these regulations, means that the policy subsystem is actually quite open. Initially, environmental protection was described as a completely new type of policy area, unaffected by traditional ideological divisions between left and right. Since the goal of environmental protection was essentially public-good provision, it was assumed that policymaking in this area would be relatively uncontentious and bipartisan. While this may have been a reasonably good description of the environmental policy subsystem in the early 1970s, these characteristics dissipated in less than a decade. Today there exists a mature environmental policy subsystem characterized by contentious and often intensely partisan debates between two competing advocacy coalitions divided by traditional ideological core beliefs. In addition to the consistently aligned participants, other groups, such as labor unions and state and local governments, often ally with one or the other advocacy coalition, depending on the issue at hand.

The *environmental quality* advocacy coalition, made up of actors whose belief systems revolve around a core that values environmental purity, represents the liberal side of the policy subsystem. Though environmental groups still make up the largest bloc of players in the environmental quality advocacy coalition (the ten largest groups had 7.8 million members in 1995 [Bosso 1997]), they can no longer be seen as a unified force. The environmental movement has matured and diversified to include large, multi-issue groups (the Sierra Club); smaller, more narrowly focused "purist" groups (Friends of the Earth); nonpartisan research and policy development centers (Resources for the Future); "radical" deep ecology groups (Earth First!);

and increasingly active independent state and local groups (Clean Water Action) (Bosso 1994). While groups share certain core values, they display a dazzling variety of policy positions and tactics.

Other actors have joined the environmental quality advocacy coalition over the past twenty years. The coalition historically has had strong advocates in Congress, and sometimes in the White House. Certain industrial groups, such as the insurance, waste disposal, and pollution control equipment companies, have also adopted a more proenvironmental stance. As evidence mounted regarding stratospheric ozone depletion, global warming, and the immunological and reproductive effects of certain toxic pollutants, large sections of the scientific community also joined the environmental quality camp. Finally, significant numbers of social scientists and civil rights activists have allied themselves with the coalition, as it has become more receptive to the concerns of economic efficiency and potential racial and class biases in environmental regulation.

At the other end of the ideological spectrum we find the *economic rationality* advocacy coalition, whose participants' belief systems reflect a core that values unfettered private enterprise. Much as environmental groups are still major players in the environmental quality advocacy coalition, industrial groups continue to dominate the economic rationality coalition. While players may have remained the same, the names and the tactics have not. During the early 1970s, industry relied heavily on umbrella groups and trade associations. As this strategy proved generally ineffective, industry moved toward reliance on lobbying by individual corporations. The late 1980s and early 1990s saw another shift: industrial coalitions setting up nonprofit corporations to lobby for regulatory change. These organizations benefit from a broad base, deep pockets, and names that invoke thoughts of civic-mindedness (e.g., the National Wetlands Coalition includes real estate, petroleum, and natural gas industries, while the National Endangered Species Act Reform Coalition was organized by electric utility and agribusiness firms) (Carney 1992). Similar to the environmental advocacy coalition, the economic rationality coalition has advocates in Congress and, sporadically, in the White House.

Two of the most interesting changes in the economic rationality advocacy coalition have been the remarkable increases in industry-supported conservative policy think tanks (e.g., the Heritage Foundation) and antienvironmental grassroots interest groups. Think tanks were nonentities twenty-five years ago, but with the increasing importance of analysis in policy debates, they now play a significant role in environmental regulation (Sabatier and Jenkins-Smith 1993; Smith 2000). An example of an antienvironmental grassroots organization is the 250 or so interest groups that march under the "Wise Use" banner, who run the gamut from true populist organizations made up of ranchers and four-wheel-drive enthusiasts, to public relations fronts for the timber, fossil fuel, and mining industries. What the groups share is a grassroots lobbying style, a sense that environmental regulation has gone too far, and an emphasis on the protection of private property rights.

Executive-Legislative
Interactions in Environmental Regulation

The president and Congress routinely clash over environmental regulation. This has been true since the beginning of the modern environmental era, when President Nixon created the EPA (largely ignoring congressional input regarding the structure of the agency) and when Congress crafted legislation empowering and directing agency activity (largely ignoring presidential wishes and, in a few instances, overriding presidential vetoes). The actions of the EPA are so central to the public's perception of governmental performance (a by-product of issue salience) and business concerns regarding economic performance that both actors still clash over the direction of environmental policy. One might chalk up this high degree of interinstitutional conflict to divided government, since party control of Congress and the presidency has been split for twenty-seven of the EPA's thirty-five year history. Divided government does not provide a full explanation for executive-legislative combat, however, since this conflict continued during periods of unified government. In a sense, the EPA is expected to serve two masters: Congress and the president.

Presidents have attempted to influence environmental regulation through administrative appointments, executive orders, budgetary requests, legislative initiatives, bureaucratic reorganizations, and the centralization of regulatory clearance. These tools have hardly been used solely in the pursuit of protecting the environment, however. While presidential interest in environmental regulation has been constant since 1970, presidential support of environmental regulation has been more sporadic. More often than not, presidents intervene in environmental regulation to advance specific environmental and economic policy goals rather than to articulate a broad vision for environmental protection (Shanley 1992). In doing so, presidents have allied themselves with different advocacy coalitions. The weight of the Nixon and Ford administrations was not lined up behind either of the advocacy coalitions in the environmental policy subsystem, largely because the subsystem itself was still in flux and advocacy coalitions had yet to become well defined. Subsequent presidents, however, have clearly associated themselves with one of the two advocacy coalitions: Reagan and both George H. W. Bush and George W. Bush with the forces of economic rationality, and Carter and Clinton with the forces of environmental quality.

Congress takes pride in exercising leadership in environmental regulation. While the EPA is generally more comfortable serving its congressional master, serving even this one master can be extraordinarily difficult and has become more difficult over time. To begin, congressional support for environmental regulation comes at the price of high levels of oversight. In addition to unusually specific legislative requirements, the agency is subject to so much oversight that the Government Accountability Office, the investigative arm of Congress, once maintained a permanent branch office at EPA headquarters.

Party positions with respect to environmental protection have diverged over time, with Democrats becoming more supportive of environmental protection while similar support has eroded among Republicans (Lowry and Shipan 1997). Currently, the parties are more polarized than ever over environmental regulation. The League of Conservation Voters (LCV) evaluates each member of Congress with respect to their support for environmental legislation, assigning scores ranging from 0 (perfect opposition) to 100 (perfect support). In 2004 the average LCV score for House Republicans was 10, while for House Democrats it was 86. In the Senate, Republicans averaged a score of 8, while Democrats averaged 85. The Republican leadership of key environmental committees in Congress is even less supportive of environmental protection than is the rank and file. In 2004 the chair of the House Energy and Commerce Committee, Joe Barton (R-TX), had an LCV score of 0, as did the chair of the House Resources Committee, Richard Pombo (R-CA), and the chair of the Senate Environment and Public Works Committee, James Inhofe (R-OK). Inhofe has gone so far as to say that global warming is a hoax, and that EPA should become a service agency for citizens and industry, rather than a regulatory agency (Kriz 2003).

Environmental support in Congress also varies substantially across regions, placing distinctly different political pressures on EPA regional offices (Kamieniecki 1995). Finally, the EPA must implement statutes that are crafted by several different congressional committees. This means that EPA bureaucrats must respond to the priorities and values of these different committees. While congressional criticism of EPA performance is constant and sometimes severe, many experts trace the problems to congressional actions themselves (i.e., the lack of an organic act, a lack of legislative priorities, overlapping committee jurisdictions and regulatory deadlines, and increasing regulatory responsibilities accompanied by a shrinking budget [NAPA 1995]).

The congressional environment within which the EPA operates changed radically after the 1994 midterm elections. For the first time, the agency faced a Congress where both chambers were controlled by a Republican majority largely hostile to the mission of the EPA. In addition, the House and, to a lesser degree, the Senate changed their committee structures, disrupting long-standing congressional-bureaucratic relationships. This restructuring did little to rationalize responsibility for environmental protection in Congress, however. At least six committees in the House of Representatives have significant jurisdiction over environmental issues—most notably the Commerce Committee and the Resources Committee—while at least five Senate committees share policy responsibility in this area, chief among them the Environment and Public Works Committee.

The Courts

As stated above, the EPA must pursue civil and criminal penalties against violators through the federal district court system. Moreover, several environmental statutes empower citizens and interest groups to act as "private attorneys general," in essence giving these actors the right to sue firms for noncompliance with environmental regulation. In addition, the appellate courts and the Supreme Court rule on the statutory fidelity and constitutionality of EPA rules and regulatory decisions. In these instances, the courts are called in to determine what the law is and how it should be enforced. In fulfilling this role, courts affect EPA behavior in three important ways. First, court decisions may set or reshape agency priorities, forcing the agency to undertake actions it might not have taken on its own. Second, court decisions can redefine the relationship between the EPA and other agencies. For example, in 1984 a federal district court determined that Department of Energy facilities were required to apply for EPA permits under the RCRA and the CWA (in *Legal Environmental Assistance Foundation v. Hodel* 1984). Third, court decisions can affect the manner in which the EPA reaches regulatory decisions. In several cases, courts have criticized the EPA for failing to rely on adequate scientific and economic analysis in crafting regulations (Fiorino 1995; Melnick 1983). Moreover, these avenues for court influence are not simply hypothetical, as James Spriggs (1997) showed that the EPA invariably changes its regulatory approach in reaction to federal court decisions.

Early in the modern environmental era, environmentalists scored many of their most important victories in the federal courts. Changes in the policymaking environment, however, have not left the courts unaffected. At the federal district court level, partisan differences have significant effects on the enforcement of environmental regulations. In their study of judicial civil penalties in environmental protection cases, Evan Ringquist and Craig Emmert (1999) found that, all other things being equal, federal judges appointed by Republican presidents levy smaller fines than do their Democratic counterparts. Similarly, the practice of appointing particularly conservative judges carried out by Presidents Reagan and Bush means that the courts are much less supportive of environmental regulation than was true in the 1970s (Kovacic 1991). Finally, charges that federal environmental regulations infringe on private property rights are increasingly being upheld by the US Claims Court, resulting in hundreds of millions of dollars in claims against the federal government for enforcing these regulations (Wenner 1997). In short, while the courts continue to be a central player in environmental policy, their role has changed substantially over time.

The Evolution of Environmental Regulation, 1970–Present

Environmental Regulation in the 1970s: Federal and Environmental Dominance

By 1970, public opinion polls showed that environmental protection was the most frequently cited public problem (Anderson, Brady, and Bullock 1977). Although Americans were still generally ignorant regarding the economic costs or technological complexity of environmental regulation, it was clear to the public that something had to be done. Political activity during this period was remarkably unified behind increased environmental protection. Congress fired the first shot in the war for the hearts and minds of environmentalists by passing the National Environmental Policy Act. Over the next several years, Congress enacted eighteen pieces of new or significantly revised environmental protection legislation. Unwilling to abdicate policy leadership in this area to Congress, Nixon consolidated all pollution control efforts in the new EPA and promoted several legislative initiatives of his own (though he vetoed the Clean Water Act).

President Nixon's nominee as the first EPA administrator, William Ruckelshaus, willingly assumed the mantle of environmental advocate and aggressively enforced environmental regulations. Ruckelshaus believed that suing violators in court was the most effective way to establish the new agency's credibility among polluters and the public. Ruckelshaus was followed at the EPA by Russell Train, a past president of the Conservation Foundation (a moderate environmental group). Train continued Ruckelshaus's legal approach to environmental regulation while cultivating an increased role for scientific research and analysis in the agency. President Carter's EPA administrator, Douglas Costle, radically altered the direction of the agency. In an effort to boost public support for the agency and provide it with additional political staying power, Costle attempted to recast the EPA as a public health agency, with limited success (Landy, Roberts, and Thomas 1994). Though each of these administrators employed different approaches in implementing environmental regulations, the 1970s established the norm of appointing committed environmental advocates to lead the EPA. One might argue that, during this period, the courts prodded the EPA to pursue environmental protection more aggressively than even EPA administrators were comfortable with, by preventing the significant deterioration of air quality (*Sierra Club v. Ruckelshaus* 1972), prohibiting dilution as a mechanism for reducing ambient pollution levels around power plants (*National Resources Defense Council v. Environmental Protection Agency* 1974a), and limiting the agency's ability to provide variances to facilities unable to comply with their pollution control permits (*National Resources Defense Council v. Environmental Protection Agency* 1973, 1974b; but see also *National Resources Defense Council v. Environmental Protection Agency* 1974c and *Train v. National Resources Defense Council* 1975).

The first rush of statutory activity during the 1970s was followed by a period of moderate retrenchment. Three factors account for this regulatory retrenchment. First, the energy crises of the 1970s placed significant strain on industries trying to reduce pollution by changing to newer, cleaner, and rarer fuels. Moreover, increased energy costs exacerbated the economic impact of the new regulations. Second, the public began to recognize the costs and difficulty associated with significant environmental progress, so public support for environmental protection dropped somewhat. Third, the forces making up the economic rationality advocacy coalition finally coalesced to pressure the federal government for regulatory relief. These developments set the stage for an entirely different era of environmental regulation in the 1980s.

Which of the three theories discussed in Chapter 2 best explain regulatory policy activity in environmental protection during the 1970s—the bureaucratic politics, subsystems, or principal-agent perspective? Elected officials obviously played an important role in regulatory decisionmaking, mostly by enacting legislation. This sort of legislative activity is unavoidable, however. Agencies can do next to nothing until they are given the statutory authority to act. Once Congress passed environmental laws, it largely stayed out of the way. To begin, the legislation itself gave broad grants of discretion to the EPA when it came to setting standards for environmental quality, devising technical standards for pollution control, and approving state implementation efforts. Moreover, the EPA experienced relatively little congressional pressure or interference when setting NAAQS, BAT standards, and the like. Additionally, the agency was able to undertake several important regulatory initiatives on its own, including a major source enforcement initiative under the CWA that dramatically increased the number of civil suits filed against polluters and the amount of fines collected by the agency (Ringquist 1995).

Three factors help explain the triumph of bureaucratic politics over principal-agent theory with respect to environmental regulation in the 1970s. First, the policy area was so new that opponents of environmental regulation had not had time to mount an effective countermobilization—either politically or scientifically—to the environmental movement (here, we see the importance of technical complexity). Second and related, the environmental quality advocacy coalition was much better developed and had a great deal of public support. In a sense, then, a friendly dominant advocacy coalition protected agency autonomy within the environmental policy subsystem. Third, one cannot discuss the early actions of the EPA without discussing the agency's first leader, Ruckelshaus. Ruckelshaus's aggressive enforcement campaigns gave the fledgling agency a legitimacy it might have otherwise lacked. Moreover, Ruckelshaus had excellent political credentials that provided the agency with critical external support. Finally, Ruckelshaus largely adopted the "mission" orientation of most EPA bureaucrats, which allowed him to be an effective manager. We want to be careful not to overplay the role of bureaucratic politics in explaining environmental regulation during the 1970s. Certainly, early Supreme Court decisions placed boundaries on agency discretion, while public and congressional support for agency actions eroded somewhat as the decade progressed. Still, our view is that the bureaucratic politics perspective provides the most complete explanation of environmental regulation during this era.

Environmental Regulation Under Reagan: Deregulation, Devolution, and Defunding

The economic rationality advocacy coalition had regrouped and expanded during the late 1970s. Industry and think tank analysts painted regulation in general and environmental regulation in particular as the cause of much of the economic hardship of the decade (MacAvoy 1979; Weidenbaum 1981). In addition, they seized on the perceived shortcomings of technology-forced regulation and missed legislative deadlines as evidence that environmental regulation was misguided. In short, the coalition argued that environmental regulation was technologically unfeasible and economically ruinous.

Changes in the broader political environment also effected change in environmental regulation. Opinion polls showed a dip in public support for environmental protection (Dunlap 1995). The electoral consequences of the economic and ideological changes of the late 1970s were that the Republican Party took control of the Senate for the first time in a generation, a coalition of Republicans and conservative Democrats established a working majority in the House of Representatives, and Ronald Reagan was elected president on an antiregulation platform. To carry out his agenda in environmental policy, President Reagan set out on a three-pronged strategy: deregulation, devolution, and defunding.

When President Reagan was unsuccessful in reducing the scope of environmental regulation through statute (his efforts to rewrite environmental laws were rebuffed by Congress), he adopted an administrative strategy aimed at the same goal. First, Reagan reduced the EPA's constant dollar budget 56 percent between 1979 and 1983 (Ringquist 1993). Second, the president appointed Anne Gorsuch-Burford as EPA administrator, the first nonenvironmentalist to head the agency. Gorsuch-Burford supported the president's budgetary requests, crippled the EPA's enforcement apparatus, and stressed voluntary compliance with pollution laws—all radical departures from the strategies of her predecessors. The president's third tactic in deregulation was Executive Order 12291, which required federal agencies to submit proposed regulations to the Office of Management and Budget for cost-benefit analysis. The EPA was singled out for particularly close attention in the implementation of EO 12291; over half of the agency's proposed regulations were rejected or revised, and several cost-benefit analyses were manipulated for admittedly political ends in an effort to scuttle environmental regulations (Smith 1984).

The second prong of President Reagan's approach to environmental regulation was devolving policy authority to state governments. In doing this, the administration served the dual goals of reducing the reach of the federal government and returning policy responsibility to a level of government historically less supportive of environmental protection. Throughout the 1970s the EPA had been reluctant to grant primacy for environmental regulations to state governments. But from 1981 to 1984 the delegation of environmental programs to the states accelerated rapidly. As the federal government devolved more responsibility to the states, however, it simultaneously slashed federal contributions to these programs. From 1979 to 1988, federal support for state air pollution control programs fell by 54 percent, and support for state water pollution control programs declined by 68 percent (CBO 1988). By the 1980s, however, state governments had experienced a remarkable transformation with respect to the stability of their financial resources, the capacity of their legislatures, and the professionalism of their administrative agencies (Van Horn 1992). Thus, most states were well equipped to shoulder additional responsibilities in pollution control, and several had become hotbeds of regulatory innovation (Lowry 1992; Ringquist 1993).

The EPA's reaction to Reagan's deregulatory initiatives was threefold. First, agency activity and enforcement levels dropped dramatically (Davies 1984; Wood 1988). Second, morale dropped precipitously (Gottron 1982). The agency's third reaction was to fight back. Internal documents were leaked to friendly members of Congress and the press to counter Gorsuch-Burford's actions (Davies 1984). Congressional investigations precipitated by these leaks uncovered numerous improprieties in the hazardous waste program at the EPA. Subsequently, over twenty EPA officials were dismissed, and Gorsuch-Burford was held in contempt of Congress, eventually resigning in March 1983 (Vig and Kraft 1984). Reagan recouped some of his losses in the Gorsuch-Burford affair by reappointing Ruckelshaus to head the EPA. Within months, he was credited with operating an open management process and restoring agency morale (Mosher 1983).

President Reagan's second term was much less eventful with respect to environmental regulation. First, Reagan appointed Lee Thomas, a career civil servant, as the first nonattorney to lead the EPA. Thomas won generally high marks for his tenure at the agency, which featured a return to emphasizing ecological science in setting EPA priorities and a new emphasis on addressing global environmental problems (Landy, Roberts, and Thomas 1994). Next, Reagan largely abandoned efforts to reduce the EPA's budget any further. Finally, Congress belatedly reasserted its leadership in environmental protection by enacting important amendments to CERCLA and the CWA, the latter over President Reagan's veto.

A concerted effort at redirecting environmental regulation through principal-agent-type relationships was mounted during Reagan's terms as president. The president himself was no environmentalist, and his enmity toward environmental regulation was supported by a Republican-controlled Senate and his first EPA administrator. These top-down controls on EPA activity were quite successful; during the early 1980s, EPA enforcement actions dropped by 30–50 percent, depending on the particular regulatory program (Wood 1988; Wood and Waterman 1991; Ringquist 1995). Moreover, the pace of issuing regulations at the EPA dropped dramatically under EO 12291 and the intense scrutiny these regulations received from the OMB.

Many of the effects of this principal-agent offensive were short-lived, however. Regulatory activity levels at the agency returned to previous levels not long after Gorsuch-Burford left office, and the pace of issuing regulations picked up as well during Reagan's second term as president. The temporary nature of these effects can be explained by three factors. First, the changes were largely administrative since Reagan was unable to change environmental statutes. This fact alone made it more likely that the changes would not outlast his administration. Second, these efforts at environmental retrenchment mobilized marginal supporters of the EPA to enter the policy subsystem in defense of the agency at the same time they produced a ground swell of public support for environmental protection. In this vein, legislation passed by Congress during this period contained extraordinarily detailed instructions and tight deadlines for the EPA. While these requirements substantially reduced agency autonomy when compared with earlier legislation, Congress did this largely to thwart administrative efforts to slow down the EPA. In effect, Congress countered the principal-oriented actions of President Reagan by acting as a principal in its own right, presenting the EPA with conflicting requirements from multiple principals. Finally, the actions of Reagan and Gorsuch-Burford provoked sabotaging behavior on the part of EPA bureaucrats; for example, leaking documents and other information to the press and administration opponents and encouraging environmental groups to bring suits against polluters where the agency had lost the resources to do so on its own (Ringquist 1995). Thus, while principal-agent theory provides a good way of understanding environmental regulation during the first few years of the Reagan presidency, subsystem politics rapidly returned the policymaking system to something close to a pre-Reagan equilibrium point.

President George H. W. Bush
and the Environment: Reagan Redux?

A number of focusing events in the 1980s turned public attention back toward the need for environmental regulation. The 1986 accident at the Chernobyl nuclear power plant in Ukraine; the 1987 accident at the Union Carbide chemical plant in Bhopal, India; the 1989 grounding of the *Exxon Valdez* in Prince William Sound; growing evidence of global warming and stratospheric ozone depletion in the late 1980s—these and other events helped push public support for environmental regulation to an all-time high by 1990 (Dunlap and Scarce 1991).

Changes in the economic and technological aspects of the regulatory environment also helped to create conditions conducive to increased environmental regulation. First, research had demonstrated that the negative economic effects of environmental regulation had been significantly overstated (CBO 1985; EPA 1991). Second, a long period of economic expansion made citizens more willing to accept whatever economic costs might be associated with increased regulation. Third, many of the technical problems with pollution control equipment had been solved by the 1980s, and there was mounting evidence that this equipment had both reduced pollution emissions and improved environmental quality (CEQ 1989). These factors provided bridges for cooperation between the environmental and economic advocacy coalitions that simply could not have existed earlier.

For example, a number of environmental groups began to listen to what economists had been saying for years: that traditional command and control regulations were a less efficient way of protecting environmental quality than were economic incentive approaches. Consequently, the Environmental Defense Fund and Resources for the Future became strong proponents of emission fees and tradable discharge permits (Kriz 1992b). On the other hand, industry began to realize that, in many instances, pollution represents productive inefficiency and that a facility could lower costs and increase profits by reducing pollution. These alterations in the positions of advocacy coalitions in response to experience and evidence are excellent examples of how policy learning takes place within subsystems (Sabatier and Jenkins-Smith 1993).

This spirit of compromise was reflected in the political arena as well. When George H. W. Bush ran for president in 1988, one of the critical issues he chose to distinguish himself from his predecessor was environmental protection. Bush promised, in fact, to be the "environmental president." The new president followed up on this promise by appointing William Reilly, then president of the Conservation Foundation and a respected environmentalist, as EPA administrator. Bush also began to restore the EPA's budget, though in real terms the 1992 budget was still barely half as large as it had been in 1978. In the policy sphere, Bush oversaw US participation in the international phase-out of chlorofluorocarbons and helped craft the first reauthorization of the Clean Air Act in thirteen years.

Despite these actions, the Bush administration was not an unqualified friend of the environment. While Bush appointed Reilly at the EPA, he appointed recognized "antienvironmentalists" to other important environmental positions within his administration—most notably Manuel Lujan at the Interior Department. Moreover, Bush continued Reagan's pattern of appointing federal judges more in tune with industrial and development interests than with environmental protection. Cracks in the uneasy alliance of advocacy coalitions in environmental regulation began to appear in 1990, soon after President Bush signed the CAA amendments. First, Bush proposed redefining wetlands in such a way that half of all remaining wetlands would have lost federal protection, a clear violation of his "no net loss of wetlands" campaign pledge (Huth 1992). Next, a presidential commission compromised the Endangered Species Act by allowing clear-cutting in the habitat of the northern spotted owl. Following in close succession were actions that allowed polluters to exceed emission limits for toxic pollutants without public notice or comment; the proposed elimination of public hearings and court challenges to oil, coal, gas, mineral, and timber sales and leases on public lands; and the weakening of several elements of the 1990 CAA. Many of these proposals emerged from the President's Council on Competitiveness, chaired by Vice President Dan Quayle. The commission, holding most of its meetings in closed session, solicited information from industry to identify excessive compliance costs as well as regulations that could be rolled back. Critics charged that this was the strongest assault on environmental regulations since Reagan's first term (Battaile 1992; Waxman 1992).

President Bush learned several good lessons from his predecessor, one of which was the counterproductive effects of a principal-agent approach to rolling back environmental regulations (though he did impose a temporary moratorium on issuing any new regulations). On the other hand, opponents of environmental regulation were too well organized and the policy subsystem in this area was too well developed to allow a return to the degree of agency autonomy present in the 1970s. Congress had learned a few lessons from the Reagan experience as well, not the least of which was that it could not always trust an EPA controlled by the opposing party to aggressively carry out legislative directions. For this reason, the 1990 CAA required the EPA to manage the nearly impossible task of writing fifty-five new regulations in two years. Overall, Congress placed over a hundred separate deadlines into the act (Rosenbaum 1994).

The most notable effort of the Bush administration with respect to our three theories of regulatory behavior was the attempt to set up a "shadow subsystem," in the form of the President's Council on Competitiveness, to reshape environmental regulation. For a time, this shadow subsystem effectively altered regulatory activity and derailed attempts by the EPA and others to implement the requirements of the 1990 CAA amendments. In the long run, however, the environmental quality coalition once again asserted itself and was able to return responsibility for policymaking back to the EPA. During the Bush administration, then, we see a slightly different version of principal-agent direction being displaced by the more enduring subsystems approach to regulatory decisionmaking.

Environmental Regulation in the Clinton Administration
The election of "New Democrat" Bill Clinton as president and avowed environmentalist Al Gore as vice president elated members of the environmental quality advocacy coalition (and enraged their opponents). The 1990s produced two trends in environmental regulation: legislative efforts aimed at rewriting environmental statutes, and administrative efforts aimed at reshaping the implementation of environmental laws. While these trends stemmed from different core values and often conflicted, they shared a common dissatisfaction with the regulatory status quo.

Redefining environmental regulation through legislation: Congress vs. Clinton.
During his first two years in office, President Clinton exerted little leadership in environmental regulation. While Clinton appointed environmental advocates Carol Browner as EPA chief and Bruce Babbitt as secretary of interior, the new administration found it difficult to articulate a clear environmental agenda. Clinton's vacillation on environmental issues ended with the midterm elections of 1994, which returned control of both houses of Congress to the Republicans for the first time in forty years. Within this new political reality, President Clinton defined an environmental agenda largely in opposition to the efforts of the new Congress.

Republican victories in the 1994 elections had two extraordinary consequences for environmental regulation. First, Republicans controlled all congressional oversight committees for the first time in the environmental era. Over the previous twenty-five years, EPA officials had built an uneasy yet predictable relationship with the majority Democrats on these committees. In fact, the agency relied on these committees for protection and support during the Reagan and George H. W. Bush administrations. Now, these traditional interinstitutional relationships were dissolved, and environmental regulators faced oversight committees stacked with lawmakers generally hostile to environmental protection.

Given the conflict in core values between EPA officials and their new legislative overseers, the situation was ripe for Congress to attempt some sort of principal-agent control over the agency. This situation led to the second consequence of the 1994 elections for environmental regulation. In a broad legislative initiative, Congress proposed far-reaching reforms of the CAA, the CWA, the Safe Drinking Water Act, the Endangered Species Act, and CERCLA, and it sought a year-long moratorium on new environmental regulations (Cushman 1995). In addition, the House passed the Risk Assessment and Cost-Benefit Analysis Act, part of the Republicans' "Contract with America," which would have required the EPA to complete comprehensive risk and cost-benefit analyses for all regulatory activities (Wildavsky 1996). Finally, committees in both the House and the Senate reported out bills that would have required the federal government to compensate owners whose property values were reduced by environmental regulations. On the one hand, supporters of these bills emphasized that they simply protected citizens' rights against the taking of private property for public use guaranteed by the Fifth Amendment. On the other hand, opponents—noting that corporations are citizens in the eyes of the law—feared that these bills would allow polluters to sue the government to recoup the costs of complying with environmental regulations. According to EPA administrator Browner, these regulatory reform bills would "undermine every single environmental and public health standard in the country" (Kraft 1997: 119).

Widespread opposition to these environmental initiatives prevented them from passing both houses of Congress. On the heels of these defeats, however, congressional Republicans employed alternative strategies to roll back environmental regulations. Members of the House attached a number of riders (unrelated amendments) to spending bills. These riders attempted, among other things, to cut the EPA's budget by one-third, ban the EPA from protecting wetlands, prevent the Interior Department from identifying and protecting new endangered species, and prevent the EPA from enforcing certain provisions of the CAA and the CWA. Rather than acquiesce to congressional demands, President Clinton vetoed these spending bills, contributing to the government shutdowns of 1996 (Kriz 1996a).

All told, Congress enjoyed little success in its campaign to significantly revise federal environmental legislation in 1995–1996. Congress and the president were able to agree, however, on a few less ambitious changes to current environmental law. For example, Congress passed legislation allowing homebuilders and real estate developers to bypass local zoning boards and state courts and sue directly in federal court if zoning ordinances or other regulations reduce the value of their properties (Freedman 1997f), and Congress and the president were able to agree on revisions to the Safe Drinking Water Act.

Reinventing environmental regulation through administrative change. Beginning in 1995, Congress attempted to weaken environmental statutes and sent clear signals that it expected the EPA to change the way it implemented these statutes in order to reduce the regulatory burden on businesses and property owners. Principal-agent theory would predict that the EPA would heed such clear signals. While the EPA did implement several initiatives in the late 1990s, few were consistent with congressional directives. First, in late 1996 the EPA publicized its intention to significantly tighten air quality standards for ozone and suspended particulates. After substantial deliberation, Clinton endorsed the EPA proposals. The case for more stringent standards was hardly clear-cut. Proponents of the tighter regulations claimed that the new particulate standard alone could avoid 64,000 premature deaths each year, but opponents noted that air quality was currently better than at any time in the previous thirty years. Even the EPA's own science advisory board suggested a range of regulatory options, from which the agency chose some of the most stringent. Congressional reaction was swift. Republicans claimed that the new regulations were not scientifically justified (though the scientific basis for the new standards was stronger than for most previous standards) and introduced legislation requiring the EPA to establish scientific certainty before issuing new regulations. Even congressional Democrats and traditional Democratic constituents (labor unions and big-city mayors) opposed the new regulations. John Dingell (D-MI), chair of the House Energy and Commerce Committee, pronounced the new regulations "asinine" and, along with several cosponsors, introduced a bill imposing a four-year moratorium while more scientific study was completed (Freedman 1997b, 1997d, 1997g).

Second, EPA officials played a prominent role in the US delegation to the 1997 global warming conference in Kyoto, Japan. At the conference, President Clinton pledged that the United States would reduce its emissions of greenhouse gases 7 percent below 1990 levels by 2012, a 15 percent reduction from current levels and a 40 percent reduction from projected levels for 2012. The Senate, however, took no action to ratify US participation in the Kyoto accords, largely because of strong Republican opposition to any global warming treaty, particularly among the leaders of environmental oversight committees in the Senate (Freedman 1997e, 1997g).

Perhaps the most important changes regarding environmental regulations at the EPA centered on Gore's "reinventing government" initiative, launched in March 1995. This initiative applied new principles of public management within federal bureaucracies with the goal of providing a government that "worked better and cost less." In general, regulatory reinvention at EPA sought to increase the flexibility of regulations, to increase the participation of business in designing and implementing these regulations, reduce paperwork and administrative delays, and improve access to environmental information. The program eventually included nearly sixty reinvention initiatives.

Two initiatives might help illustrate regulatory reinvention at EPA. First, with Project XL ("excellence and leadership"), the EPA worked with selected firms to integrate environmental permits and facilitate the development and implementation of innovative environmental management practices that moved firms "beyond compliance" with traditional environmental regulations. In return, firms received technical assistance and relief from some of the requirements of traditional environmental regulations. Second, with regulatory negotiation ("reg-neg"), the EPA replaced the traditional quasi-judicial and adversarial process of developing agency rules with a series of cooperative workshops in which all stakeholders (but particularly industry) could collaborate with the EPA in designing more effective and less onerous rules. While the Gore reinvention team did not develop reg-neg, the team enthusiastically embraced it and launched an effort to identify all environmental requirements that were candidates (Weber 1998).

While hopes were high for both Project XL and reg-neg, recent evidence indicates that in practice the successes of these programs fell far short of expectations. Project XL was plagued by low participation, extremely long and difficult negotiations between the EPA, industry, and state environmental agencies, and general frustration on the part of industry participants. Since few Project XL agreements were ever finalized and implemented, the environmental benefits of the program have been minimal (Marcus, Geffen, and Sexton 2002). In addition, a systematic review of reg-neg at the federal level found that negotiated rule making was no faster than traditional rule making, and that stakeholder satisfaction with negotiated rules was no higher than for traditional rules—that is, negotiated rules were just as likely to be challenged in court (Coglianese 1997).

In addition to reinventing its relationships with regulated industries, the EPA took steps to improve its relations with state governments. In May 1995 the EPA launched a new system for federal oversight of state environmental programs, the National Environmental Performance Partnership System (NEPPS). Under NEPPS, states with the strongest and most effective environmental programs receive more autonomy and flexibility in implementing these programs. Moreover, if the state meets negotiated environmental quality standards, federal oversight will be kept to a minimum. By mid-2004, thirty-one states had entered into agreements with the EPA under NEPPS.

We see examples of all three theoretical perspectives from Chapter 2 in environmental regulation during the Clinton years. In accordance with the principal-agent perspective, Congress attempted to redirect regulatory policy with the use of legislation, with limited success. The bureaucratic politics perspective is perhaps best illustrated in the EPA's reinvention initiatives. While the broad parameters of reinvention were set by President Clinton and Vice President Gore, it was left up to EPA personnel to develop specific reinvention initiatives. It is clear that the EPA will never again be able to exercise the degree of autonomy common in the 1970s. Given these limits, however, it is interesting to note that the EPA used its autonomy with respect to reinvention to institutionalize subsystem politics through formal stakeholder involvement in regulatory negotiation, community-based environmental protection, Project XL, and other programs. Subsystem competition within the reinvention framework has the potential to produce less adversarial policymaking, and it also affords the EPA more control over subsystem politics than is true in the more traditional forms of subsystem interaction (stakeholder interaction under reinvention, after all, takes place within an institutional framework designed and overseen by the EPA). Reinventing environmental regulation, therefore, may have ushered in the next stage in the development of subsystem politics.

George W. Bush and Environmental Regulation in the Twenty-First Century

Neither George W. Bush nor Dick Cheney come from the shrinking "Teddy Roosevelt" wing of the Republican Party, and Cheney in particular developed a reputation in Congress for significant antipathy to environmental regulation (e.g., in his last term in the US House of Representatives, Cheney received an LCV score of 0). Thus, members of both advocacy coalitions expected big changes in environmental regulation after Bush and Cheney's election as president and vice president in 2000. The terrorist attacks of September 11, 2001, and the Iraq War placed the Bush environmental agenda onto the back-burner, but since 2003 this agenda has become more pronounced.

Supporters of Bush's record in environmental protection can point to a number of notable actions in this area. For example, under President Bush the EPA has required significant reductions in air pollution from diesel-fueled heavy equipment and off-road vehicles, and accepted a Clinton-era rule reducing allowable concentrations of arsenic in drinking water. Moreover, the Bush EPA has enforced a Clinton-era requirement that General Electric dredge polychlorinated biphenyls (PCBs) from the Hudson River (the largest environmental cleanup in history), and in 2005 it negotiated the largest civil penalty in agency history (a $17 million dollar penalty levied on chemical giant DuPont). Critics of the president, however, point out that he has cut EPA's budget and personnel numbers. More important, these same critics argue that other presidential initiatives amount to the largest effort to weaken environmental regulation since the early days of the Reagan administration. In fact, the League of Conservation Voters was so disturbed by Bush's environmental initiatives that in 2004, for the first time, it devoted a majority of its election efforts to defeating a presidential candidate (historically the LCV has focused on congressional races). Most of President Bush's efforts to reshape environmental regulation focus on reforming the EPA's approach to enforcing environmental regulations, and on restructuring the regulations themselves.

Reforming enforcement at the EPA. Regulators can play one of two roles vis-à-vis the regulated industries: they can be "cops" who look for and punish violations of regulations, or they can be "consultants" who work collaboratively with industry to encourage compliance with these regulations. Historically, regulators at the EPA have taken the former approach (Clinton-era efforts at reinvention not withstanding), but the Bush administration's "Smart Enforcement" plan at EPA has moved the agency toward the latter (Stanton 2003a).

The first tactics used to change the enforcement stance at the EPA have been the familiar tools of appointments and reorganization. President Bush's first choice for the head of the agency's Office of Enforcement and Compliance Assurance was Donald Schregardus, former head of the Ohio EPA. Schregardus had to withdraw, however, after it was revealed that he had fabricated charges against an unjustly punished whistleblower critical of his performance in Ohio, and that a report by the EPA faulted Schregardus for failing to enforce environmental regulations in Ohio (Seelye 2001). Indeed, Schregardus's performance as chief enforcement officer in Ohio was so poor that in 1997, groups in that state sought to have the federal government revoke Ohio's authority to enforce federal environmental regulations (Sanjour 2001). Subsequent heads of enforcement at the EPA have included J. P. Suarez (2002–2004), an official with no previous environmental policy experience, and Granta Nakayama (2002–present), formerly an attorney for a firm defending large polluters from EPA enforcement actions. In addition, President Bush twice introduced plans to eliminate several EPA enforcement field offices, substantially reduce the EPA's enforcement personnel and budget, and hand over more enforcement authority to the states—even though many EPA and state officials feel that the agency needs more, not fewer, enforcement agents (Franz 2002; Stanton 2003b).

The second tactic used to change the enforcement stance at the EPA has been an overall reduction in traditional enforcement efforts. While civil referrals from the EPA to the Department of Justice remained essentially unchanged from 2000 to 2004, criminal investigations during this period declined 14 percent, criminal fines and restitutions declined 61 percent, and assessed prison time for convicted violators declined 47 percent. Total penalties assessed for environmental violations declined 25 percent between 2000 and 2005 (EPA 2005). On the other hand, during this same period, pollution reduction commitments from industry increased 54 percent, and the amount spent by industry to comply with EPA administrative orders increased from $1.6 billion to $10 billion. Overall, the Bush administration's new position on enforcement has caused several senior EPA enforcement officials to resign, and has led to significant morale problems among remaining career personnel (Seelye 2002; Lee 2004a).

The final tactic to reform enforcement at the EPA has been a dramatic increase in the use of voluntary compliance audits by industry and the frequency of compliance assistance efforts by EPA personnel. As part of building partnerships and employing regulatory flexibility, the Clinton administration instituted an industry self-audit program through which firms can find, disclose, and fix regulatory violations without fear of punitive penalties. Industry negotiated 437 such remediation efforts with the EPA in 2000, 1,754 in 2001, and just over 1,000 in 2005 (EPA 2005). Under the compliance assistance program, EPA inspectors truly become "consultants" rather than "cops," providing technical, legal, and administrative advice to industry. In 2000 the EPA provided compliance assistance to 351 firms. By 2004 this figure had increased to 731 (EPA 2005).

Revising environmental regulations. The Bush administration has begun significant revisions to water quality regulations, superfund cleanup standards, wetlands designation rules, and NEPA environmental impact statement requirements. The primary emphasis of the president's regulatory reform initiatives, however, has been air pollution regulations. Initially, the president sought to change these regulations legislatively through his "Clear Skies" initiative. Clear Skies proposed to replace most of the rule making, permit, and state implementation requirements of the Clean Air Act with cap-and-trade systems for sulfur dioxide, nitrous oxides, and mercury. In essence, Clear Skies applies the sulfur dioxide allowance trading scheme from the 1990 CAA to all three pollutants nationwide. Clear Skies is predicted to reduce emissions of sulfur dioxide by 90 percent, nitrous oxides by 94 percent, and mercury by 60 percent from 1970 levels by 2018, and the plan has significant support from economists and the National Academy of Sciences (Easterbook 2005; Gayer, Horowitz, and List 2005). Environmentalists, many Democrats, and several state governments, however, oppose Clear Skies, because existing requirements of the Clean Air Act are projected to produce greater reductions in these pollutants by 2012. Why, these critics ask, should the Clean Air Act be revised in a way that returns fewer environmental benefits over a longer time frame? The answer, according to the Bush administration and supporters of Clear Skies, is that the cap-and-trade approach will provide these benefits at a much lower cost than current regulations, and avoid most of the legal wrangling and delay that characterize these regulations. Democrats in Congress have offered alternatives to Clear Skies, and analyses by independent consultants and EPA staff show that these legislative proposals deliver greater pollution reductions and greater net benefits than does Clear Skies (Janofsky 2004a, 2004b, 2005). At the start of 2006, however, none of these proposals had been voted out of committee.

With his legislative agenda for revising air quality regulations thwarted, President Bush quickly turned to an administrative strategy: changing EPA rules for implementing the existing CAA. Initially, the president's appointees sought to revise the so-called New Source Review (NSR) standard. Under the original CAA, many existing sources of air pollution were exempt from installing pollution control devices. Under the NSR, any such facility (typically power plants and refineries) that upgraded its equipment to produce more power (and more pollution) was supposed to install expensive new pollution control equipment. The rub here is that too often, what regulators viewed as equipment upgrades, facility owners viewed as "routine maintenance" that was exempt from the NSR. In the late 1990s the Clinton administration brought suit against a large number of coal-fired power plants that it believed had violated NSR requirements. These violations were not trivial. In fact, the former head of the EPA's Office of Enforcement and Compliance Assurance said that these violations "were the most significant noncompliance pattern EPA had ever found" (Barcott 2004: 38). The Bush administration, however, revised NSR requirements in a way that undercut these enforcement efforts, and legalized retroactively almost all of the utilities' actions that had heretofore been illegal. Specifically, revisions to the NSR requirements now allowed power plants to spend up to 20 percent of the value of the facility each year in plant upgrades without installing pollution control equipment (an initial EPA study recommended that this threshold be set at 0.75 percent) (Barcott 2004).

Reaction to the new NSR standards was swift. Eric Shaeffer, the longtime head of clean air enforcement at the EPA, resigned in protest over the NSR changes and the subsequent abandonment of enforcement actions against utilities that had violated the earlier standard. The EPA inspector general criticized the new rule for undermining the agency's ability to enforce the CAA (Janofsky 2004b). Environmental groups howled in protest. Several Democrats in Congress, and Jim Jeffords (a former Republican and current ranking member of the Senate Environmental and Public Works committee) questioned the legality of the new NSR rule, while Senator Joseph Lieberman (D-CT) called on EPA administrator Whitman to resign (Goldreich 2002). Most state air pollution control officials believed that the new NSR rule would increase air pollution in their states. Consequently, fourteen state attorneys general and several municipalities challenged the new NSR rule in federal court, claiming that it would significantly increase air pollution crossing over into their states and cities (Barcott 2004; Lee 2004b). Industry groups, on the other hand, viewed the revisions to the NSR as reasonable and long overdue. Most important, the District of Columbia Circuit Court of Appeals generally upheld the Bush administration's position that the EPA had acted within its rights when issuing the new NSR standard (*Environmental Integrity Project v. EPA* 2005).

Despite their success in the NSR case, the Bush appointees at the EPA have not acted to implement the new NSR rule. In the view of these officials, the new NSR standard was made obsolete by the new Clean Air Interstate Rule (CAIR). The CAIR essentially takes the cap-and-trade sulfur dioxide and nitrous oxide programs from Clear Skies and puts them in place via the administrative rule-making process, rather than through legislation (though the CAIR only applies to twenty-eight eastern states and the District of Columbia). In this way, the Bush administration has been able to implement its most desired changes in air pollution control regulations without expending the political capital (or suffering the public relations drawbacks) of fighting to get Clear Skies through a divided Congress. The CAIR supplants the NSR because, true to the cap-and-trade nature of CAIR, older power plants seeking to upgrade their equipment or expand their capacity no longer need to obtain permits from the EPA, and can choose to address the increased pollution emissions from their facilities by installing pollution control equipment, changing to less-polluting fuels, or purchasing additional pollution allowances on the open market.

Soon after issuing the CAIR, the Bush administration issued the companion Clean Air Mercury Rule (CAMR). The CAMR introduces a cap-and-trade system for mercury that is projected to reduce emissions of this pollutant by 69 percent by 2018. The Clinton administration had considered and rejected a cap-and-trade program for mercury, largely because mercury is a potent neurotoxin and therefore a hazardous air pollutant (under the CAA, a cap-and-trade program for hazardous air pollutants is illegal). The Bush administration, by contrast, reclassified mercury as a nonhazardous air pollutant in crafting the CAMR (Krugman 2004; Lee 2003). Partially because of disagreements over the appropriateness of a cap-and-trade regime for mercury, and partially because existing Clinton-era regulations would have required larger and faster reductions in mercury emissions, a coalition of eleven states has sued the EPA to stop the implementation of the CAMR (O'Donnell 2005).

The period 2001–2006 provides the best example of the principal-agent perspective in explaining environmental regulatory activity. Like presidential efforts in the Reagan and George H. W. Bush presidencies, and congressional efforts during the Clinton years, elected officials have made a concerted effort since 2001 to significantly change the course of environmental regulation. Unlike these earlier periods, however, recent efforts have been much more effective for President George W. Bush, and these effects will likely be longer-lasting than similarly effective efforts early in the Reagan administration.

We can identify three reasons for this triumph of principal-agent politics. First, unlike earlier periods, since 2001 all of the elected branches of government have been controlled by Republicans intent on effecting significant changes in environmental regulation. When President Reagan attempted to make large-scale changes during the early 1980s, he was thwarted by a coalition of career EPA bureaucrats and their allies in the Democrat-controlled House of Representatives. Conversely, when the Republican Congress attempted to effect large-scale changes in the mid-1990s, they were opposed by President Clinton, Vice President Gore, and EPA administrator Carol Browner and her deputies. Since 2001, however, there has been no political counterweight to the forces of regulatory retrenchment. Second, the Reagan effort at redirecting the EPA employed overtly hostile rhetoric and tactics, while the efforts of George H. W. Bush were led by the secretive Council on Competitiveness. The first strategy mobilized public opposition to Reagan's efforts, while the second produced changes that were ephemeral (since the council could not make changes to environmental rules). President George W. Bush has employed a far superior strategy of publicizing regulatory reform efforts using positive rhetoric that emphasizes environmental improvements ("Clear Skies," "Healthy Forests") and cooperative relationships with industry, and quickly focusing on making changes in key administrative rules when his legislative strategy stalls. Finally, we believe that President Bush's efforts at regulatory reform have been aided by the terrorist attacks of September 11, 2001, and the subsequent "war on terror" and Iraq War, which have drawn public attention away from the administration's regulatory activities.

8

Regulating
the Workplace

TWO DOCTRINES EVOLVED in nineteenth-century common law to assist courts in assigning liability for workplace injuries. Assumption of risk presumed workers understood the risks inherent in their occupations and that risk was reflected in wage differentials. Contributory negligence presumed that as long as the employee (or any other employees) bore any responsibility for the accident, the employer could be absolved of liability. In the early decades of the twentieth century, states began to address this imbalance in the assignment of responsibilities with the passage of worker compensation laws that provided injured parties with a fixed payment out of a company's insurance funds, usually under the administration of a state commission. Since insurance premiums would decline in response to an exemplary safety record, the system created financial incentives for voluntary improvements in workplace safety (Fainsod, Gordon, and Palamountain 1959: 166–167).

In 1970, Congress passed the Occupational Safety and Health Act (OSH Act), creating the Occupational Safety and Health Administration and directing it "to assure so far as possible every working man and woman in the nation safe and healthful working conditions." Its "general duty clause" assigned responsibility to the employer "to furnish to each of his employees employment and a place of employment which are free from recognized hazards that are causing or are likely to cause death or serious physical harm to his employees." This new responsibility would be defined with great detail via the rule-making process and enforced through the imposition of penalties, although the general duty clause would make the employer responsible for recognizable hazards even if they were not addressed by specific OSHA regulations.

One should not assume that the normative assumptions underlying the earlier common law regime were wholly discarded. Some contemporary analysts of occupational safety and health regulation continue to argue that risks are reflected in wages determined in labor markets (see Viscusi 1983; but see also Smith 1979). Critics have also focused on OSHA performance, arguing that the agency's obsession with trivial safety regulations and its rigid legalistic style of regulation generate resentment, minimal compliance, and legal challenges that undermine its effectiveness (Bardach and Kagan 1982: 93–119; Kelman 1981). Others claim that OSHA overregulates a handful of health hazards, thereby misallocating resources that could be used more rationally to address health risks that are simply ignored (Mendeloff 1979, 1987), and that its policies are rarely sensitive to the balancing of costs and benefits. These and many other debates have made the history of OSHA a lively one.

Occupational Safety and Health Policy

The policies examined in this chapter can be conveniently divided into two categories. *Safety regulations* address the design of workplace equipment and facilities that have the goal of reducing accidents that might result in injuries and deaths. They often have an immediate impact on accidents. *Health regulations,* in contrast, seek to eliminate or minimize exposure to toxic substances in the workplace, thereby reducing the incidence of disease. They often fail to exhibit a short-term impact, because many of the regulated substances contribute to diseases that manifest themselves years or decades after exposure.

As noted in Chapter 2, it is useful to characterize regulatory politics by relative levels of salience and complexity. Occupational health and safety policy has been highly salient, particularly since the mid-1970s (see Figure 8.1). While OSHA imposes concentrated costs on business, the benefits realized by workers are relatively diffuse. This is particularly the case in health regulations that require large compliance costs while only reducing the probability of disease in some distant future. In this assignment of costs and benefits, the regulatory issue area has much in common with other social regulations. Concentrated costs create significant incentives for affected businesses to mobilize, while the diffusion of benefits would usually provide few incentives for the beneficiaries to devote resources to mobilization. Labor organizations, however, have countered the mobilization of business associations that routinely oppose OSHA policies—a perfect example of Mancur Olson's by-product theory of interest groups (1965).

Occupational safety and health is also characterized by extreme complexity, with clear economic and scientific dimensions. Despite OSHA's

Figure 8.1 The Salience of Occupational Safety and Health

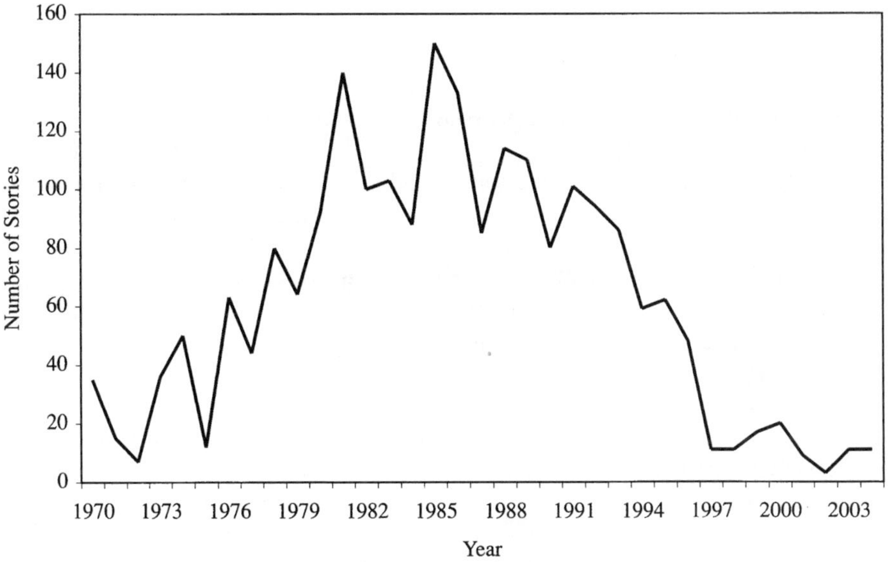

expansive mandate, the OSH Act did not require the agency to balance the benefits and costs of its regulatory actions. Section 6(b)(5) instructed the secretary of labor to promulgate the standard "which most adequately assures, to the extent feasible, on the basis of the best available evidence, that no employee will suffer material impairment of health or functional capacity." The phrase "to the extent feasible" opened the door to objections from businesses that interpreted it as mandating some consideration of cost-effectiveness (Bardach and Kagan 1982: 48). The central objective of the act—to ensure that "no employee will suffer material impairment of health or functional capacity"—is inherently problematic. One cannot achieve a risk-free economy. In practical terms, one must arrive at some implicit conclusion regarding whether the marginal utility of additional gains in workplace safety would be offset by the costs incurred. Even if there is some implicit threshold beyond which one cannot justify additional regulation, the organic legislation did not identify this threshold, nor did it require OSHA to consider the costs of its actions (Viscusi 1986).

The scientific complexities associated with occupational health regulations are significant as well. The risk-assessment process used to identify and characterize risks and determine acceptable levels of exposure is fraught with complexities. The scientific complexity has required the direct integration of scientific research into the regulation process (Rushefsky 1986). The economic and scientific complexities create a seemingly endless array of assumptions that are open to challenge and competing bodies of evidence—a situation comparable to environmental protection (see Eisner 2000: 134–169).

The Occupational Safety and Health Administration

The OSH Act unified standard-setting and enforcement authority in a new agency, OSHA, in the Labor Department (see Nobel 1986: chap. 3; Moe 1984). The act directed the secretary of labor and OSHA to promulgate and enforce standards for all private-sector employees. The Bureau of Occupational Safety in the Department of Health, Education, and Welfare was renamed the National Institute for Occupational Safety and Health (NIOSH) and assigned responsibility for conducting research used in identifying risks and developing standards. The act also established an appellate body to review contested decisions, the Occupational Safety and Health Review Commission (OSHRC). In fiscal year 2005, OSHA had a budget of $464.2 million (see Figure 8.2), with a staff of approximately 2,300.

OSHA is formally under the direction of the assistant secretary of labor for occupational safety and health (see Figure 8.3), a presidential appointee requiring Senate confirmation. Although the specific offices and divisions within the agency have undergone minor changes in name and organization

Figure 8.2 The Occupational Safety and Health Administration Budget

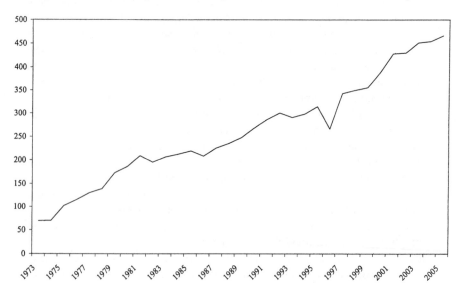

Figure 8.3 The Occupational Safety and Health Administration

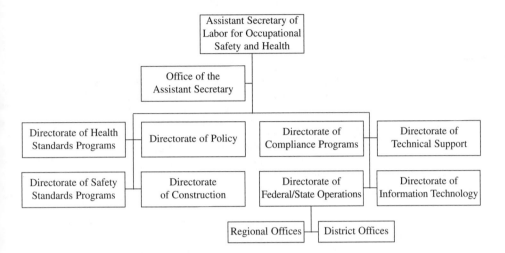

over time, they can be separated analytically into three clusters. First, a number of offices engage in planning and evaluation and conduct external relations with Congress and the Office of Management and Budget (e.g., the Directorate of Evaluation and Analysis, the Directorate of Information Technology). Second, there is a set of offices responsible for the formulation of standards (e.g., the Directorate of Construction, the Directorate of Standards and Guidance), which is subdivided into specialized units addressing specific classes of health and safety problems. Third, there are offices that provide compliance support and administer programs at the state level (e.g., the Directorate of Cooperative and State Programs). Ten regional offices implement policy along with state regulators administering OSHA-approved plans.

Given the complexity of this regulatory issue area, one would expect to encounter high levels of professionalization and, by implication, many of the organizational difficulties that exist in most professionalized agencies. Indeed, OSHA is highly professionalized, with staffs of attorneys, economists, epidemiologists, industrial engineers, industrial hygienists, and toxicologists. As noted in Chapter 2, professionalization is often the source of organizational problems. The norms inculcated through professional socialization vary widely by discipline and can be difficult to integrate. The scientific research projects that provide a basis for OSHA health standards typically take years to complete, a timetable that conflicts with the professional incentives of staff attorneys who seek to establish a litigation record. Standards that are based in scientific research and regulatory remedies designed by engineers and industrial hygienists may be difficult to justify in economic terms. Indeed, the historical dominance of industrial hygienists and health professionals at OSHA has had an impact on the design of rules. As Steven Kelman notes, professional biases have been expressed in the design of regulatory remedies:

> Officials have worked in the occupational safety and health professions (safety engineering or industrial hygiene) or take courses in these fields after joining the agencies. Members of these professions share a body of knowledge. They also tend to share like members in many professions, values that comprise a professional ideology. For occupational safety and health professionals, these are pro-protection values. They believe strongly that workers ought to be protected from hazards and that larger reductions or risk are preferable to smaller ones (without much thought of cost). (1980: 89)

The difficulties of coordinating professional staffs are exacerbated here by a physical separation that multiplies communication linkages and thus contributes to implementation problems (Nakamura and Smallwood 1980). The separation of OSHA and NIOSH has been particularly important. Past OSHA administrators have bemoaned the lack of communication with NIOSH and the resultant divergence in priorities. Researchers at NIOSH have completed studies on the risks of various substances in the workplace only to discover that there was no intention on the part of OSHA to regulate exposure. The lack of communication is of more than passing importance, given that NIOSH criteria documents often serve as a basis for setting OSHA's regulatory agenda (Singer 1975b; Gerston, Fraleigh, and Schwab 1988: 177–178).

Many of OSHA's efforts are directed toward the development, promulgation, and enforcement of safety and health standards. The vast majority of OSHA standards concern safety issues, and OSHA has relied heavily on industry codes and standard-setting organizations in developing this body of regulations. Health standards, in contrast, are designed to regulate exposure to chemical substances that contribute to disease. In order to arrive at adequate regulations, it is necessary, first, to document the causal relationship between the substance and the disease, and second, to determine the level of exposure deemed hazardous. The risk-assessment process is fraught with uncertainty. When conducting risk assessment, OSHA relies primarily on academic and federally funded research. Regulators must determine how to combine and weigh the data and analyses. This is a complicated matter. For example, the high dosages used in bioassays often produce higher estimates of risk than epidemiological studies. Thus the heavier the reliance on bioassays, the more risk-averse the resulting regulations. To complicate matters, the mathematical models used to extrapolate from animal to human populations are fraught with uncertainty (see Rushefsky 1986: 21–58).

Once risk assessment is completed, decisions have to be made about how best to manage the risks. Compliance costs can be great, particularly when regulatory remedies require the reengineering of productive facilities or the elimination of chemicals that are integral to the production process. Regulators must make broad determinations about the distribution of the burdens between employers and employees. OSHA usually relies on technical design or engineering standards rather than the less costly performance standards favored by business. This bias reflects the professional norms of its staff and the failure of the OSH Act to a systematic consideration of costs. The high and concentrated compliance costs associated with health regulations can cause great conflicts. There is usually fragmentary evidence concerning success: health regulations yield benefits decades after their introduction, due to long latency periods. Moreover, many diseases result from multiple chemical agents, some of which may not be regulated by OSHA. As a result, the causal connection between the reduction of exposure and a variation in the rate of disease may be difficult to define with any accuracy.

The development of OSHA standards is comparable to the rule-making process at other agencies. OSHA may decide to begin standard-setting on its own initiative or in response to the petitions filed by other interested parties (e.g., NIOSH, standard-setting organizations, labor or business associations). Once OSHA concludes that a standard is necessary, it relies on standing or ad hoc advisory committees to develop recommendations. To ensure that a variety of positions are considered at an early stage, all advisory committees must include representatives from labor, management, state occupational health and safety agencies, and the Department of Health and Human Services.

Within the agency, OSHA creates project teams that formulate each rule and shepherd it through the rule-making process. Once the decision has been made to propose a new standard, OSHA publishes a "notice of proposed rule making" in the *Federal Register.* The notice includes a description of the new rule and announces the length of the public comment period (usually sixty days). During this time, parties may introduce additional evidence and written analyses. If there has been no previous announcement of public hearings, interested parties may request that hearings be scheduled. Once this stage draws to a close, the project team makes necessary revisions to the rule and publishes it, in its final version, in the *Federal Register,* along with an explanation of the standard, its justification, and the date it becomes effective. Within sixty days of promulgation, affected parties have the right to petition the US Court of Appeals for judicial review of the standard. They may also appeal to OSHA for a temporary or permanent variance. OSHA may also publish a temporary emergency standard, which becomes a proposed permanent standard, and then the regular standard-setting process is engaged.

Health and safety standards are enforced through inspections. Yet OSHA has but 1,100 inspectors to cover over 7.2 million workplaces employing some 115 million workers. In 2004, OSHA conducted 39,167 federal inspections (with an additional 57,866 state inspections). OSHA targets its inspections to focus on firms that are believed to pose a higher risk, because of industry statistics or recorded lost workday rates suggesting that problems may exist. Inspections may turn up evidence of violations that range in the level of severity from the trivial to the life-threatening. When violations are deemed to be less than serious, inspectors may simply make the firm aware of the violation or recommend a nominal fine. Serious violations can result in a mandatory fine of $7,000. In those cases where the firm knows that a serious violation exists and yet fails to remedy the situation, inspectors may find that there has been a willful violation. Here the fines vary from a minimum of $5,000 to a maximum of $70,000, with additional penalties for repeat violations. If such a violation has resulted in the death of a worker, the fines can escalate to $250,000. Finally, OSHA can impose so-called egregious penalties when employers willfully subject their employees to conditions that could result in serious illness or death. In such cases, OSHA has been willing to count each unsafe piece of equipment or each worker subjected to the risk as a separate violation, with the result that fines quickly escalate into the millions of dollars. OSHA may also seek court injunctions and recommend to the court that such violations merit criminal penalties (see Keiser 1995: 207–208).

OSHA administers its regulations through a system of ten regional offices. More important, twenty-four states, the Virgin Islands, and Puerto Rico administer OSHA-approved state plans. The OSH Act authorized the agency to approve such plans when they were at least as effective as federal regulation. A mechanism was established to subsidize approved state plans with grants covering 50 percent of the costs. In 2005, OSHA transferred $91 million to the states for this purpose. Research on state enforcement provides a mixed picture. There is some evidence that it has been more effective than federal enforcement, as reflected in higher numbers of inspections and greater consistency in the level of enforcement (see Thompson and Scicchitano 1987). At the same time, other researchers (e.g., Scholz and Wei 1986; Marvel 1982) have concluded both that the state programs are more responsive to political forces and that the number of inspections tends to be inversely correlated with a state economy's reliance on manufacturing. While OSHA should be able to reduce such variation through oversight, a General Accounting Office (GAO 1994) study concluded that OSHA oversight is undermined both by the scarcity of state enforcement data and by OSHA's propensity to focus on indicators that may not be good measures of performance (e.g., inspections conducted, violations cited, penalties assigned).

The Policy Subsystem

OSHA functions within a network of interorganizational linkages, connecting it to the presidency, Congress, and the courts. There are numerous access points within each of these linkages (and within OSHA's rule-making processes) where policy can be altered in response to external demands (see Bryner 1987: 121–133). OSHA regulations are highly salient, addressing the relationship between the employer and employee and forcing concentrated costs onto businesses, thereby creating powerful incentives to mobilize. Individual firms and peak and trade associations frequently participate in rule making, lobby Congress and the executive to shape OSHA policy, and challenge rules in court. Every significant OSHA rule has resulted in court appeals; protracted litigation has become a routine response to OSHA efforts to impose multimillion-dollar fines for egregious violations. While businesses have had marked success in each of these forums, their influence at OSHA has been minimal. As Kelman (1981) notes, because OSHA develops standards in an adversarial environment, it has adopted a rigid posture in enforcement. The expectation of adversarial relations leads regulated parties to shape policy through other venues. Despite the diffusion of benefits, organized labor has also been a constant source of agency support.

The President and Congress

One of the most important tools in the president's arsenal is the power of appointment. The assistant secretary for occupational safety and health is a presidential appointee. At OSHA, the selection of the agency executive can have a major impact on the agency's regulatory posture. The history of the agency provides a number of examples of appointees who have furthered presidential agendas. There are many other points at which the president can influence OSHA policymaking. At each stage of the policy process, standards are subjected to review by the assistant secretary and the Regulation Review Committee, which scrutinize the research supporting the rule. Moreover, reviews are conducted within the Department of Labor. Of course, all proposed and final regulations are subjected to reviews conducted by other executive branch agencies, including the OMB and the entire panoply of executive review bodies discussed in Chapter 3 (see McGarity 1991).

Presidents of both parties have proven responsive to business concerns over compliance costs. Thus, even as Carter was seeking to nurture his relationship with organized labor, his Regulatory Analysis and Review Group subjected OSHA decisions to closer scrutiny in hopes of reducing the costs of regulation. In its review of a proposed rule regulating exposure to acrylonitrile, for example, RARG convinced OSHA to adopt the highest of the three exposure levels under consideration, whereby each death averted would have cost $4 million, compared with a range of $29 to $170 million for the more stringent thresholds advocated by OSHA (Bardach and Kagan 1982: 307–308). There are limits to presidential control via regulatory review. The president cannot officially require OSHA to apply cost-benefit analysis, given its organic mandate. Nevertheless, Reagan's OSHA head, Thorne Auchter, required the application of cost-effectiveness analysis during his tenure, but as one of many factors considered in regulatory design.

Congress also has a number of tools to influence the bureaucracy. These tools are relatively blunt, however, and far more effective in restraining an overzealous bureaucracy than in forcing activism. Congress appropriates funding for OSHA. As shown in Figure 8.2, OSHA has received nominal increases over its history, yet, once adjusted for inflation, the increases have been far from impressive. What of oversight? Effective congressional oversight is frequently hampered by problems of information asymmetry that become more distinct the greater the complexity of the issue area. Nevertheless, the relationship between Congress and OSHA has been highly politicized, reflecting the high levels of interest mobilization in the regulatory policy area. Beyond the budget and oversight, Congress may attempt to control OSHA through legislation. This has been a common strategy, albeit only a marginally successful one, given the highly partisan nature of the issue area. During the 1970s, members of Congress introduced numerous bills and riders to establish exemptions for small businesses, farms, and recreational facilities. Riders on appropriation bills were also employed to restrict OSHA jurisdiction and limit its budgetary discretion. In the 1990s, Congress placed riders on appropriations bills prohibiting OSHA from using funds to issue ergonomics standards (see Victor 1995a). Legislative restrictions on OSHA autonomy send clear signals concerning levels of congressional support. At the same time, they may also have a corrosive effect on OSHA authority. Businesses may fail to make investments to meet regulatory standards if congressional support for OSHA appears tenuous (Wilson 1985: 36–43).

The Courts

Virtually every OSHA health regulation results in litigation; court challenges are a de facto stage in the policy process. The ongoing role of the courts in interpreting OSHA standards and the limits of agency authority have had a predictable effect on agency decisionmaking. As Graham Wilson explains: "the framing of standards within the agency usually involves a constant quarrel between the expert advocates of a proposed standard, anxious to tackle a health problem quickly, and the lawyers of the agency, anxious to prepare the strongest possible case for the Court battles which almost certainly lie ahead" (1985: 105).

In their interaction with OSHA, the courts have been forced to address a host of complex scientific and economic issues. For example, the court considered a challenge to a 1978 revision of OSHA's benzene standard, which revised sharply downward permissible levels of exposure to this chemical agent that has been causally linked to leukemia. The 5th Circuit Court of Appeals rejected the revised standard on the grounds that OSHA had not demonstrated that a more stringent standard provided benefits that outweighed the additional costs. In *Industrial Union Department v. American Petroleum Institute* (1979), the Supreme Court affirmed this decision, noting that the OSH Act required that standards be "reasonably necessary." This would have required some evidence that more stringent exposure thresholds would provide benefits that were unattainable under the earlier standard. Without such demonstration, OSHA could not "make a threshold finding that a place of employment is unsafe."

There has been some ambiguity in the courts' treatment of economic factors, a point best developed through examples. In 1971, OSHA adopted an emergency asbestos standard (based on a NIOSH recommendation) that would be phased in over a four-year period. The American Federation of Labor–Congress of Industrial Organizations (AFL-CIO) sued, claiming that the phase-in was a politically motivated effort to minimize corporate compliance costs (see Mendeloff 1979: 58–64). Ultimately, the Court of Appeals decision in *Industrial Union Department v. Hodgson* (1974) noted that "it would comport with common usage to say that a standard that is prohibitively expensive is not 'feasible.' . . . Congress does not appear to have intended to protect employees by putting their employers out of business." However, this did not require the agency to employ cost-benefit analysis. Even if compliance costs reduced profitability and bankrupted some businesses, a standard might still be feasible until "the effect becomes more widespread within an industry."

The courts' position became even clearer in a dispute involving OSHA's 1976 decision to introduce a new standard for cotton dust, which has been linked to byssinosis. While the existing standard had established a threshold of 500 micrograms per cubic meter, OSHA decided to reduce exposure levels to 200 micrograms for yarn production and 750 micrograms for fabric production on the basis of new research. The Textile Manufacturers Association challenged the health benefits of lower exposure and claimed that the rule would mark the demise of the textile industry and thus would fail the feasibility test (Viscusi 1985). Ultimately, the Supreme Court determined that OSHA was not bound by cost-benefit considerations and concluded that Congress had already decided the issue "by placing the 'benefit' of worker health above all other considerations" (*American Textile Manufacturers Institute v. Donovan* 1981).

As these three decisions illustrate, the courts have a powerful impact on the way OSHA executes its mandate. As the benzene decision suggests, OSHA would have to place a heavy reliance on scientific evidence, showing that more stringent standards are justified on the basis of research findings. While this would appear to direct the agency toward some application of cost-benefit analysis and consideration of the marginal benefits of progressively more prohibitive thresholds, the courts have assiduously avoided this conclusion. Adopting a rather peculiar reading of feasibility, the courts have emphasized the importance of occupation safety and health over compliance costs, deferring to congressional will as expressed in the OSH Act.

The Evolution of Occupational Safety and Health Policy

OSHA has spent much of its existence embroiled in controversy—a product of its economy-wide mandate, the complexity of its regulatory duties, and the high costs it imposes. The agency has been subjected to more than its share of "horror stories," politically charged claims of regulatory excess that have rarely found an empirical basis. Moreover, given that OSHA's first decade was marked by stagflation, opportunities to associate it economic decline were legion. As we explore the politics of occupational safety and health, we again do so through the analytical lenses introduced in Chapter 2: the principal-agent perspective, the bureaucratic politics perspective, and the subsystems perspective.

The Creation, Expansion, and Professionalization of OSHA

In the early years, OSHA concentrated primarily on occupational safety issues. The OSH Act authorized OSHA to bypass normal rule-making procedures during its first twenty-eight months in order to adopt national safety and health consensus standards. Nixon's assistant secretary of labor, George Guenther, adopted some 4,400 private-sector standards wholesale after one month, many of which were widely acknowledged as irrelevant or trivial. Agency critics would ridicule OSHA by citing rules that specified that toilets have hinged, open-front seats, that all rest-room stalls have precisely placed coat hooks, and that "ice in contact with drinking water shall be made of potable water." Guenther directed OSHA to develop rudimentary enforcement priorities: inspections concentrated on longshoring, roofing and sheet-metal work, meat processing, transportation equipment manufacturing, and lumber and wood products—all industries with high injury rates. OSHA moved quickly to issue a list of more than 400 substances deemed harmful and directed businesses to keep employee exposure below the thresholds set by the American Conference of Governmental Industrial Hygienists. It also promulgated the above-noted asbestos standard. However, the damage was done: wholesale adoption of safety standards created the image of an agency obsessed with trivia (see Clark 1978b).

In some ways, OSHA's level of activism was surprising. The Nixon administration was attempting to restrain the growth of federal regulation. It imposed employment ceilings and average-grade controls, thereby undermining OSHA's efforts to recruit upper-grade health professionals. The problem was the most severe at NIOSH, which could not fill one-sixth of its authorized positions. OSHA regulation was also frustrated by Nixon's "New Federalism," which led it to set aside a large percentage of its overall budget for state grants precisely when the new agency needed to develop its own bureaucratic resources. Critics of New Federalism argued that this transfer of authority could result in wild local variations and far more conservative policies than might exist under federal administration (Culhane 1972a, 1972b). During this period, the enforcement of trivial safety standards attracted the ire of business. Labor support was tepid, given OSHA's small budget, limited enforcement efforts, lack of health regulations, and allegations that the White House was influencing enforcement to attract corporate donations. Nixon attempted to placate labor by appointing John Stender, a former international vice president of the International Brotherhood of Boilermakers (of the AFL-CIO), to replace Guenther in 1973. However, concerns over OSHA's performance continued to resound: more than eighty bills were introduced in the 93rd Congress to amend the OSH Act (Demkovich 1974).

In the face of business opposition, there were efforts to strengthen OSHA during the Ford administration. Ford appointed Morton Corn as assistant secretary. A Harvard PhD in industrial hygiene and a former professor of occupational health and chemical engineering at the University of Pittsburgh, Corn was committed to professionalization and eliminating "extraneous influences" in its enforcement efforts (Singer 1975b: 1727). Corn expanded the professional staff of the Standards Development Office to thirty and brought scientists into the agency to work with OSHA staff. He focused greater resources on serious health problems, forging closer interaction with NIOSH. Moreover, OSHA explicitly focused its inspection resources on industries with severe death, injury, and illness rates and high levels of exposure to toxic chemicals. Finally, Corn sought to prevent political conflicts by clarifying standards and expanding the congressional affairs staff. In the end, Corn's impact was limited both by Ford's brief tenure in office and the president's adoption of deregulation and regulatory reform as part of his anti-inflationary program. During 1976, Ford made numerous negative comments about OSHA, as a convenient symbol of overregulation.

Concerns that a presidential task force to streamline regulations would target OSHA had the effect of mobilizing organized labor, which quickly became OSHA's major source of support (Singer 1976; Gerston, Fraleigh, and Schwab 1988: 178–179).

The agency finally encountered a supportive political environment during the Carter presidency. At the suggestion of the AFL-CIO, Carter appointed Eula Bingham as assistant secretary. Bingham, like Corn before her, carried impressive credentials as a professor of environmental health and an associate director of the Department of Environmental Health at the University of Cincinnati School of Medicine. Bingham successfully shifted the agency's primary focus from safety regulations to health, doubling the number of health standards in four short years. OSHA promulgated permanent standards for benzene, dibromchlorpropane (DBCP), inorganic arsenic, cotton dust, acrylonitrile, and lead. The redefinition of the agency's mission placed a much higher demand on the scientific staff and required greater resources for health inspections. Given the complexity of health regulations, the number of investigations actually declined. Yet resources were increasingly directed toward serious violations. As a result, the number of serious, willful, or repeat violations increased from 9,250 in 1976 to 49,474 in 1980, with penalties growing from $12.5 million to $23.5 million (Singer 1977; Harter 1977; Meier 1985: 213–217; DOL, *Annual Report,* various years).

Bingham also transformed OSHA's approach to regulation. Thus far, it had employed a case-by-case approach to regulating workplace toxins. Given that NIOSH had recently identified some 42,000 chemical substances used in industry (including some 2,000 possible carcinogens), this approach would prove inadequate to the task at hand (Demkovich 1974: 1831). Therefore, OSHA began regulating by effect rather than substance. In 1980, OSHA released its cancer policy and a list of 207 substances that would be affected immediately. Under the cancer policy, OSHA divided potential carcinogens into two categories. Category I comprised chemicals that had been conclusively linked to cancer. Where there were substitutes, OSHA would ban these substances. Where there were no substitutes, it would set standards at the lowest feasible level. Category II comprised suspected carcinogens that could be regulated on a case-by-case basis (Rushefsky 1986: 88–94).

OSHA also initiated efforts to review for possible elimination consensus standards under the "standard deletion project." However, whereas the OSH Act authorized a fast track for adoption, there was no such process for deletion, and OSHA quickly discovered that even the most obscure standards had constituencies. The AFL-CIO demanded that each standard deletion be accompanied by public hearings. Some 90 percent of the consensus standards were commented on as part of the process. After negotiations with the AFL-CIO, OSHA identified 900 standards that were appropriate for revocation (Clark 1978a, 1978b). The practical impact was questionable, given that most of these regulations had probably never been enforced (Bardach and Kagan 1982: 202).

By the end of the Carter presidency, OSHA appeared well on its way to becoming an effective regulator. The past two administrators—appointed by a Republican and a Democrat—had been health professionals committed to the mission of the agency. OSHA's budget had increased from $59 million to $209 million in a single decade. It had developed a large professional staff and procedures for targeting enforcement resources proactively on the basis of risk. It had all the characteristics of a highly professionalized regulatory agency with a growing capacity to translate scientific research into health regulations. Things changed, however, with the 1980 election.

The Reagan-Bush Revolution and OSHA Regulations

A central component of Ronald Reagan's economic recovery program was regulatory relief. OSHA had been cited in campaign speeches as an example of a regulator that had undermined growth in the 1970s. Vice President George H. W. Bush, who assumed the chairmanship of the President's Task Force on Regulatory Relief, noted: "We recognize the Government's responsibility in the safety of the workplace. . . . But unrealistic, overzealous regulators have made a mockery of the good intentions, and by their arbitrary actions they've added tens of thousands of workers to the unemployment roles" (Bush 1981: 409). Observers were not surprised when the administration moved quickly to change the direction of OSHA.

Reagan's selection for OSHA head was Thorne Auchter, a Reagan campaign organizer in Florida and an executive in a family construction company. Citing the excesses of the past, Auchter announced his goal of transforming OSHA into a "cooperative regulator" (Wines 1981: 1985). In practical terms, this meant reducing OSHA's regulatory presence—an objective that was facilitated by significant budget cuts. During the first years of the Reagan presidency, OSHA sustained serious resource reductions (see Figure 8.2). A 1981 budget of $209 million fell to $195 million the next year, with staffing reductions of 22 percent. Staff resources would remain stagnant for the remainder of the Reagan presidency. Working under severe budget constraints, OSHA targeted firms with a lost workday rate above the national average, thereby exempting some 75 percent of the nation's firms from inspections. Approximately 19 percent of the inspections during the Carter presidency were health inspections, with the remainder addressing safety. In 1982, health inspections fell to 14.9 percent of the total and remained at approximately 15 percent for the remainder of the Reagan presidency. Penalties, which had reached $23.5 million by 1980, fell to $9.9 million in 1981 and $5.8 million in 1982. In real terms, the dollar value of the fines would not approach the 1980 level until the George H. W. Bush presidency (DOL, *Annual Report,* various years; see also Wines 1981, 1983b; Viscusi 1982).

The goal of creating a "cooperative regulator" required that a new emphasis be placed on voluntary compliance, business self-inspections, informal conferences before the issuance of fines, and the use of consulting visits. At the same time, Auchter promoted greater delegation of authority to the states. Twenty-one states were authorized to administer their own programs, thereby removing OSHA inspectors altogether (Gerston, Fraleigh, and Schwab 1988: 186–191). Despite this devolution, the funding of state plan grants fell from $44.4 million in 1981 to $40.5 million by 1988; the number of state inspections fell by 20 percent during this same period. These efforts won the resounding support of business associations while earning denunciations from labor and a host of public advocacy groups (Wines 1983b). The newfound commitment to voluntarism was combined with attempts to revise, dilute, or delay standards for benzene, cotton dust, ethylene dibromide, and noise. In most years of the Reagan presidency, the agency devoted a larger proportion of its standard-setting staff to regulatory revisions than to the development of new standards. OSHA's cancer policy was revised in 1981, such that the Category I carcinogens would not be reduced to the lowest feasible levels, as earlier suggested, but would be regulated on a case-by-case basis. At the same time, new standards on lead, asbestos, and the labeling of hazardous agents used in manufacturing actually strengthened regulation (see Wines 1983a; Keiser 1995: 219). The efforts to weaken health standards alienated many members of OSHA's scientific staff and led, ultimately, to the exodus of the professional staff and myriad extended vacancies.

Auchter resigned in 1984, and the position was filled, albeit temporarily, by Charles Rowlands, former chair of the Occupational Safety and Health Review Commission, who stepped down before confirmation and was replaced by John Pendergrass, a former 3M executive. Under Pendergrass, the earlier trajectory of regulatory withdrawal continued. In 1988, for example, OSHA proposed a rule that would establish exposure levels for 428 chemicals. Of the 200 exposure standards already recommended by NIOSH, 185 of those proposed accepted higher exposure levels. As one might expect, business embraced the proposed standards, and standards were declared for 370 of these chemicals. In the end, the AFL-CIO successfully challenged these standards in a 1992 federal appellate court case, with the result that the previous standards were once again applicable (Keiser 1995: 212–213).

Given George H. W. Bush's role in the Task Force on Regulatory Relief, one would have expected a continuation of the Reagan program at OSHA. Surprisingly, the Bush presidency witnessed a mild revitalization of

the agency with the appointment of Elizabeth Dole as labor secretary and
Gerald F. Scannell, an occupational safety and health professional with
prior corporate and OSHA experience, as assistant secretary. New leadership was combined with an expanding resource base. The agency's budget
grew from $245 million in 1989 to $304 million in 1992, a 24 percent nominal increase. Although the number of inspections declined by 27 percent
(from 58,354 in the last year of the Reagan presidency to 42,431 in 1992),
the penalties increased by 91 percent, suggesting a more effective targeting
of resources. Moreover, health inspections, which had been de-emphasized
during the Reagan presidency, came to constitute 21.4 percent by 1992, a
new record for the agency (DOL, *Annual Report,* 1988, 1992). Scannell initiated new efforts to address cumulative trauma disorders associated with
repetitive work and health care workers' exposure to hepatitis B and the
human immunodeficiency virus (HIV). Indeed, under Scannell, OSHA proposed the largest fine thus far in its history, a penalty of $7.3 million against
USX for a number of health and safety violations (Victor 1989). Penalties
reached a record $86.1 million in 1992, compared with $45 million four
years earlier. Indeed, the level of OSHA enforcement led some analysts to
note that President Bush might be remembered as the "regulatory president"
(Rauch 1991).

The Clinton Administration and OSHA

One would have anticipated a strengthening of OSHA following the election of Bill Clinton in 1992. The 1992 Democratic Party platform's plank on
worker rights proclaimed: "We will reform the job safety laws to empower
workers with greater rights and to hold employers accountable for dangers
on the job." Democrats received the support of organized labor and controlled both Congress and the White House. Clinton appointed Robert Reich
as secretary of labor, widely viewed as the most qualified occupant of the
position in a generation (see Victor 1995b). He also appointed John Dear,
formerly head of the Washington Department of Labor and Industries, as
assistant secretary in charge of OSHA. OSHA publicly committed itself to
bolstering enforcement and increasing penalties by 5 percent (Weisman
1996c).

With a Democratic president and unified Democratic control of
Congress, the stage was set for the strengthening of OSHA. Although the
fiscal year 1994 budget request of $294.5 million was only a 2.2 percent
increase over the previous year's appropriation (and thus in line with the
Bush administration's average annual increase of 2.3 percent), the fiscal
year 1995 budget increased significantly, to $312.5 million, a 5.1 percent
increase. In 1994, Representative William D. Ford (D-MI), and Senator
Edward Kennedy (D-MA) introduced legislation to strengthen the OSH Act.

Under the proposed legislation, employers with eleven or more workers would be required to create a committee of workers and managers to review health and safety procedures and identify improvements. More important, OSHA would be required to initiate investigations within twenty-four hours of a serious accident and respond to petitions for new safety or health regulations within ninety days. Where new regulations were deemed necessary, OSHA would have one year to propose the rule. OSHA would be given strengthened civil and criminal sanctions, and all state and local employees would fall under its jurisdiction. Although the legislation appeared to be on its way to passage, on April 5, 1994, OSHA proposed new regulations to ban smoking in most businesses. Following an unprecedented flow of complaints, a coalition of forty-two House members representing tobacco states demanded that Labor Secretary Reich withdraw the proposed regulations. This coalition, when combined with additional Republican opposition to empowering OSHA, effectively killed the initiative (Masci 1994a, 1994b; Sammon 1994; Camia 1994).

All regulatory agencies, OSHA included, faced a more hostile environment before the Republican majorities in the 104th Congress. The "Contract with America" promised to pass a job creation and wage enhancement act that would improve the investment environment for businesses by requiring heightened reliance on cost-benefit analysis and greater flexibility in regulatory design and enforcement. At the same time, OSHA came under renewed attacks. Drawing on an apocryphal account of a dentist who was restricted by OSHA regulations from giving a child a tooth that had been extracted, opponents decried OSHA's outlawing of the tooth fairy. OSHA also came under fire for its efforts to develop ergonomics standards to prevent repetitive motion injuries. These efforts (which, oddly enough, began during the Reagan administration) attracted great attention following the issuance of a draft standard in March 1995. A coalition of affected businesses was successful in getting the House Appropriations Subcommittee on Labor, Health, and Human Services to place a rider on the 1996 fiscal year appropriations bill prohibiting OSHA from issuing proposed or final ergonomics standards or guidelines through the end of the year (Victor 1995a). There were, in addition, numerous bills introduced specifically to reform OSHA (see Wells 1995a).

Potentially the most important challenge was the proposed Safety and Health Improvement and Regulatory Reform Act of 1995 (HR 1834), introduced by Representative Cass Ballenger (R-NC) and fifty-five cosponsors. Ballenger noted: "OSHA has become fundamentally misdirected, and instead of promoting and encouraging workplace safety and health, OSHA has become known for issuing silly regulations and is preoccupied with collecting fines from unsuspecting employers. It is time to add some common sense to OSHA's regulations and focus on promoting safety in the workplace" (*Congressional Record,* 104th Cong., 1st sess., 1995, H7076). Much of the Ballenger bill was designed to turn OSHA into a cooperative regulator, earmarking 50 percent of its funding for consultation, training, education, and compliance assistance. It would authorize certified health and safety consultants to review employer safety programs; voluntary reviews would exempt businesses from inspections for up to one year. OSHA would be prohibited from investigating in response to worker complaints unless the worker had first reported the danger to the employer. In addition, OSHA would no longer be able to assess penalties under the "general duty" clause and would be prohibited from issuing penalties unless inspectors had given "notice" of a violation and had been provided the opportunity to fix safety and health violations. HR 1834 also mandated the elimination of NIOSH and the merging of the Mine Safety and Health Administration into OSHA.

In response, the AFL-CIO started a massive campaign during the spring of 1995, funded with an assessment of $1.80 per union member. The AFL-CIO secretary treasurer described the Ballenger bill as the "Death and Injury Enhancement Act." To defeat this act, the AFL-CIO initiated a multi-point plan, which included membership education and outreach, a national petition drive, targeted activities in Washington (e.g., union attendance at all hearings tied to the Ballenger bill), grassroots activities targeting selected congressional offices, and media outreach. The efforts began in earnest with a three-day vigil at the Capitol Building, the "Campaign of Shame," designed to publicize the stories of workers who were victims of work-related injuries, deaths, and illnesses (*AFL-CIO News,* July 3, 1995, August 11, 1995). It culminated in a coordinated set of grassroots efforts targeting legislators (*AFL-CIO News,* November 17, 1995). A business coalition including the US Chamber of Commerce, the National Association of Manufacturers, and the National Federation of Independent Businesses worked unsuccessfully to counter the labor effort. Under intense pressure, the Ballenger bill failed to get the support of congressional leadership (Weisman 1996c).

In the end, the Ballenger bill may have been more successful than critics would admit (Weisman 1996c). As part of the National Performance Review, the Clinton administration unveiled *The New OSHA,* a blueprint for reinventing the agency (see OSHA 1995a). According to the document, OSHA would give businesses the choice between "partnerships" with OSHA or traditional regulation. Partners would receive technical assistance and consultation. Although inspection would not cease, the focus would be on major infractions, and penalty reductions up to 100 percent would be available depending on the vigor of the firm's efforts. Firms that refused the responsibilities of partnership would receive heightened regulatory attention. *The New OSHA* also outlined plans to "streamline and rationalize" existing regulations and to use a system of priority planning to focus future efforts. Finally, the report called for the use of "common sense" in enforcement, focusing on "results, not red tape." This was to be realized through the use of performance indicators (rather than indicators of activity), new means of targeting enforcement, and improved information dissemination.

As part of reinventing itself, in November 1998 the agency launched the OSHA Strategic Partnership Program (OSPP) to generate innovative solutions to occupational safety and health problems and leverage private sector resources. The OSPP was designed to work through collaborative agreements with various "partners" (e.g., employers, unions, state and local governments, insurance companies). Working together, OSHA and its partners could identify a safety and health problem, develop strategies for managing the problems, and maintain a system for verifying results. The partnership agreements ran for three years, with a commitment of partners to continue to support the programs after the agreements had run their course. The OSPP opened ten partnerships in 1998, with an additional twenty-eight in 1999 and fifty in 2000. As will be noted below, the OSPP continued to flourish during the George W. Bush presidency.

Reinvention appeared to many to be a conciliatory gesture in a hostile political environment in which Congress sought to restrict OSHA's actions in a number of subtle ways (Beadle 1999; Freedman 1998). The level of rule making fell to lower levels than during the previous two administrations and the agency became far more cautious with the standards it promulgated. Yet OSHA continued to develop rules, the most costly and controversial of which addressed repetitive stress injuries and the need for mandatory ergonomics programs. As noted above, industry mobilized vigorously against the standard at various points in the 1990s; some 500 companies and trade associations worked through their participation in the US Chamber of Commerce's National Coalition on Ergonomics (Stone and Jacobson 1999). Following a series of appropriation riders prohibiting the Department of Labor from issuing a rule on ergonomics, observers believed that a final rule—should it be issued at all—would be far less costly. In the event that OSHA pursued a standard that was deemed unacceptable by Congress, legislators had another weapon in their arsenal. Under the Congressional Review Act of 1996, Congress has sixty days to review major regulations (i.e., those that impose costs on the economy of $100 million or more per year). Congress could pass a resolution of disapproval, which, with the signature of the president, could rescind any new regulations (Freedman 1998).

In November 1999, following the last vote before the end of the congressional session, OSHA formally proposed its new ergonomics standards, which would take effect in one year. The standards would cover workers in manufacturing and occupations requiring heavy lifting (with the exception of the maritime, agricultural, and construction industries). Employers would be required to create ergonomics programs in response to the reporting of musculoskeletal disorders. It would also require them to compensate injured workers for six months of recovery, with 90 percent of compensation for those who were out of work. OSHA estimated that the standard would impose annual costs of $4.2 billion, but argued that these costs would be small compared to the $9.1 billion in savings from lower insurance payments, increased productivity, and the prevention of 300,000 injuries annually (Benton 1999). Under congressional pressure, the comment period was extended on the rule and OSHA released its final version in November 2000. Ultimately, the ergonomic standard became one of the midnight regulations imposed in the waning days of the Clinton presidency, and was scheduled to go into effect on January 16, 2001.

The George W. Bush Administration and OSHA

Two decades before the Bush victory, Ronald Reagan had presented OSHA as the paradigmatic case of overregulation, an agency that was in dire need of thoroughgoing reform. In contrast, George W. Bush assigned minimal importance to changing directions at OSHA. No one on Bush's transition team, for example, was assigned the duty of evaluating OSHA's activities and charting a new course. Bush's first appointment to the position of assistant secretary for occupational safety and health was John L. Henshaw. While Henshaw had strong credentials, with a quarter century of experience directing environmental, safety, and health programs in the chemical industry and as president of the American Industrial Hygiene Association (1990–1991), he lacked Washington experience.

Budgets provide important information of changing priorities or, in the case of OSHA, the lack of substantial change. In the final year of the Clinton presidency, OSHA had a budget of $381.6 million. By 2005 the budget had increased to $464.2 million, some 122 percent of what existed in 2000. Moreover, while there have been changes in budgetary priorities under Bush, they have been minor. Enforcement claimed 36.9 percent of the budget ($141 million) in 2000; as a proportion of the budget, if fell to 36.6 percent by 2005 ($169.7 million). In 2000, 3.3 percent of OSHA's resources ($12.7 million) were assigned to developing safety and health standards; by 2005, this had increased to 3.5 percent, or $16 million. Funding for state programs claimed 21.9 percent of the budget ($83.5 million) in 2000, with another 11.2 percent ($42.8 million) for state consultation grants. Five years later, support for state programs had fallen to 19.6 percent of the budget ($91 million), whereas state consultation grants had increased to 11.5 percent ($53.4 million) of the budget. The one area where change seemed the most distinct was in the support for compliance assistance. In 2000, compliance assistance commanded 14.2 percent of the budget ($54.2 million). By 2005, 15.3 percent of the budget ($70.9 million) was devoted to compliance assistance. Indeed, three general conclusions seem apparent when examining the budget. First, changes in priorities were minor compared to those that occurred in the second half of the 1990s under REGO (see Figure 8.2). Second, the budgetary changes under Bush have been largely in keeping with preexisting trends. Third, given the steady growth in OSHA's budget under Bush, every area has received an increase in funding over the period in question.

By most standard indicators, moreover, there has not been a marked shift in enforcement efforts. In fiscal year 2004, for example, there were 39,225 inspections, an increase over the 36,613 inspections in 2000, the last year of the Clinton presidency. In 2004, 55.1 percent of these inspections were targeted toward high-risk industries, a slight increase over the 50.3 percent of targeted inspections in 2000. In 2004, OSHA assigned penalties in excess of $85 million, the majority of which (71.1 percent) stemmed from serious violations. In 2000, OSHA handed out $72 million in penalties, 62.6 percent of which stemmed from serious violations (OSHA 2005; Siskind 2002).

The continuity between administrations is not limited to the budget. As noted above, under REGO, the Clinton administration increased support for compliance assistance and worked to foster cooperative relations and partnerships. Under the direction of Henshaw, the agency has embraced this new direction. The Voluntary Protection Program was extended to over 1,100 facilities, and the OSHA Strategic Partnership Program experienced significant growth. We will examine the growing emphasis on voluntarism in greater detail below, noting how the broad continuity may, in fact, obfuscate some more significant changes in OSHA policy. To understand these changes, we must begin with a discussion of regulatory standards.

One area where there has been a sharp departure from the past is in the issuance of new regulatory standards. During the first term of George W. Bush, OSHA eliminated almost five times as many pending standards as it completed. The most important rule that was rescinded was the ergonomics rule (see below). Because the Clinton administration had devoted so much time on this rule, it had left forty-four other rules that were unfinished and thus ripe for cancellation. By the end of the first year of the Bush administration, eighteen of these rules had been eliminated; an additional six were discarded by the end of 2003. The aborted rules covered a number of issues, ranging from the regulation of chemicals used in the semiconductor industry to workplace testing for tuberculosis. Significantly, in 2004, OSHA also eliminated a rule that required employers to keep a record of ergonomic injuries. At the same time, the Bush administration failed to initiate any significant health or safety rules (Brinkley 2004; Goldstein and Cohen 2004). Early on, OSHA head John Henshaw viewed the regulatory agenda he had inherited from the Clinton administration as being little more than a wish list of proposals that had languished for years. His goal was to cull the regulatory agenda to create a meaningful "to-do" list. According to OMB Watch's J. Robert Shull, "OSHA cleared the decks of its agenda. Just swept it clean" (Skrzycki 2004: 1).

Did the Bush administration simply clear the deck, or did it move purposively toward a more practical list of priorities? Neither seems to be the case. Rather, the administration appears to have a more coherent regulatory strategy that involves a retreat from the standard-driven, command and control model of the past to one that is steeped in voluntarism and partnerships. Depending on one's perspective, it is either a logical culmination of REGO or the hijacking of REGO to fundamentally transform OSHA regulation and achieve the Reagan-era goal of turning the agency into a "cooperative regulator." This point is best illustrated through a brief examination of the ergonomics standard.

As noted above, OSHA's ergonomics standard was implemented as one of the final acts of the Clinton administration. Bolstered by the results of the 2000 election, businesses renewed their lobbying efforts, this time focusing on the Congressional Review Act of 1996, which, as mentioned above, gives Congress sixty days to review major regulations and pass a resolution of disapproval, which in turn, with a presidential signature, could kill the new standard outright. Such a resolution was deemed superior to protracted legal challenges that might not bear fruit. Moreover, business interests were hopeful that Bush's decisions to place a sixty-day freeze on regulations that hadn't yet gone into effect, and stop publication in the *Federal Register* of new regulations until they could be reviewed, indicated a willingness to overturn the new ergonomics standard (Stone 2001).

The Congressional Review Act received its first use in March 2001, when Congress voted a resolution of disapproval (S.J. Res. 6). President Bush was quick to lend his support, noting in his statement: "There needs to be a balance between and an understanding of the costs and benefits associated with Federal regulations. In this instance, though, in exchange for uncertain benefits, the ergonomics rule would have cost both large and small employers billions of dollars and presented employers with overwhelming compliance challenges. Also, the rule would have applied a bureaucratic one-size-fits-all solution to a broad range of employers and workers—not good government at work" (March 21, 2001). Ironically, with a stroke of the pen, George W. Bush ended a rule that had been in development since it was initiated in the presidency of his father.

Congressional support for overturning the OSHA rule had been generated only with assurances that the administration would move quickly to develop its own policy on ergonomics. Thus, as the mandatory ergonomics rule died, Labor Secretary Elizabeth Chao announced a series of public forums for the summer of 2001 to collect information on repetitive stress injuries for a new ergonomics program at OSHA. Critics were quick to note that there was not a need for more information. After ten years of development and, in the previous year alone, ten weeks of hearings and a thousand witnesses, the only question left open was whether OSHA was going to execute its regulatory duties (Murray 2001). Organized labor had reason to be skeptical. As the "Ergo Tour" drew to a close, Bush announced that he had appointed Eugene Scalia, the son of Supreme Court justice Antonin Scalia, to serve as the Labor Department's top lawyer (Benton 2001). Scalia had gone on record as being in opposition to OSHA's ergonomics regulations, noting that "the 'science' of ergonomics is notoriously doubt-ridden and controversial," "an ergonomics rule is folly," and OSHA should "cease its general duty clause litigation" to address repetitive motion injuries (Scalia 2000: 2, 13).

In April 2002 the Department of Labor released its new policy for ergonomics to address musculoskeletal disorders in the workplace. The four-pronged approach involved industry-specific and task-specific guidelines, enforcement, outreach, and research. Subsequently, OSHA published ergonomic guidelines for the nursing home industry, retail grocery stores, and poultry processing plants, and initiated guidelines for shipyards, furniture manufacturing, and the printing industry. In each case the guidelines were developed with public comments, and in most cases with stakeholder meetings. These guidelines do not constitute enforceable standards. As OSHA notes:

> These guidelines are advisory in nature and informational in content. They are not a new standard or regulation and do not create any new OSHA duties. Under the OSH Act, the extent of an employer's obligation to address ergonomic hazards is governed by the general duty clause. 29 U.S.C. 654(a)(1). An employer's failure to implement the guidelines is not a violation, or evidence of a violation of the general duty clause. Furthermore, the fact that OSHA has developed this document is not evidence of an employer's obligations under the general duty clause; the fact that a measure is recommended in this document but not adopted by an employer is not evidence of a violation of the general duty clause. (OSHA 2004c: 3)

Of course, this is not a new position for OSHA. The guidelines for the meatpacking industry, developed a decade earlier, issued a comparable set of caveats.

OSHA backed these guidelines with ergonomics inspections (some 2,400 between 2002 and 2005). Enforcement actions have been conducted under the authority of the OSH Act's "general duty clause," which establishes the employer's obligation to "furnish to each of his employees employment and a place of employment which are free from recognized hazards that are causing or are likely to cause death or serious physical harm to his employees." This clause provides broad jurisdiction where there is no specific standard in place, as is the case with ergonomics. Nonetheless, enforcement has been paltry. During the period in question, only twenty-two firms were cited for ergonomics-related violations under the clause, according to OSHA's Integrated Management Information System.

With respect to outreach, OSHA created twenty-four strategic partnerships focused on ergonomics (see the discussion of the OSPP below) and has formed alliances with a number of associations (including the American Apparel and Footwear Association, the Airline Industry Alliance, the National Telecommunications Safety Panel, and the American Academy of Orthopedic Surgeons) to develop industry-specific ergonomics manuals. The final prong, research, has involved the creation of the fifteen-member National Advisory Committee on Ergonomics, representing industry, labor, academia, and the legal and medical professions.

The problem with the shift from enforceable standards to voluntary initiatives is evident. Voluntary efforts are purely discretionary. If corporate managers have a fiduciary responsibility to maximize shareholder wealth, the investment in ergonomics programs will be contingent on its compatibility with the bottom line. If, in fact, OSHA was correct in its early claims that the costs of ergonomics regulations would be minimal in comparison to the returns to corporations (e.g., reduced insurance payments, gains in worker productivity), there would be sufficient incentives to manage the problem absent regulation. The high levels of corporate mobilization against the ergonomics standard suggest that either OSHA overstated the benefits relative to the costs, or corporations were incapable of recognizing their own self-interest.

Even if one assumes that there is sufficient market incentive to manage ergonomic injuries, one might still have a preference for mandatory standards. Firms in price-sensitive markets may not have the resources or incentives to institute ergonomics programs absent regulatory pressures. Moreover, public regulation can force higher levels of accountability. In this context, the administration's decision to eliminate the required record-keeping of ergonomic injuries is quite interesting.

The decision to repeal the ergonomics standard was combined with a commitment to develop ergonomics programs through a series of voluntary partnerships. This model seems to be prevalent at OSHA more generally and constitutes a clear elaboration of Clinton-era REGO initiatives. Reinvention was heralded as a means of improving regulatory performance by appending a host of partnerships onto the existing regulatory structure. The Bush administration has moved beyond REGO by using partnerships as a substitute for, rather than a complement to, traditional modes of regulation.

The Bush administration retained and expanded the OSHA Strategic

Partnership Program, created in 1998. In 2004, OSHA promulgated a new OSHA directive (03-02-002) on strategic partnerships that clearly defined the place of partnerships in the larger regulatory system. This discussion is based largely on the new directive. An OSHA strategic partnership is an "extended voluntary cooperative relationship between OSHA and groups of employers, employees, employee representatives, and/or other interested stakeholders designed to encourage, assist, and recognize efforts to eliminate serious hazards and achieve a high degree of worker safety and health" (OSHA 2004b: IV-B). A strategic partnership is formalized in a written agreement that identifies the partners and their responsibilities, states the purpose and scope of the agreement and the strategies for achieving the outcomes, establishes effective performance measures and the methodology for conducting annual evaluations and verifying results, and identifies the benefits for participants (OSHA 2004c: XII).

The benefits of participation are potentially significant. Non-enforcement-related benefits include access to free on-site technical assistance and public recognition through OSHA press releases, certificates, and the use of the strategic partnership logo. The enforcement-based benefits include opportunities for receiving a 10 percent "good faith" penalty reduction (not applicable to high-gravity, serious, or willful violations, or to failure to abate or repeat citations). Participants can also receive additional enforcement-based benefits, which can be quite significant for firms subject to programmed inspections (i.e., firms that are normally targeted for higher inspection priorities due to industry injury or illness rates). In order of increasing importance, these benefits include a six-month deferral in programmed inspections, a limited scope on programmed inspections, or removal from OSHA's programmed inspection list altogether. In each case, access to greater benefits is performance-based (OSHA 2004c: XIV).

The OSPP initiated between fifty-four and fifty-seven new partnerships per year during 2001–2004. By 2005, OSHA had participated in 373 partnerships covering some 800,000 workers and 13,000 employers. Over 80 percent of the partnerships addressed high-risk industries and serious injuries or illnesses, according to OSHA's Office of Partnership and Recognition. Most of the partnerships are between OSHA and a given corporation, professional association, or set of contractors. The participation of organized labor is concentrated in large construction projects in OSHA regions I, II, and III (New England and the Mid-Atlantic) and region V (the industrial Midwest). It is almost wholly absent in other regions of the country.

Although there has been great controversy surrounding the cancellation of the ergonomics standard, OSHA has worked on reducing repetitive motion injuries through several OSPP partnerships, including two with the United Auto Workers and one with the US Postal Service (USPS), the

American Postal Workers Union (of the AFL-CIO), and the National Postal Mail Handlers Union. The latter partnership was designed to identify and control the risk factors that can cause musculoskeletal disorders to postal employees. The performance measures were analyzed for the first ten facilities (over fifty-nine USPS facilities have entered the partnership). Between January 31, 2003, and February 24, 2004, the partners analyzed 608 tasks, developed ergonomic risk-reduction processes for a subset of the tasks, and conducted training sessions for 10,484 workers. At the ten USPS facilities in question, the partnership resulted in a 19 percent reduction in injury and illness rates, a 20 percent reduction in the musculoskeletal disorder rates, and a 17 percent reduction in lost workdays.[1]

In March 2002, OSHA created its Alliance Program, under which the agency and participants (including employers, labor unions, trade or professional associations, and educational institutions) can cooperate to address workplace safety and health issues. Although comparable in many ways to the OSPP, the Alliance Program does not demand the same level of commitment on the part of participants and carries no enforcement-related benefits. Nonetheless, participants can "build trusting, cooperative relationships with the agency," "network with other groups committed to workplace safety and health," "leverage resources to maximize worker safety and health protection," and "gain recognition as a proactive leader in safety and health" (OSHA 2004a: 2). This final benefit is reinforced by an official alliance logo, which participants can place on their print and electronic media to advertise their commitment to occupational safety and health. Alliance members negotiate two-year agreements setting short- and long-term goals for training and education, outreach and communication, and promoting dialogue by sharing data. By 2005 there were over seventy alliances with signed agreements. Of this number, only one alliance included union representation (the Roadway Workzone Safety and Health Coalition). The remainder involved corporations and trade or professional associations.[2] This stands in stark contrast to the OSPP, in which many partnerships—particularly in the construction industry—include labor.

By all indicators, the Alliance Program is expanding at a pace that is well ahead of expectations. In addition to the national alliances, there is a growing network of regional alliances. By the end of 2004, 172 regional alliances were in place, with an additional 55 in development (OSHA 2004a). At first glance, there is nothing even remotely objectionable to the Alliance Program. Given the dearth of regulatory resources relative to the size of the economy, gains in occupational safety and health may well depend on voluntary efforts to find innovative solutions to common problems. Yet voluntary programs, as noted above, have an impact on outcomes only to the extent that participants implement changes in practices. To the extent that these changes are compatible with corporate profitability, they may well occur. Yet the public recognition that accompanies participation may create an impression of a commitment that does not extend to the shop floor. The lack of labor participation, when combined with the lack of an enforcement component, may create few pressures for anything more than symbolic self-regulation.

How does one make sense of the occupational safety and health regulation during the George W. Bush administration? Several indicators—budgetary priorities, inspections, penalties, support for Clinton-era reinvention initiatives—suggest great continuity with the past. Yet the abandonment of standard development, combined with an expansion of voluntary partnerships and alliances, suggests a notable departure from the past three decades and a return to an earlier vision of workplace safety as being largely a managerial prerogative, albeit one that is now reinforced by regulatory enforcement actions against the most egregious violations.

Conclusion

OSHA has survived for more than three decades in a highly conflictive environment. Given the controversies that have surrounded the agency, it is amazing that it has survived this long. Figures on levels of inspections, citations, and fines can present an imperfect picture of agency effectiveness insofar as they focus on levels of activity that are rarely good surrogates for effectiveness. In an agency like OSHA, where a citation can stem from a paperwork violation or the failure to display a poster, enforcement figures can be particularly unenlightening. There are good data on occupational injuries and fatalities. These data, while not unambiguous, suggest that OSHA's regulatory activities have in fact coincided with a reduction in occupational injury and death rates. Yet the declines in workplace injury and fatality rates appear to be relatively consistent over the course of the past century, making it difficult to claim with any certainty that OSHA has been a primary driver in this trend. Still, there is reason to believe that OSHA inspections do, in fact, impact on injury rates at the level of the firm. Research by Wayne Gray and John Scholz (1993), for example, reveals that for firms that received inspections with penalties in a given year during the period 1979 to 1985, there was a 22 percent fall in workplace injuries over the course of the next three years.

The history presented in this chapter appears to provide some real support for the principal-agent perspective. The history of OSHA is, in large part, a history of changing presidential agendas imposed through appointees. However, the exercise of political direction is itself a product of institutional design. As OSHA is a mainline regulatory agency, one would expect the president to play the dominant role in directing agency activities.

Bureaucratic factors come into play in another way. During the 1970s, OSHA became increasingly professionalized and developed a rather sophisticated set of internal processes for developing policies. One would expect a highly professionalized agency to be more capable of resisting political control. In the case of OSHA, we see an agency that has shown a remarkable degree of continuity over the course of some turbulent periods. One can attribute the consistency of regulatory focus to the fact that OSHA is a professionalized agency that embodies the norms of dominant professional groups.

How can one limit the power of a professionalized bureaucracy? Here, three strategies suggest themselves, two of which have been actively pursued. First, one may use funding restrictions to deprofessionalize an agency. This was a successful strategy during the first term of the Reagan presidency, although the recent history of OSHA has been one of funding increases rather than reductions. Second, one may introduce new decision rules that can heighten the role of cost-benefit analysis. This has been of limited efficacy due to the provisions of the OSH Act. Finally, one might promote decentralization through devolution of authority to field offices, state regulators, or the regulated themselves. Implementation of OSHA policies is highly decentralized as a result of state enforcement; the number of state inspections in any given year dwarfs federal inspections. A heavy state dependence on OSHA grants makes state enforcement vulnerable to changes directed from above. Understanding this vulnerability, one should not be surprised that those intent on reducing OSHA's activism have promoted it. More recently, decentralization has taken a new form: under regulatory reinvention, authority has been increasingly delegated to partnerships. Although these partnerships were initially viewed as a complement to mandatory regulations, increasingly they have been embraced as a substitute.

What of Congress? Given the high salience of occupational safety and health policy, there have been ongoing efforts on the part of Congress to shape and direct OSHA activities. The annual flood of legislation (most of it unsuccessful) and budget controversies have been a constant part of OSHA's environment. The highly partisan nature of the issue area and the existence of multiple veto points have limited the impact of these efforts. One might hypothesize that efforts to exercise political influence will be most successful when Congress and the presidency are controlled by the same political party. They will be least effective when the institutions are under divided control. Certainly, divided control has been a common feature of OSHA's external environment. As the events of the 1990s suggest, divided control need not result in stalemate. Rather, it can force the discovery of a compromise position in which presidential initiatives are designed, in part, to respond to potential sources of conflict. Yet with a return to unified control, efforts have been made once again to alter fundamentally the nature of occupational safety and health regulation by replacing mandatory regulations with regulatory voluntarism. Whether the current drive to transform OSHA into a "cooperate regulator" is successful, may well be determined by the outcomes of future elections.

Notes

1. See OSPP data at http://www.osha.gov/dcsp/partnerships/national/usps/usps.html.

2. See Alliance Program data at http://www.osha.gov/dcsp/alliances/national_alliances.html.

9

Regulating
Consumer Products

FOR CONSUMERS TO MAKE rational decisions, they must have adequate information. Information asymmetries are a common source of market failure. They become more serious as products become increasingly complex and consumers and producers are geographically dispersed. Thus the need for consumer protection regulation has become more distinct as the nation evolved from a decentralized agrarian economy to a mass consumption economy. Ironically, corporations may promote regulation out of their own self-interest. Take the case of the Progressive Era consumer protection regulations such as the Pure Food and Drug Act and the Meat Inspection Act of 1906. Congress suggested that it was acting in the "public interest," yet the regulatory initiatives were also supported by the largest meatpackers. Following the publication of Upton Sinclair's *The Jungle* (1906), concerns over the purity of meats had reduced demand in export markets (Snyder 1945; Kolko 1963: 98–100). The introduction of new regulations simultaneously addressed these concerns and imposed costs on smaller producers that could potentially force them into bankruptcy (see Kolko 1963; Yaeger 1981; Young 1989). There is reason to believe that corporate support for consumer protection has reflected some of the same elements at other points in history.

Although US consumer protection regulation dates back to the early years of the twentieth century, the level of concern peaked during the late 1960s and 1970s. Many trace the modern consumer movement to the publication of Ralph Nader's *Unsafe at Any Speed* (1965), an exposé of the Corvair that placed safety issues on the agenda, leading ultimately to the passage of the National Traffic and Motor Vehicle Safety Act of 1966 and the creation of the National Highway and Traffic Safety Administration four years later (see Stone 1995). In 1969, Nader founded the Center for the Study of Responsive Law and used it as a launching pad for additional reports by "Nader's Raiders," a group of young lawyers and law students who exposed regulatory failure in several regulatory agencies. A number of new consumer groups, such as Public Citizen, the Consumer Federation of America, the Consumers Union, and the US Public Interest Research Group, were formed in these years, many with the financial support of Nader. Backed by the growing consumer movement, Congress passed new regulatory statutes and created several new agencies that would play some role in consumer protection (see Harris and Milkis 1996: 53–96). There are more than forty executive branch agencies that play some role in consumer protection, with parallel agencies at the state and local levels (Brown 1995: 408–409). In this chapter, we restrict our discussion to two of the primary consumer protection regulators: the Federal Trade Commission and the Consumer Product Safety Commission. The major consumer protection statutes enforced by the FTC and the CPSC are presented in Figures 9.1 and 9.2, respectively.

Consumer Protection Policy

Minimally, consumer protection policy should provide the information necessary to make rational decisions in the market. If one accepts a subjectivist position (i.e., that consumers are the best judges of their own welfare), this might be sufficient. Fair labeling, however, may be combined with common law, which assigns liability and allows for monetary redress, thereby giving consumers the guarantee of a warranty or recourse to the courts. Regulators often adopt a far more protective stance, however, assuming that some consumers are incapable of reasoned decisions or that some products are simply too harmful to be made available. They may establish product standards and require that products prove their efficacy before entering the stream of commerce. When evidence suggests that products in circulation fail to meet these criteria, they may be recalled or banned altogether.

The complexity of consumer protection regulations is variable, depending on a number of political and technical factors. One would correctly expect conservative regulators to possess a strong market orientation and embrace a minimalist policy, whereas more liberal regulators would have a greater penchant for design standards and requirements that manufacturers prove the safety and efficacy of their products. Moreover, the complexity of regulation should reflect the complexity of the good in question (e.g., determining whether textile fiber content is correctly reflected on the label is less complex than determining whether a given medication will have the intended impact). Similarly, regulatory complexity should reflect the potential for sig-

**Figure 9.1 Major Consumer
Protection Statutes Enforced by the FTC**

Federal Trade Commission Act (15 U.S.C. §§ 41–58, as amended)

Wool Products Labeling Act (15 U.S.C. §§ 68a–68j, as amended)

Fur Products Labeling Act (15 U.S.C. §§ 69a–69j)

Textile Fiber Products Identification Act (15 U.S.C. §§ 70a–70k, as amended)

Federal Cigarette Labeling and Advertising Act of 1966 (15 U.S.C. §§ 1331–1340, as amended)

Fair Packaging and Labeling Act (80 Stat. 1296; 15 U.S.C. §§ 1451–1461)

Truth in Lending Act (15 U.S.C. §§ 1601a–1667f, as amended)

Fair Credit Billing Act (15 U.S.C. §§ 1666a–1666j)

Fair Credit Reporting Act (15 U.S.C. §§ 1681a–1681u, as amended)

Fair Credit and Charge Card Disclosure Act (15 U.S.C. §§ 1637c–1637g)

Equal Credit Opportunity Act (15 U.S.C. §§ 1691a–1691f, as amended)

Fair Debt Collection Practices Act (15 U.S.C. §§ 1692a–1692o, as amended)

Electronic Fund Transfer Act (15 U.S.C. §§ 1693a–1693r)

Consumer Leasing Act (15 U.S.C. §§ 1667a–1667f, as amended)

Magnuson-Moss Warranty/Federal Trade Commission Improvements Act (15 U.S.C. §§ 2301–2312)

Hobby Protection Act (16 U.S.C. §§ 2101–2106)

Petroleum Marketing Practices Act (15 U.S.C. §§ 2801–2841)

Postal Reorganization Act of 1970 (39 U.S.C. § 3009a)

Comprehensive Smokeless Tobacco Health Education Act of 1986 (15 U.S.C. §§ 4401–4408)

Federal Deposit Insurance Corporation Improvement Act of 1991 (PL 102-242)

Dolphin Protection Consumer Information Act (16 U.S.C. § 1385, as amended)

Energy Policy Act of 1992 (106 Stat. 2776, codified in 42 U.S.C. §§ 6201 et seq.)

Telephone Disclosure and Dispute Resolution Act of 1992 (15 U.S.C. §§ 5701 et seq.)

Violent Crime Control and Law Enforcement Act of 1994 (PL 103-322)

Telecommunications Act of 1996 (PL 104-104)

Home Equity Loan Consumer Protection Act (15 U.S.C. §§ 1637 and 1647)

Home Ownership and Equity Protection Act (15 U.S.C. § 1639)

nificant harm. More complicated regulatory proceedings should exist when a given product could result in death than when claims are simply deceptive. Finally, procedural complexity may engender regulatory complexity, even if a product might be regulated effectively through fair labeling.

The data presented in Figure 9.3 reveal that the salience of consumer protection peaked in the late 1970s, a period that witnessed a great deal of controversy in the area of regulation more generally. Salience declined precipitously between 1978 and 1985, and has since remained relatively stable.

**Figure 9.2 Major Consumer
Protection Statutes Enforced by the CPSC**

Consumer Product Safety Act (15 U.S.C. §§ 2051–2084)
Federal Hazardous Substances Act (15 U.S.C. §§ 1261–1277)
Labeling of Hazardous Art Materials Act (15 U.S.C. § 1277)
Child Safety Protection Act (PL 103-267)
Poison Prevention Packaging Act (15 U.S.C. §§ 1471–1476)
Flammable Fabrics Act (15 U.S.C. §§ 1191–1204)
Refrigerator Safety Act (15 U.S.C. §§ 1211–1214)

Figure 9.3 The Salience of Consumer Protection

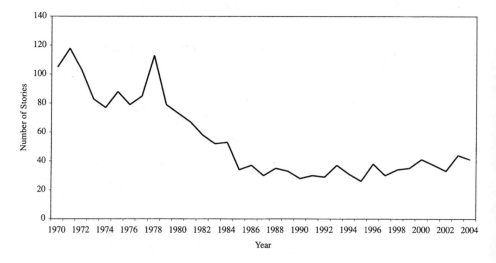

It is interesting to note that total agency stories have been largely neutral. Given the data, one would expect elected officials to pay some attention to the policy area, even if this attention would not necessarily entail explicit discussions of the agencies.

The Consumer Protection Agencies

The FTC and the CPSC are the two agencies primarily involved in consumer protection. The FTC is primarily involved with unfair, deceptive, and fraudulent practices (e.g., false advertising), whereas the CPSC regulates the safety of consumer products.

The Federal Trade Commission

Since the FTC has been addressed in some detail in Chapter 4, albeit with respect to its antitrust enforcement duties, its key organizational features can be summarized quickly. The FTC is an independent regulatory commission headed by a bipartisan commission of five. It has separate bureaus for antitrust, consumer protection, and economic analysis. The primary actor in consumer protection is the Bureau of Consumer Protection (BCP). It actively engages in rule making to specify the practices prohibited by various consumer protection statutes. The FTC also enforces the law and trade regulations through its adjudicative activities. Although the FTC is located in Washington, D.C., it places a heavy reliance on a network of ten regional offices. An organizational chart for the FTC is presented in Figure 4.5. The BCP has the mandate of protecting consumers from unfair, deceptive, and fraudulent business practices. It also works to conduct research on consumer issues and practices, educates consumers and businesses, and actively intervenes on behalf of consumers before other governmental bodies. The FTC's budget for 2005 was $205 million ($115 million for the BCP). As Figure 9.4 shows, the agency experienced periods of rapid budgetary expansion during the 1970s, periods of sharp decline during the 1980s, and recovery in recent years.

In 1969, *The Nader Report on the Federal Trade Commission* (Cox, Fellmeth, and Schultz 1969) identified a number of problems with the FTC, including a poor-quality staff, lethargic leadership, and the systematic fail-

Figure 9.4 The Federal Trade Commission Budget, by Division

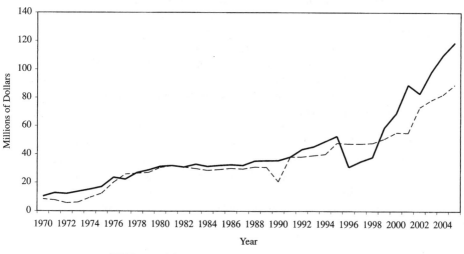

ure to establish priorities, plan actions, and allocate resources accordingly. The FTC, it was argued, was obsessed with the trivial, and as a result its policies were of no value to the population. President Nixon asked the American Bar Association to conduct its own investigation. When the ABA arrived at the same basic conclusions (ABA 1969), the administration initiated a massive reorganization of the agency. Although the FTC has had consumer protection functions since its creation in 1914, they had thus far received little support. With the 1970 reorganization, the moribund Bureau of Deceptive Practices was replaced by the new Bureau of Consumer Protection. In the next several years, this bureau was professionalized with graduates from the nation's best law schools, as was the new Bureau of Competition. The Bureau of Economics was professionalized with a staff of top economists. Henceforth, economic and legal analysis would be integrated into the areas of consumer protection and antitrust (see Eisner 1991: 163–167; Silbergeld 1995).

Reorganization and expanding resources were combined with new regulatory authority. The most important of these laws were the Alaskan Pipeline Act of 1973 and the Magnuson-Moss Warranty/Federal Trade Commission Improvements Act of 1975 (hereafter the FTC Improvements Act). Prior to the passage of these acts, the FTC regulated on a case-by-case basis. As a result, rulings were of limited impact, and enforcement stressed agency resources. The case-by-case adjudication was problematic for an additional reason: the courts had generally deferred to the supposed expertise of the commission and did not require much in the way of evidence to prove that deception or unfair practices had taken place (see West 1985: 148–150; Boyer 1989: 98).

The Alaskan Pipeline Act increased the sanctions available to the FTC by doubling the penalties for violating orders, to $10,000. The commission was also now allowed to represent itself before the courts and seek temporary or permanent injunctions and restraining orders when there was reason to believe that the law had been or was going to be violated. District courts were empowered to grant mandatory injunctions and to seek relief in equity to enforce FTC orders. Finally, the act strengthened the commission's ability to collect information as part of its investigations (Eisner 1991: 161).

The FTC Improvements Act of 1975 authorized industry-wide rule making for unfair or deceptive acts or practices and established a procedure for rule promulgation far more stringent than that imposed under the Administrative Procedure Act of 1946. It increased the penalties for the violation of rules to $10,000, with each day constituting a separate violation. With the new source of power, the FTC was transformed into one of the most powerful regulatory agencies (see Muris 1981; Ellis 1981). Would it attempt to bring proceedings with the limited evidence adopted under the old regime, or would it conduct the detailed technical and economic analysis necessary to justify and legitimize industry-wide rule making? The answer to this question would carry important political consequences (see Boyer 1989).

The BCP enforces the FTCA Section 5 prohibition of "unfair and deceptive acts and practices" and a variety of additional laws designed to protect consumers against unfair, deceptive, or fraudulent practices (see Figure 9.1). It also enforces trade regulation rules. Furthermore, the BCP conducts investigations of individual firms and industries. These investigations may be tied to rule making or enforcement or undertaken at the request of the commission or Congress. The BCP also litigates consumer protection actions both at the commission level and in the federal courts. To facilitate these duties, the bureau contains several specialized divisions for advertising practices, credit practices, enforcement, marketing practices, and service industry practices.

The BCP initiates investigations in response to complaints, requests by Congress, referrals from other agencies, or its own analyses. When its investigations support the need for a new rule, the FTC is required to abide by a process established under the FTC Improvements Act. In addition to the notice and comment requirements of the Administrative Procedure Act, the FTC must publish a notice of proposed rule making along with a justification. It must invite interested parties to submit arguments, data, and written statements—which become part of the public docket—and to hold public hearings. Should the commissioners vote to promulgate the rule, they must provide a statement of basis and purpose that notes the prevalence of the acts or practices, explains why they are unfair or deceptive, and identifies the economic impacts of the rule, especially as they affect small business and consumers. Any interested party may call for an immediate judicial review after the rule is promulgated (see Ellis 1981).

The rule-making process put in place in 1975 was extraordinarily complex. As Barry Boyer notes, "It created an elaborate procedural structure for rational decisionmaking, including hearings with cross-examination and reasoned decisions based on the evidence of record; but it incorporated so many qualifications and exceptions to these procedural rights that it was difficult to determine what opportunities to participate have actually been given or whether they would be meaningful" (1989: 101). Through a system of intervenor funding, the FTC subsidized groups that could represent important perspectives on the matter in question but might lack the resources (Boyer 1981). While the FTC was required to consider the impact of regulated practices and the economic ramifications of the regulation, it was given "no guidance on how to weigh these potentially conflicting factors or what evidence should be collected" (Boyer 1989: 101).

Enforcement actions may originate from private complaints, referrals from state and federal agencies, and economic market studies. Prior to initiating formal investigations, potential cases are assessed in screening and evaluation committees comprised of attorneys and economists. When the BCP believes there is evidence of a violation, it requests that the commission file a formal complaint. Economic impacts have become far more important in determining whether enforcement would be "to the interest of the public." Once a complaint is issued, attorneys work as a team with staff economists to compile evidence and prepare a case, which is ultimately adjudicated before an administrative law judge. The commission usually issues a cease and desist order on the basis of the adjudicative decision. Violation of a cease and desist order may result in a fine of $10,000 per day. In the 1990s the FTC worked closely with other federal and state officials to mount "sweeps" designed to attack multiple actors involved in a given practice simultaneously and with maximum publicity.

The Consumer Product Safety Commission

Congress passed the Consumer Product Safety Act (CPSA) in 1972, creating the CPSC. Under the act, the commission was given the broad mandate to "protect the public against unreasonable risks or injuries and deaths associated with consumer products." The CPSC has jurisdiction over some 15,000 kinds of consumer products, excluding those that were exempted by the organic act (i.e., tobacco, aviation and boating equipment, motor vehicles, foods and drugs, cosmetics, insecticides, fungicides, and rodenticides) or subsequent reauthorizations (e.g., guns and ammunition, fixed amusement rides). Although the CPSC disseminates information on product safety and works closely with industry and consumer groups in the development of voluntary standards, it has recourse to the full range of regulatory tools discussed above. A lack of resources and expertise combined with an economy-wide mandate have led many critics to claim that the agency is incapable of executing its mission. Indeed, while the contemporary commitment to working closely with "industry to voluntarily improve the safety of its products in lieu of mandatory regulations" may be justified as a component of successful governmental reinvention, it is something of a necessity (CPSC 1994: 1). The CPSC, with a budget of $62 million (see Figure 9.5) and 471 full-time employees in 2005, is one of the smallest agencies in the federal government.

The CPSC is an independent commission located in Bethesda, Maryland. Although it was originally headed by a bipartisan commission of five (appointed by the president, subject to Senate confirmation), the commission was reduced to three in 1985 (see Figure 9.6). The chairman of the CPSC is selected by the president. The CPSC has a number of offices that address issues of management (e.g., the Office of the Executive Director, the Office of the Budget, the Office of Planning and Evaluation). Additional

Figure 9.5 The Consumer Product Safety Commission Budget

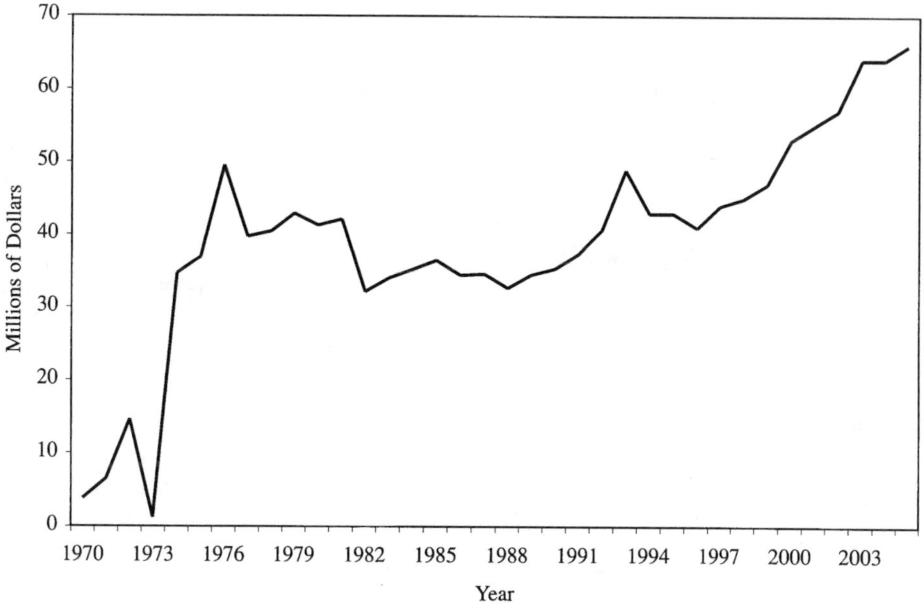

offices bear the bulk of the CPSC's regulatory duties. The Office of Hazard Analysis and Reduction has line authority over the Directorate for Epidemiology, the Directorate for Health Sciences, the Directorate for Engineering Sciences, the Directorate for Laboratory Sciences, and the Directorate for Economics. These directorates provide critical support in developing the technical data required for the identification and assessment of hazards and the design of standards. The Office of Compliance, staffed by attorneys and compliance specialists, investigates product safety hazards and works with companies to secure voluntary corrective actions, where possible. It also conducts litigation before the CPSC's administrative law judges, where necessary in pursuit of remedial actions. Finally, the Directorate for Field Operations executes the CPSC's mission through three regional centers and field offices in cities across the country. As with other regulatory agencies, the CPSC places a great reliance on cooperative efforts with state and local officials and private associations. Under this partnership, the CPSC and state or local agencies agree to a free exchange of information and cooperation in inspections, recalls, enforcement, and informational campaigns. The CPSA authorized the CPSC to commission state and local officers to conduct investigations, inspections, and sample collections on behalf of the agency and to train state and local officials who wish to be commissioned.

Figure 9.6 The Consumer Product Safety Commission

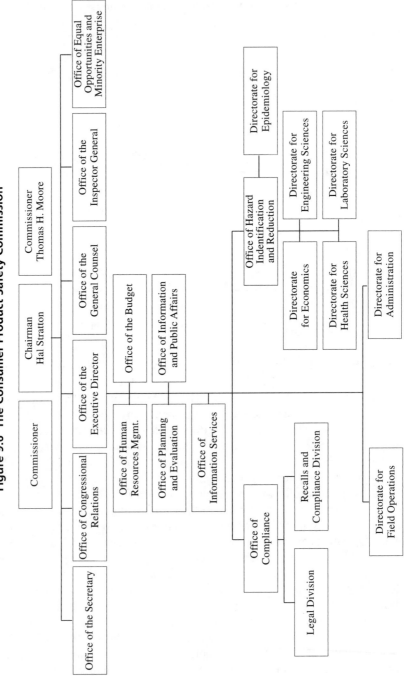

The primary duty of the CPSC is the enforcement of the CPSA's broad mandate (and several other laws listed in Figure 9.2). As noted above, the Office of Hazard Analysis and Reduction compiles data on death and injuries to develop appropriate regulatory responses. These data come from several sources, including the National Electronic Injury Surveillance System, which collects data from a statistically representative sample of hospital emergency rooms covering hundreds of product categories. Other sources of information include the death certificates provided by state health departments, hot-line reports, and in-depth investigations of specific product-related injuries. When developing many of its rules, the CPSC conducts a form of risk assessment. Using these data sources, the CPSC must identify the causal relationship between the product in question and related injuries and disease, the level of exposure or use likely to have adverse effects, and the number of consumers affected. This provides a clear picture of the magnitude of the problem in question.

The CPSC's duties do not end with scientific analysis. Under the Consumer Product Safety Act, the CPSC was directed by Congress to be certain that its rules were "reasonably necessary" to reduce or eliminate the risk of injury and that the "adverse effects" on business be minimized. In a 1978 circuit court decision, the CPSC was informed that it would have to provide "substantial evidence" that "the benefit [of the standard] has a reasonable relationship to the disadvantages" (*Aqua Slide "N" Dive v. CPSC* 1978). As a result, the agency has paid greater attention to the economic impact of its regulations. Once the risk has been characterized, the CPSC compiles data on the costs associated with various regulatory responses as they would impact on consumers and industry actors. When the determination of costs is completed, the CPSC can arrive at some determination as to whether the benefits justify the costs and use this determination to support the chosen response (Bryner 1987: 156–157). The CPSC has a range of options, from the provision of information to technical standards and, in the most severe cases, product recalls and bans (see Fise 1995: 277–279).

With Sections 7 and 10 of the CPSA, Congress chose to maximize participation in rule making. Under Section 10, any person can petition for a rule establishing safety standards for specific products. The CPSC is required to respond within 120 days. Reasons for denials had to be published in the *Federal Register* and were subject to review by a district court. Given that the decision would be reviewed de novo, the decision to deny a petition had to be firmly justified. Under Section 7, the CPSC was required to observe a new process for developing rules. The CPSC was required to publish its intention to proceed with rule making in the *Federal Register,* identifying the justification for a new standard. All interested parties were then invited to submit existing standards or offer to develop new standards.

Under the so-called offeror system, the CPSC was required to accept such offers when the offeror provided evidence of competence, a reasonable timetable for completion of the rule (under 330 days), and a plan detailing how all interested parties would participate in standard development. In addition, the CPSC was required to maximize participation through intervenor funding. A standard developed by an offeror had to be published in the *Federal Register* so that the CPSC could solicit additional comments and evidence. A standard could not be subsequently modified without engaging the offeror process once again (see Congressional Quarterly 1982: 43; Bardach and Kagan 1982: 181–182).

The decision to maximize participation carried a high cost. In the words of Jerry Mashaw, the "progressive logic of participation" became "the progressive logic of disaster." He continues: "That is certainly a reasonable description of CPSC regulation. Petitions for rules have swamped the agency in unproductive investigations of useless subjects and destroyed its capacity to set a reasonable agenda for regulation. The offeror process has produced inordinate delay and has made the commission the virtual captive of the industries it was meant to regulate" (1985: 262–263). The offeror system rightly came under criticism quite early. In December 1977 the GAO noted that the process had produced only three mandatory standards in the agency's history (regulating swimming-pool slides, matchbook covers, and architectural glass) and that the standard development took an average of 834 days, compared with the 330-day limit mandated by the CPSA. Congress responded in 1978 by increasing CPSC discretion to decide whether to develop its own standards or initiate the offeror process. In the 1981 reauthorization, the offeror process was abolished for mandatory rules, although it was still applied for voluntary standards. This, however, was part of a larger effort to emphasize the use of voluntary standards over mandatory rules. The CPSC must now show that voluntary standards either would fail to provide adequate reductions in injuries or would not be routinely complied with. In practice, the CPSC will seek voluntary standards before considering mandatory standards (Congressional Quarterly 1982: 53; Bryner 1987: 146–149).

Much of what constitutes enforcement at the CPSC takes the form of information dissemination, education, and industry guidance in compliance. This educational mission translates into a higher level of cooperation between the CPSC and companies. This cooperation does not foreclose traditional enforcement, however. If hearings convince commissioners that a given product constitutes a substantial hazard to consumers, the CPSC can order companies to repair or replace the product or refund the purchase price. In 2004 the CPSC identified and corrected 386 violations related to fire hazards (including 91 recalls involving some 10 million product units), 35 products that presented a risk of electrocution (including 34 recalls involving 1.7 million product units), and 312 voluntary corrective actions for products that presented a substantial risk of injury for children (including 91 recalls involving 11 million product units). Usually the CPSC involves affected companies in the design of corrective remedies. The CPSC may also pursue civil penalties. In 2004 the commission imposed fines of some $4.2 million (CPSC 2005). Civil penalties are the remedy of choice when there is evidence that manufacturers "knowingly failed to properly report defects in products that could create a substantial risk of injury, or that presented an unreasonable risk of serious injury or death," as required under the CPSA, or "violated mandatory safety requirements" (CPSC, *Annual Report,* 1996: 15).

The Policy Subsystem

Because consumer protection is characterized by concentrated costs and diffuse benefits, one should not expect traditional agency capture. At the same time, the open rule-making processes, intervenor funding, norms of consultation, emphasis on voluntary standards, and expanded access to the courts have all provided multiple venues for interest group influence. Both the FTC and the CPSC have been criticized for the delays. This is unavoidable, however, given that the institutions were designed to maximize participation and regulate it through a highly legalistic process.

The modern consumer movement consists of a number of highly professionalized interest associations, including the Consumer Federation of America (itself an association representing some 240 groups), the Consumers Union, the US Public Interest Research Group, and Public Citizen. Working as a coalition, these groups have been rather effective in promoting legislation and active participants in rule making. Some groups (e.g., the first three above) actively conduct research on safety issues and petition the agencies to initiate formal investigations and rule making. These groups express a strong interest in vigorous consumer protection regulation, in part reflecting the roles they played during the passage of key pieces of legislation. They actively promote increased agency budgets, oppose reductions in regulatory authority, and file suits to force regulators to promulgate rules when necessary.

Businesses have strong incentives to interact with the agencies, given the potential costs of regulation. The CPSC developed ties with businesses quite early—a product of the offeror process and the emphasis on voluntarism. Often, business associations will work with the CPSC to secure standards that will minimize compliance costs. Take the example of child-resistant caps on medicine. Under the Poison Prevention Packaging Act of 1970, the CPSC required that such caps be placed on medicine containers.

When a smaller manufacturer patented a reversible cap that could be used either in a child-resistant mode or an easy-access mode (for those with arthritis), large manufacturers of the childproof caps argued that the reversible model would endanger children. The CPSC agreed, thereby preserving the market share of the established manufacturers (Bardach and Kagan 1982: 200–201).

The FTC, in contrast, embraced an adversarial relationship with business in the 1970s, particularly on the consumer protection side. In large part, this can be attributed to the ruling ethos at the agency following the reorganization of 1970. Many of the commission officials who had developed friendly relationships with business did not survive the reorganization, in response to the charge that the FTC deferred to the businesses it was supposed to regulate. They were replaced by activist attorneys with ties to the consumer movement (Boyer 1989: 207–208). This has since changed, as the FTC has placed greater emphasis on self-regulation, and, more recently, has relied on workshops to promote participation. In addition, the growing role of economic analysis in regulatory decisionmaking has made the FTC appear much more reasonable to many of the interests that once sought its elimination.

The president's relationship with the FTC and the CPSC is structured by a set of formal linkages. The president, with the advice and consent of the Senate, appoints commissioners at both agencies, who will also serve as chairs. There are many recent examples of presidents using the power of appointment to further their policy agendas. As a generalization, Republican presidents have selected chairs who have emphasized self-regulation and voluntary standards combined with a greater adherence to cost-benefit analysis. Democratic presidents, in contrast, have appointed heads who have been more skeptical of self-regulation and the efficacy of market governance and more supportive of an activist regulatory mission.

Congress arguably has a more intimate relationship with the agencies, given their formal independence. As with the president, Congress's relationship with the two agencies is structured, in large part, by a set of formal linkages. There are important differences, however, in its formal relationship with the two agencies. One of the chief concerns in designing the CPSC was preserving its independence from the president and maximizing congressional influence. As a means to this end, the CPSA explicitly limited presidential control over the chairmanship. Once confirmed, the chair could not be removed by the president. Although this restriction was subsequently relaxed to allow a newly elected president to name the chair, this was combined with new restrictions; no officials in the CPSC below the level of commissioner are to be subject to review by the executive. In addition, CPSC budgets are to be submitted simultaneously to the OMB and Congress (Bryner 1987: 151).

Congress routinely interacts with the agencies through oversight and the budgetary process—venues that can be used to influence agency priorities and enforcement agendas. In the Senate, primary oversight responsibilities fall under the jurisdiction of the Commerce Science and Transportation Committee's Subcommittee on Consumer Affairs. In the House, the agencies fall under the jurisdiction of the Commerce Committee's Subcommittee on Telecommunications, Trade, and Consumer Protection. While oversight has often been routine, potentially high regulatory compliance costs have frequently led to highly politicized hearings and direct congressional intervention into agency rule making and agency investigations. In both agencies, Congress has delivered contradictory messages, pushing the agencies to higher levels of activism, only to punish them for zealotry. Thus the House Commerce Committee's oversight subcommittee accused the CPSC of being derelict in failing to set standards for home insulation and prodded it to be more vigorous in its regulatory actions, only to turn around a few years later to amend a commission rule on power lawnmowers in response to industry pressures (see Bryner 1987: 171). A similar cycle has occurred with the FTC, where expansive budget increases and supportive cues resulted in higher levels of consumer regulation, only to stimulate industry mobilization and the passage of the FTC Improvements Act of 1980, which placed serious restraints on the agency.

Much of the new social regulatory legislation of the 1970s provided expanded standing in the courts, allowing interests that were not materially affected to sue the agencies for their failure to execute their nondiscretionary duties. In the consumer protection agencies—as in the Environmental Protection Agency and the Occupational Safety and Health Administration—expanded standing resulted in a large number of suits and greater opportunities for judicial intervention. The CPSC and the FTC have been subject to ongoing litigation such that they can realistically expect that court challenges will be part of the policy process. The heavy reliance on settlements and voluntary regulation has somewhat reduced the vulnerability to the courts. However, they remain important features of the policy subsystem.

The Evolution of Consumer Protection, 1970–Present

The recent history of consumer protection regulation can be divided into four periods: the 1970s, when Congress strongly supported consumer protection, albeit with variable support from the president; 1981 to 1992, when Republican presidents sought to reduce the regulatory authority and budgets; the Clinton presidency, when attention returned to consumer protection issues and regulatory reinvention; and the presidency of George W. Bush.

Consumer Protection in the 1970s

The 1970s can be considered the decade of consumer protection, insofar as it witnessed the creation of the FTC's Bureau of Consumer Protection and the CPSC, as well as the passage of a number of key regulatory statutes. The FTC was expanded, professionalized, and armed with vast new regulatory powers during the 1970s, such that many correctly referred to it as being among the most powerful of the regulators. The CPSC, in contrast, was perpetually weak, characterized by a lack of professional resources, serious budget constraints, limited regulatory authority, and a policy process that was so complex as to stall serious regulation.

The reorganization of 1970 was a transformative event for the FTC—a rebirth for the "Little Old Lady of Pennsylvania Avenue." With the support of the American Bar Association report, Nixon appointed strong chairmen to the FTC, Caspar Weinberger, who served for seven months, followed by Miles Kirkpatrick, the head of the ABA commission responsible for the 1969 report. Ford continued this pattern with the appointment of Lewis Engman. Reorganized and revitalized, the FTC enjoyed a period of growing resources and statutory authority. Even if Nixon and Ford believed that the costs of regulation often outweighed the benefits, there was little evidence of overt intervention in hopes of reining in the FTC. Moreover, even Republican appointees were seeking to expand the reach of the FTC. For example, during the chairmanship of Kirkpatrick, the FTC initiated the concept of advertising substantiation, such that the failure to have proof of an advertising claim constituted a violation of the FTCA of 1914. Such a reversal of burdens was indicative of the new agency activism (Kinzler 1979). With the election of Jimmy Carter, the FTC was placed under the chairmanship of Michael Pertschuk, an energetic consumer advocate and former head of the Senate Commerce Committee's staff. Congress, for its part, strongly supported the FTC, approving the growing budgets and, as noted above, providing a number of important new powers. Congress used oversight hearings to call on the agency to be more vigorous in its regulatory duties (Kovacic 1987).

The FTC responded to this supportive environment by becoming increasingly vigilant in enforcement and seeking to push consumer protection well beyond existing parameters. It embraced the new powers, basing many of its actions on the Fairness Doctrine, "a vague and open-ended concept which the Commission began to utilize in the mid-1960s as a justification for its consumer protection actions" (West 1985: 147). A flurry of new investigations and rule-making proceedings began, many of which pitted the FTC against well-established interests. Rules addressed a vast array of products and activities, including prescription and over-the-counter drugs, mobile homes, vocational education, food advertising, and hearing aids. Rules required the disclosure of important information (e.g., octane values in gasoline, care instructions for home furnishings, energy labeling for home appliances, R-values in thermal insulation, warranty coverage in used cars, cost disclosure in funeral services). The FTC challenged occupational self-regulation of physicians, dentists, and optometrists, arguing that prohibitions on advertising simply facilitated price-fixing. It also initiated an investigation of advertising aimed at children—the so-called Kidvid investigation—under the concern that such advertisements fell under the prohibition of unfair practices. As part of this investigation, the commission actively considered several alternative remedies, including regulating advertisement frequency and techniques, disclosure of nutritional information, and outright prohibition of ads aimed at children (see Singer 1979; Kinzler 1979; Pertschuk 1982).

Under Pertschuk, the FTC became a symbol of overregulation, despite the fact that Congress had repeatedly pushed it to fully explore the limits of the law and thirteen of the seventeen rule-making proceedings at the time had been fully initiated by the commission during Republican presidencies (with a fourteenth mandated by Congress itself). Because rule making took between three and five years (creating records in excess of 40,000 pages), a flood of new rules would soon be in effect, many of which would affect actors on an industry-wide basis. Understanding that time was short to prevent the new regulations, business mobilized a massive lobbying effort, which included the US Chamber of Commerce, the National Association of Manufacturers, the American Medical Association, the National Association of Broadcasters, the Grocery Manufacturers of America, the Association of National Advertisers, the National Automobile Dealers Association, and the National Funeral Directors Association. Interest group mobilization was combined with higher levels of media coverage, much of which portrayed the FTC as an overly intrusive "national nanny." Given that every member of Congress had optometrists, funeral directors, attorneys, dentists, physicians, and used-car dealers in his or her district, the demands for change reverberated through the House and Senate. Intense lobbying was backed by millions of dollars in new campaign spending, creating an irresistible combination of forces. Howard W. Cannon (D-NV), chair of the Commerce, Science, and Transportation Subcommittee, warned Pertschuk and other commissioners to expect "the most vigorous oversight that you've ever seen. . . . This is a partnership created by Congress and it can be amended or terminated at any time" (Singer 1979: 1680). The level of mobilization was not the only factor involved, of course. The House and Senate commerce committees had become ideologically more conservative as a result of deaths, retirements, and electoral defeats (see Kovacic 1987; Weingast and Moran 1982).

As the pressure on the FTC built, Congress failed to pass the legislation authorizing the agency's budget from 1977 to 1980, resulting in a need for continuing resolutions for funding and periods when Congress actually allowed the FTC to be closed. More important, it began considering new legislation that would restrain FTC activism. The Federal Trade Commission Improvements Act of 1980 was the final result, requiring that new trade regulation rules be submitted to Congress sixty days before going into effect, subject to a two-chamber legislative veto. The rule-making process was made more complicated through additional procedural requirements. The balance of interests effectively shifted away from the consumer advocacy groups and toward business. The intervenor funding program was effectively curtailed (Sarasohn 1980). More significant, cost-benefit analysis was elevated in importance. The FTC was now required to provide preliminary and final regulatory analyses that would explain the need for and objectives of the rule, review the costs and benefits of the rule, and provide other reasonable alternatives. Failure to submit these analyses was explicitly cited as grounds for the courts to set aside the new rule. Finally, the act placed restrictions on current and future activities, explicitly exempting some interests from FTC rules and restricting the regulation of children's advertising to issues of deception so that appeals to the Fairness Doctrine ceased, as did an investigation of the insurance industry and a Lanham Act proceeding against Formica designed to remove its trademark status (Silbergeld 1995: 117; Eisner 1991: 178–179; West 1985: 150–155). The decade that began with a firm commitment to the FTC ended with a resounding effort to hobble the runaway regulator.

*   *   *

The 1970s witnessed a similar pattern of events with respect to the CPSC, even if this agency never achieved the powers of its more established counterpart. In 1968, President Lyndon Johnson responded to the growing salience of consumer protection issues by creating the National Commission of Product Safety, which reported that there were some 20 million consumers injured each year—including 110,000 permanent disabilities and 30,000 deaths. In 1970 it called for the creation of a consumer protection agency, arguing that it could prevent some 4 million injuries and 6,000 deaths per year (Congressional Quarterly 1982: 53–53). Nixon believed that the best approach to consumer protection would involve education and the development of voluntary standards. Such activities could be assigned, he argued, to the FDA or the Department of Health, Education, and Welfare. Consumer advocates argued that anything short of formal independence would increase the agency's vulnerability to industry influences. Congress responded to intense consumer group lobbying and created an independent commission, the CPSC, in 1972.

Reflecting his opposition to an independent agency, Nixon failed to appoint the full contingent of five commissioners until some five months into the life of the CPSC. He appointed Richard O. Simpson, an engineer with government experience at the Commerce Department, as chairman. Simpson faced some significant challenges. First, the CPSC inherited its staff from existing agencies: 586 workers were transferred from the Department of Health, Education, and Welfare, the Commerce Department, and the FTC. The new agency also inherited fourteen fully staffed FDA regional offices. Contemporary observers believed that these transfers were used strategically by the agencies in question as a means of ridding themselves of unqualified workers protected by the civil service. In addition to staffing problems, Simpson was forced to fend off White House attempts to exert control over top appointees by making Civil Service Commission approval contingent on political clearance. Simpson circumvented the system by hiring appointees as agency consultants and ultimately went public with his criticism of the efforts to limit agency independence (*CQWR* 1978b: 391–392).

The politics surrounding the CPSC placed Simpson in an untenable position. His efforts to exert independence undermined presidential support (President Ford, when his term officially expired in October 1975, was silent about whether Simpson would be reappointed, thus undercutting his legitimacy as chair). At the same time, he could not rely on consumer advocates who viewed his appointment with suspicion from the beginning and were suing the CPSC to force more vigorous enforcement. Simpson unwisely structured expectations early, promising 100 mandatory standards by 1982. After its first four years, the CPSC, mired in the complexity of the offeror process, had produced but two final standards (Johnson 1990: 75). In the end, Simpson's single greatest success came in convincing Congress to amend the CPSA in the 1976 reauthorization to strengthen CPSC independence both by permitting agency attorneys to initiate civil proceedings if the DOJ failed to act on referrals within forty-five days, and by exempting top appointees from White House clearance. The CPSA reauthorization also reduced some of the political opposition by providing an exemption of firearms while strengthening the exemption of tobacco products.

After a prolonged stay in political limbo, Simpson resigned, and Ford selected S. John Byington, deputy special assistant to the president for consumer affairs, as chair. Concerns that Byington was selected by virtue of his friendship with Ford provided an opening for consumer and labor group mobilization. The Senate Commerce Committee shelved the nomination, leading Ford to renominate Byington for an unexpired term of two and a half years. Although the Senate initially rejected the nomination (33 to 37), it voted again to narrowly approve the nomination (Congressional Quarterly 1982: 52–53). The new CPSC chair adopted a minimalist mission, noting that the CPSA "does not say we are to make sure all consumer products are safe [but] simply to remove unreasonable risk." Risks were deemed unreasonable when they were not obvious to the consumer, when they could be eliminated without impacting on price or function, or when they affected special classes of consumers (children, the elderly). Product liability and tort law were the mainstays of consumer protection; the CPSC might "give the process a significant push" (Byington 1977: 33, 35).

Byington's chairmanship was marred by a series of critical assessments of the CPSC, issued by the GAO and the House Commerce Committee's Oversight and Investigation Subcommittee, which painted a portrait of an agency that was incapable of setting regulatory priorities, effectively allocating its resources, and enforcing the few standards it had managed to produce. The failures, it was agreed, stemmed in part from the complexities of the offeror process. These critical conclusions were combined with a Civil Service Commission report alleging widespread violation of personnel rules and employee dissatisfaction with performance, as well as with an internal management study that concluded that the CPSC had fallen far short of reasonable levels of performance, given the resources at its disposal (Congressional Quarterly 1982: 52–53). In response to this dismal record, Representative Bob Eckhardt (D-TX) and Senator Wendell H. Ford (D-KY), chairmen of the consumer subcommittees in the two chambers, called for Byington's resignation, arguing that his mismanagement had damaged the agency's credibility. Byington complied in hopes that it would "depoliticize" the congressional hearings (*CQWR* 1978b: 392).

Given the poor performance of the CPSC, President Carter considered abolishing the agency. Following vigorous consumer group lobbying, however, he accepted a three-year reauthorization, albeit with changes in the CPSC, such that newly elected presidents would now have the right to select a new chair. Carter appointed Susan B. King to a vacancy in January 1978 and elevated her to the chairmanship in June when Byington's resignation took effect. Trained as a political scientist and with no experience in consumer protection, King lacked the credentials to suggest effectiveness in the position. Nevertheless, her successful tenure as chair was a key factor in the CPSC's survival. Under King's direction, the CPSC's performance record improved significantly. She introduced a number of priorities to guide CPSC action, focusing attention on potentially serious household hazards, products designed for children, and energy conservation products. Indeed, under King the CPSC narrowed its priorities from an unmanageable list of 150 to 15 (Demkovich 1978). In addition, the agency streamlined its product recall procedures and tightened its use of cost-benefit analysis in regulatory decisionmaking. Although the pace of standard setting would never fulfill the promise made by Simpson, the CPSC produced seven mandatory standards (including toy design, lawnmower safety, refuse bins, electrocution hazards from antennas, and unvented gas space heaters). In addition, it supervised the development of thirty-seven new voluntary standards. The CPSC estimated that its actions had prevented 300 deaths and 215,000 injuries per year. Although the CPSC would find itself embroiled in litigation, it was victorious in seventeen of twenty-one challenges (Swallow 1981; CPSC, *Annual Report,* various years).

As noted earlier, the FTC was under heavy fire in the final years of the Carter presidency. Its regulatory activism under Chairman Pertschuk and effective mobilization by business resulted in the constriction of its regulatory mandate. The CPSC had not, at that time, realized a level of activism sufficient to draw the attention of opponents—nor would it ever. However, under King its performance record improved markedly. With the inauguration of Ronald Reagan and the window of opportunity provided by reauthorization hearings, it too would experience significant challenges to its regulatory authority.

Consumer Protection in the Reagan-Bush Presidencies

The Reagan presidency was premised on a broad economic program in which deregulation and regulatory reform played a central role. The administration sought to realize changes in regulation through several means, including appointment of loyalists to key agency positions, significant budget cuts, and the application of cost-benefit analysis (see Eisner 2000: 170–201). The administration pursued this three-pronged strategy in consumer protection. After a decade-long process of professionalization, reform at the FTC would require a heavier reliance on economics in regulatory decisionmaking. A strategy of appointments would prove critical in this respect, although the FTC was also forced to endure its share of budget cuts. In the case of the CPSC, where bureaucratic resources were far less developed, regulation could be curtailed through a combination of budget cuts and appointments, particularly once the agency's mandate had been restricted.

The FTC Improvements Act of 1980—a rebuke for the activism of the 1970s—was only the beginning. The Reagan administration's transition team called for a 25 percent reduction in the FTC's budget and the elimination of the field offices. In addressing the consumer protection activities, the team called for the FTC to emphasize the economic merits of its regulatory proceedings and "terminate all cases based on 'social theories.'" To this end, it also recommended that the Bureau of Economics be elevated to a gatekeeping function, signing off on the economic merits of all new actions (*Antitrust and Trade Regulation Report* 999 [January 29, 1981]: G1–G3). As noted in Chapter 4, a coalition consisting of consumer advocates in Congress, the Small Business Legislative Council, the National Federation of Independent Businesses, the ABA, state attorneys general, and a number of consumer groups preserved the field offices and blunted the severity of the budget cuts. However, in consumer protection, as in antitrust, economics would rapidly be elevated in importance.

Reagan appointed James C. Miller III, the head of the FTC transition team and a central actor in the saga of the regulatory reform of the 1970s, as chair. As the first PhD economist on the commission, he used his executive powers to pursue regulatory change within the FTC. As an independent commission, the FTC was not subject to Executive Orders 12291 and 12498 (see Chapter 3). Miller had to achieve the same ends through administrative means. Economists and lawyers with economic training were appointed to key positions throughout the agency. Administrative changes were introduced to centralize control in the chairmanship and strengthen the coordination between the Bureau of Economics and the litigating bureaus. Timothy Muris—who had openly questioned whether the FTC should be abolished— was appointed director of the FTC's Bureau of Consumer Protection (see Clarkson and Muris 1981: 307–315). Agency attorneys, many of whom had entered the commission during the consumer heyday of the 1970s, were sent a clear message: the economic merits of proposed actions would be determinative. As the FTC noted in 1982, the consumer protection mission would place "emphasis on those practices that may unreasonably restrict or inhibit the free exercise of consumer choice" and, in so doing, would have a strong bias for "market-oriented remedies" (FTC, *Annual Report,* 1982: 7). The transition team's recommendations had been implemented through administrative means (see Eisner 1991: 212–220).

Chairman Miller's approach to consumer protection was a direct expression of economics. As he noted: "A central tenet of the Reagan platform . . . was that the best consumer protection possible is provided by a well-functioning marketplace" (Miller 1989: 9). For the market to function effectively, however, there must be adequate information and a supportive institutional structure, including common law rules against false advertising and breach of contract (Miller 1989: 11). Thus conceived, the FTC's role was clear: "to enhance the functioning of competitive markets, not to supplant them" (Miller 1989: 13). As noted above, the FTCA prohibits "unfair and deceptive" practices and authorizes regulatory actions when they are in the "public interest." Yet the determination of what constituted an unfair or deceptive practice was highly subjective, and the FTC had failed to articulate clear standards. Under Miller's direction, the determination of whether a given practice was unfair *and* subject to an industry-wide rule was based on four criteria: (1) the practice had to be prevalent, (2) it had to result in significant harm, (3) the rule would have to be effective in reducing the harm, and (4) benefits would have to exceed cost (Miller 1989: 25). There might be cases in which a given practice resulted in harm that was significant and widespread, yet for which, due to the limits of the existing regulatory remedies, product liability laws or class actions might provide the best remedy.

The Miller commission also adopted simple criteria for determining whether a practice was deemed deceptive and worthy of FTC action: a deceptive act or practice was defined as a material representation that "is likely to mislead consumers, acting reasonably in the circumstances, to their detriment" (Miller 1989: 27). The focus turned from whether claims were literally true and substantiated, to whether a *reasonable* person would be able to distinguish truth claims from the puffery common in advertising campaigns. If a reasonable person might arrive at the wrong conclusion, would the harm be great enough to warrant action? Something might be truly deceptive but of insufficient significance to make regulation in the public interest. In such cases, deception would be punished by the market (see Dahringer and Johnson 1984).

The application of the new market-based criteria occasionally resulted in decisions that became the object of horror in the consumer advocacy community (Wines 1983b). Concerns over unethical, immoral, and exploitative behavior that were common in the FTC of the 1970s were rarely aired in the 1980s, and when they were, it was by the remaining Carter appointees, Pertschuk and Patricia Bailey. To be certain, the continued expansion of the Bureau of Economics and the assignment of an economist to each proposed rule provided greater technical support for the regulatory process. However, the analytical requirements were so great as to obstruct the regulatory process (see Harris and Milkis 1996: 197–200). In the area of consumer protection, new rules fell to a virtual standstill.

When Miller left the FTC in 1985 to assume the leadership of the OMB, he was replaced by Daniel Oliver, whose experience at the Department of Education and as an editor of the *National Review* suggested modest qualifications for the position. Although the commissioners were now all Reagan appointees, Oliver's efforts to further centralize power in the chairmanship created ongoing conflict in the commission. The FTC became stagnant in its regulatory activities, and the efforts to redefine doctrine and create a new theoretical basis for consumer protection essentially ceased. Yet as economics had become integrated into all facets of the FTC's regulatory activities, it was doubtful that executive leadership would play as central a role as some might have expected (see Eisner 1993).

*   *   *

The record was comparable at the CPSC. In 1981 the agency had the misfortune of being the first regulatory agency up for reauthorization following the Reagan inauguration. David Stockman, OMB director, believed that this would provide an indicator of the administration's deregulatory commitment. The administration considered three options: eliminating the CPSC altogether, placing it in the Commerce Department, or severely reducing its budget. The elimination of the commission did not carry much support in Congress or in the business community, which found the CPSC preferable to individual state consumer agencies. Representatives Henry Waxman (D-CA) and John Dingell (D-MI) successfully built a congressional coalition to foreclose the option of transferring the agency to the Commerce Department (Swallow 1981). The third option became, by default, the reality. The CPSC suffered significant budget reductions: its budget fell from $42 million in 1981 to $32 million in 1982. Equally important, the reauthorization placed new and onerous restrictions on the agency.

The 1981 CPSA amendments reauthorized the agency for two years. They eliminated three organizations: the Product Safety Advisory Council, the National Advisory Committee for the Flammable Fabrics Act, and the Technical Advisory Committee on Poison Prevention Packaging. The offeror process was abolished, as was the requirement that the CPSC act on petitions for new safety standards within 120 days. Now, rule making would be initiated by issuing advanced notices of proposed rule making, which had to include detailed findings regarding the necessity of the standard. At the same time, the commission had to invite the development of voluntary industry standards and provide technical assistance. If a voluntary standard was deemed adequate and it was determined that compliance was probable, the CPSC was required to terminate mandatory rule making. If there was no voluntary standard deemed adequate by the CPSC, it could develop mandatory standards. However, Congress prohibited design standards, restricting the agency to performance standards, warnings, and instructions. All mandatory rules were subject to a legislative veto. Congress also directed the CPSC to amend its lawnmower standard and banned regulation of amusement rides that were permanently fixed (CPSC, *Annual Report,* 1981: 4).

A 24 percent budget cut and new restrictions were combined with a new regulatory philosophy, as exemplified by a series of Reagan appointees to the chairmanship. Nancy Steorts, former consultant to the US Office of Consumer Affairs and special assistant for consumer affairs at the USDA, served as chair from August 1981 to October 1984. Steorts articulated a number of regulatory priorities, which applied to such areas as furniture and bedding flammability, smoke detectors, child safety, and indoor air pollution. However, she wanted to emphasize a partnership with business involving a higher reliance on industry self-policing and reporting of product hazards and high levels of cooperation (Steorts 1983). This position was shared by Terrance Scanlon, Steorts's successor. He minimized the importance of budget cuts: "The law requires manufacturers and retailers to report potential hazards to us, and this continues no matter what our budget. We are stressing voluntary development of standards. We want to work *with* companies to solve problems, not *against* them." Reiterating the case for voluntarism, he noted: "You get more protection in a shorter period of time. It takes less government staff, there's less litigation, and therefore the costs are lower" (Scanlon 1985: 74).

The new emphasis on voluntarism found an expression in CPSC activities. Consider the example of 1985. The CPSC created a senior staff position in the Office of the Executive Director to coordinate voluntary standards activities and participated in and monitored the development of fifty-three voluntary standards, while issuing no final mandatory standards. It terminated its mandatory standard development for chainsaws when it determined that voluntary standards would prove sufficient. It encouraged industry to develop voluntary standards for all-terrain vehicles, despite the dire safety record. Finally, the CPSC hoped to amend its voluntary standards policy to recognize voluntary safety standards set by industry without commission participation—a proposal that was withdrawn in response to criticism (CPSC, *Annual Report,* 1985: 18).

The support for regulatory voluntarism might be understandable given the CPSC's troubled relationship with Congress. The 1981 reauthorization had stripped away much of the agency's independence and instructed it to emphasize voluntary standards. Moreover, it had been forced to endure severe budget cuts, such that by 1988 the CPSC's budget, in real terms, was less than 60 percent of what it had been in 1981. Following the departure of two commissioners, Sandra Brown Armstrong and Stuart M. Statler, in 1986, Congress failed to appropriate funds for their replacements and their staffs. Henceforth the CPSC would be a commission of three (CPSC, *Annual Report,* 1986). The CPSC's status was not elevated, however, by the lapses of the successive chairs who would be charged by critics (including fellow commissioners of both parties!) with the misallocation of resources for personal and frivolous purposes, efforts to circumvent commission decisions through administrative trickery, and conflicts of interest (see Shapiro and Golden 1987; Donner and Ledbetter 1988; *Harper's,* February 1985: 17–18). Moreover, there were examples of deregulatory excess, including Scanlon's efforts to get the CPSC to allow firms to export goods that failed US safety standards. In response to critics who believed that products (such as children's pajamas dyed with Tris, a chemical suspected of causing cancer) that were deemed hazardous should be removed from the stream of foreign commerce as well, Scanlon asked, "Are we expected to be international nannies?" (Cifelli 1984: 176).

*   *   *

The antiregulatory fervor of the Reagan administration was tempered during the presidency of George H. W. Bush. President Bush named Janet

Steiger, a moderate with experience in both Democratic and Republican administrations, to chair the FTC. Although Steiger worked to repair the FTC's reputation and relationships with key constituents, the commission remained severely divided between moderates and Reagan loyalists, thus limiting the speed with which a move to the center could be executed (see Harris and Milkis 1996: 302–331). Following a decade of budgetary retrenchment, Congress began increasing the BCP's budget. Between 1989 and 1993, the budget was increased by 28 percent, more than twice the inflation rate. Under Steiger, the FTC became far more active in consumer protection. In 1990, for example, the FTC filed sixty-one consumer protection complaints and assessed thirty civil penalties worth more than $1.6 million. It was successful in obtaining $72 million worth of consumer redress (FTC, *Annual Report,* 1990). By way of contrast, in 1985 the FTC had issued three consumer protection complaints. While it imposed eleven civil penalties worth $2.9 million—a figure that was inflated by a single penalty worth $1.6 million—its actions resulted in a mere $3.8 million in consumer redress (FTC, *Annual Report,* 1985). At the CPSC, the trajectory established by the Reagan administration was halted, if not fully reversed. Bush appointed Jacqueline Jones-Smith as chair, an attorney with a litigation record established at the FCC and as assistant county attorney for Montgomery County, Maryland, where she was responsible for civil prosecutions involving health, safety, and environmental protection laws (CPSC, press release 90-12). In addition, the 1991 reauthorization of the CPSC expanded its regulatory authority and sanctions. Companies were now required to inform the CPSC of products that were the subject of at least three civil actions alleging death or grievous injury and of those for which at least three of the actions led to a settlement or judgment for the plaintiff. In addition, firms were now required to report any information that reasonably supported a conclusion that a product failed to meet voluntary product safety standards or created an unreasonable risk of death or serious injury. These reporting requirements were backed by civil penalties of up to $1.25 million. In addition to the new authority, Congress provided the first successive budget increases every year from 1989 through 1993, such that the budget for fiscal year 1993 was 42 percent greater than that which existed in 1989, a rate of increase more than triple the inflation rate.

Under Jones-Smith, the CPSC continued the emphasis on voluntary standards—congressional preferences remained unambiguous in this area. However, the commission once again began enforcing its mandate and pursuing consumer protection. In 1990 the CPSC was successful in obtaining 101 corrective orders and requiring 148 recalls, in addition to the 59 million products that were voluntarily recalled. It imposed $782,000 in civil penalties. Moreover, the CPSC began making rules again, proposing three new rules and providing an advance notice of proposed rule making in another matter. To be certain, the CPSC continued its emphasis on voluntary standards, assisting in the development of eleven new standards (CPSC, *Annual Report*, 1990). But five years earlier, voluntary standards had been the primary focus of CPSC efforts. There were but eighty-two recalls ordered that year and no new administrative adjudicative proceedings calling for corrective action (CPSC, *Annual Report*, 1985).

Consumer Protection and the Clinton Presidency

The extent to which the Clinton administration's commitment to consumer protection could be expressed in a new pattern of regulatory actions was constrained by resources. Despite the budgetary support during the Bush presidency, the 1992 budget for the CPSC was 66.8 percent of what it had been a decade earlier. Indeed, accounting for inflation, the budget for the CPSC would have to have been $98.5 million, more than twice its 1992 level, for the agency to have had the same resources as were available in 1974! The FTC's Bureau of Consumer Protection had fared better. Its 1992 budget of $43.5 million was only slightly less than its 1982 budget, adjusted for inflation. Once again, in real terms, the FTC's 1992 budget was almost exactly what it had been in 1974.

Unlike the CPSC, the FTC of the 1980s sought to establish new doctrines in consumer protection grounded heavily in economics. The new decision rules drew on the analytical resources developed within the agency through the professionalization program in the decade following the reorganization of 1970, suggesting that the changes would have greater permanence. Indeed, the definitions of deception and unfairness that were developed in the 1980s stood the test of time (Starek 1997: 3–4). Nonetheless, the determination of how much economic evidence is necessary to justify enforcement is highly impressionistic and difficult to codify. The high analytic thresholds imposed in the 1980s effectively inhibited regulatory action. By the Clinton presidency, the ideological aversion to regulation had ceased to find an expression in insurmountable thresholds. Although Clinton was slow to signal his support for the FTC, he ultimately named Robert Pitofsky as chairman. A law professor at the Georgetown University Law Center, he had served as an FTC commissioner during the Carter presidency and as director of the BCP from 1970 to 1973. Having experienced the congressional reaction of the late 1970s firsthand, he struck a moderate position (Pitofsky 1996: 2). Pitofsky named Jodie Bernstein as director of the BCP. Her previous experience included environmental positions in the corporate world and senior positions in the government, as deputy director of the Department of Health and Human Services and acting director of the BCP in the 1970s. Under the direction of Pitofsky and Bernstein, consumer protection was revitalized.

Intervenor funding was a victim of the difficulties the commission encountered in the late 1970s. Yet participation became important at the FTC in the 1990s as part of the REGO effort. Beginning in 1993 the commission began relying heavily on workshops for framing new rules, considering targets for regulatory reform (see below), and initiating cooperative ventures. These workshops integrated a host of "stakeholders," including consumer groups, industry actors, experts, and representatives from other agencies, at a very early point and without the procedural rigidity of the rule-making process (Azcuenaga 1996: 6–7). At the same time, they are a useful means of promoting self-regulation: businesses can become aware of FTC expectations and use industry associations to pursue regulatory objectives to prevent direct government regulation. As one FTC commissioner, Roscoe B. Starek III, noted: "Direct government regulation—while sometimes necessary—often is not the best solution to consumer protection problems. Self-regulation can be an extremely effective way to protect consumers, particularly when it is complemented by carefully selected government law enforcement actions" (1997: 10).

By the end of Clinton's second term, the FTC was once again pursuing an active agenda. Activities expanded in two areas that were indicative of the changing economy. First, there was growing attention to the international dimensions of consumer protection. The International Marketing Supervision Network, founded in the final year of the George H. W. Bush presidency, linked criminal and civil law enforcement agencies involved in consumer protection. The network, which included the FTC and its counterparts in Europe, Canada, Mexico, Japan, Australia, and New Zealand, became increasingly important in tracking consumer protection problems involving transactions across national borders (Starek 1995). In 1996 the FTC began working with other members of NAFTA to discuss revision and harmonization of national rules to facilitate trade (FTC, *Annual Report,* 1996). It also hosted conferences on cross-border fraud and signed an agreement with Canada creating the joint Task Force on Cross-Border Fraud (Azcuenaga 1996: 3). Second, the FTC turned to the role of the Internet, which raises a host of nettlesome problems. Consumers may execute transactions with companies in other nations without realizing that they do not fall under the jurisdiction of US laws. Moreover, given the speed of transactions, consumers have less time to consider the veracity of advertising claims. Finally, because the barriers to entry are virtually nonexistent, small entrepreneurs could open operations without understanding advertising law (Starek 1995; Varney 1996). The FTC's regulatory strategy evolved during the 1990s. In 1997 it created the Consumer Response Center to receive consumer complaints. The complaints were subsequently entered into the Consumer Information System databases, where they could be analyzed by the FTC to identify patterns and better target enforcement resources. By the end of 2000, some 834 thousand complaints had been entered into the database. The information was used, for example, to generate 149 cases of Internet fraud between 1995 and 2000. By combining enforcement actions, the promotion of self-regulation, and education, the FTC estimated that it brought 83 percent of the actors in targeted industries into compliance in 2000 (FTC 2001b). Information analyzed from the databases also allowed for greater cooperation in enforcement actions both at the national and international levels. Consider one of the FTC initiatives involving telemarketing fraud. Under the authority provided in the Telemarketing and Consumer Fraud and Abuse Act of 1994, the FTC adopted a new "telemarketing sales rule" enforceable by itself and state agencies. The FTC enforced the rule through "sweeps"—multiple and simultaneous enforcement actions executed by state and federal officials. For example, in July 1996 the FTC orchestrated the efforts of the US Postal Service and state attorneys general to enforce the rule against fraudulent sweepstakes promotions. "Operation Jackpot" resulted in fifty-six enforcement actions involving defendants in seventeen states and Canada. These sweeps were designed to have maximum impact and media exposure with minimal resources (Azcuenaga 1996: 1–3; Varney 1996). In 1996 there were a total of ten sweeps as part of the FTC antifraud effort, resulting in 65 FTC cases and a total of 222 cases when state and federal cases were combined (FTC 1997: app. 3). Between 1995 and 2000 the FTC led 60 sweeps resulting in 1,576 law enforcement actions, including 376 cases by the FTC. In its performance report for fiscal year 2000, the FTC estimated that its actions to stop fraudulent practices, when taken as a whole, had saved consumers $263 million (FTC 2001b). While the Clinton FTC was far more active in enforcement than the FTC of the Reagan-Bush years, it did not retreat from the new emphasis placed on competition and economic analysis. It formalized and continued revising and rescinding rules deemed to be harmful to competition. In 1992 the commission officially established its regulatory reform program. By 1996 it had rescinded twenty-seven rules and guidelines and revised an additional nineteen, constituting more than half of the rules and guidelines that were in effect in 1993 (FTC, *Annual Report,* 1996). Efforts were made to target rules that have ceased to have the intended effect due to changes in technology and markets. In hopes of limiting the need for such recisions and revisions in the future, the FTC placed a twenty-year sunset on all administrative rules in 1995. Effective January 2, 1996, existing orders were also slated to terminate automatically after twenty years, as long as no violations had been alleged.

*   *   *

President Clinton nominated Ann Brown, vice president of the Consumer Federation of America, to head the CPSC. Despite Brown's commitment to consumer protection, the agency was forced to work within significant budgetary constraints. In 1997 the CPSC released its strategic plan, *Saving Lives and Keeping Families Safe*, pursuant to the Government Performance and Results Act. The report identified a number of regulatory goals (e.g., to reduce the rate of head injury to children under fifteen years old by 10 percent from 1996 to 2006), and strategies that would be used to achieve them. These strategies, as ranked by the commission, included promoting voluntary action, using risk-based decisionmaking, providing clear compliance standards, building successful partnerships, encouraging market-oriented solutions, using educational and information campaigns, and promoting harmonization of international safety standards (CPSC 1997: 3).

As one might suspect given the pattern of regulation since 1981, a great emphasis was placed on the use of voluntary standards and public-private partnerships. The CPSC strategic plan was quite frank in discussing the impact of existing budget constraints. After describing the "significant downsizing" whereby the current "budget has 60 percent less purchasing power than the agency's first budget in 1974," the commission noted that "it will be extremely difficult to fund future increases in the costs of doing business." While "fostering partnerships . . . stretches [the] CPSC's resources and allows the Commission to do more with less," there are limits: "if the agency's basic funding does not keep pace with price increases or information technology needs, achievement of the strategic goals and objectives may be jeopardized" (CPSC 1997: 40–41). Despite the budgetary constraints, Brown's tenure as CPSC chair was broadly recognized as a period of activism in consumer protection (Javitt and DeFrancesco 2001). The CPSC developed several new rules per year, some of which were initiated during the George H. W. Bush administration. At the same time, it continued to support voluntary standard-setting. In 1993 the CPSC provided technical support for the development of eleven voluntary standards; by 1996 it was providing direct support or monitoring the development of some fifty-one standards. There was also greater aggressiveness in enforcement. In 1993 the CPSC imposed $255,000 in civil penalties and secured 367 corrective actions (e.g., recalls) involving some 28 million consumer products. By 1996 there were 375 corrective actions affecting 85.1 million consumer product units, and civil penalties reached $1.5 million. In the last year of the Clinton presidency the CPSC was providing technical support for 63 voluntary standards, 29 of which were completed (new, revised, and reaffirmed). There were two new mandatory standards (bunk beds and multipurpose lighters). With respect to enforcement, there were over 500 inspections, 288 corrective actions affecting 90 million consumer product units, and $2.8 million in civil penalties (see CPSC, *Annual Report,* 1993, 1996, 2000. The key question was whether this level of activism would survive a change in administrations.

Consumer Protection and
the Presidency of George W. Bush

As noted in Chapter 4, President George W. Bush appointed Timothy Muris as FTC chair, the first in the agency's history to hold the top positions in the Bureau of Competition and the Bureau of Consumer Protection. Although Muris had been at the center of the Reagan revolution at the FTC of the 1980s, few expected significant changes in the pattern of consumer protection activities. The changes initiated in the 1980s were still largely in place. Indeed, many of the current initiatives (e.g., the antifraud activities) were shaped by Muris when he was in charge of the BCP (Mayer and Grimaldi 2001). The BCP was placed under the direction of J. Howard Beales III, an economist. Consumer advocates were concerned that Beales's past work as a consultant to R. J. Reynolds would make him unfit for the position. Indeed, his analysis denying any connection between advertising and smoking among children was used to defend Joe Camel from earlier FTC actions (Labaton 2001c). In the end, as the *Wall Street Journal* noted, Muris "unexpectedly emerged as perhaps most aggressive and effective regulator in [the] Bush administration" (Wilke 2003: 1). The team of Muris and Beale would leave a strong legacy of consumer protection regulation that was not dissimilar from that of the previous administration.

During George W. Bush's first term, the FTC's consumer protection mission sustained strong budgetary growth, with increases from $78 million in 2001 to $104 million in 2004. The growth in resources was used to promote an aggressive record of enforcement. As noted above, by 2000 some 834,000 complaints had been entered, in aggregate, into the FTC's database, which is used to target enforcement actions. In 2001 an additional 430,000 complaints were added; by 2004 the annual additions reached 994,000 (including 314 complaints of identity theft, a growing source of concern for the commission). One of the indicators that the FTC adopted to measure its success was the dollar savings for consumers from FTC actions against fraud. In the period 2001–2004 the aggregate savings exceeded $2 billion. Moreover, a steady stream of federal court actions against fraud resulted in aggregate consumer redress of $1.66 billion (FTC 2001b, 2002a, 2002b, 2003b, 2004, 2005a).

The FTC's actions created new precedents with respect to the levels of consumer redress. In August 2002 the FTC finalized a settlement with Citigroup Inc. in response to charges that subsidiaries Associates First Capital Corporation and Associates Corporation of North America had engaged in deceptive marketing practices to induce consumers into refinancing existing debts with high interest rates and fee home loans and credit insurance. The settlement required Citigroup to pay $215 million in refunds to affected consumers, making it the largest consumer settlement in the agency's history. Similarly, the FTC targeted First Alliance Mortgage

Company for its lending practices, generating some $63 million in consumer redress (FTC 2002b: 2). In November 2002 the FTC reached a settlement to shut down the Psychic Readers Network for misleading consumers through the use of deceptive advertising, billing, and collections. The settlement resulted, additionally, in a $5 million fine and an agreement to forgive a staggering $500 million in outstanding charges (Mayer 2002b).

During the 1990s the FTC had responded to technological trends by turning its attention to Internet fraud. This focus expanded under the direction of Muris, as the FTC became involved in initiatives against "pretexting" (the practice of using false pretenses to obtain customer financial information), identity theft, and false advertising through computer spam. In its most high-profile initiative, however, the FTC targeted telemarketing, a powerful industry with annual revenues of $293.5 billion in 2001. In 2002 the FTC amended its Telemarketing Sales Rule to create a national "do not call" registry. Under the rule, marketers are charged $7,250 for access to the complete national registry and face a maximum penalty of $11,000 for each call placed in violation of the rule. As one might expect, the industry responded by filing court challenges, initially with some success. After the US District Court for the Western District of Oklahoma found that Congress had not given the FTC the authority to establish the registry, Congress passed the Do Not Call Implementation Act of 2003. Within hours of its passage, the US District Court in Denver ruled that the regulations violated the free speech rights of telemarketers—a decision that was subsequently overturned by the US Court of Appeals for the 10th Circuit in Denver. In October 2004 the US Supreme Court refused to hear challenges to the registry, letting stand the appellate court decision.

Few consumer advocates would have expected a strong enforcement record (some 258 federal district court cases), unprecedented settlements worth billions in consumer redress, and high-profile regulatory initiatives from a veteran of the Reagan FTC and an economist who had worked for the tobacco industry. Yet, as Muris explained, his commitment to vigorous enforcement stemmed from a belief that "the rules are there to make free markets work" (Wilke 2003: 1). In the summer of 2004, Muris and Beale announced their resignations from the commission and a return to the academy. President Bush appointed Deborah Platt Majoras, a former deputy assistant attorney general at the Antitrust Division, to serve as the new FTC chair. Lydia B. Parnes, a twenty-four-year veteran of the commission and former deputy director of the Bureau of Consumer Protection, was elevated to the position of director. There is every indication that the second Bush term will be marked by continuity with what appears to be a well-established and stable regulatory consensus.

*   *   *

In 2001, President Bush nominated Mary Sheila Gall to serve as chair of the CPSC. Gall, a ten-year veteran of the commission, had been appointed during the presidency of George H. W. Bush. During the 1990s, she regularly questioned the CPSC's core mission. She argued repeatedly that many of the injuries and deaths that are attributed to product safety are more correctly the result of a lack of personal responsibility on the part of the consumer. She consistently opposed new safety standards for baby walkers and bath seats, for example, by arguing that injuries and deaths resulted from a lack of parental supervision rather than flawed product designs (Javitt and DeFrancesco 2001). Gall stated in a 1999 letter to *USA Today* that it was "frustrating . . . to witness the procession of proclamations issued by [the CPSC] on behalf of the federal Nanny State" (Mayer 2001a: 23). Confirmation of Gall was imperiled by the return of Senate control to Democrats following the defection of Jim Jeffords from the Republican Party (Labaton 2001b). The Consumers Union, the Children's Defense Fund, and the US Public Interest Research Group lobbied heavily against Gall, noting in a letter to Congress that she "repeatedly refused to act when faced with evidence of deaths and injuries to children from dangerous products, often blaming the parents, not the products" (Mayer 2001b: 1). In August 2001 the Senate Commerce Committee, in a party-line vote of 12 to 11, rejected Gall, handing President George W. Bush his first defeated nominee (Mayer 2001c). As President Bush considered demoting Brown from her chairmanship, she decided to resign her position. Subsequently, Bush successfully nominated Harold Stratton, former New Mexico attorney general (and cochairman of Lawyers for Bush in New Mexico) to the position (Barnes 2001). Although Stratton lacked consumer protection credentials, he began his term as CPSC chairman with fanfare, announcing a $1 million civil penalty against General Electric for failing to promptly report product defects and stating that the fine "puts companies on notice that they must notify CPSC without delay when they learn of product hazards or consumer injuries." In a subsequent statement, he announced his intention to review the adequacy of the legislative caps on civil penalties ($1.65 million), which he viewed as insufficient given the net worth of companies like GE (the maximum civil penalty was subsequently increased to $1.825 million, effective January 1, 2005). Stratton also questioned the adequacy of the budget, noting that the commission lacked the legal resources to prosecute industrial giants (Mayer 2002a). Despite initial concerns that consumer protection would not fare well during the Bush presidency, the performance of the CPSC has been largely on par with the levels achieved at the end of the Clinton presidency. During the Bush presidency, the CPSC began to present its activities as they related to specific problems, setting goals and reporting achievements for each year. A comparison of 2001–2004 with the last year of the Clinton presidency reveals few shifts in levels of rule making and participation in voluntary standards and code revisions. The one area where there was a marked shift in emphasis was in corrective actions and recalls. Under the goal of reducing fire-related deaths, the average number of recalls or other corrective actions for 2001–2004 was 409, compared with 529 in 2000. Recalls and corrective actions were higher, on average, for carbon monoxide poisoning (an average of 5 for 2001–2004, compared with 2 for 2000), chemical hazards (an average of 124.5 for 2001–2004, compared with 68 for 2000), and household and recreational hazards (an average of 108.5 for 2001–2004, compared with 53 for 2000). The percentage of recalls that were initiated within twenty days (under the Fast-Track Program) increased slightly, from 94 percent in 2000 to an annual average of 95.25 percent from 2001 to 2004 (CPSC 2004). Indicative of the consistency in CPSC activity, when the Senate Commerce Committee initiated a hearing on CPSC reauthorization, consumer groups did not mount an attack on the adequacy of the enforcement record under Bush. Rather, they focused on the perennial concerns over CPSC budgetary authority and the size of civil penalties. As with the FTC, the politics of consumer protection under Bush appear far less divisive than they were in the early 1980s, when the CPSC's very survival was in question.

Conclusion

Consumer protection regulation provides important lessons regarding the sources of regulatory policy change. First, as the case of the FTC would suggest, Congress and the president can successfully increase the level and vigor of regulation by providing funds for agency professionalization and broader legislative mandates. At the same time, a lack of such resources—as the case of the CPSC suggests—can make effective regulation difficult. Congressional vulnerability to the mobilization of business interests can lead Congress to quickly retract its support, leading to a second important lesson: vigorous regulation may be decisive in undermining the political support for regulation. The "Little Old Lady of Pennsylvania Avenue" enjoyed a quiet political environment for decades. But as soon as the FTC received an expanded mandate and took this mandate seriously, it became more of a liability to Congress than a testament to what is possible when rhetoric concerning the public interest is combined with resources.

A third lesson: bureaucracy matters. Our comparison of the FTC and the CPSC reveals that whereas the former pursued a sustained program of agency professionalization and institution building, the latter languished as a repository of bureaucrats who were not retained—often quite purposively—by the agencies with which they once worked. This had important implications for the strategies of regulatory change adopted during the

1980s. In the case of the FTC, Miller and his appointees were able to draw on the resources of the Bureau of Economics to bolster the regulatory reforms they envisioned. Critics of the FTC might have disagreed with the direction of consumer protection policy, but they rarely had reason to question the commitment of the agency's executives or the quality of the underlying analyses. In the case of the CPSC, declarations regarding the need for new partnerships with business, the virtues of voluntarism, and the adequacy of business self-reporting were combined with regulatory inaction and a hemorrhaging of resources. The CPSC became little more than a clearinghouse for voluntary standard-setting, characterized by a dearth of leadership and a sense of political irrelevancy. Finally, leadership should be viewed as operating within organizational parameters. As noted in Chapter 2, leadership is an important and often underemphasized factor in the history of regulation. A series of strong executives at the FTC has imparted an ongoing sense of mission. Given the evolution of the FTC bureaucracy and the integration of economics at each stage of the policy process, the success of current and future executives to realize their visions of policy will be largely a product of whether these visions can be reconciled with the bureaucratic culture. Whereas the FTC of the Clinton and George W. Bush presidencies has consistently articulated a more activist vision of consumer protection than that which prevailed in the 1980s, it is far more sensitive to the importance of economic analysis than was the case during the 1970s. At the CPSC, where bureaucracy building was never a priority, executives have greater latitude but fewer bureaucratic resources at their disposal, making the future of the CPSC in some ways less certain, and in some ways more certain, than that of its more established partner in consumer protection.

10

Regulating
Energy

AS OF LATE 2003, more than a dozen federal agencies over-saw more than 150 energy-related programs. These programs generally address one of eight activity areas: (1) energy supply, (2) the effect of energy production and consumption on environmental quality, (3) low-income energy assistance, (4) basic energy research, (5) development and maintenance of the energy delivery infrastructure, (6) energy conservation, (7) energy security, and (8) energy market competition (Wells, Cooksey, and Crothers 2005). It is impossible to address each program in each area in a single chapter. Our focus here is federal and state regulatory activity with respect to energy supply, conservation, infrastructure, and market competition.

Federal energy policy has been likened to "a five-ring circus with a sideshow" (Davis 1993: 20), in that "energy policy" is really five or six separate policies dealing with individual sources of energy, which rarely have been coordinated as part of an overall plan for dealing with the question of energy supply. The relative independence of these energy policies notwithstanding, regulation of the production, distribution, and utilization of energy have at least two common characteristics, regardless of the energy source in question. First, nearly every scholar of energy policy concludes that policy-making in this area is best explained as subsystem politics, with a single producer–controlled dominant coalition (Chubb 1983; Davis 1993; Katz 1984; Rosenbaum 1989; Yergin 1991). While the relative power and impermeability of these producer coalitions have eroded somewhat since the mid-1970s, the politics of energy regulation can still provide glimpses of the "iron triangles" of old. Second, with the exception of several crisis events in the past three decades, energy policy generally ranks very low with respect

257

to salience. Unless prices rise rapidly, foreign supplies are threatened, or a huge accident occurs in the production or transportation of energy, the public rarely thinks about where its energy comes from or how it is produced (see Figure 10.1). This low degree of salience, of course, helps explain the dominant coalition subsystem politics that characterizes the policy area.

According to David Davis (1993), in order to understand energy policy, one must first understand three sets of factors that affect these policies: the physical characteristics of the fuel source, the market forces affecting the fuel source (e.g., conditions of supply, economies of scale), and the general political environment in place during the period in which the energy source first came to prominence (since the politics surrounding each energy source is a reflection of the politics in place at policy inception). Given the fractured nature of energy policy, we begin with a brief primer on the physical nature of the major fuel sources subject to regulation. Second, we discuss the policy subsystems and substance of policy for each fuel type prior to the 1973–1974 oil embargo. Third, we address the embargo itself, the effect it had on energy policy subsystems, and the changes in energy policy pursued by the Nixon and Ford administrations in response to the embargo. Fourth, we explore in detail the Carter administration's efforts to impose order on the entropy of energy policy, since these efforts shape the character of national energy policy even today. Fifth, we present changes in the regulation of energy in each of the presidential administrations since 1980. Sixth,

Figure 10.1 The Salience of Energy Policy

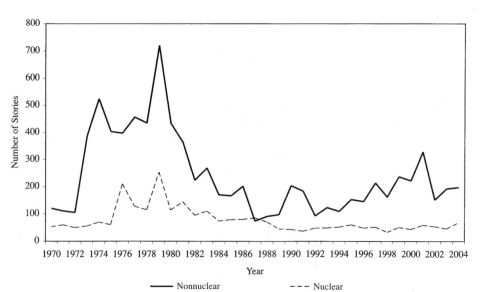

we discuss recent efforts to deregulate the generation and distribution of electricity, a process that spans three presidential administrations and includes both the federal and state governments. We close with some concluding thoughts about the effect of recent changes in the energy policy subsystem and likely directions for future energy policy.

A Primer on Energy: Physical and Market Characteristics

While the United States contains about 5 percent of the world's population, Americans consume more than a quarter of all energy used worldwide. At present growth rates, about 2 percent a year, energy consumption in the United States will double by 2040. The industrial sector uses the largest share of energy consumed in the United States (33 percent), followed by the transportation sector (28 percent), households (21 percent), and the commercial sector (18 percent) (EIA 2005). With respect to the source of this energy, most comes from petroleum (40 percent) and natural gas (23 percent), with a significant amount also being provided by coal (22 percent). About 11 percent of all energy consumed in the United States is in the form of electricity produced from nuclear and hydroelectric power (EIA 2005).

To a large extent, economic systems, social structures, and social institutions are built around the characteristics of the dominant energy sources and the pathways by which these sources are used. Changing the dominant energy source, or even the mix of energy sources, has enormous implications for existing social and economic institutions. Regulating the production and use of these energy sources has similar implications.

Ring One: Coal

Coal is the fossilized remains of ancient lowland plant matter. In terms of chemical structure, coal is simply long chains of carbon atoms with other associated compounds (e.g., sulfur, water, cadmium). Nearly three-quarters of all coal used in the United States is used to generate electricity. Most of the remainder is used as coke in the smelting of steel. While almost all coal can be used in its natural form, not all coal is created equal, and differences in grades of coal have important consequences for energy policy. Anthracite and bituminous coal are the most desirable types of coal from the perspective of energy production, since they contain the most potential energy per pound. Subbituminous coal and lignite (or brown coal), on the other hand, are less desirable on this criterion, since they contain less potential energy and (generally) higher concentrations of water.

What the lower grades of coal lack in potential energy, however, they make up for in other areas. For example, the lower grades of coal also usually have much lower levels of sulfur, so it is easier for electric utilities and others using this coal to meet air pollution standards (see Chapter 7). In addition, the higher grades of coal are generally found far underground, and mining this coal is dangerous, labor intensive, and relatively inefficient. Subbituminous coal and lignite, however, are generally found closer to the surface and can be "strip-mined." Rather than sinking thousand-foot shafts into underground coal seams, strip mining literally lifts the top hundred or so feet of soil and rock off of the coal seam so that long draglines can scoop out the coal. While neither type of mining is technologically complex, strip mining is safer and less labor intensive, and can extract over 90 percent of the available coal.

In terms of the distribution of the resource, the United States is literally "the Saudi Arabia of coal," with nearly a quarter of the world's coal reserves. Anthracite and bituminous coal are concentrated in the eastern and midwestern states, while lower grades of coal are concentrated in the western states. Given the relative abundance of coal, the relative simplicity of extraction and use, and its primitive distribution network (i.e., railroads and river barges), most coal regulations focus on the mining hazards and the environmental consequences of coal production. Differences in regulating different types of coal, however, will have obvious consequences with respect to regional and state political economies.

Ring Two: Petroleum
Petroleum is a complex mix of various hydrocarbon molecules in liquid form. Like coal, oil is found underground and is the residue from partially decayed lipids from ancient organic matter. Petroleum generally migrates underground into porous rock formations (e.g., sandstone and limestone) or shale formations. Unlike coal, petroleum cannot be used in its natural form. The different hydrocarbons in oil must be separated and refined through the application of heat, pressure, and the use of several chemical catalysts. The end results of refining petroleum are products like grease, kerosene, motor oil, gasoline, diesel fuel, and jet fuel. Over half of all petroleum consumed in the United States is used in transportation, with roughly 10 percent being used directly in industry, 10 percent in the generation of electricity, and 10 percent in the production of petrochemicals.

Not all oil wells are "gushers." In fact, in most wells, natural pressure is not great enough to force the oil up out of the ground—it has to be pumped, and a large percentage of petroleum present in oil fields remains trapped in the rock formations (how much depends on the grade of oil and the extent to which advanced oil recovery techniques, like flooding oil fields with water or steam, are used). While the technology of oil exploration and drilling has advanced dramatically in the past fifteen years, becoming much more complex, the basic technology for refining petroleum has not changed much in fifty years. The biggest technological hurdle in producing petroleum is finding it in the first place, and the second challenge is getting petroleum products (i.e., gasoline and diesel fuel) to the consumer. Because there are large economies of scale in refining and because the end users of the refined product are widely distributed, there is a complicated distribution network for these fuels.

Like coal, oil is not evenly distributed around the globe or across the country. Nations in the Middle East, led by Saudi Arabia, are home to over 30 percent of known petroleum reserves. Russia and other countries once part of the former Soviet Union are home to another quarter (or more) of world reserves. The United States, even with its vast oil fields in Alaska, Texas, Oklahoma, and the Gulf of Mexico, is home to less than 8 percent of world petroleum reserves. Indeed, US oil production from these limited reserves has been unable to meet domestic demand. Compared with coal, for which it is a net exporter, the United States imports about 60 percent of the crude oil it consumes. Since petroleum is relatively scarce, requires significant effort to refine into useful products, and entails a complicated distribution network, government regulations have at one time or another targeted production, refining, and distribution.

Ring Three: Natural Gas

Natural gas is also a mix of several different hydrocarbon compounds, but these compounds are much simpler than those in oil (e.g., the dominant hydrocarbon in natural gas is methane, or CH_4) and are in gaseous form. Roughly 40 percent of natural gas is used for space heating by homeowners, businesses, and industry. Another 30 percent is used directly as fuel by industry, or to produce petrochemicals. Roughly 22 percent of the natural gas used in the United States goes to produce electricity, and this figure has increased by half over the past fifteen years as electric utilities moved to take advantage of this clean-burning energy source (EIA 2005). Natural gas shares characteristics with both coal and oil. Like coal, natural gas can be used right out of the ground, though it is typically purified or "sweetened" before entering the distribution network. Natural gas and petroleum are sometimes considered twins separated at birth, because they are almost invariably found in the same rock formations (Davis 1993). In fact, the pressure of natural gas trapped in these rock formations is what forces out most of the free-flowing petroleum in oil wells. Thus the technology for tapping natural gas is no more complex than the technology for drilling for oil. There are economies of scale in the production of natural gas, similar to those for oil, but the end users are widely distributed. Therefore, a vast and complicated distribution network exists for this fuel as well.

Originally, oil companies found natural gas a nuisance—due to its toxicity, high flammability, and low commercial value given its low energy content with respect to volume. Most early oil producers, in fact, either vented or "flamed off" the natural gas found in their oil wells, and this is still done in remote oil fields like those in Alaska, Russia, and parts of the Middle East. With the advent of pipelines capable of containing natural gas, and the more recent advances in liquefying natural gas through a combination of supercooling and pressurization, natural gas is now arguably more valuable than petroleum (although the technology of distribution is also more complicated). Finally, since oil and gas are often found together, world and domestic distribution of this fuel are similar to those of oil. Some countries and regions, however, are home to substantially more gas than oil (e.g., Russia, Canada, Mexico, most of Europe). The United States is a large importer of natural gas, with most of this gas coming from Canada and Mexico. Given these characteristics, regulation has focused on the production and distribution of natural gas.

Ring Four: Nuclear Power

There are two kinds of nuclear energy: nuclear fission (where energy is released from splitting heavy atoms like uranium) and nuclear fusion (where energy is released from fusing light atoms like hydrogen). Both are chain reactions (i.e., they are self-sustaining), and while we have dreams of someday using nuclear fusion (the reaction that powers the sun) as an energy source, we currently use only nuclear fission, and only to produce electricity at centralized locations. An uncontrolled fission reaction produces an explosion like that which leveled Hiroshima in the waning days of World War II. Although the bombs dropped on Hiroshima and Nagasaki will always link military with civilian uses of nuclear power in the minds of average citizens, a controlled fission reaction such as that used in nuclear power plants could never explode like an atomic bomb. It simply produces a lot of heat. At a nuclear power plant, a moderated fission reaction is used to boil water, which produces steam, which is then pressurized and used to run a turbine, which in turn produces electricity. The United States is the world's largest producer and user of nuclear power. There are roughly 104 operating nuclear reactors in the country, and they produce about 20 percent of the nation's electricity.

Since coal, oil, and natural gas are also used to produce the pressurized steam that runs turbines, the only difference between nuclear power plants and other power plants is the way in which they boil water—but what a difference this is. Nuclear power is by far the most technologically complicated energy source commonly used around the world.

The first step in the nuclear fuel cycle is mining uranium ore, a majority of which is found on public lands and Native American reservations. This ore must be crushed and "milled" in order to extract the metallic uranium (commonly known as yellowcake). Next, the yellowcake is "enriched" in order to concentrate the uranium further into uranium hexafluoride. Through a series of steps, the uranium hexafluoride is converted into fuel pellets for nuclear reactors (uranium dioxide). Uranium milling, enrichment, and the production of uranium fuel pellets all take place at government-owned facilities. In fact, the federal government owns all nuclear fuel produced and used in the United States. The fuel pellets, for all intents and purposes, are leased (below cost) to utilities, which use them to produce electricity. After the uranium fuel has served its useful life (i.e., after it has become so contaminated with radiation that it can no longer sustain a reaction), it is moved to temporary storage ponds at the power plants. Even the used fuel pellets, commonly referred to as high-level radioactive wastes or transuranic wastes, remain the property of the federal government, and it is the government's responsibility to properly dispose of these wastes permanently. Unless these wastes are reprocessed, they will have to be isolated from the environment for more than 100,000 years in order to prevent contamination. Eventually, the power plants themselves will become so radioactive that they will have to be decommissioned and disposed of as high-level radioactive waste. Federal policy can and does affect the production of nuclear power at each stage of the nuclear fuel cycle.

Ring Five: Electricity

Electricity is a secondary energy source. With the exception of lightning, we do not find "deposits" of electricity in nature. Electricity, however, is the most versatile of all energy sources. It can be used for transportation, lighting, space heating, industrial and medical lasers, even for smelting metal. Each of the energy sources discussed above can be used to produce electricity, and for coal and nuclear power this is their primary purpose. To the extent that these fuels are used to produce electricity, then, regulations regarding these fuels govern electricity as well. The production and transmission of electricity itself, however, is the subject of much government regulation. There are at least four reasons for this. First, the generation, transmission, and distribution of electricity have generally been assumed to be natural monopolies, and government regulation can and does target each of these activities. Second, in some cases the federal government determined that the lack of universal and reliable electrical service was a hindrance to economic and social development, so it stepped in to provide this service on its own (e.g., the Tennessee Valley Authority [TVA]). Third, the majority of electric utilities in the United States are owned by public entities, generally municipalities (though few of these municipal utilities actually generate electricity, focusing instead on distribution). Thus, government policy has had to address the constant tension between private power providers and advocates of the public provision of electricity at the local level. Finally, electricity is a commodity, produced by a monopoly, that is often sold across state lines. The federal government had to devise a way to regulate these sales in order to carry out its twin mandates of antitrust enforcement and the regulation of interstate commerce.

The Sideshow: Renewable Energy

Each of the energy sources discussed above can be classified as nonrenewable; once it is used, it cannot be replaced (at least not for hundreds of millions of years). There are other energy sources, however, classified as renewable. While there are literally dozens of renewable energy sources—from crops to tidal power to hydrogen produced from seawater—we focus here on the five most common: hydropower, biofuels, solar power, wind power, and energy conservation. By some accounts, renewable energy contributes over 20 percent of all energy consumed in the United States (Brower 1992). More typical accounting techniques, however, put the figure at around 6 percent (EIA 2005). The most common of these are hydropower (i.e., electricity produced by falling water at large dams) and biofuels (e.g., ethanol produced from crops and added to gasoline). Whereas solar power can also be used for space heating, the most commonly discussed use of both solar and wind power is the production of electricity. Most commonly, solar energy is used in photovoltaic arrays, where electricity is produced when sunlight strikes the surface of specially prepared silicon chips. Wind power produces electricity by using the wind to turn a turbine.

With the exception of photovoltaic technology, the production of energy from renewable sources is not complex. Moreover, even with respect to hydroelectric dams, there appear to be few economies of scale with respect to renewable energy sources: personal windmills, dams, and photovoltaic arrays are just as efficient as large centralized power plants, maybe more so (Brower 1992). Thus the infrastructure necessary for producing and distributing energy from renewable sources is vastly different from the infrastructure needed for any of the energy sources discussed previously, with all that this implies for social and economic institutions. With the exception of promoting hydroelectricity, government policy generally ignored renewable energy sources until the mid-1970s. Since that time, regulations have focused only limited attention on the production of power from these sources.

A Brief History of the Development of Federal Energy Policies

Prior to the 1970s, policies for all energy sources were made by well-insulated and relatively independent fuel-based subsystems. Within this unifor-

mity, however, substantial variation exists with respect to the types of policies that govern particular fuels. One prominent explanation for these differences can be found in the general political context that dominated in the
era during which the energy source first came to prominence (Davis 1993).
For example, coal reached its heyday during the laissez-faire period of the
industrial revolution. Thus it comes as no surprise that this energy source is
dominated by private producers or that many of the regulations imposed on
this industry are the consequences of labor unrest. On the other hand,
hydroelectric power blossomed during the New Deal, while petroleum came
to prominence during World War II. Consistent with the politics of the
times, both energy sources are characterized by a high degree of government involvement in rationalizing their production and distribution. In this
section, we sketch the major actors within each energy policy subsystem,
identify those factors most responsible for early policymaking in these
areas, and discuss the general character of regulatory policies in the preem-
bargo era.

Coal

The policy subsystem for coal has been dominated by a few large coal companies, coal-producer trade associations (e.g., Bituminous Coal Operators
Association [BCOA]), officials within the Office of Coal and the Bureau of
Mines in the Department of Interior, and the United Mine Workers (UMW).
In its early history, the "regulation" of coal consisted of providing subsidies
to coal producers. Two of the most important subsidies were low-cost leases
to mine coal on federal lands, and the research and development into more
effective methods of searching for and mining coal undertaken by the
Bureau of Mines. On the labor front, at least after 1937, coal policy historically sought to protect the interests of the UMW as well. Allied with the
BCOA, the UMW worked to maintain union jobs at the largest mines, keep
the price for coal steady, and drive small, nonunion mines out of business
(Tugwell 1988: 33–37). The BCOA and the UMW were aided in their
efforts by the Interior Department's Bituminous Coal Advisory Council.
The BCOA-UMW alliance was relatively successful at preserving union
jobs and avoiding strikes, but the union continued to push for safer working
conditions in the mines (coal mining was dominated by underground
anthracite and bituminous mines during this period). Congress passed land-
mark underground mine safety legislation in 1941, 1952, and 1969 that
required mine owners to provide miners with safety gear and implement
safety improvements. The first and last of these acts significantly reduced
mining deaths (Lewis-Beck and Alford 1980).

Several factors worked to destabilize the carefully crafted equilibrium
in the coal policy subsystem in the 1960s and early 1970s. First, underground mining became increasingly mechanized. Second, an ever greater

share of US coal production came from strip mines in western states with low levels of labor union membership. Both of these developments made organized labor a less important part of the coal subsystem. In addition, with the recognition of the environmental consequences of mining and burning coal, policy debates in this area increasingly came to emphasize environmental protection. The environmental impact of mining introduced a new set of players to the coal subsystem: environmental interest groups (see below).

Petroleum

Similar to coal, the policy subsystem surrounding oil policy was for decades dominated by petroleum producers and bureaucrats within the Interior Department—initially, those in the Bureau of Mines, and after World War II, personnel in a separate Oil and Gas Division in the department.

Through most of the twentieth century, government policy with respect to petroleum focused on two goals: promoting oil exploration and regulating the production of oil. Government policy aimed at limiting production is a fine example of industry seeking regulation from the government. Petroleum is an excellent example of an "open access" or "common pool" resource. Unfettered access to such resources results in the familiar "tragedy of the commons," where the pursuit of individual self-interest leads to suboptimal social outcomes. In the case of oil, fields containing this resource cross property lines, so that wells drilled on one person's property can extract oil from under another person's property. In this situation, each property owner has a strong incentive to extract as much oil as quickly as possible, since leaving the oil in the ground probably ensures that one's neighbor will extract the oil instead. This rush to extract oil has two effects. First, oil floods the market and drives down prices (and industry profits). Second, rapid oil extraction reduces the amount of oil that can be recovered from a field, wasting some of the resource.

After several attempts at industry self-regulation had failed, petroleum producers persuaded Texas and Oklahoma to regulate the market for crude oil. Oklahoma, after failing to enforce a minimum price for oil, moved to production controls. The Texas Railroad Commission followed suit, going one better than its neighbor and using martial law to police production and maintain price levels (Yergin 1991: 248–252; Davis 1993). While such practices were successfully challenged in lower courts, the Supreme Court eventually accepted the conservation arguments put forth by Oklahoma, upholding a state's right to regulate production in the interests of conservation of public resources (Nash 1968; Davis 1993).

World War I provided the context in which the groundwork for an oil policy subsystem was laid. A predictable supply of oil was indispensable to the conduct of the war, and President Woodrow Wilson established the National Petroleum War Service Committee (NPWSC) to coordinate oil production for the duration of the war (Nash 1968: 24–28; Yergin 1991: 178). Working with the producer-dominated NPWSC, the US Fuel Administration and its Oil Division pooled production, allocated outputs, and controlled the rate at which oil was pumped—the very activities prohibited by antitrust regulation. The Oil Division was so successful at its job that it attracted the attention of the Federal Trade Commission, which threatened to file charges of monopoly and profiteering against oil-industry actors. The FTC and the Fuel Administration reached a compromise in which the latter agreed to police price rises more carefully and the former was allowed to pursue a more limited set of charges against Standard Oil of Indiana (Nash 1968: 29–38; Davis 1993).

Following the war, the NPWSC, renamed the American Petroleum Institute (API), absorbed many of the high-ranking government employees of the disbanded Fuel Administration and continued to search for ways to manage the production of oil to guarantee reasonable profits (Nash 1968: 41–43). Despite these efforts, oil boom was followed by bust, prices fluctuated wildly, and the business was more cutthroat than ever. In response, the government created the Federal Oil Conservation Board, charged with controlling production and ensuring an adequate supply of fuel for the US Navy. The functioning of the Conservation Board appeared to be in the cartel tradition of its government predecessor, the Fuel Administration. Over time, however, the board increasingly stressed conservation above industry profit, resulting in API opposition to the efforts at government coordination and regulation (Davis 1993: 72).

Disappointed with the Conservation Board, oil producers turned their attention to taxation, lobbying Congress for the adoption of a *depletion allowance* (Engler 1961: 23–24, 30–31). A depletion allowance is explicit recognition that the value of a capital investment dwindles as capital ages. The IRS allows businesses to deduct the costs of such investments—primarily machinery—at a set rate based on the expected life-span of the investment. The problem with treating oil wells as a capital investment is that there is no standard "life-span" of an oil well. Arguing that the IRS's case-by-case determination was unfair, the petroleum industry convinced Congress to base the depletion figure on annual gross oil sales. Eventually, Congress voted to allow oil companies to deduct 27.5 percent of their gross sales from taxable income, providing the figure did not exceed 50 percent of taxable income (Nash 1968: 34–35, 85–86; Davis 1993: 73). In addition, companies were allowed to deduct from their taxable income the miscellaneous costs associated with exploration, drilling, and the development of wells. While changes in tax policy proved quite lucrative to the petroleum industry, they did nothing to stop the destructive competition.

For a brief moment, the New Deal institutionalized the cartel arrangements long sought by the petroleum industry under the auspices of the National Recovery Administration (Nash 1968: 128–156). Declared unconstitutional by the Supreme Court in 1935, the NRA arrangements were replaced by the Interstate Compact to Conserve Oil and Gas, which left regulation to state governments and the API. By the early 1950s, 10 percent of oil consumption came from foreign sources, and members of the interstate compact secured the backing of the Eisenhower administration for a voluntary 12 percent limit on imports in 1954 (Yergin 1991: 512–513). Cheating on the quota was so widespread, and domestic producers' lobbying so intense, that President Eisenhower reluctantly imposed an official import quota in 1959 (Nash 1968: 205–206; Yergin 1991: 537–538). Sometimes referred to as the "drain America first" policy, the quota limited oil imports to 12 percent of oil consumption east of the Mississippi River and charged the Interior Department with approving applications for the import of oil. The end result of these policies was a regulatory system that encouraged domestic production, inflated prices, and allowed exorbitant industry profits.

Natural Gas

The policy subsystem with respect to natural gas is almost identical to that for oil. The major difference between the two is that transmission companies (i.e., pipeline owners) are important private-sector players in the natural gas subsystem. Because of its physical characteristics, gas regulation started out as a local concern (Tussing and Tippee 1995: 23–51). The local distribution of gas was deemed a natural monopoly because the resources required to put together a citywide distribution system necessitated a sizable initial investment that could be recouped only over time. Local distributors were awarded franchises by city governments that closely controlled pricing to guarantee universal service and a fair rate of return to gas companies. The extraction of natural gas was only loosely regulated by the states, in much the same fashion as oil. Since gas could not be reliably moved very far from its origins, most states ignored the extractive process. This left a gap in regulation once electronic welding made interstate sales of gas possible. The result, as might be expected, was classic monopolistic behavior by pipeline operators (Sanders 1981: 27–36; Davis 1993: 137). Indeed, just a decade after perfecting pipeline technology, there was significant vertical integration in the industry, and ten companies controlled the interstate transmission of gas.

The New Deal targeted this concentration of economic power, outlawing vertical integration in the natural gas industry with the Public Utility Holding Company Act of 1935. More important, Congress passed the Natural Gas Act in 1938, which allowed the Federal Power Commission

(FPC) to regulate the price of gas and the construction of distribution networks (i.e., pipelines) (Sanders 1981: 22–23; Tussing and Tippee 1995: 33–36). The FPC approach to licensing created localized pipeline monopolies, which posed significant problems for transporting gas when the market was later deregulated (De Vany and Walls 1995). Gas companies fought the FPC tooth-and-nail on its regulation of prices, but in *FPC v. Hope Natural Gas Company* (1944), the Supreme Court backed the FPC efforts to regulate prices charged in the interstate transportation of gas (Sanders 1981: 79–81). When the FPC attempted to extend its price-setting authority to the price of natural gas at the wellhead, Senator Robert Kerr (D-OK), founder of the energy giant Kerr-McGee, secured the passage of legislation removing FPC rate-making authority. Vetoed by Truman, the passage of the legislation was a strong enough message to convince the FPC to studiously avoid further price-setting activity (Sanders 1981: 88–93).

Throughout the 1960s, the few price increases granted by the FPC did not keep up with increased demand for natural gas, and gas became seriously underpriced. As a result, producers began hoarding gas pumped from public lands, selling only the minimal levels required by their leases (Tussing and Tippee 1995: 172–184). In response to the scarcity, pipelines from Canada and Mexico brought imported gas to the US market. In addition to the traditional means of moving gas to market, the development of a process by which natural gas was liquefied, greatly reducing its volume and making it transportable in specially constructed container vessels, allowed the importation of natural gas from the Middle East and Far East. While this new technology was not cheap, the scarcity of gas on the US East Coast made it a viable option. The intrastate market for gas suffered no similar shortage, because prices were not regulated, with the effect that gas was available at a higher price in states in which it was produced (Sanders 1981).

Nuclear Power

At its inception, proponents of the civilian use of nuclear power promised that it would provide electricity that was "too cheap to meter" (Morone and Woodhouse 1989). Government policy for much of the postwar era has made a concerted effort to make this promise come true, though without much success. The policy subsystem surrounding nuclear power is the most closed and secretive of any energy source. Of course, this is a result of the dangers posed by the fuel and wastes from nuclear energy, and the sensitive military applications of nuclear technology. In fact, it is not an exaggeration to suggest that the nuclear power subsystem is the closest thing to a traditional iron triangle found in any area of regulatory policy. The industry arm of this triangle originally consisted of electric utilities and reactor manufacturers like Westinghouse and General Electric (these actors later created a trade association, the Atomic Industrial Forum). The congressional arm of this triangle, the Joint Committee on Atomic Energy (JCAE), dealt with all legislation regarding the military or civilian use of atomic power. The administrative arm of the triangle was the Atomic Energy Commission (AEC), a five-member independent regulatory commission created in 1946 to oversee the development of atomic energy for military and civilian purposes (the same act created the JCAE). While the AEC was supposed to both encourage the development of civilian nuclear power and regulate its safety, the agency was stocked with refugees from the Manhattan Project and other supporters of atomic energy, so it quite naturally pursued the first mandate aggressively while ignoring the second. In their zeal to promote the fledgling industry, members of the AEC consistently downplayed, classified, or covered up any information that questioned the safety and viability of nuclear power (Morone and Woodhouse 1989).

Nuclear energy is unique not just because of the process involved in producing it and the cloistered nature of its subsystem. It is also the only energy source that began as, and remains, a primarily public enterprise. The federal government provided all initial research and development costs, built and operated several demonstration reactors, provided free uranium fuel (later reduced to subsidized fuel) to nuclear power plants, purchased the first reactors produced by private industry, absorbed nearly all of the costs of researching waste disposal methods, absorbed nearly all the costs of waste disposal, and under the Price-Anderson Act, limited a utility's financial liability in the case of an accident to $560 million. In short, it is extraordinarily unlikely that civilian nuclear power would exist without government support. Private utilities can own and operate nuclear power plants, but only after receiving construction and operating licenses from the federal government. These licenses are limited to the expected safe life-span of a nuclear power plant (originally thirty-five years). Government policy continued to promote and underwrite the development of nuclear power well into the 1970s.

Electricity

The provision of electricity can be thought of as having three elements: generation of electricity at a power plant, transmission of electricity from the power plant to population centers, and distribution of electricity to end users. Traditionally, each element was viewed as a natural monopoly requiring government regulation. Consequently, electric utilities in the United States developed as local, vertically integrated monopolies that combined all three elements. Government involvement in electricity generally takes one of three forms: regulation of rates and conditions of service, regulation of interstate sales, and direct provision of service. The first, which focuses on the generation and distribution elements described above, is almost always the responsibility of state and local governments. By 1922, every state but one had regulated the production of electricity, and state public utility commissions generally set rates using a "cost-plus," or the somewhat misnamed "guaranteed rate of return," formula. Price gouging on the part of electric utilities was rarely a problem, since through the mid-1960s utilities almost invariably asked for rate decreases as economies of scale forced down the price of electricity. Regulation of interstate sales of electricity, or the transmission element, has historically been the responsibility of the federal government (these rates were initially set by the Federal Power Commission, the same entity that set prices for interstate sales of natural gas, and are now set by its successor, the Federal Energy Regulatory Commission [FERC]).

Perhaps the most important development in electricity regulation prior to the 1970s was the enactment of the 1935 Public Utilities Holding Company Act (PUHCA). The 1920s and early 1930s saw two important developments in the relatively new electricity industry. First, small generation and transmission facilities were bought up and consolidated under the control of large, multistate holding companies. In time, a large proportion of the nation's total generating and transmission capacity came to be controlled by a small number of holding companies, which in many cases charged excessive prices. Because these holding companies were engaged in interstate commerce, however, they were largely immune to the regulatory efforts of state public utility commissions. Second, utility holding companies engaged in a number of nonelectricity business activities, such as oil and gas production (which created large, horizontally integrated energy companies that could exert market power over substitute energy sources) and real estate. During the Great Depression, the failure of these nonutility business investments forced many utility holding companies to declare bankruptcy, with disastrous consequences for utility customers. To prevent these problems in the future, the PUHCA restricted the size and geographic scale of utility holding companies (making them subject to state regulation), and prevented them from investing in nonutility businesses (to protect the reliability of electrical service).

The regulation of natural monopolies is a familiar refrain in this text, but what sets electric power generation apart is the existence of public providers of electrical power that operate alongside private producers. In fact, there are nearly 3,000 public or semipublic electric utilities in the United States, and only about 260 or so private utilities—though these private power plants account for almost 80 percent of all electricity generated (Davis 1993). The federal government also produces a substantial amount of power through entities like the Tennessee Valley Authority. The TVA originated as an economic development scheme to bring construction jobs, irrigation, recreation opportunities, and, most important, hydroelectric power to impoverished areas of the southeastern United States. While the TVA is regional in character, it soon outgrew its hydroelectric origins and now produces electricity from power plants using all types of fuel. Using the TVA as a model, the federal government developed similar regional power authorities in the Pacific Northwest and the south-central plains region, and it has constructed scores of hydroelectric and irrigation projects under the auspices of the Bureau of Reclamation and the Army Corps of Engineers.

Another influence of the TVA was the creation of the Rural Electrification Administration (REA). Adopting a stance similar to the Reconstruction Finance Corporation, the REA sought to make low-cost loans to private energy providers to encourage them to extend electrical service to rural areas (Rudolph and Ridley 1986: 79–84). Private providers balked at the idea, arguing that such activity was inherently unprofitable. When municipal providers offered to step in and fill the gap, the courts issued a series of rulings that questioned the legality of their offering service beyond their geographic boundaries. The end result was the creation of energy cooperatives, associations of rural users who pooled together to buy electricity from established producers, building their own transmission lines with government loans and, in some cases, their own transmission facilities as well. REA efforts were bolstered by the Public Utility Holding Company Act of 1935, which gave the FPC the power to regulate the transmission and sale of electricity to cooperatives (Rudolph and Ridley 1986: 77–89; Davis 1993: 177–179).

The final area in which the federal government regulates electricity is in the interstate sale of power. For decades the FPC encouraged the creation of regional power grids, or power pooling, in which utilities in areas with low electricity consumption can sell their excess power to areas with high electricity consumption. The FPC determined the price and conditions of sale for electricity in these power pools. While power pooling can result in the more efficient use of generating capacity and lower electricity prices for consumers, one drawback is that if part of the regional power grid fails, the entire grid may crash. During the high-growth period of the 1960s, electric utilities suffered through a series of blackouts that were traced to weak links in the regional power grids (Rudolph and Ridley 1986: 131–132; Davis 1993). Congress reacted to the blackouts by introducing legislation calling on the FPC to require more reliable systems, while private power companies insisted that self-policing would be more effective. Nine regional power councils were combined into the North American Electric Reliability Council, charged with the oversight of pooling arrangements and developing policy to ensure an adequate supply of electricity. Despite these efforts, interstate power grids are still susceptible to catastrophic failure, as evidenced by the large blackout in the eastern United States during 2003 that was caused by the failure of one part of the grid in Ohio.

* * *

Without exception, subsystems in energy policy prior to the Organization of Petroleum-Exporting Countries (OPEC) oil embargo of 1973–1974 were dominated by producer groups and administrative officials who shared the values of these groups. In most instances, the policy decisions made by these subsystems subsidized the production of energy, protected producers from domestic and international competition, and generally went to great lengths to guarantee the profitability of the energy industry. Where the tools of regulation were employed, they were always the price and entry tools typical of traditional economic regulation rather than the health and safety requirements of the new social regulation. Even the price and entry controls, moreover, were demanded by the regulated industry (e.g., production quotas with respect to domestic petroleum) at least as often as they were imposed on the industry against its will (e.g., pipeline price controls for natural gas). This system of dominant coalition subsystem politics is exactly what we would expect, given the low salience and generally low levels of technical complexity that characterize energy policy.

Energy Policy in a Postembargo World

The oil embargo of 1973–1974 was the defining moment for modern energy policy, and neither traditional energy policies nor traditional energy policy-making subsystems would ever be the same.[1] To begin, the oil embargo made energy policy salient for the first time in a long while. Long gas lines, shortages of natural gas and heating oil, skyrocketing fuel prices, and the attendant inflation these increases produced all caught the attention of American citizens, who now wanted to know just what the government was going to do (and had been doing) to ensure them an adequate supply of cheap energy. Second, the embargo forced Congress and the president for the first time to consider the virtues of a coordinated energy policy. In fact, every president since Richard Nixon has made an effort to integrate actions across the disparate energy policy subsystems. Third, coming on the heels of the heyday of the environmental movement, this "energy crisis" threw into stark relief the connection (perhaps even the trade-off) between energy use and a clean environment.

Nixon Responds to the Energy Crisis

In 1974, President Nixon identified the energy crisis as the number one national problem. He created the Energy Research and Development Administration (ERDA), consolidating almost all of the federal government's research and development efforts in the area of energy in an effort to move research and development responsibilities and personnel out of the traditional fuel source subsystems. Coinciding with this effort, Congress dismantled the AEC, giving its research and development responsibilities to ERDA and placing its responsibilities for inspecting and licensing nuclear power plants in the new Nuclear Regulatory Commission. While Nixon's proposal for a new cabinet-level Department of Energy and Natural Resources was rebuffed by Congress, the creation of ERDA and the NRC was a significant development in breaking the producer-dominated fuel source fiefdoms in energy policy.

The president's proposal to lodge control over the allocation of energy supplies in the White House did not pass congressional muster. He did, however, convince Congress to lower the national speed limit to fifty-five miles per hour as an energy-saving measure. He also placed controls on the price of oil. While this may have protected some consumers from higher fuel prices, it also had the effect of keeping demand for gasoline and other fuels artificially high (as any subsidy will do) and almost certainly exacerbated fuel shortages. The most important policy action taken by the Nixon administration, however, was "Project Independence," jointly authored by the federal government, the Ford Foundation, and researchers from the RAND Corporation. The goal of Project Independence was to make the United States free from dependence on foreign oil by 1980. The project's blueprint called for increasing coal consumption dramatically and more than doubling US nuclear power capacity. In Project Independence, we see the first example of the common practice of defining energy problems as problems of inadequate supply rather than excess demand. The blueprint made little mention of energy conservation or renewable energy sources as a way of meeting the goal of energy independence. The recommendations from the project were never codified in legislation, and while the recommendations themselves bore the unmistakable mark of the producer groups that traditionally dominated energy policymaking, Project Independence was the first time in recent memory in which these groups thought about coordinating their policy demands to pursue a common goal.

In addition to capping prices for oil, Nixon attempted to deal with the apparent shortage of natural gas by deregulating the price of this fuel. Nixon and others believed the regulator-enforced low price paid for natural gas meant exploration for gas alone was an unprofitable proposition. The Democrat-controlled Congress resisted the deregulation of gas prices, however, arguing that the industry was an oligopoly that must be regulated.

Rather than backing deregulation, Democrats allied with consumer rights activists, and municipal utilities represented by the American Public Gas Association advocated for the extension of FPC price regulation to intrastate sales of gas. In the face of congressional resistance, Nixon decided to pursue an administrative strategy. Relying on those of his FPC appointees who were allied with the American Gas Association, the lead producer group, the FPC issued a three-tier pricing structure, adjusted annually for inflation. The pricing scheme was intended to wean customers from artificially low prices yet maintain FPC price oversight to protect consumers (Sanders 1981: 167–179; Tussing and Tippee 1995: 156–184).

Ford Responds to the Energy Crisis

By the time Gerald Ford took over the presidency after Nixon's resignation, the OPEC oil embargo had ended. Energy prices were still high, however, and the policy response to shortages was still a central issue in the minds of politicians and voters alike (as one indication of this, more than a thousand energy-related bills were introduced in Congress in 1975) (Katz 1984). Whereas Nixon's most enduring legacy lay in integrating elements of disparate fuel-based subsystems, Ford made his mark with the passage of the Energy Policy and Conservation Act (EPCA).

The act temporarily rolled back environmental protection standards to allow the use of more coal at electric power plants and lower grades of domestic petroleum at refineries. More important, the act established the Strategic Petroleum Reserve, the corporate average fuel economy (CAFE) standards, and appliance efficiency standards. The Strategic Petroleum Reserve is a government-owned oil reserve (originally 500 million barrels, expanded to 1 billion in 1992). The federal government buys this oil on the open market and then stores it in underground geologic formations on public land (among other places). The government can release oil from this reserve in the event of an interruption in the supply of foreign oil. The CAFE standards require automakers to meet an average fuel efficiency standard (27.5 miles per gallon since 1990) across all cars they sell (the act also imposed a "gas guzzler tax" on the least-efficient vehicles). The manufacturers can meet this standard by improving the fuel efficiency of all of their vehicles or by providing incentives for purchasing more efficient vehicles. Manufacturers that do not meet these fuel efficiency goals are subject to fines. EPCA also set minimum energy efficiency standards for most major household appliances and required manufacturers to place energy efficiency labels on these appliances. The CAFE and appliance efficiency standards constitute the first example of the federal government promoting energy efficiency as a means of dealing with the energy crisis. Finally, Ford extended the natural gas policies of the Nixon administration to oil by placing price controls on newly discovered oil supplies while planning for the eventual decontrol of oil prices.

The Moral Equivalent of War:
Energy Policy in the Carter Administration

No president has made energy policy as central to his administration as did Jimmy Carter. In part, Carter's emphasis on energy policy was a reflection of his sincere belief that the United States faced a serious energy crisis and that the country could avoid ruin only through aggressive and unprecedented government action. In addition, the Carter administration had the misfortune of having to deal with two of the most potent crises in the history of US energy policy: the 1979 oil embargo precipitated by the Islamic revolution in Iran and the near meltdown of a reactor at the Three Mile Island nuclear power plant that same year.

Unlike previous presidents, Carter was willing to tackle the energy problem from the demand side, arguing strenuously for increases in energy conservation and reductions in energy demand. This demand-side focus did not sit well with energy-producer groups, and Carter expended a great deal of precious political capital trying to force subsystem participants to follow his wishes with respect to energy policy. Carter's inability to deal assuredly with the consequences of the second oil embargo in 1979 helped seal his fate in the 1980 presidential election. While most of Carter's unconventional policy initiatives were never enacted, he did manage to substantially increase federal spending for conservation and renewable energy.

Reorganizing energy policy subsystems.   Carter's most enduring legacy in this area is the federal Department of Energy. Carter and his advisers believed that they would never be able to overcome the objections of entrenched producer groups and coordinate federal energy policy within the existing framework of isolated fuel-based policy subsystems. While Carter was not the first president to propose such a department, he was the one who succeeded in creating it, in 1977. The new department merged the Federal Energy Administration, ERDA, and the FPC, and took various energy-related functions from almost a dozen other federal departments and offices. At least as important as the functions included in the new department were the functions left outside its control. The Department of Energy did not get the power to set prices for electricity, oil, and natural gas. Rather than place these sensitive functions under presidential control, Congress placed these responsibilities of the old FPC within the new five-member Federal Energy Regulatory Commission. Second, the DOE did not receive the authority to administer coal and oil leases on federal lands and the outer continental shelf, which remained with the Department of Interior. Finally, the department did not receive authority to regulate nuclear power plants, which remained with the NRC. Nevertheless, with the creation of the DOE, the federal government for the first time had most of its energy responsibilities within one agency, where they were both visible and more easily coordinated.

Carter and his first energy secretary, James Schlesinger, knew that it would take more than a change of address to break up the traditional fuel-based subsystems. Thus, as originally constituted, the DOE was organized without respect to fuel sources. Schlesinger, in particular, felt that organizing the department according to fuel sources would simply reinforce the independent and insular nature of policymaking in this area. Instead, the DOE was organized along functional lines, with offices for basic research, development, commercialization, and information (the Office of Information later came to be called the Energy Information Administration). The hope was that such an organizational structure would facilitate the integration of energy policy across fuel sources. While the effort to dismantle previous energy policy subsystems was admirable, Carter underestimated the power of energy producers and their supporters in Congress. By 1980 the DOE had been reorganized three times, resulting in a structure organized along traditional subsystem lines, with offices of coal, oil, gas, and so forth—a structure it maintains to this day (see Figure 10.2).

Energy policy development in the Carter administration. The same legislation that created the DOE also required the president to produce five- and ten-year comprehensive energy plans. Carter's initial attempt was the first National Energy Program (NEP I), submitted to Congress early in 1977. NEP I aimed to solve the nation's energy crisis by increasing energy conservation, increasing the use of renewable sources of energy, and increasing (somewhat) the consumption of coal. NEP I reflected the legislative priorities of environmental groups, aiming to solve the nation's energy problems by reducing the demand for energy rather than by increasing supply. The plan also would have levied taxes on energy consumption, increased automotive CAFE standards, and dramatically increased federal research and development spending for renewable energy.

Although NEP I was approved with few changes in the Senate, it was dismembered in the House and sent out to a dozen different committees. In the end, only a very few parts of the plan passed both houses of Congress. In addition to the Public Utility Regulatory Policy Act (PURPA) of 1978 (discussed below), one remnant of NEP I prohibited new electric power plants from burning oil or natural gas (in order to conserve these fuels) and strongly encouraged existing power plants burning these fuels to convert their boilers to coal. A second remnant of NEP I provided tax credits to individuals, businesses, and industries that invested money in energy conserva-

Figure 10.2 The Department of Energy

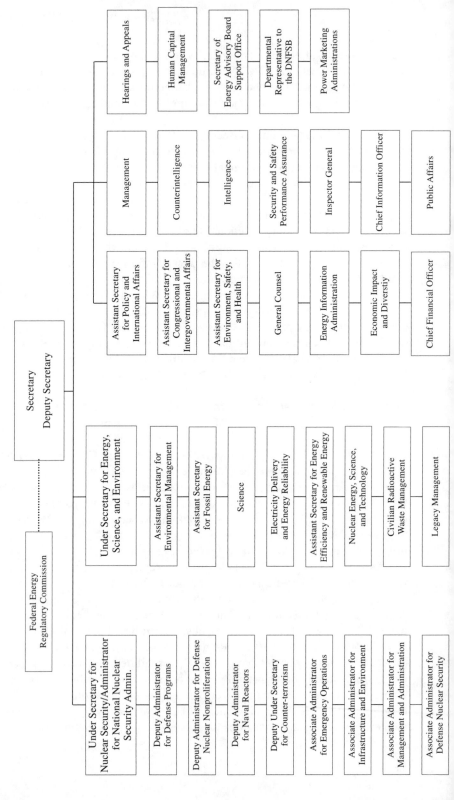

tion and renewable energy technologies. These tax credits spurred a boom in energy conservation and renewable energy development.

After the price of oil more than doubled in 1979 following the Islamic revolution in Iran, NEP II was introduced in Congress. Learning a lesson from the failure of NEP I, Carter consulted with representatives of the energy industries and with key members of Congress from energy-producing states. NEP II focused more on increasing energy supplies of coal and nuclear power than on managing the demand for energy. Much to the dismay of environmentalists and conservationists, energy conservation and renewable sources of energy received little attention. NEP II extended price controls on oil and natural gas into the mid-1980s and instituted the "windfall profits tax," designed to recapture some of the record profits of the oil industry that would occur after the planned phase-out of oil price controls. Finally, NEP II created the Synfuels Corporation, a multibillion-dollar public-private partnership aimed at producing nontraditional or synthetic petroleum substitutes (e.g., shale oil, coal liquefaction, ethanol). Most of these synthetic fuels were projected to be hugely expensive, and almost all posed substantial threats to the environment. Since traditional energy producers like Exxon would receive Synfuels subsidies, however, this portion of NEP II received much support. In the end, NEP II passed Congress and was signed into law by Carter.

President Carter did not ignore environmental concerns regarding energy use, as evidenced by his efforts to regulate coal mining. The Surface Mining Control and Reclamation Act outlines nationwide standards to protect against environmental devastation associated with strip mining, the actual design and implementation of which are left to state regulators. State regulators must submit their regulatory plans to the Office of Surface Mining (OSM), within the Interior Department, for approval. If states refuse to submit plans or fail to gain approval for their plans, the OSM steps in to enforce the act. This created much tension between state regulators and the OSM at the time the act was implemented, as well as with mine operators who viewed the OSM as an overly stringent regulator.

In the area of gas policy, Carter moved toward further deregulation of gas prices, alienating a sizable contingent of his own party in the process. The Natural Gas Policy Act of 1978, passed after an enormous lobbying effort on the part of the White House, set prices for this fuel using a maze of intricate formulas. Not coincidentally, once the act was signed, the shortage disappeared as producers scrambled to bring gas to market (Sanders 1981: 174–189). By the early 1980s, prices had risen so high that demand began to drop, a trend that continued throughout the decade.

Carter, a trained nuclear engineer, was surprisingly cool to the expansion of nuclear power. Most notably, Carter remained a steadfast opponent of breeder reactor technology (in addition to producing electricity, a breeder reactor transforms uranium into plutonium, in effect producing more fissionable material than it consumes). While breeder technology promised an almost unlimited supply of atomic fuel, Carter opposed it on environmental and national security grounds (i.e., he feared increasing the availability of plutonium, which can be used to build atomic weapons). With respect to traditional fission technology, Carter's initial energy plan called for reducing the nation's reliance on atomic fission, and he changed this outlook only after the failure of NEP I and heavy lobbying on the part of the atomic energy industry. The policy debate regarding increased reliance upon nuclear power was effectively settled in 1979 by something neither the president nor Congress could control: the partial reactor meltdown at the Three Mile Island nuclear power plant. This experience soured the American public on nuclear power, and no new reactors have been ordered in the United States since 1979.

While the expansion of the nuclear power industry effectively ended after the Three Mile Island incident, existing power plants were still producing tons of radioactive waste from all steps in the nuclear fuel cycle. Congress and the Carter administration took action to deal with several of these wastes. The 1978 Uranium Mill Tailings Reduction Act required the waste from uranium mining to be turned into solids and placed in abandoned mines, with the federal government picking up 90 percent of the costs. A second class of radioactive wastes, low-level wastes, was also largely unregulated prior to the Carter administration. Utilities produce only about half of these wastes, with the remainder coming from hospitals, research labs, and the like. Most low-level radioactive wastes are placed in landfills, either before or after incineration. The 1980 Low Level Waste Policy Act makes disposing of these wastes the responsibility of state governments and encourages them to enter into interstate waste disposal compacts. Most state governments subsidize the disposal of low-level radioactive wastes.

The aforementioned Public Utility Regulatory Policy Act of 1978 was the most notable piece of electricity-focused legislation passed in twenty-five years. PURPA was Carter's attempt to force state public utility commissions to adopt policies that would conserve energy and favor individual consumers over industrial consumers. As originally introduced, PURPA required electric utilities to institute an increasing of *block pricing*—that is, charging large power consumers higher prices to encourage conservation (utilities did just the opposite)—and to offer reduced prices during off-peak hours in order to encourage consumers to spread their power use throughout the day. This would reduce the need to build new power plants to meet peak electrical demands. Second, PURPA required electric utilities to purchase power generated by independent power producers (i.e., industrial facilities that produced both steam and electricity, or average folks with windmills in their backyards). In the final legislation, however, Congress made the increasing of block pricing optional and left it up to state utility commissions to set the price at which they would buy power from independent producers. Nevertheless, PURPA was the first step toward promoting competition in the production of electricity.

What Energy Crisis?
Ronald Reagan and National Energy Policy
In energy policy, as in most areas, Ronald Reagan was yin to Jimmy Carter's yang. While Presidents Nixon, Ford, and Carter all believed there was an energy crisis and that the federal government ought to take action to solve it, Reagan believed neither of these things. Instead, Reagan felt that the "energy crisis" was largely the result of misguided federal interventions into the market for energy. Thus the crisis would solve itself only if government would get out of the way. The Reagan energy model was microeconomics at its most simple: if government decontrolled the price of energy, prices would rise. These price increases would stimulate the search for more energy (a supply-side solution), encourage energy conservation on the part of consumers (a demand-side solution), and make renewable sources of energy more competitive (an environmental solution).

Reagan proposed five tactics for effecting this sea change in energy policy. First, he ordered the immediate decontrol of oil and gas prices and eliminated all remaining import and production restrictions, abandoning the phased decontrol policies of Carter. Second, he proposed to dismantle the DOE. Reagan's first energy secretary, James B. Edwards, initially supported abolishing the department, but his perspective changed once he found out that many energy producers supported keeping the department. Moreover, abolishing the DOE required an act of Congress, and a bootleggers-and-Baptists coalition of energy-producer supporters and environmentalists lobbied to keep the department (Axelrod 1984). Third, he reduced federal support for renewable energy research and development by 80 percent over three years, while also cutting spending for coal, oil, and natural gas research and development by half (see Figure 10.3). Fourth, the administration vastly increased the leasing of oil, gas, and coal reserves on federal land at bargain-basement prices (Axelrod 1984). Finally, since the tax code could also distort the market for energy, Reagan eliminated tax credits for investments in conservation and renewable energy, and even eliminated many of the tax advantages enjoyed by the oil industry (Burnbaum and Murray 1987).

The market discipline advocated by the Reagan administration was compromised in at least two areas: the production of synthetic fuels and the establishment of appliance efficiency standards. From a market perspective, the Synfuels Corporation, established by Carter's NEP II, was an abomina-

Figure 10.3 Federal Energy Subsidies

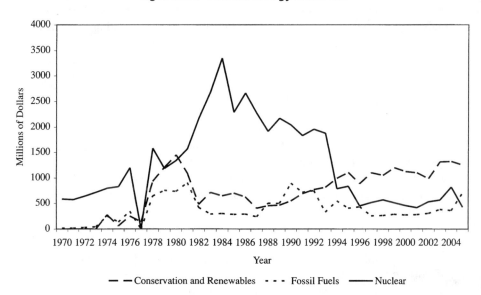

Conservation and Renewables   Fossil Fuels   Nuclear

tion, spending billions of dollars of public money to produce fuel at more than twice the price of traditional energy sources. On the other hand, these billions were being transferred to large and politically powerful energy producers like Exxon and the Atlantic Richfield Company to develop new energy technologies and demonstration projects. At first, the lure of the oil barrel overwhelmed the logic of the market, and Reagan endorsed federal support for the Synfuels Corporation (Uslaner 1989). Later, however, after even the energy companies soured on the program, the Synfuels Corporation was eliminated. Similarly, from a market perspective, implementing appliance efficiency standards (or at least requiring manufacturers to advertise appliance efficiency) makes perfect sense, as it gives consumers information with which to make more rational purchasing decisions. But the Reagan administration, citing the cost to industry, refused to establish appliance standards until forced to by the Supreme Court (the administration also prevented state governments from setting their own standards; see Axelrod 1984).

If Reagan's commitment to a free market in energy was compromised with respect to synthetic fuels and appliance efficiency standards, it disappeared altogether when it came to nuclear power. Rather than eliminate the multiple sources of federal support that kept the nuclear power industry afloat, Reagan increased budgetary appropriations for this energy source (see Figure 10.3). Moreover, Reagan pushed forward with a federal demonstration project for breeder reactor technology at Clinch River, Tennessee, previously opposed by President Carter. Reagan took an even more aggressive approach to nuclear power promotion within the NRC. First, Reagan appointees substantially reduced the inspection and enforcement activities of the NRC (Wood and Waterman 1991). Second, under Reagan, the NRC eliminated the avenue by which state and local governments could delay the licensing of new nuclear power plants. Third, in 1987 the NRC unilaterally doubled the licensing period for all nuclear power plants to seventy years, effectively sidestepping the costly and unresolved problem of reactor decommissioning (of course, this also meant that many nuclear power plants would continue operating beyond their designed life expectancy). Congress joined the fray in 1982, passing the Nuclear Waste Policy Act, which outlined federal policy for the disposal of high-level radioactive waste, requiring the construction of two permanent disposal facilities—one east of the Mississippi, the other west. The first disposal facility was to open in 1998, at which time the federal government would take title to all high-level radioactive waste in the country and pay for storage and monitoring of these wastes.

The market-based policies of the Reagan administration had the desired effect: the price for energy initially increased, which spurred increased oil and gas exploration domestically. Increases in exploration, however, could not keep pace with increases in the consumption of energy, and thus this development had little effect on reducing US dependence on foreign oil. Luckily, large oil and gas discoveries in non-OPEC nations and defections on the part of OPEC cartel members produced a crash in world oil prices in 1986, so increased reliance on foreign sources of these fuels was neither as costly nor as dangerous as in the 1970s.

Energy Regulation in the Administration of George H. W. Bush

Ronald Reagan oversaw the end of the synthetic fuels program, encouraged utilities to reexplore the nuclear energy option, decontrolled oil and gas prices, and pushed for increases in the production of oil and gas on public lands. As might be expected, the Bush administration continued many of these trends, aided in part by the outbreak of war in the Middle East following Iraq's invasion of Kuwait. Still, George H. W. Bush signaled a break of sorts with his predecessor's laissez-faire approach with the appointment of James Watkins to head the DOE. Watkins announced that energy conservation and efficiency were to be the cornerstones of the Bush DOE. The problem with Watkins's vision was that it clashed with that of Bush's chief of staff, John Sununu, a proponent of a Reaganesque market strategy that opposed all conservation measures as government interference (Kuntz 1991).

While Bush proclaimed himself the "environmental president" and spoke in glowing terms of the need to conserve energy, his service in the congressional delegation of Texas, not to mention his business experience in oil, meant he was also an ally of the petroleum industry. The result was that the Bush administration, while trying to assert its role as principal in setting the energy agenda, often appeared to be speaking out of both sides of its mouth.

Bush's effort to set the energy agenda took the form of the National Energy Strategy Act, introduced in 1991. This proposal called for boosting domestic oil production, most notably in the Arctic National Wildlife Refuge (ANWR), and increasing nuclear power production. The Senate Energy and Natural Resources Committee, however, was not about to let the president assume the role of principal unchallenged. The chair of the committee, J. Bennett Johnston (D-LA), was joined by the ranking minority member, Malcolm Wallop (R-WY), and the two cosponsored their own energy bill. The Senate effort, titled the National Energy Security Act, contained a package that called for increased production of fossil fuels balanced with conservation measures (Mills 1991a). The primary legislative vehicle in the House was actually a series of five bills sponsored by Philip R. Sharp (D-IN), chair of the Subcommittee of Energy and Commerce. Sharp had cut his energy teeth guiding Jimmy Carter's proposals through the House in the 1970s, and his legislation reflected the conservation ideals of the former president. As if to prove nothing is ever easy in the House, the Sharp bill was challenged by Leon Panetta (D-CA), who introduced legislation that attempted to balance conservation and production goals in a package that straddled the middle ground (Idelson 1991a).

The four energy packages contained several common points. All sought to expand the Strategic Petroleum Reserve, increase CAFE standards, promote the use of alternative fuel–powered public transit, and encourage research and development of renewable energy technologies. Commonalities aside, the administration package was clearly the most energy-producer friendly, although the Senate version was a close second. Only the House bills stressed conservation over production, laying the groundwork for a protracted debate over the course of energy policy. All the would-be agenda setters recognized the primacy of oil and gas in the debate; where they disagreed was over how to treat these energy sources. The Senate and administration bills solved the problem by opening the ANWR to production and relaxing prohibitions against drilling in the outer continental shelf (Idelson 1991a: 702), drawing protests from environmental groups and residents of coastal states. The administration and the Senate also advocated easing regulations on pipeline construction and import and export restrictions on natural gas (Idelson 1991a: 701–702). The Panetta bill left natural gas regulation untouched, while the Sharp legislation eased licensing of pipelines but left the environmental review process intact.

In the area of nuclear power, the president proposed speeding up licensing by consolidating the two-step process—construction approval followed by reactor licensing—into a single preconstruction step. The Senate went one step further, arguing that the NRC already had the power to grant a license in a single step. While the industry welcomed regulatory relief regarding licensing, the major stumbling block to nuclear energy production involved disposing of the high-level radioactive waste. The problem of disposing of the growing volume of these wastes paralyzed Congress. No member wanted to be known as the legislator who brought the nuclear dump home. It was probably no coincidence that of the three states mentioned as possible sites, Texas and Washington managed to get themselves removed from the list while members of their congressional delegations served as Speaker and majority leader of the House. With only the Yucca Mountain site in Nevada left in the running, the debate became quite heated. While the choice of a site did present Congress and the DOE with some complex engineering and geology problems, the process of siting the waste was a classic example of the "not in my backyard" (NIMBY) syndrome. In an effort to move the question of a waste dump to some resolution, the administration proposal empowered the Department of Energy to proceed with a study of Yucca Mountain as a waste repository unencumbered by state environmental review.

In the realm of electricity, both the administration and the Senate proposed simplifying the licensing of hydroelectric projects and eliminating FERC oversight of small dams. The administration also proposed extending tax breaks to all plants using renewable or waste energy. In an effort to attract new entrants into electricity generation, both the administration and the Senate called for easing the restrictions on the size, structure, and geographic areas of service in the 1935 Public Utility Holding Company Act. In one final effort to realize complete electricity privatization, the administration sought to end subsidies for the Bonneville, Southeastern, Southwestern, and Western Area Power Administrations (Idelson 1991a: 702–703).

None of the preceding proposals went anywhere in the first session of the 102nd Congress. The problem was that there were multiple would-be principals attempting to set the energy policy agenda. While policy was moving in a subsystem mode, the politicking undertaken in the House was typical of that of transitory coalitions. Bush flirted with acting as the energy agenda setter, while Philip Sharp did his best to maintain the primacy of the Energy and Commerce Committee. His job was complicated by the role of the full committee chair, John Dingell (D-MI). Dingell was antagonistic toward CAFE standards, alternative fuels, or anything that appeared to threaten the primacy of the automobile and petroleum in American life. This brought him into direct conflict with his subcommittee chair, Sharp, although it did provide a bridge to the White House. Dingell's soft spot for petroleum-producing interests also made him a natural ally of Johnston in the Senate. Despite a challenge from Senator George Mitchell and the Environment and Public Works Committee, Johnston managed to maintain control of the issue in the Senate (Idelson 1991b). Even though nothing came of the 1991 energy proposals, they laid the groundwork for a second round of efforts to restructure energy policy.

If the oil embargoes of the 1970s had provided the catalyst for reassessing energy policy two decades earlier, the invasion of Kuwait by Iraq performed a similar role in 1991. The Gulf War set up the president as the natural agenda setter, focused attention anew on the lack of a coherent energy policy, and forced the various warring industry factions and congressional committees to think seriously about formulating a compromise (Idelson 1991c). Johnston got the ball rolling in the Senate, dropping provisions for increasing CAFE standards and drilling in the ANWR. In order to keep the administration on board, the Johnston bill sped up nuclear licensing and increased the pace of oil and gas pipeline construction. Conservationist concerns were reflected in the portions of the bill that increased the energy research and development budget and funding for alternative fuels and energy-efficient technology (Idelson 1992a). The Senate passed the Johnston bill in a 94 to 4 vote, sending it to the House.

Consideration of an omnibus energy bill in the House pitted George Miller (D-CA), the new Interior Committee chair, against Dingell's Commerce Committee. Miller, an ally of environmentalists, clearly sought to regain control of turf that he felt the former chair, Morris Udall (D-AZ), had let slip away (Idelson 1992g). Miller sought to widen the scope of the conflict, preferring to carry the debate to the floor of the chamber. Dingell, in the words of Science and Technology Committee chair George Brown (D-CA), "really [did not] want to engage in a negotiating process, [preferring] to keep the bill solely within his committee's jurisdiction" (Idelson 1992e: 1244). Dingell won a partial victory when the Rules Committee made Energy and Commerce the committee of origin for the House energy bill. The victory was not complete, since the Rules Committee allowed portions of the bill to be considered by eight additional committees (Idelson 1992g). The legislation passed in the House 381 to 37, leading to a conference to iron out the differences between the House and Senate bills.

Unusual for its size (more than a hundred members) and the diversity of preferences among its members, the conference committee hardly resembled the classic political principal. Rather than proceeding with the fuel-based subsystems designing policy with little or no coordination, the Energy Policy Act of 1992 was a concerted effort to fashion an all-encompassing energy policy. What this meant was that the various subsystems had to strike bargains with one another, as well as with environmental, consumer, and conservationist interests. The driving goal was to reduce US dependence on oil imports. Linked to this was a shifting consensus backing renewable resources, conservation, and continued price deregulation. While there was not universal backing for all of this, majority coalitions could be assembled for various combinations of the three.

Senator Johnston took control of the conference, hammering out a compromise that passed the House (363 to 30) and the Senate (84 to 8), though some senators threatened a filibuster over Nevada losing the struggle against a high-level nuclear waste depository (Idelson 1992i). Nuclear energy was clearly a winner, with its image refurbished by that portion of the Energy Policy Act providing increased funding for research and development of advanced commercial reactors. The act contained a number of provisions funding alternative fuels research and mandating the use of alternative fuel fleets by particular government agencies, alternative fuel producers, and state and municipal government entities. Energy efficiency standards were put in place for federal, state, and local government buildings, and the DOE was instructed to draw up a set of voluntary efficiency guidelines for the private sector. At the insistence of some members of the House delegation, the act directed the Department of Energy to study additional ways to reduce the consumption of imported oil and make regular reports to Congress on its progress (Idelson 1992i: 3728). This was a clear attempt by the House to institutionalize oversight and manage DOE activities in particular policy areas.

The Energy Policy Act contained very little that dealt directly with oil. House language banning drilling in the ANWR and the outer continental shelf was dropped as veto bait. The Strategic Petroleum Reserve was expanded to 1 billion barrels, and the president was given additional powers to sell oil from the reserve during crises. Similarly, action on the natural gas front was minimal. Import restrictions on Canadian natural gas were relaxed, and congressional support for price deregulation was reiterated. Like nuclear energy, coal got a boost from the act. Money was set aside for research and development of clean coal technology and for the export of such technology. The act sought to increase the export of US coal, as well as research for new uses for coal.

The most radical change came in the realm of electric utilities. The Energy Policy Act created a class of wholesale power producers exempt from the 1935 Public Utility Holding Company Act (addressed below). In addition, hydroelectric operations on public lands are subjected to increased National Park Service oversight designed to protect public lands and waterways. Similarly, the Bureau of Land Management and the US Forest Service were given veto authority over the building of roads, pipelines, and transmission lines that would run across lands under their jurisdiction (Idelson 1992i: 3724). In the end, incoming vice president Al Gore summed it up best when he characterized the Energy Policy Act as "the last of the big production bills" (Idelson 1992b: 397).

More of the Same:
President Clinton and the Republican Revolution

The energy subsystems were subject to new shocks in the 1990s. First, the election of Bill Clinton as president in 1992 unseated an incumbent Republican who had seemed invincible just a year before. A change in administration is a potential disturbance to any subsystem. In the case of the Clinton administration, the threat to the subsystem came not from the president, but from his running mate, Al Gore. Vice President Gore was singularly preoccupied with the effects of burning fossil fuels and the phenomenon of global warming (see Chapter 7). Gore's experience in the Senate, coupled with the power-sharing style of the new president, made the vice president a potentially important actor in the energy drama. The second shock occurred in Congress, where in 1994 the Republican Party gained control of both houses for the first time in nearly half a century. The new Republican majority vowed to change traditional ways of governing, something that did not bode well for most subsystems. What is interesting about these two potentially subsystem-shattering events is that neither had much of an impact on the various energy subsystems. Why this is so has to do with the resilience of subsystems, the rarity of the conditions necessary for any single player to act as a principal, and the complexity of the energy field itself.

The 1990s were remarkable, at least following the end of the war with Iraq, for abundant energy supplies and low energy prices. Because of this, Clinton was able to focus on cutting energy programs seen as wasteful or environmentally unfriendly, and shifting priorities from fossil fuel and nuclear programs to conservation and renewables (Healey 1994a). For example, Clinton attempted to eliminate many of the advanced nuclear reactors funded by the National Energy Act passed just two years before (Masci 1994c, 1994d, 1994e, 1994f). While the nuclear subsystem was not able to protect all of these projects (funding for one reactor design was eliminated), it still managed to survive the budget cuts quite nicely, but not as nicely as did oil.

The oil and natural gas subsystems came through the Clinton administration virtually unscathed. The administration proposed privatizing the Naval Petroleum Reserve, allowing commercial drilling and exploration to boost domestic production of oil. If this was not a big enough boon to the fortunes of oil, the tax breaks contemplated by the Senate for offshore exploration certainly were. Never really neglected by its congressional representatives, the oil subsystem positively thrived under Johnston. Ever the vigilant guardian of oil, the Louisiana senator was feeling so good about the position of oil that he led an attack against the ethanol requirement in the Clean Air Act. In a battle that pitted members of the oil subsystem against the agriculture subsystem, Johnston enlisted the support of environmental groups and anti-Clinton Republican legislators. Demonstrating that the protection of subsystem interests is more important than party lines, Johnston recruited Republican legislators who simply wanted to make life hard for Archer Daniels Midland, the largest producer of ethanol and a major Clinton (and Democratic Party) donor. Oil interests were upset over losing an estimated 10 percent of the gasoline market to ethanol producers. Eventually Johnston backed off from these efforts in the face of stiff resistance from agriculture state senators, and the ethanol requirements remained in place (Gettinger, Hosansky, and Katz 1994).

The 1994 midterm elections introduced a new potential principal on the scene in the form of the Republican Party. The limits of the "Republican revolution" in energy policy were especially pronounced when freshman Republicans attempted to upset the energy applecart. Along with dismantling the Department of Energy, the freshmen called for privatizing the energy labs conducting nuclear energy research, the five federal power administrations, and the government petroleum reserves (Freedman 1995a). The majority of the House and Senate were taken aback by the proposals.

Particularly unenthusiastic about the proposals for change were the Republican Party members who now chaired the committees and subcommittees that claimed energy as their turf. While Robert Walker, the new chair of the Science and Technology Committee, wished to redirect DOE research and policy priorities, he had no desire to oversee the dismantling of the agency. Striking a middle ground between those who wanted to dismantle the DOE and those who would leave it untouched, Walker moved to stop funding applied research, calling it "corporate welfare," in favor of money for basic research in areas such as hydrogen-fusion reactors (Babson 1995b). While Walker was concerned with cutting deals with the fiscal conservatives in the House, his Senate counterparts were less inclined in this regard. True, Senate majority leader Bob Dole was game to play along with the House proposals. Dole was no doubt already thinking of a run for the White House, and the impressive showing of the Republican Party in the House was not lost on him. But the Senate is a very different place than the House, and Dole's wishes carried little weight with the senators tied to the various energy subsystems. To make this point perfectly clear to both Dole and the House, Pete Domenici (R-NM) shepherded an energy bill through the Senate that authorized $1.5 billion more in spending than did the House (Freedman 1995c, 1995d). In the end, however, no significant pieces of energy legislation were enacted during Clinton's two terms as president.

George W. Bush and the Return
of Producer-Dominated Subsystems

Traditional energy interests have never been better represented than within
the administration of George W. Bush, at least during the post–World War II
period. Both the president and the vice president, Dick Cheney, come from
large fossil fuel–producing states (Texas and Wyoming). Moreover, both
men have had extensive personal and professional experience in the energy
industry: Bush as the principal partner in an independent oil exploration
firm, and Cheney as the chairperson of Haliburton, the world's largest energy services company. It should come as no surprise, then, that the president's first domestic policy priority, after tax cuts, was reshaping the
nation's energy policy.

On January 29, 2001, President Bush created the National Energy
Policy Development Group (NEPDG), chaired by Vice President Cheney,
and charged the group with developing "a national energy policy designed
to help the private sector, and government at all levels, promote dependable,
affordable, and environmentally sound production and distribution of energy in the future" (Robinson and Reese 2003: 1). The NEPDG released its
final report in May 2001, containing over a hundred recommendations for
executive actions and new legislation to increase the nation's energy supply.

The NEPDG report was developed over several months, largely with
the input of scores of representatives from coal, oil, and natural gas companies, as well as electric utilities, in closed-door meetings. By all accounts,
environmental groups and advocates for nontraditional energy policies were
not invited to participate. The NEPDG was roundly criticized by these
groups because they were not included in the process, and they disagreed
with the group's recommendations. More important, the NEPDG was also
criticized by "good government" groups and many members of Congress
for the secretive (i.e., nontransparent and apparently undemocratic) nature
of its deliberations. Concerns over the actions of the NEPDG were so serious that the US Government Accountability Office (GAO), the investigative
arm of Congress, was asked to examine the process by which the final
report was produced and to estimate the total cost to the government of
developing that report. When the GAO asked for documents used in
NEPDG deliberations and records of meetings held by the NEPDG, the
Office of the Vice President refused to release the records, claiming that the
GAO had no statutory authority to examine them. Moreover, when the GAO
asked to interview government officials who participated in the NEPDG
meetings, the Office of the Vice President refused to allow the GAO access
to these officials (Robinson and Reese 2003). The vice president made the
claim that since NEPDG meetings took place outside the normal processes
of government policymaking (i.e., the meetings were not part of
Congressional legislative decisionmaking, nor were they part of a formal

agency rule-making process), the actions of the group were not under the jurisdiction of the GAO. In effect, the vice president was arguing that since the NEPDG was simply an advisory body to the president, open-meeting laws, the GAO's statutory authority guaranteeing it access to government records, and the Freedom of Information Act did not apply. Fearing that not challenging this position would set a dangerous precedent, the GAO sued the Office of the Vice President in federal district court. The court dismissed the case on jurisdictional grounds, and after meeting with Republicans and Democrats in Congress, the GAO decided not to appeal this decision (Robinson and Reese 2003).

The central conclusion of the NEPDG report was that excessive government regulations, particularly environmental regulations, were to blame for potential energy shortages in the United States. Indeed, the report claims that past inattention to increasing domestic supplies of energy from fossil fuels and nuclear power had led to "the worst energy crisis in decades" (Kahn 2001: A1). Key regulatory targets identified by the NEPDG included eliminating restrictions for oil and gas drilling on the outer continental shelf and the ANWR, eliminating land-use restrictions governing energy development in the Rocky Mountains, and eliminating environmental regulations and reviews that were slowing down the construction of new or refurbished power plants and oil refineries (i.e., the New Source Review requirements of the Clean Air Act—see Chapter 7).

Each year after the release of the NEPDG report in 2001, the president backed a comprehensive energy bill in Congress that embodied the recommendations of the report. No energy bill was passed by Congress in 2001 or 2002, however, as the terrorist attacks of September 11, 2001, focused congressional attention away from energy policy, and because a leading Republican on environmental and energy issues, Jim Jeffords (I-VT), abandoned the Republican Party, eliminating the Republican majority in the Senate necessary for pushing through the president's plan. Congressional inaction did not completely stymie presidential efforts in this area, however, as President Bush issued two executive orders in 2001—apparently drafted by energy industry lobbyists—that directed federal agencies to accelerate the approval of permits to develop oil, gas, and coal on federal lands, and to build new power plants, refineries, and pipelines (Van Natta 2002). Energy bills embodying the president's plan were again introduced in 2003 and 2004, but once again Congress was unable to craft majorities in support of this legislation. In addition to being preoccupied with waging the Iraq War in 2003, major obstacles to enacting the energy bill were the provisions allowing oil and gas development in the ANWR, and liability protection provided to the manufacturers of methyl tertiary butyl ether (MTBE), a chemical gasoline additive that had leaked from storage facilities and contaminated several drinking-water aquifers around the country (the largest manufacturer of MTBE happened to be located in the district of House majority leader Tom DeLay [R-TX]).

In late 2005, Congress was finally able to agree on comprehensive energy legislation, and the president signed into law the Energy Policy Act of 2005. If one simply counts the recommendations contained in the NEPDG report, one will find that it contains more recommendations for renewable energy, conservation, and efficiency programs (forty-two) than for traditional energy sources (thirty-five). With respect to the substantive effect and cost of the recommendations, however, the priorities of the report clearly lie with increasing supplies of traditional energy sources. For example, as identified by the report, the most important obstacles to increasing energy supplies and improving energy security in the United States all focus on fossil fuels and nuclear power (Kahn 2001). A budgetary analysis by the nonpartisan watchdog group Taxpayers for Common Sense concluded that the 2005 Energy Policy Act would spend $12.7 billion on traditional fossil fuel sources, $12.6 billion on energy efficiency programs and renewable energy sources, $5.8 billion on ethanol production (ethanol is used as a gasoline additive), $5.0 billion on nuclear power, and $4.0 billion on the development of hydrogen as a future energy source (in the bill, the hydrogen is obtained from coal, natural gas, and nuclear power) (Taxpayers for Common Sense 2005). In addition, the act provides more than $8.0 billion in tax incentives, and while the exact distribution of these incentives is difficult to assess, historically more than 90 percent of such tax advantages have gone to traditional sources of energy (Wells, Cooksey, and Crothers 2005).

The Energy Policy Act of 2005 contains literally hundreds of sections and provisions. Here we summarize only a few of the most important provisions relevant to each of the energy sources discussed in the first section of the chapter. With respect to conservation and renewable sources of energy, the act requires a 20 percent increase in the energy efficiency of all federal buildings by 2015, requires the use of energy-efficient technologies, building techniques and materials, and vehicles at all National Park Service and Fish and Wildlife Service units (among others), and proposes to install 20,000 solar photovoltaic arrays on federal buildings by 2015. In the area of fossil fuels, the act requires federal agencies to conduct comprehensive assessments of oil and gas reserves in the United States, identify government policies and regulations that restrict the development of these reserves, and eliminate or modify these regulations to facilitate the domestic production of fossil fuels. In addition, the act provides for the categorical exclusion of certain energy development projects from the environmental review and environmental impact statement requirements of the National Environmental Policy Act (see Chapter 7). Coal is treated especially well in the Energy Policy Act. In addition to providing billions for clean coal technology research, the act specifically emphasizes the need to develop and perfect technologies for creating natural gas and liquid fuels from coal (recall that the Synfuels program of the late 1970s and early 1980s embodied the same goals—a program that cost tens of billions of dollars and produced no appreciable increases in energy supplies). The act also empowers the Department of Interior to increase the number, size, and length of coal leases on federal land. Finally, in a nod toward growing concerns about climate change, the act provides support for research, demonstration projects, and voluntary industry efforts aimed at carbon sequestration (Burns 2005).

Some of the most far-reaching changes embodied in the 2005 Energy Policy Act address nuclear power and the generation and transmission of electricity. With respect to nuclear power, the act extends the protections of the Price-Anderson Act to 2025, and limits the liability of nuclear power plants to $95.8 million dollars for any nuclear accident. The Energy Policy Act also extends the license period for new nuclear power plants to forty years, and provides increased support for research and development into new methods for disposal of high-level radioactive waste. Most important, the act establishes the "Next Generation Nuclear Plant Project," aimed at developing modular nuclear reactors that are able to generate both electricity and hydrogen. In the area of electricity, the act gives FERC the authority to set and enforce reliability standards for state and regional electric power grids (this will facilitate effective competition for electricity), and allows FERC to override the objections of state governments in granting authority to construct new transmission lines within designated "national interest electric corridors." Moreover, the act amends PURPA to require utilities to provide customers with "net metering" (i.e., at a customer's request, utilities must install meters that record both the power consumed by a customer and the power generated by that customer and channeled to the electric grid), and provide time-of-day pricing to customers. The first change will encourage the generation of electricity from small-scale generators, while the second will encourage customers to reduce their demand for electricity during peak consumption periods. Both changes will reduce the need to build large new power plants. On the other hand, and just as important, the act eliminates the PURPA requirement that utilities purchase electricity from small, independent power producers. In effect, in most cases these small producers must find customers for their power on the open market— presumably a difficult proposition for all but the largest of the independent power producers (IPPs) (McGarvey and Murphy 2005).

Finally, one of the most important and least-discussed sections of the 2005 Energy Policy Act actually repeals the 1935 Public Utility Holding Company Act. Recall that this act was put in place to limit the size of public utility holding companies, to prevent these holding companies from engaging in nonutility businesses, and to allow federal regulators to govern the business practices of these firms and state regulators to govern the prices they could charge for electricity. Each of these restrictions in the PUHCA was put in place to protect consumers from the exercise of monopoly power by utility holding companies. Nearly all observers expect that repealing the PUHCA will result in a raft of mergers and a dramatic consolidation among utility companies in the United States. Supporters of such consolidation believe that it will result in lower electricity prices for consumers, as larger holding companies take advantage of economies of scale and are better able to invest in expensive improvements required to upgrade the nation's electricity grid. Opponents of repealing PUHCA point out that it will protect utility holding companies from regulation by state public utility commissions, and fear that the resulting consolidation will substantially increase the abilities of utilities to manipulate electricity prices through the exercise of market power.

Deregulating Electric Utilities

While PURPA required utilities to purchase the electricity generated by small, independent power producers (IPPs), the amount of power generated by these facilities was minimal. In the early 1990s, then, the electric utility industry was still characterized by local, vertically integrated monopolies that generated electricity, transmitted it to population centers, and distributed it to consumers. In return for this government-sanctioned monopoly, utilities accepted prices and terms of service that were set by state and federal regulators. Economic, technical, and political changes were taking place, however, that fundamentally changed this state of affairs, leading to the rapid deregulation (and re-regulation) of the utility industry that continues today.

Economic, Technical, and
Political Changes in the Utility Sector

Electricity generation historically had experienced large economies of scale, particularly with respect to coal-fired power plants. These economies of scale posed a significant barrier to entry for smaller power producers, and contributed greatly to the idea that electricity generation was a natural monopoly. In the 1980s, however, new technologies for generating electricity (for example, combined-cycle natural gas systems) eliminated these economies of scale. Combined with historically low natural gas prices, combined-cycle systems allowed for the production of cheap electricity from small, quickly constructed plants. In fact, IPPs using these new technologies could produce electricity at 2–3 cents per kilowatt hour—on a par with coal-fired power plants, and significantly cheaper than the 6–8 cents per kilowatt hour associated with many nuclear facilities, or the up to 10 cents per kilowatt hour some utilities had to pay for power generated from PURPA facilities (in some states, utilities were forced to purchase power from PURPA facilities at the retail peak price for electricity, which is far above the average generation price). Utilities in many states—saddled with costly power from nuclear and PURPA facilities—found themselves under pressure from potential competitors employing cheaper technologies. If customers could choose to buy power from these IPPs (which they could not, given the vertically integrated monopolies discussed above), presumably their electricity bills would drop dramatically.

Natural gas combined-cycle power generators were not considered "qualifying facilities" under PURPA, and therefore utilities were not obligated to purchase power from them. PURPA could have been amended to cover these IPPs, but given their large size, most utilities opposed this. For their part, the IPPs preferred to enter the electricity market directly, selling their power to wholesale customers and competing with traditional utilities. To make such competition a reality, IPPs needed access to transmission lines, as well as some way to monitor, manage, and balance hundreds of power purchases and sale orders in real time. Tremendous advances in power router technology, computing power, information technology systems, and energy modeling meant that both requirements could be met in the mid-1990s.

The relative success of deregulation in the airline, trucking, and telecommunications industries during the 1970s and 1980s—and the conservative turn in national politics—created powerful political constituencies in favor of deregulation in general. By the mid-1990s, electric utilities were one of the last industries—and definitely the largest industry—still governed by old-style price and entry regulations. Thus the utilities made a tempting target for the proponents of deregulation.

Federal Steps Toward Electric Utility Deregulation
As mentioned above, the federal government took the first steps toward deregulating the electric utility industry with the PURPA requirements that regulated utilities' purchase power produced by qualifying facilities. The first major move toward deregulation at the federal level, however, occurred in 1992 with the Energy Policy Act. This act created a class of exempt wholesale generators (EWGs) that could produce and sell electricity in competition with traditional utilities. EWGs had to apply to FERC to obtain access to interstate transmission lines, and FERC was responsible for making sure that the prices charged by EWGs were "just and reasonable," but in these respects, EWGs were treated no differently than traditional utilities (Timney 2004). The Energy Policy Act introduced an era of wholesale com-

petition into the electricity utility industry, because for the first time large customers could contract for electricity from EWGs instead of being forced to purchase power from regulated utilities at rates set by state public utility commissions.

The 1992 Energy Policy Act was a good first step, but IPPs and EWGs still needed some way to deliver power to end users. While the generation of electricity was no longer a natural monopoly, the transmission of electricity was. Thus, to further the development of competition in electricity, in 1996 FERC issued Order 888, requiring all utilities to provide "open and nondiscriminatory access" to transmission grids to all power generators. Order 888 also recommended that states and utilities band together to create independent system operators (ISOs) to coordinate the supply and demand for electricity across regional power grids (Moot 2004). FERC continued pushing for deregulation in 1999 with the issuance of Order 2000, which strongly encouraged states and utilities to create regional transmission organizations (RTOs) that would coordinate and facilitate the buying and selling of power across wide areas (in effect, RTOs were larger ISOs, managed by ISO-style personnel). Curiously, FERC did not make the adoption of RTOs compulsory, nor did it impose any requirements on their structure. Consequently, few RTOs were adopted, and those that were adopted exhibited oddly shaped service areas (Moot 2004). In 2001, after the election of George W. Bush and the California electricity crisis (see below), FERC abandoned Order 2000 and initiated a rule-making procedure to create uniform, standardized market designs for RTOs (the so-called SMD rule). Thus far, the SMD rule has not been implemented.

State Efforts Toward Utility Deregulation: The Case of California

By 1999, Congress and the FERC had set the stage for significant deregulation of the electric utility industry. However, since most regulations governing price, entry, and conditions of service were issued by state governments, complete deregulation required state action. In 1994, California was the first state to propose deregulation of its market for electricity. The state enacted the necessary legislation in 1996 and implemented its restructuring plan in 1998. Deregulation in California had several important implications. First, it allowed IPPs access to state power grids. Second, it allowed large industrial and wholesale customers and bundled retail customers to choose their electricity provider. Third, it allowed prices for electricity to be set by the market, not by the state public utility commission. By 2001, twenty-two states had followed California's lead and begun to restructure their electricity markets to allow for competition (Timney 2004).

California's restructuring plan was fairly complex, but we can summarize its key elements here. First, in order to enter the competitive market for electricity, all traditional utility monopolies had to divest themselves of generating facilities. The state's largest utilities—Pacific Gas and Electric, Southern California Edison, and San Diego Gas and Electric—did this by selling power plants to large, out-of-state companies (e.g., Duke Power in North Carolina, Cinergy in Texas), and by creating independent holding companies and transferring ownership of power plants to these entities. In essence, the above-mentioned three largest utilities became power transmission and delivery companies that purchased their power from private producers on the open market. A few municipal utilities, however, refused to divest, and thus did not enter the new electricity market. Second, traditional utilities were allowed to recover "stranded costs" (i.e., the money still owed on nuclear and other power plants that produced electricity at a price too high to be competitive in the new marketplace) by imposing a surcharge on electric bills. However, the prices these utilities could charge their customers were capped until the stranded costs were recouped and the surcharge was eliminated. Finally, utilities were prevented from purchasing power through long-term contracts with generators. Instead, they had to contract for power purchases no more than one day ahead of time on the "spot market" managed by the California Power Exchange (Wolak 2005).

This is not the place for a full recounting of the disastrous consequences of electricity deregulation in California. Interested readers can find several excellent discussions of this topic (e.g., Timney 2004; Wolak 2005). We only discuss the broad outline of the catastrophe here. In 2000–2001 the wholesale price of electricity on the California spot market rose from around $25 per megawatt to over $250 per megawatt (some days, the price peaked above $750 per megawatt). Utilities that had entered the electricity market and recouped their stranded costs, San Diego Gas and Electric, responded with a several-fold increase to their electricity rates (Timney 2004). Municipal utilities that had not divested and remained outside the market continued to generate and sell electricity to their customers at regulated rates. The two largest utilities, however— Pacific Gas and Electric, and Southern California Edison (and others)— had divested and entered the market, but had not recouped their stranded costs. Thus they were prohibited from raising their electricity rates to compensate for the dramatic rise in wholesale electricity prices. These utilities began hemorrhaging cash at an alarming rate. Pacific Gas and Electric went bankrupt—the largest utility bankruptcy in US history—and Southern California Edison faced bankruptcy but avoided it. The California ISO ordered rolling blackouts, as utilities could not afford to purchase power to meet system demand.

Responding to the crisis, California governor Gray Davis first asked the federal government for help, requesting that FERC cap the prices being charged by generators on the spot market. FERC refused. California then took a multipronged approach to addressing the problem on its own. First, the state purchased the transmission grid of Southern California Edison for $2.7 billion (this infusion of cash is what allowed the utility to avoid bankruptcy). Second, the state entered into long-term (ten-year) contracts to purchase power from out-of-state generators. Third, the state issued $5 billion in bonds that allowed it to purchase, build, and lease its own generating facilities. Finally, the state suspended customer choice and assigned customers to utilities in order to guarantee that the state and other utilities had enough customers to remain solvent (Timney 2004; Wolak 2005).

In some ways, the California electricity crisis was "the perfect storm," in that several causes coincided to create the catastrophe. For example, 2000 saw a drought and low snowpack in the Pacific Northwest, which reduced the amount of hydroelectric power that California could import from Oregon and Washington. In addition, several companies engaged in illegal market manipulation (e.g., El Paso Natural Gas Company) or outright fraud (e.g., Enron) that drove up the price of electricity in California (Timney 2004). Regulators and policymakers could do little to avoid these problems. On the other hand, the California crisis does provide some excellent lessons for policymakers and regulators in that the actions of both contributed significantly to the depth of the crisis.

The nature of electricity makes electricity markets especially susceptible to manipulation through the exercise of market power. That is, very small changes in the supply of electricity over a short period of time can lead to dramatic increases in price (and profit) (Griffin and Puller 2005; Joskow 2005). Electric utilities therefore face terrific incentives to withhold supply in the hope of obtaining the rents present in imperfect markets. In this way, electric utilities are unlike airlines, telecommunications, or any other industry that has undergone successful deregulation. The actions of state and federal officials exacerbated the already substantial potential for the exercise of market power in the California electricity market, and several experts view these actions as the primary cause of the magnitude of the crisis (Wolak 2005).

For their part, policymakers in California facilitated the exercise of market power by electricity utilities by requiring them to purchase their power on the spot market. This forced the utilities to be price takers in a market dominated by a few providers, or run the risk of crashing the power grid due to an inadequate supply of electricity. In the electricity market, long-term contracts are an effective hedge against this exercise of market power by producers (Wolak 2005).

At the federal level, the regulators at FERC could have prevented the crisis, or at least significantly mitigated it, by capping the spot market price for electricity. Recall that the primary role of FERC is to ensure that prices for the interstate sale of electricity are "just and reasonable" (Kelliher 2005). Historically, FERC had determined rates using a cost-plus formula similar to those used by state public utility commissions. Under deregulation, however, FERC defined "just and reasonable" rates using market prices. The assumption here is that in a perfectly competitive market, prices are set at or just above marginal costs, and are therefore by definition "just and reasonable." The obvious problem with this procedure is that the market for electricity in California was anything but perfectly competitive. Between 1999 and 2001 the California Market Supervisory Committee had sent more than a half dozen reports to FERC illustrating the imperfect nature of the electricity market in the state and pointing out the potential for electricity utilities to exercise large amounts of market power. FERC ignored the recommendations in each of these reports, thereby exacerbating the crisis in California (Wolak 2005).

Now that the dust has settled, we can identify four ironies stemming from California's experiment with electricity deregulation. First, while deregulation was supposed to reduce electricity bills, it actually increased these bills several-fold for almost all consumers. Second, while deregulation was supposed to reduce the role of the state, it actually increased it. The state of California now owns a large electricity transmission grid, owns or is in the process of building several electric generating facilities, is the single largest purchaser of electricity in the state, and allocates customers among utility companies. None of these things were true in the prerestructuring period. Third, rather than serving as a model for other states to follow, California's experience with electricity deregulation has caused all other states to halt electric utility restructuring (Timney 2004). Finally, FERC's desire to facilitate further deregulation through its SMD rule has been halted by opposition from members of Congress and several state governments who fear California-like disasters in other states—a disaster that FERC itself helped create. Indeed, the California experience has led some scholars to draw the lesson that traditional industry deregulation may not be possible with electric utilities. Due to the nature of the product and the industry, some significant government oversight may be inevitable in order to avoid the exercise of market power. At the very least, effective deregulation will require better tools, better policy design, and better regulator choices than were exhibited in California (Bushnell 2005).

Conclusion

Regulating energy policy is an incredibly complex undertaking. This is due, in part, to the fact that energy policy involves a mix of actors, public and private, operating in multiple subsystems. In this regard, energy policy is quite unlike the other policy areas considered in this volume, with perhaps the exception of environmental policy. Different too are the tasks and tools of the various bureaus involved in the energy policy arenas. Some have fairly straightforward regulatory responsibilities—licensing nuclear reactors (the AEC and its successor, the NRC), or regulating electricity rates (the various state public utility commissions and the FERC). Still, much of energy policy involves no real regulation at all—for example, granting mineral leases for oil, gas, or coal production, or developing hydroelectric sites. Rather, energy policy takes on distributive overtones typical of policymaking in producer-dominated subsystems. Because of the mix of policy types, public actors, and private interests, it is hard to speak of energy policy in the same way one refers to consumer protection, financial regulation, or other endeavors. In the end, energy policy is often the sum total of what occurs, or does not occur, in five separate yet interconnected subsystems.

The analysis here suggests that salience can and does change all this. During times of crisis—war, economic downturn, or shortages—various actors think and act in terms of *energy*. Thinking "holistically" about energy is the first step in attempting to assume the mantle of principal agenda setter. Historically, this is a role reserved for the president and one that various presidents have been able to assume because of a larger crisis. World Wars I and II both created the conditions necessary for the chief executive to serve as a principal vis-à-vis the various energy subsystems. They also provided the context necessary for people to speak and think in terms of energy, as opposed to oil, gas, or hydroelectric power. Still, these crises are short-lived, and once they are over, energy policy returns to its multiple-subsystem norm. Witness the inability of the chief executive to maintain the role of agenda setter in lesser crises—the various oil embargoes—despite the willingness of some members of Congress to thrust the role upon him. In this regard, an important finding of our study of energy policy is that whereas crises are a necessary condition to move policymaking from a subsystems to a principal-agent mode, they are not a sufficient condition.

When a crisis pits industry factions against one another, consumers against producers, or conservationists against users, policymaking tends to assume a subsystem format. Congressional committees jealously guard their turf, agencies side with their industry charges, and policy involves dividing distributive goodies. This latter condition seems the norm in energy policy. Occasional crises may punctuate this equilibrium, but over time, politics returns to the multiple-subsystem norm (Baumgartner and Jones 1993). This is not to say that punctuating events do not alter policymaking; the environmental movement's influence on energy policy is the best example of the very real effect of such events. Rather, it is simply recognition that subsystem arrangements, once established, are long-lasting even if they do fluctuate over time.

Note

1. The embargo actually resulted in less than a 5 percent reduction in the world supply of oil. This small marginal change in supply, however, was enough to more than double the spot market price of crude oil.

11

Making Sense of Regulation in a Deregulatory Era

"A SPECTRE IS HAUNTING the United States—the spectre of Regulation."[1] This statement might have been lifted wholesale from the arguments made by deregulatory and antiregulatory zealots in the 1970s and 1980s, who attributed all stripes of political, economic, and moral carnage to the excesses of regulation. The solution, it was asserted, was to be found in the market. The chapters in this volume have told a somewhat different story. Regulations may serve purposes that are both laudable and, in our judgment, essential in a capitalist market system, even if performance is not always what one might hope. Moreover, if we replace the abstraction of regulation with the actual patterns of action that constitute regulatory policies, there is some reason for cheer. To be certain, excesses in both directions and periods of lethargy mark the records of the agencies surveyed here. But it is unsound—even if convenient—to generalize from the extremes to arrive at a universal judgment about regulation, and our goal in this book has not been to arrive at such conclusions. We will leave that task to others who are so inclined. Instead, we are concerned with a more direct question: How can we understand the patterns of action that constitute regulation?

Why Regulate?

Why do we regulate? Some argue that governments regulate to further "the public interest," preventing or compensating for various forms of market failure. Others suggest that regulations reflect, instead, industry demands for wealth transfers. Vote-maximizing politicians and budget-maximizing bureaucrats continue to produce regulations as a means of pursuing their self-interest. Finally, one might observe that regulations are a product of the competition among regional political economies. As Chapter 1 suggested, each of these responses, while incomplete, provides insights into the history of regulation and can be quite useful when seeking to understand the multiple facets of policy and administration.

In Chapter 2 we turned to another question: How do we explain regulatory change? Recent scholarly debates over regulation have been cast, typically, in the conceptual frameworks introduced by three competing perspectives on regulation and, more generally, on politics. The bureaucratic politics perspective attributes policy change to forces that are internal to the bureaucracy (e.g., organization, budgets, expertise, staffing patterns) or factors that affect an agency's relationships with key external constituencies and other political actors. The principal-agent perspective, in contrast, is concerned with political-bureaucratic relations, albeit in a somewhat more restricted sense. Elected officials seek to direct bureaucratic actions in the hope of bringing them into alignment with their own ideological proclivities or of maximizing votes. The subsystems perspective views bureaucratic organizations as part of a dense network of organizations exercising common policy prerogatives, congressional subcommittees, and interested constituencies. These subsystems or policy communities play an important role in shaping the parameters of policy change over time. As we confessed in Chapter 2, we share a mild bias in support of the subsystems explanation, in large part because it avoids the narrower focus of the alternative perspectives. At the same time, we believe that the subsystems perspective can benefit from greater attention to the variables identified by these competing perspectives. As a result, it makes sense to consider the three perspectives simultaneously, understanding that their explanatory value may vary from case to case.

We also argued that it is essential to contextualize regulatory politics by considering complexity and salience. We predicted that the principal-agent perspective would be most useful for policies of high salience and low complexity. Salience should attract elected officials, while low levels of complexity will not repel them. As the level of complexity increases, the propensity to exert principal-agent-like controls will diminish. At high levels of complexity, there will be high (and potentially prohibitively high) barriers to entry. Moreover, serious problems of information asymmetry would lead elected officials to place a greater emphasis on the expertise of bureaucrats and other subsystem actors. We expect to see far fewer attempts at principal-agent direction in low-salience policies, reflecting the lack of electoral incentives. Where low salience is combined with low complexity, regulatory politics will be dominated by street-level bureaucrats and regulated parties, creating a situation ripe for regulatory capture. We would also expect to see, at best, a modest role for subsystems. Under conditions of low public salience and high technical complexity, we expect to see little evidence of principal-agent controls. Not only is the lack of salience important in reducing the electoral gains from intervention, but the technical barriers to entry are high as well. We would expect upper-level bureaucrats with a high degree of technical expertise to exercise control, supported by interest groups and a few members of Congress with similar expertise.

The case studies in this book have offered a useful context for considering the relative merits of the three perspectives and the role of salience and complexity in shaping regulatory politics. Given that we have adopted qualitative case studies, the extent to which any of the perspectives suffices is a product of interpretation. Moreover, given that we are primarily concerned with contemporary regulation, we are somewhat limited in our ability to draw on the longer historical record. Certainly, the rich history of an agency like the Federal Trade Commission, spanning some ninety years, would offer lessons that are unavailable when one adopts a shorter horizon. Yet as Chapter 3 suggested, the contemporary history of regulation is both intrinsically interesting and important. Government agencies have been called on to regulate ever more complicated problems requiring the synthesis of policy with scientific and social scientific analysis. Regulatory advocates and opponents have become ever more adept at shaping agency performance through institutional design. Moreover, despite the cries of excessive regulatory spending, there has been a significant reduction in the budgetary support for regulation. As Figure 11.1 reveals, inflation-adjusted dollars spent on the activities of the agencies surveyed in this volume peaked in 1978 and have remained relatively stable since the end of Reagan's first term in office. The lack of budgetary growth is dramatic, given that today's economy is some two and a half times the size of that which existed in 1970 as measured by inflation-adjusted gross domestic product.

Before discussing the individual case studies, it is useful to consider the characterization of the policies along dimensions of salience and complexity (see Figure 11.2). Given that policies may shift in complexity and salience over time, the placement of these policies is largely a product of interpretation, albeit one that is supported by salience data and our substantive understanding of the technical dimensions of the policies under consideration. When the salience data from each of our case studies are compared, it becomes clear that the only policies that one might view as being highly salient throughout the period are occupational safety and health and environmental protection. One should not be surprised by the high levels of salience attached to these policies, considering the high regulatory compliance costs, the sharp partisan battles, and the large number of issues that have environmental implications. Other policies, however, have been of variable salience.

As Figure 11.2 suggests, most of the issue areas can be characterized as

Figure 11.1 Regulatory Spending

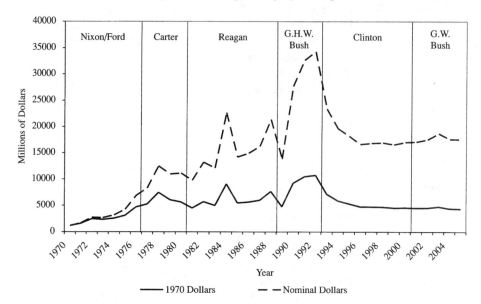

complex. There is a distinct "northern drift" in the placement of regulatory policy areas. The lack of policy areas in the low-complexity cells reflects two factors. First, many of the low-complexity policies became the targets of deregulation. For example, the Interstate Commerce Commission's regulation of railroads and trucking and the Civil Aeronautics Board's regulation of air transportation were both characterized by low levels of complexity. In each case, regulators functioned much as George Stigler (1971) suggested. Given the low complexity and the salient claims that regulations contributed to economic stagflation, both were ripe for deregulation. Both have been eliminated, their functions either privatized or assigned elsewhere in the regulatory bureaucracy.

There is a second factor, however, that helps explain this clustering of regulations at the high end of the complexity continuum. Contemporary regulatory policies rely heavily on scientific and social scientific expertise. The regulation of various chemical agents by the Environmental Protection Agency and Occupational Safety and Health Administration requires policymakers to have some understanding of the underlying science. Understanding the impact of new regulations on businesses requires some understanding of economic analysis and some expertise in cost-benefit analysis. Similarly, antitrust, communications, and banking regulation demand careful economic analysis. Even if legislation does not explicitly impose high analytical thresholds, the demands of regulatory oversight and

Figure 11.2 Regulatory Complexity and Salience

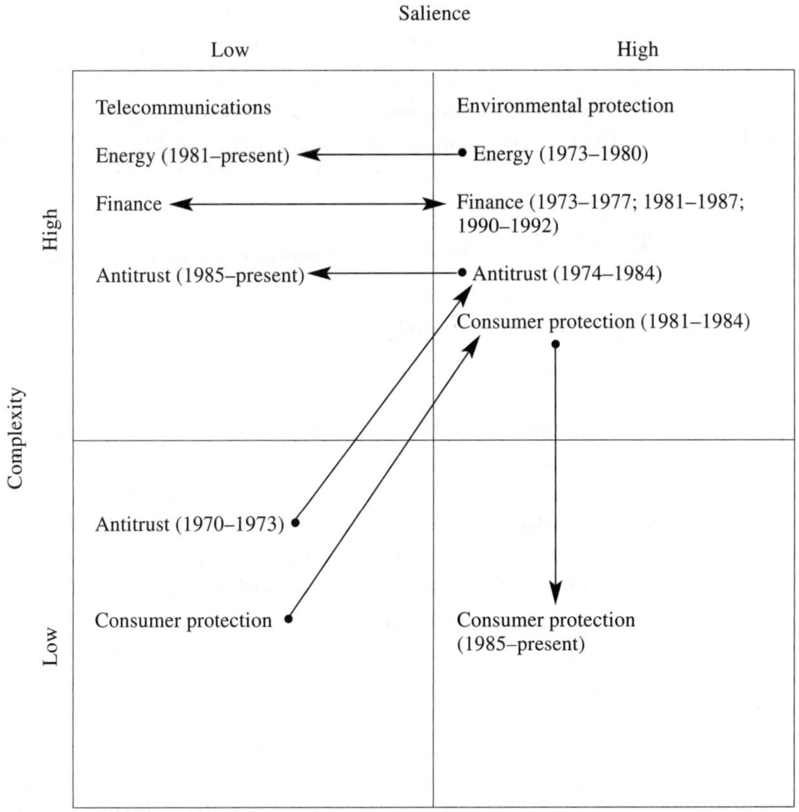

Salience

Low	High

High

Telecommunications

Energy (1981–present) ◄————————• Energy (1973–1980)

Finance ◄————————► Finance (1973–1977; 1981–1987; 1990–1992)

Antitrust (1985–present) ◄————• Antitrust (1974–1984)

Environmental protection

Consumer protection (1981–1984)

Antitrust (1970–1973) •

Consumer protection •

Consumer protection (1985–present)

Complexity

Low

potential litigation have had this effect. One result of this growing complexity is that the agencies have been forced to develop greater levels of bureaucratic expertise. The old vision of regulatory agencies as the repositories of incompetence has been replaced by a new reality of highly professionalized agencies drawing on the nation's best law schools and doctoral programs. A second result is equally clear: bureaucracies and policy subsystems have come to play a far greater role than in the past, limiting the efficacy of principal-agent controls.

This raises an interesting question regarding the whole issue of policy complexity. Complexity is, in many ways, a product of perception. What some might understand as a simple illness may appear to specialists to be the complex interaction of biological systems and pathogens that can be fully appreciated only through a detailed knowledge of microbiology. Many can identify an illness, but diagnosis and treatment may require expertise.

Expertise is an important bureaucratic resource, and bureaucrats clearly understand that the more complicated an issue, the greater the likelihood that elected officials will defer judgment to specialists. Much of the complexity surrounding regulatory policies has been generated by subsystem actors and regulators themselves, one suspects, the former seeking to insulate the debates from political outsiders, the latter seeking both to maximize insulation and to legitimize their actions before attentive audiences. To the extent that complexity reduces the impact of salience and allows subsystem actors to minimize exogenous shocks, one should expect to see greater policy complexity over time.

Contemporary Regulatory Politics

Before drawing broad conclusions from the agencies examined in this volume, it is useful to summarize briefly the case studies. We began with the case of antitrust, in Chapter 4. Antitrust has undergone some major transformations since the passage of the Sherman Act. In the contemporary period, a policy, previously defined through a confusing series of court decisions, has been given greater coherence through a growing reliance on economic expertise. The agencies have undergone a process of economic professionalization. Economic analysis has been integrated into every stage of the regulatory process, reflecting the evolution of subsystem debates and the growing role of economics in judicial decisionmaking. Increasingly, the agencies became hesitant to enforce provisions of the antitrust laws for which an economic justification could not be found, thus leaving much of antitrust unenforced. During the 1990s the agencies discovered a new mission, attacking trade barriers that might negatively impact on US firms in international markets or domestic consumers victimized by foreign corporations. The continuity of enforcement priorities across the Clinton and George W. Bush presidencies suggests that a firm consensus regarding policy has replaced the rather harsh battles of the Reagan presidency.

In Chapter 5 we turned to the regulation of financial intermediaries. Financial regulation is deeply embedded in a set of beliefs concerning the sanctity of "other people's money" (Worsham 1997). Historically, these beliefs took their programmatic incarnation as the series of regulatory mandates contained in New Deal (Glass-Steagall) regulation. A coalition consisting principally of large financial intermediaries, and led by the Office of the Comptroller of the Currency, began tinkering with these mandates in the 1980s. By 2000 they were joined by midsized financial institutions, most members of the banking committees, large securities firms, and the Securities and Exchange Commission in modifying the understanding of banking as different from other forms of economic enterprise. That said, the transformation has not been complete. Conflicting coalitions have stymied complete abandonment of Glass-Steagall, although some of the major provisions dividing banking from securities and insurance underwriting have been relaxed. Regulators have led these changes, deregulating the financial services industry in a disjointed administrative manner. Currently, any further talk of deregulation is enough to raise the hackles of either the Financial Services Committee (Banking in the Senate) or Energy and Commerce (Commerce in the Senate), and often both, as they compete to maintain their turf. Still, regulators continue to test the deregulatory waters, while opponents caution against moving too fast or too slow, and the subsystem sits mired in a stalemate produced by competing coalitions.

Chapter 6 examined the evolution of telecommunications regulation. Universal service, the central goal of telephone regulation, has had its meaning altered over time. The Telecommunications Act of 1996 was another instance of redefining this central goal. In this case, universal service now means more than efficacy of phone service. It currently involves a variety of operations, from standard phone service to lines for computers and video equipment. Much of the dynamic of phone regulation concerns different interpretations of universal service and the regulation necessary to achieve this ideal. In this respect, the Federal Communications Commission has always been torn between multiple congressional and executive overseers claiming the role of principal and insisting on their interpretation of this central tenet of phone regulation as the correct reading. The problem from the FCC vantage is clear: rarely do the three—the president, the House, and the Senate—speak with the same voice. The 1996 act appeared to settle some of the cacophony produced by multiple principals, in that it brokered a deal among the Clinton administration, the House, and the Senate. More important, it removed the federal district court from its longtime oversight role. That said, the act did not anticipate the pace of technological changes effecting data transmission, as well as voice transmission, nor were its predictions of competition in local service realized. As a result, telecommunications policy is increasingly characterized by regulator-led deregulation, or at least adaptation, to the changing technological context. The result of this is a subsystem that has managed to eliminate, at least for the near future, the transitory phenomenon of presidential and court involvement. That said, interchamber competition involving the House and Senate commerce committees appears to be the norm for the foreseeable future.

The flagship social regulatory agency, the Environmental Protection Agency, was the subject of Chapter 7. Since 1970, environmental protection has been at the forefront of the regulatory policy agenda, and the EPA has grown to become the largest single regulatory bureaucracy within the federal government. As such, broader trends with respect to regulation in general, such as the push for deregulation and regulatory reinvention, are amplified with respect to the EPA. The policy subsystem is characterized by two powerful competing advocacy coalitions. The relative balance between these coalitions, coupled with strong public support for environmental protection, has frustrated efforts of external principals to weaken or redirect environmental regulation. This is not to say that environmental regulation has not changed in the face of external pressures. The past two decades have brought changes in regulatory tools, agency enforcement styles, and relationships with stakeholders. However, historically the agency has been able to draw on public support, technical expertise, and unified and committed personnel to address these changes on its own terms. This characterization of regulatory politics at the EPA may be outdated. Solid Republican majorities in both chambers of Congress, a president and vice president committed to significant changes in environmental regulation, and a public with greater policy priorities than environmental protection have set the stage for what is potentially the most effective exercise of principal-agent-style discipline in the history of the EPA. How the agency responds to these efforts over the next few years will hold great interest for students of regulatory policy and public administration.

In Chapter 8 we considered another important legacy of the 1970s, the Occupational Safety and Health Administration. As with the EPA, OSHA is regulating at the intersection of science, economics, and the law. The breadth of its regulatory mandate combined with the complexity of the scientific and social scientific expertise required to develop health standards had some important implications for OSHA. First, OSHA regulations were continually embroiled in controversy. Businesses claimed that the high costs of regulation were unjustified by the potential health gains, which, due to the complexities of the underlying scientific research, were at all times probabilistic. Moreover, given that the Occupational Safety and Health Act did not require the agency to weigh the costs and benefits of its regulations, opponents claimed that the agency often overregulated, imposing marginal costs that greatly exceeded marginal benefits. Second, OSHA's regulatory mandate placed a premium on bureaucratic resources. Without a sufficiently large professional staff, the agency would be unable to develop new standards. Advances during the Ford and Carter administrations were largely vitiated during the Reagan presidency, as efforts were made to transform OSHA into a cooperative regulator and reduce its funding. Although the agency received a new influx of resources in the George H. W. Bush and Clinton presidencies, ongoing congressional intervention took an increasing toll. Most recently, the George W. Bush administration's reliance on partnerships and voluntarism—pursued, often, in lieu of vigorous enforcement of mandatory rules—suggests that OSHA may be evolving into the cooperative regulator first envisioned by the Reagan administration.

Chapter 9 turned to the consumer protection policies administered by the Consumer Product Safety Commission and the Federal Trade Commission. The past several decades have revealed the extent to which Congress and the president can influence independent regulatory commissions. In the case of the FTC, a revitalization of the agency in the 1970s increased its level of regulatory activism, thereby stimulating high levels of business mobilization and new legislation to strip the agency of many of its hard-earned powers. When combined with the antiregulatory posture of the Reagan appointees, it appeared all but certain that the FTC would no longer be in the business of consumer protection. The CPSC faced a similar fate, albeit without the financial, professional, and legal resources of its counterpart. Forced from the beginning to place a premium on business voluntarism, it appeared to be an agency designed for failure. To be certain, the FTC underwent a second revitalization in the 1990s, redefining its mission to emphasize the international dimensions of consumer protection and the impact of electronic commerce. Its regulatory mandate and enforcement efforts continued to expand during the presidency of George W. Bush. The CPSC has been far less successful in this regard, and remains an understaffed and underfunded shadow of the FTC.

Chapter 10 considered the morass that constitutes energy policy. Energy policy is rivaled only by environmental regulation in its breadth. We suggested that Frank Baumgartner and Bryan Jones's notion of punctuated equilibrium (1993) describes the course of energy policy quite well. First, energy policy is conducted in a subsystems setting. Indeed, there are many energy policies, each formulated in a fuel-based subsystem. The subsystems bring a certain stability to the process, the identity of actors, the nature of policy produced, and the like. This feature of energy policy accounts for the equilibrium part of the model. To say energy policy is the sum total of what occurs in fairly stable and autonomous subsystems is not to claim it is static. Events in the larger environment have punctuated otherwise stable subsystem-induced equilibria. Most notably in the aftermath of crises (e.g., the 1973 and 1979 oil embargoes, the 2001 California electricity crisis, and the spike in oil prices in 2005), presidents have tried to coordinate and integrate policymaking across these disparate subsystems. During the first two crises excluded stakeholders (e.g., environmental groups and renewable energy producers), in a traditional move, attempted to gain entry into these subsystems. By contrast, the latter two crises were notable for the extent to which actors in control of the energy policy agenda sought to exclude these stakeholders from decisionmaking. These crises have produced important and relatively enduring changes in the process of policymaking and the substantive aspects of energy policy. With the exception of the nuclear power and electricity subsystems, however, these efforts have had only minimal effect; and in the case of electricity, most of the major policy changes have been producer-driven. Of all the regulatory arenas examined in this book, energy may provide the clearest remaining example of producer-dominated subsystem politics.

The Lessons

What do these case studies tell us about regulation? First and foremost, they reveal the impact of complexity and salience. The importance of salience is no surprise. Politicians are attracted to salient issues for the same reason the notorious bank robber Willie Sutton was attracted to banks: that's where the money is. What is particularly interesting is the impact of complexity. High levels of complexity create barriers to effective mobilization and control, place a premium on bureaucratic resources, render agencies more dependent on funding, and increase the importance of the subsystems. We present here twelve key lessons that can be drawn from the case studies.

1. *Low levels of complexity accentuate the impact of salience.* Where there were high levels of salience but lower levels of complexity, agencies were subject to ongoing efforts at political control. In the case of consumer protection, the agencies were subjected to the kinds of pressures that principal-agent theories of regulation might predict (e.g., budget cuts, legislative riders limiting agency discretion, and political appointees working to prevent new rules and enforcement actions). These pressures prevented the CPSC from becoming an effective regulator. The FTC's survival may be a function of its antitrust responsibilities and the higher levels of professionalization that occurred in this connection.

2. *Salience is variable over time and often reflects the impact of exogenous forces.* Consider the case of energy. During times of crisis, traditionally quiescent stakeholders take an interest in the politics of energy, thereby increasing the variety of actors involved in regulatory politics and creating an opportunity for experiments in regulatory design. The deregulatory and reform efforts of the 1970s and 1980s were possible, in part, because stagflation and OPEC embargoes had increased the salience of regulation. Because regulators or members of the policy subsystem cannot control exogenous forces such as war and recession, they are at all times vulnerable. Exogenous shocks can create new opportunities for political control.

3. *Regulators and subsystem actors may exploit exogenous forces to their advantage.* In Chapter 2 we noted the importance of agency leadership. In several of the case studies, regulatory executives effectively exploited forces in the larger environment to enhance the power or prestige of their agencies. This occurred in the 1970s, when the EPA recast itself as a

public health agency and thereby tapped into growing concerns over cancer. It occurred in the 1990s, when OSHA turned its attention to HIV and when the antitrust agencies expanded their international activities. In each case, new missions justified greater financial and bureaucratic resources. Agencies that failed to redefine their missions over time often became lethargic and moribund—a state that made them ripe for deregulation or outright elimination.

4. *High levels of salience may create incentives for nonsubsystem actors to promote policy change.* Crises may create the opportunity for recasting policies in ways that cut across existing subsystems and create space for elected officials to play a far greater role and potentially exert political control over regulatory bureaucracies. Consider, once again, the case of energy. The OPEC embargoes created opportunities for presidents to speak "holistically" about energy rather than focusing on oil, gas, or hydroelectric power—conceptualizations that would reinforce existing subsystems. The insulation afforded by subsystems disappeared, albeit temporarily. Leadership—within traditional subsystem agencies and agencies seeking entry—often makes the difference between temporary subsystem turbulence and enduring policy change.

5. *Crises may be short-lived and may not be of sufficient duration to alter permanently the configuration of forces within policy subsystems.* When a crisis pits factions against one another (e.g., consumers versus producers versus conservationists), dominant coalitions weaken. Traditional subsystem participants jealously guard their turf and protect their interests, making policymaking much more contentious. If the crises are relatively short-lived, or if policy entrepreneurs are unable to translate increased public salience into significant policy change, the dominant coalition may reassert itself. As several of the case studies suggest, while crises are a necessary condition to move policymaking from a subsystems to a principal-agent mode, they are not sufficient. In short, not all crises are crises. This is not to say that punctuating events do not alter policymaking—as exhibited by environmental policy, energy policy, finance, consumer protection, and occupational safety and health. Rather, it is simply recognition that subsystem arrangements, once established, are long-lasting.

6. *High levels of complexity promote the development of bureaucratic resources.* In many agencies addressed in this book, high levels of complexity required the development of internal bureaucratic resources. One cannot regulate corporate organization and conduct, finance, and telecommunications without economists; one cannot regulate pollution and workplace health hazards without access to a broad panoply of professionals.

7. *Bureaucratic professionalization promotes policy complexity.* As professional bureaucrats play a more central role, they recast the regulatory debates in their own specialized idioms, thereby further insulating their

debates from external actors. This allows them to control the direction and rapidity of policy change.

8. *Agencies regulating complex problems or sectors have not been free from efforts at political control.* The high levels of salience associated with their policies have affected OSHA and the EPA in particular. They have been ongoing targets of partisan attacks. However, lacking a sufficient understanding of the underlying expertise, elected officials are often limited in the kinds of changes they can advocate. Regulatory horror stories may attract political attention, but they do not provide a basis for much more than obstructionism. Of course, for many opponents of regulation, stopping further regulatory actions may be sufficient.

9. *Professionalized bureaucracies have a greater capacity to resist efforts at political control.* Even during periods of retrenchment, we witnessed several instances of bureaucrats retaining a commitment to their policy mandates and a regulatory presence. Agencies are often staffed with specific kinds of professional bureaucrats for strategic reasons. The professional values of environmental scientists and industrial hygienists, to take two examples, reinforce the missions of the agencies that employ them. To the extent that agencies are professionalized with groups that share a commitment to the broader mission, they can be programmed to act in specific ways. This would seem to reinforce a bureaucratic politics explanation of regulation, albeit one that recognizes that bureaucratic design is often a tool of political control.

10. *Professionalized bureaucracies may prove highly vulnerable to resource constraints.* To be certain, the strategy of regulatory changes adopted in the 1980s suggests that opponents of the EPA and OSHA in the Reagan administration and Congress clearly understood the importance of bureaucratic resources in preserving agency mandates. This should be no surprise: complexity creates some insulation from political control efforts, while the premium it places on professionalization enhances the vulnerability to budgetary control. But as with our previous point, this is a tool of limited utility: one may be able to restrain an overzealous bureaucracy with budget cuts, but one cannot use them to chart a positive course of policy change.

11. *Subsystem resources may support agency efforts to resist political control.* Why did OSHA and the EPA survive the 1980s and 1990s with their missions and regulatory capacity largely intact, whereas other agencies did not? Perhaps it was because the efforts were not pursued in earnest. Most of the budget cuts came early in Reagan's first term in office. Thereafter, budgets either grew slowly or remained more or less stable. Indeed, George H. W. Bush's label as the "regulatory president" was earned largely because of the resurgence of budgetary growth and regulatory output during his term in office (Rauch 1991). But that raises a more provoca-

tive question: Why were these efforts at political control so short-lived? It is here that we return to subsystem explanations. The regulators examined in this book are situated in dense networks linking actors from agencies, congressional committees, interest groups, and the larger policy communities. These subsystems affect the pace and direction of regulatory change. Moreover, as policy complexity has increased, debates within the subsystems have become far more grounded in relevant bodies of expertise, such that questions of regulatory design may turn as much on scientific and social scientific research as on calculations of naked self-interest. To the extent that subsystem actors adopt a long-term perspective and seek to preserve their control over key policies, they will limit the efforts to bring changes that are both rapid and politically motivated.

12. *The combination of bureaucratic and subsystem politics explains the overwhelming continuity in regulatory policy.* The period examined in this volume witnessed the most concerted political efforts to eliminate regulations in the nation's history. Yet the antiregulatory zeal of the 1980s and the "Contract with America" in the 1990s failed to tear the regulatory system out by its roots—despite the proclamations and promises of so many powerful political actors. The history of regulation in the contemporary period is more a story of continuity than a story of change. After all the hyperbolic claims, regulatory horror stories, and appeals to the marvels of the market have been aired, there remain actors, institutions, and interests, all linked together in the patterns of action that constitute regulatory policy.

*   *   *

These lessons are by no means exhaustive. Yet they provide us with insights into regulatory politics that are simply unavailable to those who espouse a single theoretical perspective or, worse yet, adopt assumptions that simplify out of existence bureaucratic organizations and the complicated subsystems within which they are enmeshed. If public policy is, as we argued in Chapter 1, best understood as consisting of patterns of governmental action and inaction, we cannot dispense with the complex organizations and interagency relationships that shape these patterns. This, in the end, may be the greatest lesson one can learn from contemporary regulatory policies.

Note

1. Of course, the opening line of the *Communist Manifesto* reads: "A spectre is haunting Europe—the spectre of Communism" (Marx and Engels 1962: 32). We reprint it here only because we have looked long and hard and cannot find one of our students who had actually read what we once thought was an indispensable political treatise.

Acronyms

AAG	assistant attorney general
ABA	American Bar Association
AEC	Atomic Energy Commission
AFL-CIO	American Federation of Labor–Congress of Industrial Organizations
ANWR	Arctic National Wildlife Refuge
API	American Petroleum Institute (formerly the NPWSC)
AT&T	American Telephone and Telegraph
ATM	automated teller machine
BAT	best available pollution control technology
BCOA	Bituminous Coal Operators Association
BCP	Bureau of Consumer Protection (FTC)
BPT	best practicable pollution control technology
CAA	Clean Air Act
CAB	Civil Aeronautics Board
CAFE	corporate average fuel economy
CAIR	Clean Air Interstate Rule
CAMR	Clean Air Mercury Rule
CBO	Congressional Budget Office
CEA	Council of Economic Advisers
CEQ	Council on Environmental Quality
CERCLA	Comprehensive Environmental Response, Compensation, and Liability Act
COWPS	Council on Wage and Price Stability
CPSA	Consumer Product Safety Act
CPSC	Consumer Product Safety Commission

CQWR	*Congressional Quarterly Weekly Report*
CWA	Clean Water Act
DBCP	dibromchlorpropane
DIDMCA	Depository Institutions Deregulation and Monetary Control Act
DOE	Department of Energy
DOJ	Department of Justice
DOL	Department of Labor
DSL	digital subscriber line
EIA	Energy Information Administration
EIS	environmental impact statement
EO	executive order
EPA	Environmental Protection Agency
EPCA	Energy Policy and Conservation Act
EPCRTKA	Emergency Planning and Community Right-to-Know Act
EPO	Economic Policy Office (Justice Department, Antitrust Division)
ERDA	Energy Research and Development Administration
EWG	exempt wholesale generator
FACA	Federal Advisory Committee Act
FCC	Federal Communications Commission
FDA	Food and Drug Administration
FDIC	Federal Deposit Insurance Corporation
FERC	Federal Energy Regulatory Commission
FFIEC	Federal Financial Institutions Examination Council
FHLBB	Federal Home Loan Bank Board
FIFRA	Federal Insecticide, Fungicide, and Rodenticide Act
FINE	*Financial Institutions and the Nation's Economy* (government study)
FPC	Federal Power Commission
FQPA	Food Quality Protection Act
FRC	Federal Radio Commission
FSLIC	Federal Savings and Loan Insurance Corporation
FTC	Federal Trade Commission
FTCA	Federal Trade Commission Act
GAO	General Accounting Office
GAO	Government Accountability Office
HIV	human immunodeficiency virus
HSWA	Hazardous and Solid Waste Amendments
IBAA	Independent Bankers Association of America
ICC	Interstate Commerce Commission
IIAA	Independent Insurance Agents of America
IPP	independent power producer

IRC	independent regulatory commission
IRS	Internal Revenue Service
ISO	independent system operator
JCAE	Joint Committee on Atomic Energy
LATA	local access and transport area
LCV	League of Conservation Voters
MMF	money market fund
MTBE	methyl tertiary butyl ether
MWTGP	Municipal Wastewater Treatment Grant Program
NAAQS	national ambient air quality standards
NAB	National Association of Broadcasters
NAFTA	North American Free Trade Agreement
NAPA	National Academy of Public Administration
NCUA	National Credit Union Association
NEP	National Energy Plan
NEPA	National Environmental Policy Act
NEPDG	National Energy Policy Development Group
NEPPS	National Environmental Performance Partnership System
NIMBY	"not in my backyard"
NIOSH	National Institute for Occupational Safety and Health
NOW	negotiated order of withdrawal
NPDES	National Pollutant Discharge Elimination System
NPL	National Priorities List
NPWSC	National Petroleum War Service Committee
NRA	National Recovery Administration
NRC	National Research Council
NRC	Nuclear Regulatory Commission
NSR	New Source Review
OCC	Office of the Comptroller of the Currency
OEM	original equipment manufacturer
OIRA	Office of Information and Regulatory Affairs
OMB	Office of Management and Budget
OPEC	Organization of Petroleum-Exporting Countries
OSH Act	Occupational Safety and Health Act
OSHA	Occupational Safety and Health Administration
OSHRC	Occupational Safety and Health Review Commission
OSM	Office of Surface Mining
OSPP	OSHA Strategic Partnership Program
OTS	Office of Thrift Supervision
PCB	polychlorinated biphenyl
PL	Public Law
PSD	prevention of significant deterioration
PUHCA	Public Utilities Holding Company Act

PURPA	Public Utility Regulatory Policy Act
RARG	Regulatory Analysis and Review Group
RCRA	Resource Conservation and Recovery Act
REA	Rural Electrification Administration
REGO	reinventing government
RIA	regulatory impact analysis
RTO	regional transmission organization
S&L	savings and loan
SARA	Superfund Amendments and Reauthorization Act
SCP	structure-conduct-performance
SEC	Securities and Exchange Commission
SMD	standardized market design
TAC	Technological Advisory Council
TRI	Toxics Release Inventory
TVA	Tennessee Valley Authority
UMW	United Mine Workers
USDA	US Department of Agriculture
USLSI	US League of Savings Institutions
USPS	US Postal Service
VoIP	Voice-over-Internet Protocol
WQA	Water Quality Act
WRC	World Radiocommunication Conference

Bibliography

Court Cases

American Bankers Association v. Connell, 194 U.S. App. D.C. 80 (1980).
American Textile Manufacturers Institute v. Donovan, 452 U.S. 490 (1981).
Aqua Slide "N" Dive Corp. v. CPSC, 569 F.2d 831 (5th Cir. 1978).
Barnett Bank of Marion County, N.A. v. Nelson, 517 U.S. 25 (1996).
Continental T.V., Inc., et al. v. GTE Sylvania, Inc., 433 U.S. 36 (1977).
Environmental Integrity Project, et al. v. EPA, No. 04-1083 (D.C. Cir. 2005).
FPC v. Hope Natural Gas Company, 320 U.S. 591 (1944).
Hartford Fire Insurance Co. v. California, 113 U.S. 2891 (1993).
Humphrey's Executor v. United States, 295 U.S. 602 (1935).
Industrial Union Department v. American Petroleum Institute, 448 U.S. 607 (1979).
Industrial Union Department v. Hodgson, 499 F.2d 467 (1974).
Legal Environmental Assistance Foundation, Inc. v. Hodel, 586 F.Supp. 1163 (US Dist. 1984).
Montsanto Co. v. Spray-Rite Service Corp., 465 U.S. 752 (1984).
Munn v. Illinois, 94 U.S. 278 (1877).
Natural Resources Defense Council v. Environmental Protection Agency, 478 F.2d 875 (1st Cir. 1973).
Natural Resources Defense Council v. Environmental Protection Agency, 489 F.2d 390 (5th Cir. 1974a).
Natural Resources Defense Council v. Environmental Protection Agency, 494 F.2d 519 (2nd Cir. 1974b).
Natural Resources Defense Council v. Environmental Protection Agency, 507 F.2d 905 (9th Cir. 1974c).
Sierra Club v. Ruckelshaus, 344 F.Supp. 253 (D.D.C. 1972).
State of New York v. Microsoft Corp., No. 98-1233 (D.D.C. 1998).
Train v. Natural Resources Defense Council, 421 U.S. 60 (1975).
United States v. American Telephone and Telegraph, 552 F.Supp. 131 (1982).
United States v. Microsoft, 87 F. 2d 30, No. 98-1232 (D.D.C. 2000).
United States v. Western Electric Company, Civil Action No. 17-49 (US Dist. for

N.J. 1956; US Dist. 4076; 1956 Trade Cas. [CCH] P68, 246 [January 24, 1956]).

Government Documents

Beth, Richard S. 2001. "Disapproval of Regulations by Congress: Procedure Under the Congressional Review Act." *CRS Report for Congress* (RL31160), October 10 (Washington, D.C.: Library of Congress, Congressional Research Service).

Bush, George. 1981. "Remarks of the Vice President at the Annual Republican Senate-House Dinner." April 7. *Weekly Compilation of Presidential Documents* 17, no. 5: 407–412.

CBO (Congressional Budget Office). 1985. *Environmental Regulation and Economic Efficiency.* Washington, D.C.

———. 1988. "Environmental Federalism: Allocating Responsibilities for Environmental Protection." Staff working paper. September.

CEQ (Council on Environmental Quality). 1989. *Environmental Trends.* Washington, D.C.

Clinton, William Jefferson. 1996. "Remarks by the President at 25th Anniversary of Earth Day." Address delivered at the Park at Concord Lighthouse, Havre de Grace, Md., April 21, 1995. *Weekly Compilation of Presidential Documents,* vol. 32. Washington, D.C.: Office of the Federal Register.

CPSC (Consumer Product Safety Commission). 1994. *Annual Report to Congress.* Document no. 114. Washington, D.C.

———. 1997. *CPSC Strategic Plan: Saving Lives and Keeping Families Safe.* Washington, D.C.

———. 2004. *Performance and Accountability Report, Fiscal Year 2004.* Washington, D.C.

———. 2005. *2006 Performance Budget Request.* Washington, D.C.

———. Various years. *Annual Report.* Washington, D.C.

DOJ (Department of Justice). 1978. *Annual Report of the Attorney General of the United States.* Washington, D.C.

———. 1979. *Antitrust Division Manual.* Washington, D.C.

———. 1982. *Annual Report of the Attorney General of the United States.* Washington, D.C.

———. 1994. *Antitrust Division Annual Report for Fiscal Year 1994.* Washington, D.C.

———. 1996. *Opening Markets and Protecting Competition for America's Businesses and Consumers: Goals and Achievements of the Antitrust Division, U.S. Department of Justice.* Washington, D.C.

———. 1997. "Revision to the Horizontal Merger Guidelines Issued by the U.S. Department of Justice and the Federal Trade Commission." April 8. Unpublished.

———. 2001. "Department of Justice and Microsoft Corporation Reach Effective Settlement on Antitrust Lawsuit." Press release.

———. 2005a. *Antitrust Division Workload Statistics, FY 1995–2004.* Washington, D.C.

———. 2005b. *Appropriations Figures for the Antitrust Division, Fiscal Years 1903–2005.* Washington, D.C.

DOJ and FTC (Federal Trade Commission). 1994. "Antitrust Enforcement Guidelines for International Operations." Unpublished.

DOL (Department of Labor). Various years. *Annual Report of the Department of Labor.* Washington, D.C.

EIA. 2005. *Annual Energy Outlook 2005.* Washington, D.C.

EPA (Environmental Protection Agency). 1988. *Environmental Progress and Challenges: EPA's Update.* Washington, D.C.

————. 1990. *National Water Quality Inventory: 1988 Report to Congress.* Washington, D.C.: Office of Water.

————. 1991. *Managing Environmental Results: A Status Report on EPA's Environmental Indicator Program.* Washington, D.C.

————. 1997. "Summay of EPA's FY 1998 President's Budget." http://www.epa.gov/ocfo/1998bib.pdf.

————. 1998. "Reinventing Environmental Protection." http://www.epa.gov/reinvent.

————. 2003a. *National Biennial RCRA Hazardous Waste Report.* Washington, D.C.

————. 2003b. *2003–2008 EPA Strategic Plan: Directions for the Future.* Washington, D.C.

————. 2004. *EPA FY 2004 End of Year Enforcement and Compliance Assurance Results.* Washington, D.C.: Office of Enforcement and Compliance Assurance.

————. 2005. *EPA FY 2004 End of Year Enforcement and Compliance Assurance Results.* Washington, D.C.: Office of Enforcement and Compliance Assurance.

FDIC. 2006a. *Call Report and Thrift Financial Report.* Washington, D.C.

————. 2006b. *Quarterly Banking Profile, Fourth Quarter 2005.* Washington, D.C.

FTC (Federal Trade Commission). 1997. *The Federal Trade Commission: Implementing the Results Act.* Draft FTC strategic plan under the Government Performance and Results Act for fiscal years 1997–2002. June.

————. 2001a. *Federal Trade Commission Fiscal Year 2002 Congressional Justification: Budget Summary.* Washington, D.C.

————. 2001b. *Performance Report Fiscal Year 2000.* Washington, D.C.

————. 2002a. *Federal Trade Commission Fiscal Year 2003 Congressional Justification: Budget Summary.* Washington, D.C.

————. 2002b. *Performance Report Fiscal Year 2002.* Washington, D.C.

————. 2003a. *Federal Trade Commission Fiscal Year 2004 Congressional Justification: Budget Summary.* Washington, D.C.

————. 2003b. *A Positive Agenda for Consumers: The FTC Year in Review.* Washington, D.C.

————. 2004. *Federal Trade Commission Fiscal Year 2005 Congressional Justification: Budget Summary.* Washington, D.C.

————. 2005a. *Federal Trade Commission Fiscal Year 2006 Congressional Justification: Budget Summary.* Washington, D.C.

————. 2005b. *FTC Appropriation History.* Washington, D.C.

————. Various years. *Annual Report of the Federal Trade Commission.* Washington, D.C.

GAO (General Accounting Office). 1987. *Superfund: Extent of Nation's Potential Hazardous Waste Problem Still Unknown.* Washington, D.C.

————. 1994. *Occupational Safety and Health: Changes Needed in the Combined Federal-State Approach.* GAO/HEHS-94-10. Washington, D.C.

————. 1995. *Regulatory Reform: Information on Costs, Cost-Effectiveness, and Mandated Deadlines for Regulations.* GAO/PEMD-95-18BR. Washington, D.C.

————. 1996a. *Paperwork Reduction-Burden Reduction Goal Unlikely to Be Met.* GAO/T-GGD/RCED-960-186. Washington, D.C.

————. 1996b. *Regulatory Burden: Measurement Challenges and Concerns Raised by Selected Companies.* GAO/GGD-97-2. Washington, D.C.

OSHA (Occupational Safety and Health Administration). 1995a. *The New OSHA: Reinventing Worker Safety and Health.* National Performance Review. May.

————. 1995b. "The Cumulative Impact of Current Congressional Reform on American Working Men and Women." Prepared for Secretary of Labor Robert B. Reich. August.

————. 1996. "The OSHA Priority Planning Process, February 5, 1996." http://www.osha.gov/oshinfo/priorities.

————. 2004a. *Alliance: An OSHA Cooperative Program.* Washington, D.C.

————. 2004b. *Annual Report on the Alliance Program: October 1, 2003, to September 30, 2004.* Washington, D.C.

————. 2004c. *Guidelines for Poultry Processing: Ergonomics for the Prevention of Musculoskeletal Disorders.* Washington, D.C.

————. 2004d. *OSHA Strategic Partnership Program for Worker Safety and Health.* Directive CSP 03-02-002. Washington, D.C.

————. 2005. *OSHA Facts: December 2004.* http://www.osha.gov/as/opa/oshafacts. html.

————. n.d. "Standards Development." http://www.osha-slc.gov/ocis/stand_dev. html.

OTS (Office of Thrift Supervision). 1998. *Annual Report.* Washington, D.C.

Pertschuk, Michael. 1984. *The Performance of the Federal Trade Commission, 1977–84.* Report to the Subcommittee on Oversight and Investigations, House Committee on Energy and Commerce. September. Mimeo.

Siskind, Frederic B. 2002. "20th Century OSHA Enforcement Data: A Review and Explanation of the Major Trends." Washington, D.C.: OSHA.

US Congress, House. 1975. *Financial Institutions and the Nation's Economy (FINE): "Discussion Principles."* 94th Cong., 1st and 2nd sess.

Secondary Sources

ABA (American Bar Association). 1969. *Report of the ABA Commission to Study the Federal Trade Commission, September 15, 1969.* Chicago.

————. 1989. *Report of the American Bar Association Section on Antitrust Law Task Force on the Antitrust Division of the U.S. Department of Justice.* Reprinted as *Supplement to Antitrust and Trade Regulation Report* 57, no. 1425 (July 20).

————. 2005. *The State of Federal Antitrust Enforcement—2004.* Chicago.

Aberbach, Joel D. 1990. *Keeping a Watchful Eye: The Politics of Congressional Oversight.* Washington, D.C.: Brookings Institution.

Aberbach, Joel D., and Bert A. Rockman. 1976. "Clashing Beliefs Within the Executive Branch: The Nixon Administration Bureaucracy." *American Political Science Review* 70: 456–468.

Ackerman, Bruce, and William Hassler. 1981. *Clean Coal, Dirty Air.* New Haven: Yale University Press.

Adams, Walter. 1982. "Public Policy in a Free Enterprise Economy." In *The Structure of Industry,* 6th ed., ed. Walter Adams. New York: Macmillan.

Adams, Walter, and James W. Brock. 1986. *The Bigness Complex: Industry, Labor, and Government in the American Economy.* New York: Pantheon.

Alberini, Anna, and K. Segerson. 2002. "Assessing Voluntary Programs to Improve Environmental Quality." *Environmental and Resource Economics* 22: 157–187.

Alchian, Armen A., and Harold Demsetz. 1972. "Production, Information Costs, and Economic Organization." *American Economic Review* 62 (December): 777–795.

Anderson, James E. 1984. *Public Policy-Making*. 3rd ed. New York: Holt, Rinehart, and Winston.

Anderson, James E., David W. Brady, and Charles S. Bullock. 1977. *Public Policy and Politics in America*. N. Scituate, Mass.: Duxbury.

Andewelt, Roger B. 1985. "Organization and Operation of the Antitrust Division." *Antitrust Law Journal* 54, no. 1: 109–115.

Andrews, Richard N. L. 1984. "Economics and Environmental Decisions, Past and Present." In *Environmental Policy Under Reagan's Executive Order: The Role of Benefit-Cost Analysis,* ed. V. Kerry Smith. Chapel Hill: University of North Carolina Press.

Arnold, Thurman W. 1937. *The Folklore of Capitalism*. New Haven: Yale University Press.

Arrow, Kenneth J. 1963. *Social Choice and Individual Values*. New York: Wiley.

Auerbach, Carl A. 1964. "The Federal Trade Commission: Internal Organization and Procedure." *Minnesota Law Review* 48 (January): 383–522.

Averch, Harvey. 1990. *Private Markets and Public Intervention: A Primer for Policy Designers*. Pittsburgh: University of Pittsburgh Press.

Axelrod, Regina. 1984. "Energy Policy: Changing the Rules of the Game." In *Environmental Policy in the 1980s,* eds. Norman Vig and Michael Kraft. Washington, D.C.: Congressional Quarterly.

Azcuenaga, Mary L. 1996. "Developments in Consumer Protection at the Federal Trade Commission: Achieving Customer Satisfaction in a Government Law Enforcement Agency." Remarks before the Promotion Law/Marketing Conference of the Promotion Marketing Association of America, Hyatt Regency Washington on Capitol Hill, Washington, D.C.

Babson, Jennifer. 1995a. "Rules Panel Reaches Agreement on 'Corrections' Calendar." *Congressional Quarterly Weekly Report* 53, no. 24 (June 17): 1712.

———. 1995b. "In Picking Rules to 'Correct,' Consensus Is Hard to Find." *Congressional Quarterly Weekly Report* 53, no. 28 (July 15): 2038.

Baker, Donald I., and William Blumenthal. 1984. "Ideological Cycles and Unstable Antitrust Rules." *Antitrust Bulletin* 31, no. 2: 323–339.

Ball, Howard. 1984. *Controlling Regulatory Sprawl: Presidential Strategies from Nixon to Reagan*. Westport: Greenwood.

Balogh, Brian. 1991. *Chain Reaction*. Cambridge: Cambridge University Press.

Balto, David. 2001. "Professor at the Helm: How Will Timothy Muris Change the FTC's Enforcement Priorities?" *Legal Times* (July 30): 26.

Banks, Jeffrey, and Barry Weingast. 1992. "The Political Control of Bureaucracies Under Asymmetric Information." *American Journal of Political Science* 36, no. 2 (May): 509–524.

Barcott, Bruce. 2004. "Changing All the Rules." *New York Times* (April 4): sec. 6, p. 38.

Bardach, Eugene, and Robert A. Kagan. 1982. *Going by the Book: The Problem of Regulatory Unreasonableness*. Philadelphia: Temple University Press.

Barnes, Julian E. 2001. "Bush to Name Lawyer to Lead Safety Panel." *New York Times* (October 31): A13.

Barzel, Yoram. 1989. *Economic Analysis of Property Rights*. Cambridge: Cambridge University Press.

Battaile, Janet. 1992. "Bush Overrides Agency on Pollution Restrictions." *New York Times* (May 17): 19.

Baumgartner Frank R., and Bryan D. Jones. 1993. *Agendas and Instability in American Politics.* Chicago: University of Chicago Press.

Bawn, Kathleen. 1995. "Political Control Versus Expertise: Congressional Choices About Administrative Procedures." *American Political Science Review* 89: 62–73.

Beadle, Andrew D. 1999. "Bills Would Curb Union 'Salting,' Defray Companies' Legal Costs." *Congressional Quarterly Weekly Report* 57, no. 31 (July 30): 1880.

Bell, Robert. 1985. "Professional Values and Organizational Decisionmaking." *Administration and Society* 17 (May): 21–60.

Bendor, Jonathan, and Terry Moe. 1985. "An Adaptive Model of Bureaucratic Politics." *American Political Science Review* 79: 755–774.

Bendor, Jonathan, Serge Taylor, and Roland Van Gaaleen. 1987. "Stacking the Deck: Bureaucratic Missions and Policy Design." *American Political Science Review* 81: 873–896.

Benenson, Bob. 1995a. "House Panels Take Quick Action on Risk Assessment Provisions." *Congressional Quarterly Weekly Report* 53, no. 6 (February 11): 450–453.

———. 1995b. "House Easily Passes Bills to Limit Regulators." *Congressional Quarterly Weekly Report* 53, no. 9 (March 4): 679–682.

———. 1995c. "GOP Sets 104th Congress on New Regulatory Course." *Congressional Quarterly Weekly Report* 53, no. 24 (June 17): 1693–1697.

———. 1995d. "Procedural Overhaul Fails After Three Tough Votes." *Congressional Quarterly Weekly Report* 53, no. 29 (July 22): 2159–2162.

Bensel, Richard F. 1984. *Sectionalism and American Political Development.* Madison: University of Wisconsin Press.

Benton, James C. 1999. "Proposed Ergonomics Rules Rub GOP the Wrong Way." *Congressional Quarterly Weekly Report* 57, no. 46 (November 24): 2843.

———. 2001. "Bush Upsets Unions by Choosing Scalia." *Congressional Quarterly Weekly Report* 59, no. 30 (August 11): 1964.

Bernstein, Marver H. 1955. *Regulating Business by Independent Commission.* Princeton: Princeton University Press.

Berry, Jeffrey M. 1984. *The Interest Group Society.* Boston: Little, Brown.

Bettelheim, Adriel. 2000a. "New Corporate Incentives Bills Compete with Regulatory Relief As a Way to Spur Internet Access." *Congressional Quarterly Weekly Report* 58, no. 14 (April 1): 766.

———. 2000b. "High-Speed Internet Access Bill Appears Stalled Until Next Year by Regulatory and Business Concerns." *Congressional Quarterly Weekly Report* 58, no. 30 (July 22): 1810.

———. 2001a. "Promising a Lighter Regulatory Touch, FCC's Powell Indicates He Might Loosen Restrictions on Media Concentration." *Congressional Quarterly Weekly Report* 59, no. 13 (March 31): 723.

———. 2001b. "Tauzin's Push to Deregulate High-Speed Internet Service Meets Resistance from Bell's Critics." *Congressional Quarterly Weekly Report* 59, no. 17 (April 28): 922.

———. 2001c. "Turf Battles, Lobbying Blitz Roil 'Broadband' Deregulation." *Congressional Quarterly Weekly Report* 59, no. 18 (May 5): 1012–1013.

———. 2001d. "High-Speed Internet Access Bill Emerges from House Commerce Panel with Less Momentum Than Tauzin Hoped." *Congressional Quarterly Weekly Report* 59, no. 19 (May 12): 1082–1084.

———. 2001e. "Fate of House 'Broadband' Bill Handed to Rules by Judiciary." *Congressional Quarterly Weekly Report* 59, no. 24 (June 16): 1434–1435.

————. 2002a. "Final Lobbying Push Is Under Way As Vote on Broadband Bill Nears." *Congressional Quarterly Weekly Report* 60, no. 7 (February 16): 456–457.

————. 2002b. "House Sends Broadband to Senate with Wink and Nod to FCC." *Congressional Quarterly Weekly Report* 60, no. 9 (March 2): 581–585.

————. 2002c. "Future of High-Speed Internet Service Rides on Competing Senate Bills." *Congressional Quarterly Weekly Report* 60, no. 20 (May 18): 1303–1305.

Blais, André, and Stéphane Dion, eds. 1991. *The Budget Maximizing Bureaucrat: Appraisals and Evidence.* Pittsburgh: University of Pittsburgh Press.

Blakely, Steve. 1987a. "Panel Approves $5 Billion FSLIC Rescue Plan." *Congressional Quarterly Weekly Report* 45, no. 14 (April 4): 635–636.

————. 1987b. "Rescue of S&L Insurance Fund Imperiled by Banking Dispute." *Congressional Quarterly Weekly Report* 45, no. 17 (April 25): 779.

Bobelian, Michael. 2004. "Group Aims to Update Antitrust Law; Critics Say It Doesn't Adequately Represent Consumer Interests." *National Law Journal* (July 12): 8.

Bork, Robert H. 1978. *The Antitrust Paradox: A Policy at War with Itself.* New York: Basic.

Bosso, Christopher J. 1987. *Pesticides and Politics: The Life Cycle of a Public Issue.* Pittsburgh: University of Pittsburgh Press.

————. 1994. "After the Movement: Environmental Activism in the 1990s." In *Environmental Policy in the 1990s,* 2nd ed., eds. Norman Vig and Michael Kraft. Washington, D.C.: Congressional Quarterly.

————. 1997. "Seizing Back the Day: The Challenge to Environmental Activism in the 1990s." In *Environmental Policy in the 1990s,* 3rd ed., eds. Norman Vig and Michael Kraft. Washington, D.C.: Congressional Quarterly.

Boyer, Barry B. 1981. "Funding Public Participation in Agency Proceedings: The Federal Trade Commission Experience." *Georgetown Law Review* 70: 51–172.

————. 1989. "The Federal Trade Commission and Consumer Protection Policy: A Postmortem Examination." In *Making Regulatory Policy,* eds. Keith Hawkins and John M. Thomas. Pittsburgh: University of Pittsburgh Press.

Brinkley, Joel. 2004. "Out of Spotlight, Bush Overhauls U.S. Regulations." *New York Times* (August 14): 1.

Brouhle, Keith, Charles Griffiths, and Ann Wolverton. 2004. "The Use of Voluntary Approaches for Environmental Policymaking in the U.S." Working Paper no. 2004-05. Washington, D.C: National Center for Environmental Economics.

Brower, Michael. 1992. *Cool Energy: Renewable Solutions to Environmental Problems.* Cambridge: MIT Press.

Brown, James L. 1995. "Contemporary Consumer Protection." In *Regulation and Consumer Protection,* 2nd ed., eds. Kenneth J. Meier and E. Thomas Garman. Houston: DAME.

Browne, William P. 1988. *Private Interests, Public Policy, and American Agriculture.* Lawrence: University Press of Kansas.

Browne, William, and Won Paik. 1993. "Beyond the Domain: Recasting Network Politics on the Postreform Congress." *American Journal of Political Science* 37: 1054–1078.

Browning, Graeme. 1991. "Getting the Last Word." *National Journal* 11, no. 37 (September 14): 2194–2199.

————. 1997a. "Burning His Bridges?" *National Journal* 29, no. 23 (June 7): 1130–1131.

————. 1997b. "Busy Signal." *National Journal* 29, no. 31 (August 2): 1552–1554.

Brunner, Thomas W., Thomas G. Krattenmaker, Robert A. Skitol, and Ann Adams Webster. 1985. *Mergers in the New Antitrust Era.* Washington, D.C.: Bureau of National Affairs.

Bryner, Gary C. 1987. *Bureaucratic Discretion: Law and Policy in Federal Regulatory Agencies.* New York: Pergamon.

Burnbaum, Jeffrey H., and Alan S. Murray. 1987. *Showdown at Gucci Gulch.* New York: Random House.

Burns, Helen. 1974. *The American Banking Community and the New Deal Banking Reforms.* Westport: Greenwood.

Burns, Robert. 2005. *Summary of H.R. 6—Energy Policy Act of 2005: Title XII: Electricity.* Columbus, Ohio: National Regulatory Research Institute.

Bushnell, James. 2005. "Looking for Trouble: Competition Policy in the U.S. Electricity Industry." *Electricity Deregulation: Choices and Challenges,* eds. James Griffin and Steven Puller. Chicago: University of Chicago Press.

Byington, S. John. 1977. "What the Government Can—and Cannot—Do to Protect the Public." *U.S. News and World Report* 83, no. 17 (October 24): 33–35.

Caldwell, Lynton. 1982. *Science and the National Environmental Policy Act.* Tuscaloosa: University of Alabama Press, 1982.

Calmes, Jacqueline. 1984a. "Interstate Forays by Big Banks Revive Interest in Legislation." *Congressional Quarterly Weekly Report* 42, no. 18 (May 5): 1025–1030.

———. 1984b. "St. Germain Jettisons Bank Deregulation Bills." *Congressional Quarterly Weekly Report* 42, no. 38 (September 22): 2342.

———. 1985. "House Committee Easily OKs Nationwide Banking." *Congressional Quarterly Weekly Report* 42, no. 35 (August 31): 1713–1715.

Calvert, Randall, Matthew D. McCubbins, and Barry R. Weingast. 1989. "A Theory of Political Control and Agency Discretion." *American Journal of Political Science* 33: 588–611.

Camia, Catalina. 1994. "Indoor Air Measure Out of Breath." *Congressional Quarterly Weekly Report* 52, no. 39 (October 8): 2870.

Camia, Catalina, Jeanne Ponessa, and Alissa J. Rubin. 1994. "Republican Agenda: Capital Gain May Cause Division Within GOP." *Congressional Quarterly Weekly Report* 52, no. 45 (November 19): 3342–3344.

Campbell, John L. 1988. *Collapse of an Industry: Nuclear Power and the Contradictions of U.S. Policy.* Ithaca: Cornell University Press.

Cargill, Thomas F., and Gillian G. Garcia. 1985. *Financial Reform in the 1980s.* Stanford: Stanford University Press.

Carney, Dan. 1996. "Congress Fires Its First Shot in Information Revolution." *Congressional Quarterly Weekly Report* 54, no. 5 (February 3): 289–294.

Carney, Elizabeth. 1992. "Industry Plays the Grassroots Card." *National Journal* 24, no. 5 (February 1): 281–282.

Carson, Rachel. 1962. *Silent Spring.* Boston: Houghton Mifflin.

Cater, Douglass. 1964. *Power in Washington: A Critical Look at Today's Struggle to Govern in the Nation's Capital.* New York: Random House.

Chandler, Alfred D., Jr. 1962. *Strategy and Structure: Chapters in the History of the American Industrial Enterprise.* Cambridge: MIT Press.

Chin, Andrew. 1997. "A Summary Judgment Analysis of Innovation-Market-Based Merger Challenges." Unpublished ms., Yale Law School, New Haven.

Chubb, John E. 1983. *Interest Groups and the Bureaucracy.* Stanford: Stanford University Press.

Cifelli, Ann. 1984. "Nanny to the World." *Fortune* 109, no. 9 (April 30): 175–176.

Clark, Drew. 2001. "Behind the Microsoft Deal." *National Journal* 33 (November 17): 3603.

Clark, Timothy B. 1978a. "The 'Facts' About OSHA's 1,100 Revoked Regulations." *National Journal* 10, no. 28 (August 12): 1298–1299.

———. 1978b. "What's All the Uproar Over OSHA's 'Nit-Picking' Rules?" *National Journal* 10, no. 40 (October 7): 1594–1596.

———. 1981. "If Reagan Wants to Trump the Regulators, Here's OMB's Target List for Openers." *National Journal* 13, no. 3 (January 17): 94–98.

Clarkson, Kenneth W., and Timothy J. Muris, eds. 1981. *The Federal Trade Commission Since 1970: Economic Regulation and Bureaucratic Behavior.* Cambridge: Cambridge University Press.

Cloud, David S. 1995. "Industry, Politics Intertwined in Dole's Regulatory Bill." *Congressional Quarterly Weekly Report* 53, no. 18 (May 6): 1219–1224.

Cochran, Clarke E., Lawrence C. Mayer, T. R. Carr, and N. Joseph Cayer. 1990. *American Public Policy: An Introduction.* 3rd. ed. New York: St. Martin's.

Coglianese, Cary. 1997. "Assessing Consensus." *Duke Law Journal* 46: 1255–1349.

Coglianese, Cary, and Jennifer Nash. 2005. "Management Based Strategies for Improving the Private Sector's Environmental Performance." Working Paper no. RPP2005-03. Cambridge: John F. Kennedy School of Government, Harvard University.

Cohn, Peter. 2003a. "Principals in Broadband Debate in No Hurry to Rejoin Battle." Congressional Quarterly Weekly Report 61, no. 4 (January 25): 202–204.

———. 2003b. "New FCC Broadband Rules a Mixed Victory for Authors of Telecommunications Rewrite." *Congressional Quarterly Weekly Report* 61, no. 9 (March 1): 513.

Cole, Richard L., and David A. Caputo. 1979. "Presidential Control of the Senior Civil Service: Assessing the Strategies of the Nixon Years." *American Political Science Review* 73: 391–413.

Congressional Quarterly. 1982. *Regulation: Process and Politics.* Washington, D.C.

Conte, Christopher. 1979. "A Reluctant Congress Faces a New Debate on Banking Law." *Congressional Quarterly Weekly Report* 37, no. 2 (July 7): 1364–1369.

Cox, Edward F., Robert C. Fellmeth, and John E. Schultz. 1969. *The Nader Report on the Federal Trade Commission.* New York: Baron.

CQWR (Congressional Quarterly Weekly Report). 1978a. "Senate Votes Overwhelmingly to Curb FTC." *CQWR* 36, no. 6 (February 2): 368–369.

———. 1978b. "Byington Departure Reflects Continued Criticism of Product Safety Commission." *CQWR* 36, no. 7 (February 18): 389–392.

Crandall, Robert W. 1983. *Controlling Industrial Pollution.* Washington, D.C.: Brookings Institution.

Crandall, Robert W., and Leonard Waverman. 1995. *Talk Is Cheap: The Promise of Regulatory Reform in North American Telecommunications.* Washington, D.C.: Brookings Institution.

Cranford, John. 1988a. "Senate Panel Approves Bank Deregulation Bill." *Congressional Quarterly Weekly Report* 46, no. 10 (March 5): 566.

———. 1988b. "Energy/Commerce Panel Seeks Tight Reins on New Bank Powers." *Congressional Quarterly Weekly Report* 46, no. 39 (September 24): 2659–2660.

———. 1989a. "Bush's Thrift Plan Greeted with Caution on Hill." *Congressional Quarterly Weekly Report* 47, no. 6 (February 11): 255–258.

———. 1989b. "Bush Faces Powerful Foes As Bailout Battle Nears." *Congressional Quarterly Weekly Report* 47, no. 7 (February 18): 303–305.

———. 1989c. "102 Conferees Appointed in S&L Bill." *Congressional Quarterly Weekly Report* 47, no. 25 (June 24): 1530.

——. 1990a. "Deposit Insurance System Under Close Scrutiny." *Congressional Quarterly Weekly Report* 48, no. 7 (February 17): 520–525.

——. 1990b. "Partisan Knives Are Drawn As Thrift Crisis Builds." *Congressional Quarterly Weekly Report* 48, no. 25 (June 23): 1937–1941.

——. 1991a. "Financial System's Wounds May Only Be Bandaged." *Congressional Quarterly Weekly Report* 49, no. 5 (February 2): 284–289.

——. 1991b. "Administration Spells Out Plan to Reform Financial System." *Congressional Quarterly Weekly Report* 49, no. 6 (February 9): 357–361.

——. 1991c. "Hill Maneuvers Threaten Delay of Massive Overhaul Bill." *Congressional Quarterly Weekly Report* 49, no. 28 (July 13): 1882.

——. 1991d. "Fate of Overhaul in Doubt As Conflicts Solidify." *Congressional Quarterly Weekly Report* 49, no. 38 (September 21): 2677–2679.

Cuff, Robert D. 1973. *The War Industries Board: Business-Government Relations During World War I.* Baltimore: Johns Hopkins University Press.

Culhane, Charles. 1972a. "Administration Works to Shift Safety, Health Programs to States Despite Labor Criticism." *National Journal* 4, no. 26 (June 24): 1041–1049.

——. 1972b. "Labor, Business Press Administration to Change Safety and Health Programs." *National Journal* 4, no. 27 (July 1): 1093–1102.

Cushman, John. 1995. "Congressional Republicans Take Aim at an Extensive List of Environmental Statutes." *New York Times* (February 22): A14.

Dahringer, Lee D., and Deise R. Johnson. 1984. "The Federal Trade Commission Redefinition of Deception and Public Policy Implications: Let the Buyer Beware." *Journal of Consumer Affairs* 18, no. 2 (Winter): 320–342.

Davidson, Roger H. 1981. "Subcommittee Government: New Channels for Policy Making." In *The New Congress*, eds. Thomas E. Mann and Norman J. Ornstein. Washington, D.C.: American Enterprise Institute.

Davies, J. Clarence. 1984. "Environmental Institutions and the Reagan Administration." In *Environmental Policy in the 1980s,* eds. Norman J. Vig and Michael E. Kraft. Washington, D.C.: Congressional Quarterly.

Davis, David. 1993. *Energy Politics.* 4th ed. New York: St. Martin's.

Davis, Kenneth Culp. 1969. *Discretionary Justice: A Preliminary Inquiry.* Baton Rouge: Louisiana State University Press.

De Vany, Arthur, and David Walls. 1995. *The Emerging New Order in Natural Gas: Markets Versus Regulation.* Westport: Quorum.

Demkovich, Linda E. 1974. "OSHA Launches Dual Effort to Reduce Job Health Hazards." *National Journal* 6, no. 49 (December 7): 1831–1839.

——. 1978. "King and Her Court at the Consumer Product Safety Commission." *National Journal* 10, no. 43 (October 28): 1732–1733.

Derthick, Martha, and Paul J. Quirk. 1985. *The Politics of Deregulation.* Washington, D.C.: Brookings Institution.

Domhoff, G. William. 1970. *The Higher Circles: The Governing Class in America.* New York: Random House.

Donner, Frank, and James Ledbetter. 1988. "Deregulation by Sleaze." *Nation* 246, no. 6 (February 6): 163–166.

Dorman, Peter. 1996. *Markets and Morality: Economics, Dangerous Work, and the Value of Human Life.* Cambridge: Cambridge University Press.

Dower, Roger. 1990. "Hazardous Waste Policy." In *Public Policies for Environmental Protection,* ed. Paul Portney. Washington, D.C.: Resources for the Future.

Downs, Anthony. 1967. *Inside Bureaucracy.* Boston: Little, Brown.

————. 1972. "Up and Down with Ecology: The Issue-Attention Cycle." *Public Interest* 28, no. 3: 38–50.

Drew, Elizabeth. 1994. *On the Edge: The Clinton Presidency.* New York: Simon and Schuster.

Dudley, Susan E. 2001. "Reversing Midnight Regulations." *Regulation* 24, no. 1 (Spring 2001): 9.

Dunlap, Riley. 1995. "Public Opinion and Environmental Policy." In *Environmental Politics and Policy,* 2nd ed., ed. James Lester. Durham, N.C.: Duke University Press.

Dunlap, Riley, and Rik Scarce. 1991. "Environmental Problems and Protection." *Public Opinion Quarterly* 55, no. 3: 651–672.

Dye, Thomas R. 1992. *Understanding Public Policy.* 7th ed. Englewood Cliffs, N.J.: Prentice Hall.

Eads, George C., and Michael Fix. 1984. *Relief or Reform? Reagan's Regulatory Dilemma.* Washington, D.C.: Urban Institute Press.

Easterbrook, Gregg. 2005. "Clear Skies, No Lies." *New York Times* (February 16): A21.

Edelman, Murray. 1964. *The Symbolic Uses of Politics.* Urbana: University of Illinois Press.

Eggertsson, Thrainn. 1990. *Economic Behavior and Institutions.* Cambridge: Cambridge University Press.

Ehrenhalf, Alan. 1983. "The Unfashionable House Rules Committee." *Congressional Quarterly Weekly Report* 41, no. 2 (January 15): 151.

Eichler, Ned. 1989. *The Thrift Debacle.* Berkeley: University of California Press.

Eisner, Marc Allen. 1990. "Institutional History and Policy Change: Exploring the Origins of the New Antitrust." *Journal of Policy History* 2, no. 3 (Fall): 261–289.

————. 1991. *Antitrust and the Triumph of Economics: Institutions, Expertise, and Policy Change.* Chapel Hill: University of North Carolina Press.

————. 1993. "Bureaucratic Professionalization and the Limits of the Political Control Thesis: The Case of the Federal Trade Commission." *Governance* 6, no. 2 (April): 127–153.

————. 1994. "Economic Regulatory Policies: Regulation and Deregulation in Historical Context." In *Handbook of Administrative Law and Regulation,* eds. David H. Rosenbloom and Richard D. Schwartz. New York: Dekker.

————. 1995. *The State in the American Political Economy: Public Policy and the Evolution of State-Economy Relations.* Englewood Cliffs, N.J.: Prentice Hall.

————. 2000 *Regulatory Politics in Transition.* 2nd ed. Baltimore: Johns Hopkins University Press.

Eisner, Marc Allen, and Kenneth J. Meier. 1990. "Presidential Control Versus Bureaucratic Power: Explaining the Reagan Revolution in Antitrust." *American Journal of Political Science* 34: 269–287.

Eisner, Marc Allen, Jeff Worsham, and Evan Ringquist. 1996. "Crossing the Organizational Void: The Limits of Agency Theory in the Analysis of Political Control." *Governance* 9, no. 4 (October): 407–428.

Ellerman, A. Denny, Paul Joskow, Richard Schmalensee, Juan-Pablo Montero, and Elizabeth Bailey. 2000. *Markets for Clean Air.* New York: Cambridge University Press.

Ellis, Dorsey D., Jr. 1981. "Legislative Powers: FTC Rule Making." In *The Federal Trade Commission Since 1970,* eds. Kenneth W. Clarkson and Timothy J. Muris. Cambridge: Cambridge University Press.

Elving, Ronald. 1987. "Conferees Agree to $8.5 Billion FSLIC Plan." *Congressional Quarterly Weekly Report* 45, no. 27 (July 4): 1450.

Engler, Robert. 1961. *The Politics of Oil.* Chicago: University of Chicago Press.

Eskridge, William N., Jr., and John Ferejohn. 1992. "Making the Deal Stick: Enforcing the Original Constitutional Structure of Lawmaking in the Modern Regulatory State." *Journal of Law, Economics, and Organization* 8: 165–189.

Fainsod, Merle, Lincoln Gordon, and Joseph C. Palamountain Jr. 1959. *Government and the American Economy.* 3rd ed. New York: Norton.

Fehner, Terrence R., and Jack M. Holl. 1994. *Department of Energy, 1977–1994: A Summary History.* DOE/HR-0098. Oakridge, Tenn.: Office of Scientific and Technical Information.

Fiorina, Morris P. 1989. *Congress: Keystone of the Washington Establishment.* 2nd ed. New Haven: Yale University Press.

Fiorina, Morris P., and Kenneth Shepsle. 1982. "Equilibrium, Disequilibrium, and the General Possibility of a Science of Politics." In *Political Equilibrium,* eds. Peter Ordershook and Kenneth Shepsle. The Hague: Kluwer-Nijhoff.

Fiorino, Daniel. 1995. *Making Environmental Policy.* Berkeley: University of California Press.

———. 1999. "Rethinking Environmental Regulation: Perspectives on Law and Governance." *Harvard Environmental Law Review* 23: 441–468.

Firestone, David, and Richard Perez-Pena. 2003. "The Blackout of 2003: The Context; Failure Reveals Creaky System, Experts Believe." *New York Times* (August 15): A1.

Fise, Mary Ellen R. 1995. "Consumer Product Safety Regulation." In *Regulation and Consumer Protection,* 2nd ed., eds. Kenneth J. Meier and E. Thomas Garman. Houston: DAME.

Fox, Pauline. 1988. "Antitrust Economics and the Courts: The 'When' and 'How' of Judicial Miseducation." *Antitrust Law and Economics Review* 20, no. 3: 95–99.

Frank, John N. 1981. "New Competitors Zero in on Savings Market." *Savings and Loan News* 102 (April): 36–41.

Franz, Neil. 2002. "Lawmakers Reject Bush's EPA Enforcement Shift." *Chemical Week* 164, no. 42: 58.

Frater, Elisabeth, and Michael Steel. 2001. "Federal Trade Commission Profiles." *National Journal* 33, no. 25 (June 23): 2024–2025.

Freedman, Allan. 1995a. "Proposal to Abolish Department Tests GOP As Agent of Change." *Congressional Quarterly Weekly Report* 53, no. 7 (February 18): 516–517.

———. 1995b. "Senate Passes Removal of Ban on Exports of Alaskan Oil." *Congressional Quarterly Weekly Report* 53, no. 20 (May 20): 1416–1417.

———. 1995c. "Energy Agency Fares Better in Senate Spending Bill." *Congressional Quarterly Weekly Report* 53, no. 30 (July 29): 2251–2252.

———. 1995d. "Senate Passes Energy, Water Bill with Billion-Dollar Problem." *Congressional Quarterly Weekly Report* 53, no. 31 (August 5): 2354–2355.

———. 1995e. Property Rights Bill Advances but Faces Uncertainty." *Congressional Quarterly Weekly Report* 53, no. 50 (December 23): 3884–3885.

———. 1997a. "GOP Cautious on Easing Rules Despite Clinton's Forays." *Congressional Quarterly Weekly Report* 55, no. 3 (January 18): 168–170.

———. 1997b. "Latest Fight on Clean Air Rules Centers on Scientific Data." *Congressional Quarterly Weekly Report* 55, no. 9 (March 1): 530–532.

———. 1997c. "Congress Prepares New Assault on Troubled Superfund Sites." *Congressional Quarterly Weekly Report* 55, no. 26 (June 28): 1502–1507.

————. 1997d. "Democrats Show Divisions on New Clean Air Rules." *Congressional Quarterly Weekly Report* 55, no. 26 (June 28): 1512–1513.

————. 1997e. "Clinton's Global Warming Plans Take Heat from Congress." *Congressional Quarterly Weekly Report* 55, no. 42 (October 25): 2598.

————. 1997f. "Property Rights Advocates Climb the Hill to Success." *Congressional Quarterly Weekly Report* 55, no. 42 (October 25): 2591–2613.

————. 1997g. "Forecast Is Dim in the Senate for Global Warming Treaty." *Congressional Quarterly Weekly Report* 55, no. 49 (December 13): 3068–3069.

————. 1998. "GOP's Secret Weapon Against Regulations: Finesse." *Congressional Quarterly Weekly Report* 56, no. 35 (September 4): 2305, 2314–2320.

Freeman, J. Leiper. 1955. *The Political Process: Executive Bureau–Legislative Committee Relations.* New York: Random House.

————. 1965. *The Political Process: Executive Bureau–Legislative Committee Relations.* Rev. ed. New York: Random House.

Freidson, Eliot. 1986. *Professional Powers: A Study of the Institutionalization of Formal Knowledge.* Chicago: University of Chicago Press.

Friedman, Barry D. 1995. *Regulation in the Reagan-Bush Era: The Eruption of Presidential Influence.* Pittsburgh: University of Pittsburgh Press.

Friedman, Milton. 1962. *Capitalism and Freedom.* Chicago: University of Chicago Press.

Fry, Richard. 1989. "How Bush Is Keeping the Radical Right Inside the Tent." *Business Week* (June 19): 45.

Gahee, Michelle. 1995. "Clinton Would Veto Arctic Drilling Bill." *Congressional Quarterly Weekly Report* 53, no. 31 (August 5): 2359.

Gardner, Judy. 1972. "Consumer Report: FTC Seeks Wider Impact in Antitrust Work, Puts New Emphasis on Planning." *National Journal* 4, no. 29 (July 15): 1151–1159.

Gattuso, James L. 2004 "Reining in the Regulators: How Does President Bush Measure Up?" *Heritage Foundation Backgrounder* no. 1801 (September 28).

Gayer, Ted, John Horowitz, and John List. 2005. "When Economists Dream, They Dream of Clear Skies." *Economist's Voice* 2, no. 2: art. 7.

Gerber, Brian J., and Paul Teske. 2000. "Regulatory Policymaking in the American States: A Review of Theories and Evidence." *Political Research Quarterly* 53, no. 4: 849–886.

Gerston, Larry N., Cynthia Fraleigh, and Robert Schwab. 1988. *The Deregulated Society.* Pacific Grove, Calif.: Brooks/Cole.

Gettinger, Stephen, David Hosansky, and Jeffrey L. Katz. 1994. "Oil-State Senator Tosses Match into Gasoline Additive Debate." *Congressional Quarterly Weekly Report* 52, no. 28 (July 16): 1940–1941.

Goldberg, Victor P. 1976. "Regulation and Administered Contracts." *Bell Journal of Economics* 7, no. 2 (Spring): 426–441.

Goldreich, Samuel. 2002. "EPA Relaxes Clean Air Rules for Coal Plants. *Congressional Quarterly Weekly Report* 60, no. 44 (November 23): 3085.

Goldstein, Amy, and Sarah Cohen. 2004. "Bush Forces a Shift in Regulatory Thrust: OSHA Made More Business-Friendly." *Washington Post* (August 15): 1.

Goodnow, Frank J. 1900. *Politics and Administration.* New York: Macmillan.

Gorinson, Stanley M. 1985. "Antitrust Division Reorganized." *Antitrust* 7, no. 1 (October): 18–19.

Gormley, William T. 1986. "Regulatory Issue Networks in a Federal System." *Polity* 18, no. 4 (Summer): 595–620.

————. 1989. *Taming the Bureaucracy.* Princeton: Princeton University Press.

Gottron, Martha V., ed. 1982. *Regulation: Process and Politics.* Washington, D.C.: Congressional Quarterly.

Gramling, Robert. 1996. *Oil on the Edge: Offshore Development, Conflict, Gridlock.* Albany: State University of New York Press.

Gray, Wayne B., and John T. Scholz. 1993. "Does Regulatory Enforcement Work? A Panel Analysis of OSHA Enforcement." *Law and Society Review* 27, no. 1: 177–213.

Green, Donald, and Ian Shapiro. 1994. *Pathologies of Rational Choice Theory: A Critique of Applications in Political Science.* New Haven: Yale University Press.

Green, Harold P. 1963. *Government of the Atom.* New York: Atherton.

Green, Mark J., Beverly C. Moore Jr., and Bruce Wasserstein. 1972. *The Closed Enterprise System: Ralph Nader's Study Group Report on Antitrust Enforcement.* New York: Grossman.

Greenwood, Ted. 1984. *Knowledge and Discretion in Government Regulation.* New York: Praeger.

Griffin, James, and Steven Puller. 2005. "A Primer on Electricity and the Economics of Deregulation." In *Electricity Deregulation: Choices and Challenges,* eds. James Griffin and Steven Puller. Chicago: University of Chicago Press.

Grimaldi, James V. 2000. "Judge Orders Microsoft Split in 2." *Washington Post* (June 8): 1.

Gruenwald, Julianna. 1995. "Sharp Criticism Prompts Delay of Regulatory Overhaul Bill." *Congressional Quarterly Weekly Report* 53, no. 14 (April 4): 1022.

———. 1997. "New FCC Panel Members Face Pressure Over '96 Overhaul." *Congressional Quarterly Weekly Report* 55, no. 40 (October 4): 2390–2392.

Hager, George. 1995a. "Congress, Administration Agree on Finance Industry Reform." *Congressional Quarterly Weekly Report* 53, no. 9 (March 4): 678.

———. 1995b. "Furor over First Spending Bills Promises a Stormy Summer." *Congressional Quarterly Weekly Report* 53, no. 28 (July 15): 2041–2044.

———. 1995c. "As They Cut Appropriations, Add a Stiff Dose of Policy." *Congressional Quarterly Weekly Report* 53, no. 30 (July 29): 2245–2249.

Hamilton, James. 2005. *Regulation Through Revelation.* New York: Cambridge University Press.

Hammond, Bray. 1957. *Banks and Politics in America from the Revolution to the Civil War.* Princeton: Princeton University Press.

Hammond, Thomas H., and Jack H. Knott. 1992. "Presidential Power, Congressional Dominance, and Bureaucratic Autonomy in a Model of Multi-Institutional Policymaking." Michigan State University, East Lansing. Mimeo.

Hansen, Nancy Richardson, Hope Babcock, and Edwin Clark. 1988. *Controlling Nonpoint Source Water Pollution: A Citizen's Handbook.* Washington, D.C.: Conservation Foundation.

Hanushek, Eric A., and John E. Jackson. 1977. *Statistical Methods for Social Scientists.* Orlando, Fla.: Academic Press.

Harris, Richard A. 1985. *Coal Firms Under the New Social Regulation.* Durham, N.C.: Duke University Press.

Harris, Richard A., and Sidney M. Milkis. 1989. *The Politics of Regulatory Change: A Tale of Two Agencies.* New York: Oxford University Press.

———. 1996. *The Politics of Regulatory Change: A Tale of Two Agencies.* 2nd ed. New York: Oxford University Press.

Harter, Philip J. 1977. "In Search of OSHA." *Regulation* 1 (September–October): 33–39.

Hasin, Bernice Rothman. 1987. *Consumers, Commissions, and Congress: Law, Theory, and the Federal Trade Commission, 1968–85.* New Brunswick, N.J.: Transaction.

Hawley, Ellis. 1981. "Three Facets of Hooverian Associationalism: Lumber, Aviation, and Movies, 1921–1930." In *Regulation in Perspective: Historical Essays,* ed. Thomas K. McCraw. Cambridge: Harvard University Press.

Healey, Jon. 1994a. "Highlights on President's Proposals Listed According to Functions." *Congressional Quarterly Weekly Report* 52, no. 6 (February 12): 299–303.

———. 1994b. "New Telecommunications Age Hits a Snag in the Senate." *Congressional Quarterly Weekly Report* 52, no. 26 (July 2): 1776–1780.

———. 1994c. "Senate Sponsors Reinforce Communications Bill." *Congressional Quarterly Weekly Report* 52, no. 32 (August 13): 2322–2325.

———. 1995a. "Push Is on for Commercial Panel to Devise Overhaul Plan." *Congressional Quarterly Weekly Report* 53, no. 11 (March 18): 802–804.

———. 1995b. "GOP Dealing Wins the Vote for Deregulatory Bill." *Congressional Quarterly Weekly Report* 53, no. 21 (May 27): 1496–1498.

———. 1995c. "Regional Bells Ring GOP Theme with Calls for Deregulation." *Congressional Quarterly Weekly Report* 53, no. 29 (July 22): 2175–2176.

———. 1996. "Telecommunications Highlights." *Congressional Quarterly Weekly Report* 54, no. 7 (February 17): 406–420.

Heclo, Hugh. 1977. "Issue Networks and the Executive Establishment." In *The New American Political System,* ed. Anthony King. Washington, D.C.: American Enterprise Institute.

Herring, Pendelton. 1936. *Public Administration in the Public Interest.* New York: McGraw-Hill.

Higgins, Richard S., William F. Shughart II, and Robert D. Tollison. 1987. "Dual Enforcement of the Antitrust Laws." In *Public Choice and Regulation,* eds. Robert J. MacKay, James C. Miller III, and Bruce Yandle. Stanford: Hoover Institution.

Hilliard, Robert L. 1991. *The Federal Communications Commission: A Primer.* Boston: Focal.

Hofstadter, Richard. 1966. "What Happened to the Antitrust Movement? Notes on the Evolution of an American Creed." In *The Business Establishment,* ed. Earl F. Cheit. New York: Wiley.

Holden, Matthew. 1966. "Imperialism in Bureaucracy." *American Political Science Review* 60: 943–951.

Hook, Janet. 1994. "Bank Regulatory Consolidation." *Congressional Quarterly Weekly Report* 52, no. 1 (January 8): 7–8.

Hosansky, David. 1997a. "Wall Between Financial Services Dealt First Blow in House." *Congressional Quarterly Weekly Report* 55, no. 25 (June 21): 1431–1433.

———. 1997b. "Paralyzed Congress on Sidelines in Financial Services Evolution." *Congressional Quarterly Weekly Report* 55, no. 39 (September 27): 2292–2296.

———. 1997c. "House Financial Services Bill Faces Hurdles Before Floor." *Congressional Quarterly Weekly Report* 55, no. 43 (November 1).

Huber, John D., Charles R. Shipan, and Madelaine Pfahler. 2001. "Legislatures and Statutory Control of Bureaucracy." *American Journal of Political Science* 45, no. 2: 330–345.

Hughes, Siobhan. 2003a. "With Shelby at Senate Banking Helm, Privacy Protections Will Be Center Stage." *Congressional Quarterly Weekly Report* 61, no. 4 (January 25): 206–207.

————. 2003b. "Financial Privacy Legislation Approved by Senate Committee After Shelby Changes Course." *Congressional Quarterly Weekly Report* 61, no. 37 (September 27): 2359.

————. 2004. "House Passes Banking Bill Despite Feud over Regulation of Industrial Loan Companies." *Congressional Quarterly Weekly Report* 62, no. 12 (March 20): 702.

Huntington, Samuel P. 1952. "The Marasmus of the ICC." *Yale Law Journal* 61 (April): 467–509.

Hurst, James Willard. 1982. *Law and Markets in U.S. History: Different Modes of Bargaining Among Interests.* Madison: University of Wisconsin Press.

Huth, Tom. 1992. "The Incredible Shrinking Swamp." *Conde Nast Traveler* (September): 134–138, 184–191.

Idelson. Holly. 1991a. "Comparison of Proposals." *Congressional Quarterly Weekly Report* 49, no. 11 (March 16): 701–704.

————. 1991b. "Varying Interests Tie Hopes to Fast-Moving Omnibus." *Congressional Quarterly Weekly Report* 49, no. 11 (March 16): 669.

————. 1991c. "Energy Politics Emerge as Oil Crisis Subsides." *Congressional Quarterly Weekly Report* 49, no. 24 (June 15): 1569–1574.

————. 1992a. "Johnston Works to Clear Path for Revamped Energy Bill." *Congressional Quarterly Weekly Report* 50, no. 6 (February 8): 297–299.

————. 1992b. "Senate Passes Energy Bill, 94–4." *Congressional Quarterly Weekly Report* 50, no. 8 (February 22): 397–399.

————. 1992c. "Environmentalists Get a Boost from Committees' Markups." *Congressional Quarterly Weekly Report* 50, no. 15 (April 11): 941–942.

————. 1992d. "Panels Race to Rework Comprehensive Bill." *Congressional Quarterly Weekly Report* 50, no. 18 (May 2): 1152–1154.

————. 1992e. "House Leaders Urged to Forge Comprehensive Floor Bill." *Congressional Quarterly Weekly Report* 50, no. 19 (May 9): 1244.

————. 1992f. "Nuclear Industry Wins Points in House Policy Rewrite." *Congressional Quarterly Weekly Report* 50, no. 21 (May 23): 1436–1439.

————. 1992g. "House Gives Energy Bill Big Win." *Congressional Quarterly Weekly Report* 50, no. 22 (May 30): 1530–1532.

————. 1992h. "Conference Tackles Huge Bill, but Thorniest Issues Remain." *Congressional Quarterly Weekly Report* 50, no. 36 (September 12): 2710–2711.

————. 1992i. "National Energy Strategy Provisions." *Congressional Quarterly Weekly Report* 50, no. 47 (November 28): 3722–3730.

Ingraham, Patricia. 1987. "Building Bridges or Burning Them? The President, the Appointees, and the Bureaucracy." *Public Administration Review* 47, no. 5 (September–October): 425–435.

Jacobson, Louis. 1999. "Heavy Lifting on OSHA Regulations." *National Journal* 33, no. 14 (April 3): 899.

Janofsky, Michael. 2004a. "Study Ranks Bush Plan to Cut Air Pollution As Weakest of 3." *New York Times* (June 10): A16.

————. 2004b. "Inspector General Says EPA Rule Aids Polluters." *New York Times* (October 1): A12.

————. 2005. "EPA Backs Bush Plan to Cut Air Pollution by Power Plants." *New York Times* (October 28): A15.

Jasanoff, Sheila. 1990. *The Fifth Branch: Science Advisers as Policymakers.* Cambridge: Harvard University Press.

Javitt, Gail, and Susan DeFrancesco. 2001. "Just Be More Careful? CPSC Chair-Nominee Mary Sheila Gall Would Leave Many Unsafe Products in Many Unprotected Hands." *Legal Times* (June 18): 30.

Jenkins-Smith, Hank C. 1988. "Analytical Debates and Policy Learning: Analysis and Change in the Federal Bureaucracy." *Policy Sciences* 21: 169–211.

Jensen, Michael C., and William H. Meckling. 1976. "The Theory of the Firm: Managerial Behavior, Agency Costs, and Ownership Structure." *Journal of Financial Economics* 3, no. 4: 305–360.

Johnson, Cathy Marie. 1990. "New Wine in New Bottles: The Case of the Consumer Product Safety Commission." *Public Administration Review* 50, no. 1 (January–February): 74–81.

———. 1992. *The Dynamics of Conflict Between Bureaucrats and Legislators.* Armonk, N.Y.: Sharpe.

Jones, Charles O. 1975. *Clean Air.* Pittsburgh: University of Pittsburgh Press.

Joskow, Paul. 2005. "The Difficult Transition to Competitive Electricity Markets in the United States." In *Electricity Deregulation: Choices and Challenges,* eds. James Griffin and Steven Puller. Chicago: University of Chicago Press.

Kahn, Joseph. 2001. "The Energy Plan: The Details; Excessive Regulation Is Blamed for Energy Woes." *New York Times* (May 18): A1.

Kamieniecki, Sheldon. 1995. "Political Parties and Environmental Policy." In *Environmental Politics and Policy: Theories and Evidence,* 2nd ed., ed. James Lester. Durham, N.C.: Duke University Press.

Katz, James Everett. 1984. *Congress and National Energy Policy.* New Brunswick, N.J.: Transaction.

Katz, Jeffrey L. 1996. "GOP Dulls Its Cutting Edge, but Democrats Unsatisfied." *Congressional Quarterly Weekly Report* 54, no. 24 (June 15): 1675–1676.

Katzmann, Robert A. 1980a. "Capitol Hill's Current Attack Against the FTC." *Wall Street Journal* (May 7): 26.

———. 1980b. *Regulatory Bureaucracy: The Federal Trade Commission and Antitrust Policy.* Cambridge: MIT Press.

———. 1984. "The Attenuation of Antitrust." *Brookings Review* (Summer): 23–27.

Kaufman, George S., and Roger C. Kormendi, eds. 1986. *Deregulating Financial Services: Public Policy in Flux.* Cambridge, Mass.: Ballinger.

Kaufman, Herbert. 1960. *The Forest Ranger.* Baltimore: Johns Hopkins University Press.

Kauper, Thomas E. 1984. "The Role of Economic Analysis in the Antitrust Division Before and After the Establishment of the Economic Policy Office: A Lawyer's View." *Antitrust Bulletin* 29 (Spring): 111–132.

Keiser, Lael. 1995. "Workplace Safety and Health Regulation." In *Regulation and Consumer Protection,* 2nd ed., eds. Kenneth J. Meier and E. Thomas Garman. Houston: DAME.

Kelliher, Joseph. 2005. "Market Manipulation, Market Power, and the Authority of the Federal Energy Regulatory Commission." *Energy Law Journal* 26, no. 1: 1–33.

Kelman, Steven. 1980. "Occupational Safety and Health Administration." In *The Politics of Regulation,* ed. James Q. Wilson. New York: Basic.

———. 1981. *Regulating America, Regulating Sweden: A Comparative Study of Occupational Safety and Health Policy.* Cambridge: MIT Press.

———. 1987. *Making Public Policy: A Hopeful View of American Government.* New York: Basic.

Kennedy, Susan E. 1973. *The Banking Crisis of 1933.* Lexington: University of Kentucky Press.

Kettl, Donald F. 1986. *Leadership at the Fed.* New Haven: Yale University Press.

Khademian, Anne. 1993. *The SEC and Capital Market Regulation: The Politics of Expertise.* Pittsburgh: University of Pittsburgh Press.

King, David C. 1997. *Turf Wars: How Congressional Committees Claim Jurisdiction.* Chicago: University of Chicago Press.

Kingdon, John W. 1984. *Agendas, Alternatives, and Public Policies.* Glenview, Ill.: Scott, Foresman.

Kinzler, Peter. 1979. "How Business Ambushed the FTC." *Business and Society Review* 32 (Winter): 14–16.

Klein, Joel. 2000. "Inside a Mega-Case (Interview with Joel Klein)." *National Journal* 32, no. 22 (May 27): 1694–1695.

Klevorick, Alvin. 2005. "The Oversight of Restructured Electricity Markets." In *Electricity Deregulation: Choices and Challenges,* eds. James Griffin and Steven Puller. Chicago: University of Chicago Press.

Knott, Jack H., and Gary J. Miller. 1987. *Reforming Bureaucracy: The Politics of Institutional Choice.* Englewood Cliffs, N.J.: Prentice Hall.

Kolb, Charles. 1993. *White House Daze: The Unmaking of Domestic Policy in the Bush Years.* New York: Free Press.

Kolko, Gabriel. 1963. *The Triumph of Conservatism: A Reinterpretation of American History, 1900–1916.* New York: Free Press.

———. 1965. *Railroads and Regulation, 1877–1916.* Princeton: Princeton University Press.

Kovacic, William E. 1987. "The Federal Trade Commission and Congressional Oversight of Antitrust Enforcement: A Historical Perspective." In *Public Choice and Regulation,* eds. Robert J. MacKay, James C. Miller III, and Bruce Yandle. Stanford: Hoover Institution.

———. 1991. "The Reagan Judiciary and Environmental Policy: The Impact of Appointments to the Federal Courts of Appeals." *Boston College Environmental Affairs Law Review* 18, no. 2: 669–713.

Kraft, Michael. 1997. "Environmental Policy in Congress: Revolution, Reform, or Gridlock?" In *Environmental Policy in the 1990s,* 3rd ed., eds. Norman Vig and Michael Kraft. Washington, D.C.: Congressional Quarterly.

Krehbiel, Keith. 1991. *Information and Legislative Organization.* Ann Arbor: University of Michigan Press.

Krim, Jonathan. 2001. "Microsoft Makes Offer to Holdouts: Firm Says It Will Pay Legal Fees if Attorneys General Join Settlement." *Washington Post* (November 16): 1.

Kriz, Margaret. 1988. "Pesticidal Pressures." *National Journal* 20, no. 50 (December 10): 3125–3127.

———. 1992a. "Poison Gamesmanship." *National Journal* 24, no. 16 (April 18): 930–933.

———. 1992b. "The New Eco-Nomics." *National Journal* 24, no. 30 (May 30): 1280–1285.

———. 1996a. "Not-So-Silent Spring." *National Journal* 28, no. 10 (March 9): 522–526.

———. 1996b. "War Over Wastes." *National Journal* 28, no. 11 (May 11): 1042–1046.

———. 2003. "Regulators Beware." *National Journal* 35, no. 10 (March 8): 741–743.

Krugman, Paul. 2004. "The Mercury Scandal." *New York Times* (April 6): A23.

Kuntz, Phil. 1991. "Watkins: Energy Glasnost." *Congressional Quarterly Weekly Report* 49, no. 5 (February 2): 297–298.

Labaton, Stephen. 2001a. "Bush Is Putting Team in Place for a Full-Bore Assault on Regulation." *New York Times* (May 23): C1.

————. 2001b. "Senate Switch Alters Outlook for Businesses." *New York Times* (May 25): C1.

————. 2001c. "The Regulatory Signals Shift; F.T.C. Serves as Case Study of Differences Under Bush." *New York Times* (June 12): C1.

Ladd, Everett Carll, ed. 1995. *America at the Polls, 1994.* Storrs, Conn.: Roper Center.

Lambright, W. Henry, and Albert H. Teich. 1978. "Scientists and Government: A Case of Professional Ambivalence." *Public Administration Review* 38, no. 2 (March–April): 133–139.

Landy, Marc K., Marc J. Roberts, and Stephen R. Thomas. 1990. *The Environmental Protection Agency: Asking the Wrong Questions.* New York: Oxford University Press.

————. 1994. *The Environmental Protection Agency: Asking the Wrong Questions.* 2nd ed. New York: Oxford University Press.

LCV (League of Conservation Voters). 1998. *1998 National Environmental Scorecard.* http://www.lcv.org/images/client/pdfs/scorecard98.pdf.

Lee, Jennifer. 2003. "New Policy on Mercury Pollution Was Rejected by Clinton EPA." *New York Times* (December 16): A31.

————. 2004a. "3 Top Enforcement Officials Say They Will Leave EPA." *New York Times* (January 6): A20.

————. 2004b. "Most States Expect Pollution to Rise if Regulations Change." *New York Times* (February 6): A16.

Letwin, William. 1965. *Law and Economic Policy in America: The Evolution of the Sherman Antitrust Act.* New York: Random House.

Lewis-Beck, Michael, and John Alford. 1980. "Can Government Regulate Safety? The Coal Mine Example." *American Political Science Review* 74, no. 3: 745–756.

Liebeler, Wesley J. 1981. "Bureau of Competition: Antitrust Enforcement Activities." In *The Federal Trade Commission Since 1970,* eds. Kenneth W. Clarkson and Timothy J. Muris. Cambridge: Cambridge University Press.

Lindblom, Charles E. 1977. *Politics and Markets: The World's Political-Economic Systems.* New York: Basic.

————. 1982. "The Market at Prison." *Journal of Politics* 44, no. 2: 324–336.

Lipsky, Michael. 1980. *Street-Level Bureaucracy: Dilemmas of the Individual in Public Services.* New York: Sage.

Litan, Robert E. 1987. *What Should Banks Do?* Washington, D.C.: Brookings Institution.

Livingston, James. 1986. *Origins of the Federal Reserve System.* Ithaca: Cornell University Press.

Long, Norton E. 1962. *The Polity.* Ed. Charles Press. Chicago: Rand McNally.

Lowi, Theodore J. 1964. "American Business, Public Policy, Case Studies, and Political Theory." *World Politics* (July): 677–715.

————. 1969. *The End of Liberalism; Ideology, Policy, and the Crisis of Public Authority.* New York: Norton.

————. 1979. *The End of Liberalism: The Second Republic of the United States.* 2nd ed. New York: Norton.

Lowry, William. 1992. *The Dimensions of Federalism: State Governments and Pollution Control Policies.* Durham, N.C.: Duke University Press.

Lowry, William, and Charles Shipan. 1997. "Congress and the Environment: A Longitudinal Analysis." Paper delivered at the annual meeting of the Midwest Political Science Association, Palmer House Hilton, Chicago, April 10–12.

Lyon, Thomas, and John Maxwell. 2004. *Corporate Environmentalism and Public Policy.* New York: Cambridge University Press.

Maas, Arthur. 1951. *Muddy Rivers: The Army Engineers and the Nation's Rivers.* New York: Oxford University Press.

MacAvoy, Paul W. 1979. *The Regulated Industries and the Economy.* New York: Norton.

Macey, Jonathan R. 1992. "Organizational Design and Political Control of Administrative Agencies." *Journal of Law, Economics, and Organization* 18, no. 1: 93–118.

MacLeod, William C., and Robert A. Rogowsky. 1989. "Consumer Protection at the FTC During the Reagan Administration." In *Regulation and the Reagan Era: Politics, Bureaucracy, and the Public Interest,* eds. Roger E. Meiners and Bruce Yandle. New York: Holmes and Meier.

Mallory, Maria. 1987. "Susan King: A Stone Thrower Who Moved into a Glass House." *Business Week* (August 17): 59.

Manson, Patricia. 2005. "Antitrust Enforcement Wins Praise from ABA Panel." *Chicago Daily Law Bulletin* (February 7): 1.

March, James G., and Johan P. Olsen. 1989. *Rediscovering Institutions: The Organizational Basis of Politics.* New York: Free Press.

Marcus, Alfred A. 1980a. "Environmental Protection Agency." In *The Politics of Regulation,* ed. James Q. Wilson. New York: Basic.

———. 1980b. *Promise and Performance: Choosing and Implementing an Environmental Policy.* Westport: Greenwood.

———. 1984. *The Adversary Economy: Business Responses to Changing Government Requirements.* Westport: Quorum.

Marcus, Alfred A., Donald A. Geffen, and Ken Sexton. 2002. *Reinventing Environmental Regulation: Lessons from Project XL.* Washington, D.C.: Resources for the Future.

Marcuse, Herbert. 1964. *One Dimensional Man: Studies in the Ideology of Advanced Industrial Society.* Boston: Beacon.

———. 1969. *An Essay on Liberation.* Boston: Beacon.

Martin, Janet M. 1992. "George Bush and the Executive Branch." In *Leadership and the Bush Presidency: Prudence or Drift in an Era of Change?* eds. Ryan J. Barilleaux and Mary E. Stuckey. Westport: Praeger.

Marvel, Mary K. 1982. "Implementation and Safety Regulations." *Administration and Society* 14, no. 1 (May): 5–14.

Marx, Karl, and Friedrich Engels. 1962. "Manifesto of the Communist Party." In *Selected Works,* vol. 1. Moscow: Foreign Language Publishing House.

Masci, David. 1994a. "House Panel Begins Revamp of Workplace Safety Law." *Congressional Quarterly Weekly Report* 52, no. 9 (March 5): 553.

———. 1994b. "Overhaul of Job Safety Law Gains Committee Approval." *Congressional Quarterly Weekly Report* 52, no. 10 (March 12): 610.

———. 1994c. "Cutbacks in Nuclear Research Get Committee Approval." *Congressional Quarterly Weekly Report* 52, no. 21 (May 28): 1379.

———. 1994d. "Energy, Water Bill Passes with Fusion Funds Intact." *Congressional Quarterly Weekly Report* 52, no. 24 (June 18): 1604–1605.

———. 1994e. "Science Projects May Take Hits in Energy and Water Bill." *Congressional Quarterly Weekly Report* 52, no. 25 (June 25): 1696.

———. 1994f. "Conferees Cut Nuclear Reactor from Energy and Water Bill." *Congressional Quarterly Weekly Report* 52, no. 31 (August 6): 2244.

———. 1996a. "Panel Expected to Approve OSHA Overhaul Efforts." *Congressional Quarterly Weekly Report* 54, no. 9 (March 2): 560.

———. 1996b. "Panel OKs OSHA Changes, but Bill Has Uphill Fight." *Congressional Quarterly Weekly Report* 54, no. 10 (March 9): 625.

Mashaw, Jerry L. 1985. *Due Process in the Administrative State.* New Haven: Yale University Press.

Mayer, Caroline E. 2001a. "CPSC Nominee to Bring a Hands-Off Approach; Regulatory Restraint Likely to Define Agency." *Washington Post* (April 20): 23.

———. 2001b. "CPSC Choice Provokes Controversy." *Washington Post* (July 24): 1.

———. 2001c. "Bush's CPSC Choice Is Rejected; Senate Panel's Party-Line Vote Hands President First Nomination Loss." *Washington Post* (August 3): 1.

———. 2002a. "New CPSC Chairman Has No Patience with Scofflaws." *Washington Post* (August 30): 1.

———. 2002b. "Psychic Network Loses Future, Fortune; Companies Behind Miss Cleo Give Up $500 Million in Charges in FTC Settlement." *Washington Post* (November 15): 3.

Mayer, Caroline E., and James V. Grimaldi. 2001. "Bush Pick for FTC Was on '80s Staff." *Washington Post* (March 22): 1.

Mayer, Martin. 1974. *The Bankers.* New York: Ballentine.

Mayhew, David R. 1973. *Congress: The Electoral Connection.* New Haven: Yale University Press.

Mazmanian, Daniel, and Jeanne Nienaber. 1979. *Can Organizations Change? Environmental Protection, Citizen Participation, and the Corps of Engineers.* Washington, D.C.: Brookings Institution.

Mazmanian, Daniel, and Paul Sabatier. 1983. *Implementation and Public Policy.* Genview, Ill.: Scott, Foresman.

McConnell, Grant. 1966. *Private Power and American Democracy.* New York: Knopf.

McCraw, Thomas K. 1984. *Prophets of Regulation.* Cambridge: Harvard University Press.

McCubbins, Matthew D. 1985. "The Legislative Design of Regulatory Structure." *American Journal of Political Science* 29: 721–748.

McCubbins, Matthew D., Roger Noll, and Barry Weingast. 1987. "Administrative Procedures as Instruments of Political Control." *Journal of Law, Economics, and Organization* 3: 243–277.

McCubbins, Matthew D., and Thomas Schwartz. 1984. "Congressional Oversight Overlooked: Police Patrols Versus Fire Alarms." *American Journal of Political Science* 28: 165–179.

McDavid, Janet L., and Robert F. Leibenluft. 2001. "What Impact Will Bush Have?" *National Law Journal* (February 5): B8.

McGarity, Thomas O. 1991. *Reinventing Rationality: The Role of Regulatory Analysis in the Federal Bureaucracy.* Cambridge: Cambridge University Press.

McGarvey, Joe, and Mike Murphy. 2005. *Summary of the Energy Policy Act of 2005.* Columbus, Ohio: National Regulatory Research Institute.

Meier, Kenneth J. 1985. *Regulation: Politics, Bureaucracy, and Economics.* New York: St. Martin's.

———. 1987. *Politics and the Bureaucracy: Policymaking in the Fourth Branch of Government.* 2nd ed. Monterey, Calif.: Brooks/Cole.

———. 1988. *The Political Economy of Regulation: The Case of Insurance.* Albany: State University of New York Press.

Meier, Kenneth J., and E. Thomas Carman. 1995. *Regulation and Consumer Protection.* Houston: DAME.

Melnick, R. Shep. 1983. *Regulation and the Courts: The Case of the Clean Air Act.* Washington, D.C.: Brookings Institution.

Mendeloff, John. 1979. *Regulatory Safety: An Economic and Political Analysis of Occupational Safety and Health Policy.* Cambridge: MIT Press.

———. 1987. *The Dilemma of Toxic Substance Regulation: How Overregulation Causes Underregulation.* Cambridge: MIT Press.

Mervin, David. 1996. *George Bush and the Guardianship Presidency.* New York: St. Martin's.

Miller, Gary, and Terry Moe. 1983. "Bureaucrats, Legislators, and the Size of Government." *American Political Science Review* 83: 297–322.

Miller, James C., III. 1977. "Lessons of the Economic Impact Statement Program." *Regulation* 1 (July–August): 14–21.

———. 1989. *The Economist as Reformer: Revamping the FTC, 1981–1985.* Washington, D.C.: American Enterprise Institute.

Mills, Mike. 1991a. "Johnston Mixes Oil and Gas." *Congressional Quarterly Weekly Report* 49, no. 6 (February 9): 365.

———. 1991b. "Baby Bells' Fate Dangling Before Congress, Courts." *Congressional Quarterly Weekly Report* 49, no. 8 (February 23): 458–463.

———. 1993. "Clinton's Computer 'Highway' to Spur Information Age." *Congressional Quarterly Weekly Report* 51, no. 14 (April 3): 827–832.

———. 1994a. "Spirit of Cooperation Breaks Media Industry Gridlock." *Congressional Quarterly Weekly Report* 52, no. 2 (January 15): 64–69.

———. 1994b. "Communications Overhaul Gets Panels' Approval." *Congressional Quarterly Weekly Report* 52, no. 9 (March 5): 535–537.

———. 2002. "'New Era' for Communications Short-Lived." *Congressional Quarterly Weekly Report* 60, no. 9 (March 2): 584.

Mints, Lloyd. 1945. *A History of Banking Theory.* Chicago: University of Chicago Press.

Mitnick, Barry M. 1984. "The Bureaucrat as Agent." Paper presented at the annual meeting of the American Political Science Association, Washington, D.C., September.

Moe, Terry M. 1984. "The New Economics of Organization." *American Journal of Political Science* 28, no. 3: 739–777.

———. 1985. "Control and Feedback in Economic Regulation: The Case of the NLRB." *American Political Science Review* 79: 1094–1116.

———. 1987. "An Assessment of the Positive Theory of Congressional Dominance." *Legislative Studies Quarterly* 12 (November): 475–500.

———. 1988. "The Politics of Structural Choice: Toward a Theory of Public Bureaucracy." Paper presented at the annual meeting of the American Political Science Association, Washington, D.C., September.

———. 1989. "The Politics of Bureaucratic Structure." In *Can the Government Govern?* eds. John E. Chubb and Paul E. Peterson. Washington, D.C.: Brookings Institution.

———. 1990. "Political Institutions: The Neglected Side of the Story." *Journal of Law, Economics, and Organization* 6 (special issue): 213–253.

Moore, W. John. 1993. "Rough Ride." *National Journal* 25, no. 49 (December 4): 2874–2879.

Moot, John. 2004. "Economic Theories of Regulation and Electricity Restructuring." *Energy Law Journal* 25, no. 2: 273–318.

Morone, Joseph G., and Edward J. Woodhouse. 1989. *The Demise of Nuclear Energy? Lessons for Democratic Control of Technology.* New Haven: Yale University Press.

Mosher, Frederick C. 1968. *Democracy in the Public Service.* New York: Oxford University Press.

Mosher, Lawrence. 1983. "Ruckelshaus Is Seen As His Own Man in Battle to Renew Clean Water Act." *National Journal* 15, no. 29 (July 15): 1497–1500.

Mueller, Charles E. 1992. "Step 1 in Reforming U.S. Antitrust: Abolish the Economics Units at Justice and the FTC." *Antitrust Law and Economics Review* 24, no. 2: 1–20.

———. 1994. "For Want of an Advocate: Salvaging Small Business While Waiting for the Clinton Antitrust Revival." *Antitrust Law and Economics Review* 25, no. 2: 1–18.

Munro, Neil. 1998. "The New Deal." *National Journal* 30, nos. 47–48 (November 21): 2768–2772.

———. 2001a. "Microsoft 'Tied' in Knots." *National Journal* 33, no. 27 (July 7): 2175.

———. 2001b. "Microsoft Makes a Deal." *National Journal* 33, no. 45 (November 10): 3524.

Muris, Timothy J. 1981. "Statutory Powers." In *The Federal Trade Commission Since 1970,* eds. Kenneth W. Clarkson and Timothy J. Muris. Cambridge: Cambridge University Press.

Murray, Mark. 2001. "'Ergo Tour' Hits the Road." *National Journal* 33, no. 28 (July 14): 2254.

Nadel, Mark V. 1983. "Making Regulatory Policy." In *Making Economic Policy in Congress,* ed. Allen Schick. Washington, D.C.: American Enterprise Institute.

Nader, Ralph. 1965. *Unsafe at Any Speed: The Designed-In Dangers of the American Automobile.* New York: Grossman.

Nakamura, Robert T., and Frank Smallwood. 1980. *The Politics of Implementation.* New York: St. Martin's.

NAPA (National Academy of Public Administration). 1995. *Setting Priorities, Getting Results: A New Direction for the Environmental Protection Agency.* Washington, D.C.

Nash, Gerald D. 1968. *United States Oil Policy, 1890–1964.* Pittsburgh: University of Pittsburgh Press.

Nathan, Richard P. 1983. *The Administrative Presidency.* New York: Wiley.

Neale, A. D., and D. G. Goyder. 1980. *The Antitrust Laws of the U.S.A.: A Study of Competition Enforced by Law.* 3rd ed. Cambridge: Cambridge University Press.

Nelson, Michael. 1982. "A Short, Ironic History of Bureaucracy." *Journal of Politics* 44, no. 3: 747–778.

Neustadt, Richard E. 1980. *Presidential Power: The Politics of Leadership from FDR to Carter.* New York: Wiley.

Niskanen, William A. 1971. *Bureaucracy and Representative Government.* Chicago: Aldine-Atherton.

———. 1996. "Clinton's Regulatory Record." *Regulation* 19 (May–June): 25.

Nitschke, Lori. 1996. "Panel Speeds Construction at Yucca Waste Site." *Congressional Quarterly Weekly Report* 54, no. 11 (March 16): 694.

Nitschke, Lori, and Daniel J. Parks. 1999. "Who Wins if the Barriers Fall?" *Congressional Quarterly Weekly Report* 57, no. 41 (October 23): 2504–2506.

Nobel, Charles. 1986. *Liberalism at Work: The Rise and Fall of OSHA.* Philadelphia: Temple University Press.

Noll, Roger. 1985. "Government Regulatory Behavior: A Multidisciplinary Survey and Synthesis." In *Regulatory Policy and the Social Sciences,* ed. Roger Noll. Berkeley: University of California Press.

O'Donnell, Michelle. 2005. "States Challenge Break on Mercury for Power Plants." *New York Times* (May 19): B9.

Ogul, Morris. 1976. *Congress Oversees the Bureaucracy.* Pittsburgh: University of Pittsburgh Press.

Olson, Mancur. 1965. *The Logic of Collective Action: Public Goods and the Theory of Groups.* Cambridge: Harvard University Press.

Opatrny, Dennis J. 2002. "Reaction Mixed on Microsoft Decision." *The Recorder* (November 4): 1.

Ordover, Janusz A. 1997. "Bingaman's Antitrust Era: The Division's Intensified Enforcement and Internationalization Agenda." *Regulation* 20, no. 2 (Spring): 21.

Ornstein, Norman J., Thomas E. Mann, and Michael J. Malbin. 1990. *Vital Statistics on Congress, 1989–90.* Washington, D.C.: American Enterprise Institute.

Osborne, David, and Ted Gaebler. 1992. *Reinventing Government: How the Entrepreneurial Spirit Is Transforming the Public Sector.* Reading, Mass.: Addison-Wesley.

Ota, Alan K. 1998. "Congress May Sharpen Scrutiny of Giant Corporations." *Congressional Quarterly Weekly Report* 56, no. 42 (October 23, 1998): 2893–2894.

———. 1999a. "As Hill Considers Law's Failings, Companies See Their Opening." *Congressional Quarterly Weekly Report* 57, no. 6 (February 6): 331–333.

———. 1999b. "Senate Measure Seeks Speedier Merger Rulings." *Congressional Quarterly Weekly Report* 57, no. 19 (May 8): 1089.

———. 2000. "Industry Wants '99 Law Changed." *Congressional Quarterly Weekly Report* 58, no. 13 (March 25): 638.

———. 2002. "Hollings Fights Administration Antitrust Plan." *Congressional Quarterly Weekly Report* 60, no. 2 (January 18): 192.

Parks, Daniel J. 1999a. "United at Last, Financial Industry Pressures Hill to Clear Overhaul." *Congressional Quarterly Weekly Report* 57, no. 39 (October 9): 2373–2375.

———. 1999b. "Financial Services Bill in the Final Stretch." *Congressional Quarterly Weekly Report* 57, no. 41 (October 23): 2498–2503.

Parks, Daniel J., and Chuck Conlon. 1999. "Financial Services Overhaul." *Congressional Quarterly Weekly Report* 57, no. 45 (November 20): 2797–2801.

Peltzman, Sam. 1976. "Toward a More General Theory of Regulation." *Journal of Law and Economics* 19, no. 2 (August): 211–240.

Pertschuk, Michael. 1982. *Revolt Against Regulation: The Rise and Pause of the Consumer Movement.* Berkeley: University of California Press.

Peters, B. Guy. 1993. *American Public Policy: Promise and Performance.* 3rd ed. Chatham, N.J.: Chatham House.

Pfiffner, James P. 1988. *The Strategic Presidency.* Belmont, Calif.: Dorsey.

———. 1990. "Presidential Control of the Bureaucracy." In *Current Issues in Public Administration,* ed. Frederick S. Lane. New York: St. Martin's.

Pitofsky, Robert. 1979. "The Political Content of Antitrust." *University of Pennsylvania Law Review* 127, no. 4 (April): 1051–1075.

———. 1996. "An Antitrust Progress Report for the FTC: Past, Present, and Future." Remarks by the chairman of the Federal Trade Commission before the Antitrust 1996 Conference, Business Development Associates, Inc., Washington, D.C., March 4.

Ponessa, Jeanne. 1995. "Regulatory Freeze Stalls Paperwork Bill Advance." *Congressional Quarterly Weekly Report* 53, no. 6 (February 11): 453–454.

Portney, Paul R. 1984. "The Benefits and Costs of Regulatory Analysis." In *Environmental Policy Under Reagan's Executive Order: The Role of Benefit-Cost Analysis,* ed. V. Kerry Smith. Chapel Hill: University of North Carolina Press.

Portz, John. 1991. "Economic Governance and the American Meatpacking Industry." In *Governance of the American Economy,* eds. John L. Campbell, J. Rogers Hollingsworth, and Leon N. Lindberg. Cambridge: Cambridge University Press.

Posner, Richard A. 1974. "Theories of Economic Regulation." *Bell Journal of Economics and Management Science* 5, no. 3 (Autumn): 337–352.

———. 1976. *Antitrust Law: An Economic Perspective.* Chicago: University of Chicago Press.

———. 1979. "The Chicago School of Antitrust Analysis." *University of Pennsylvania Law Review* 127, no. 4 (April): 925–948.

Priest, George L. 1981. "Special Statutes: The Structure and Operation of the Magnuson-Moss Warranty Act." In *The Federal Trade Commission Since 1970,* eds. Kenneth W. Clarkson and Timothy J. Muris. Cambridge: Cambridge University Press.

Pytee, Alyson. 1989. "Baby Bell Regulators Struggle for Power." *Congressional Quarterly Weekly Report* 47, no. 34 (August 26): 2209–2214.

———. 1990. "Proposal to Unleash 'Baby Bells' Gets Mixed Reviews in House." *Congressional Quarterly Weekly Report* 48, no. 10 (March 10): 744–745.

Rabe, Barry. 1994. *Beyond NIMBY: Hazardous Waste Siting in Canada and the United States.* Washington, D.C.: Brookings Institution.

Rauch, Jonathan. 1991. "The Regulatory President." *National Journal* 23, no. 48 (November 30): 2902–2906.

Reder, Melvin W. 1982. "Chicago Economics: Permanence and Change." *Journal of Economic Literature* 20 (March): 1–38.

Redford, Emmette S. 1969. *Democracy in the Administrative State.* New York: Oxford University Press.

Reich, Charles A. 1970. *The Greening of America.* New York: Random House.

Revkin, Andrew. 2004. "Panel of Experts Finds That Anti-Pollution Laws Are Outdated." *New York Times* (January 30): A15.

Ricci, David. 1993. *The Transformation of American Politics: The New Washington and the Rise of Think Tanks.* New Haven: Yale University Press.

Riker, William H. 1962. *The Theory of Political Coalitions.* New Haven: Yale University Press.

———. 1990. "Political Science and Rational Choice." In *Perspectives on Positive Political Economy,* eds. James E. Alt and Kenneth A. Shepsle. Cambridge: Cambridge University Press.

Ringquist, Evan J. 1993. *Environmental Protection at the State Level: Politics and Progress in Controlling Pollution.* Armonk, N.Y.: Sharpe.

———. 1995. "Political Control and Policy Impact in EPA's Office of Water Quality." *American Journal of Political Science* 39, no. 2: 336–363.

Ringquist, Evan J., and Craig Emmert. 1999. "Judicial Policy Making in Published and Unpublished Decisions: The Case of Environmental Civil Litigation." *Political Research Quarterly* 52, no. 1: 7–38.

Ringquist, Evan J., Jeff Worsham, and Marc Allen Eisner. 1994. "Double Agents: Who Is Working for Whom? Building a More Realistically Grounded Theory of Influence in the Bureaucracy." Paper presented at the annual meeting of the Midwest Political Science Association, Palmer House, Chicago, April 14.

Ripley, Randall B., and Grace A. Franklin. 1982. *Policy Implementation and Bureaucracy.* Pacific Grove, Calif.: Brooks/Cole.

———. 1986. *Policy Implementation and Bureaucracy.* 2nd ed. Pacific Grove, Calif.: Brooks/Cole.

Robertson, Ross. 1968. *The Comptroller and Bank Supervision.* Washington, D.C.: Office of the Comptroller of the Currency.

Robinson, Robert, and Peg Reese. 2003. *Process Used to Develop the National Energy Policy 03-894.* Washington, D.C.: Government Accountability Office.

Rogowsky, Robert A. 1989. "Sub Rosa Regulation: The Iceberg Beneath the Surface." In *Regulation and the Reagan Era: Politics, Bureaucracy, and the Public Interest,* eds. Roger E. Meiners and Bruce Yandle. New York: Holmes and Meier.

Rom, Mark Carl. 1996. *Public Spirit in the Thrift Tragedy.* Pittsburgh: University of Pittsburgh Press.

Romer, Thomas, and Howard Rosenthal. 1987. "Modern Political Economy and the Study of Regulation." In *Public Regulation: New Perspectives on Institutions and Policies,* ed. Elizabeth E. Bailey. Cambridge: MIT Press.

Rose-Ackerman, Susan. 1992. *Rethinking the Progressive Agenda: The Reform of the American Regulatory State.* New York: Free Press.

Rosenbaum, Walter. 1989. "The Bureaucracy and Enviromental Policy." In *Environmental Politics and Policy: Theories and Evidence,* ed. James Lester. Durham, N.C.: Duke University Press.

———. 1994. "The Clenched Fist and the Open Hand: Into the 1990s at EPA." In *Environmental Policy in the 1990s,* 2nd ed., eds. Norman Vig and Michael Kraft. Washington, D.C.: Congressional Quarterly.

Rosenbloom, David H. 2000. *Building a Legislative-Centered Public Administration.* Tuscaloosa: University of Alabama Press.

Rourke, Francis E. 1984. *Bureaucracy, Politics, and Public Policy.* 3rd ed. Boston: Little, Brown.

Rubin, Alissa J. 1991. "Panel Members Put Obstacles in Way of Overhaul Bill." *Congressional Quarterly Weekly Report* 49, no. 37 (September 14): 2608.

———. 1996. "Debt-Limit Provisions." *Congressional Quarterly Weekly Report* 54, no. 13 (March 30): 872.

Rudolph, Richard, and Scott Ridley. 1986. *Power Struggle: The One Hundred–Year War over Electricity.* New York: Harper and Row.

Rueschemeyer, Dietrich. 1983. "Professional Autonomy and the Social Control of Expertise." In *The Sociology of the Professions: Lawyers, Doctors, and Others,* eds. Robert Dingwall and Philip Lewis. New York: St. Martin's.

Rushefsky, Mark E. 1986. *Making Cancer Policy.* Albany: State University of New York Press.

Sabatier, Paul A. 1977. "Regulatory Policy Making: Toward a Framework of Analysis." *National Resources Journal* 17 (July): 415–460.

———. 1987. "Knowledge, Policy Oriented Learning, and Policy Change." *Knowledge* 8: 649–692.

———. 1988. "An Advocacy Coalition Framework of Policy Change and the Role of Policy-Oriented Learning Therein." *Policy Sciences* 21: 129–168.

Sabatier, Paul A., and Hank Jenkins-Smith. 1993. *Policy Change and Learning: An Advocacy Coalition Approach.* Boulder: Westview.

Sabatier, Paul A., and Neil Pelkey. 1987. "Incorporating Multiple Actors and Guidance Instruments into Models of Regulatory Policy-Making." *Administration and Society* 19, no. 2 (August): 236–292.

Sammon, Richard. 1994. "Focus of 'Reform' Effort Shifts to Ending Hill's Exemptions." *Congressional Quarterly Weekly Report* 52, no. 27 (July 9): 1855–1856.

Sanders, Elizabeth. 1981. *The Regulation of Natural Gas: Policy and Politics, 1938–1978.* Philadelphia: Temple University Press.

———. 1986. "Industrial Concentration, Sectional Competition, and Antitrust Politics in America, 1880–1980." *Studies in American Political Development* 1 (Fall): 142–214.

———. 1987. "The Regulatory Surge of the 1970s in Historical Perspective." In *Public Regulation: Perspectives on Institutions and Policies,* ed. Elizabeth E. Bailey. Cambridge: MIT Press.

Sanjour, William. 2001. "Bush Environmental Enforcement Appointee Is Bad News." *Tom Paine.com.* http://www.pwp.lincs.net/sajour,shregardus.htm.

Sarasohn, Judy. 1980. "Critics Successful in Reducing Funds for Public Participation." *Congressional Quarterly Weekly Report* 38, no. 44 (November 1): 3273–3276.

Scalia, Eugene. 2000. "OSHA's Ergonomics Litigation Record: Three Strikes and It's Out." In *Cato Policy Analysis.* Washington, D.C.: Cato Institute.

Scanlon, Terrance. 1985. "We Want to Work with Companies, Not Against Them." *U.S. News and World Report* 98, no. 14 (April 15): 74.

Schattschneider, E. E. 1935. *Politics, Pressures, and the Tariff: A Study of Free Private Enterprise in Pressure Politics, As Shown in the 1929–1930 Revision of the Tariff.* New York: Prentice-Hall.

———. 1960. *The Semisovereign People. A Realist's View of Democracy in America.* New York: Holt, Rinehart, and Winston.

Scheberle, Denise. 1998. *Federalism and Environmental Policy: Trust and the Politics of Implementation.* Washington, D.C.: Georgetown University Press.

Scher, Seymour. 1960. "Congressional Committee Members as Independent Agency Overseers: A Case Study." *American Political Science Review* 54: 911–920.

Schiesel, Seth. 1997. "At FCC Confirmation Hearings, Emphasis Will Be on Competition." *New York Times* (September 29): C1, C10.

Schlozman, Kay Lehman, and John T. Tierney. 1986. *Organized Interests in American Democracy.* New York: Harper and Row.

Schoenbrod, David. 1994. *Power Without Responsibility: How Congress Abuses the People Through Delegation.* New Haven: Yale University Press.

Scholz, John T., and Feng Heng Wei. 1986. "Regulatory Enforcement in a Federal System." *American Political Science Review* 80: 1249–1270.

Seelye, Katharine. 2001. "EPA Enforcement Nominee Withdraws." *New York Times* (September 18): A16.

———. 2002. "Top EPA Official Quits, Criticizing Bush's Policies." *New York Times* (March 1): A19.

Seiberg, Janet. 2001. "Bush Trust-Busters Staying the Course." *National Law Journal* (September 3): A18.

———. 2002. "FTC Has Warning for Merging Companies." *New York Law Journal* (June 20): 5.

Seidman, Harold, and Robert Gilmour. 1986. *Politics, Position, and Power.* 4th ed. New York: Oxford University Press.

Shanahan, John. 1997. "Regulating the Regulators: Regulatory Process Reform in the 104th Congress." *Regulation* 20 (January–February): 27.

Shanley, Robert. 1992. *Presidential Influence and Environmental Policy.* Westport: Greenwood.

Shapiro, Joseph P., and Sharon Golden. 1987. "Crossing Swords over Consumer Safety." *U.S. News and World Report* 103, no. 17 (October 26): 28.

Sharma, Amol. 2004. "Internet Phoning Pulls Congress Back into the Telecom Fray." *Congressional Quarterly Weekly Report* 62, no. 8 (February 21): 491–494.

Shipan, Charles R. 1998. "Keeping Competitors Out: Broadcast Regulation from 1927–1996." In *A Communications Cornucopia,* eds. Roger G. Noll and Monroe E. Price. Washington, D.C.: Brookings Institution.

Silbergeld, Mark. 1995. "The Revitalization of the Federal Trade Commission." In *Regulation and Consumer Protection,* 2nd ed., eds. Kenneth J. Meier and E. Thomas Garman. Houston: DAME.

Sinclair, Upton. 1906. *The Jungle.* New York: Doubleday, Page.

Singer, James W. 1975a. "FTC Planning Office Plays Role in Decisionmaking." *National Journal* 7, no. 37 (September 13): 1298–1302.

———. 1975b. "New OSHA Head May Signal Change in Agency's Approach." *National Journal* 7, no. 51 (December 27): 1725–1734.

———. 1976. "New OSHA Task Force: Political Payoff or False Alarm?" *National Journal* 8, no. 28 (July 10): 973–975.

———. 1977. "A New OSHA Tries to Put Its Pieces Back Together Again." *National Journal* 9, no. 27 (July 2): 1046–1049.

———. 1979. "The Federal Trade Commission: Business's Government Enemy No. 1." *National Journal* 13, no. 41 (October 13): 1676–1680.

Siskind, Frederic B. 2002. *20th Century OSHA Enforcement Data: A Review and Explanation of the Major Trends.* Washington, DC: Occupational Safety and Health Administration.

Skrzycki, Cindy. 2004. "OSHA Withdraws More Rules Than It Makes, Reviews Find." *Washington Post* (October 5): 1.

Smith, Mark. 2000. *American Business and Political Power.* Chicago: University of Chicago Press.

Smith, Robert S. 1979. "Compensating Wage Differentials and Public Policy: A Review." *Industrial and Labor Relations Review* 32: 339–396.

Smith, V. Kerry. 1984. *Environmental Policy Under Reagan's Executive Order: The Role of Cost-Benefit Analysis.* Chapel Hill: University of North Carolina Press.

Snyder, Louis L. 1945. "The American-German Pork Dispute, 1879–1891." *Journal of Modern History* 17, no. 1: 16–28.

Spriggs, James. 1997. "Explaining Federal Bureaucratic Compliance with Supreme Court Opinions." *Political Research Quarterly* 50, no. 3: 567–594.

Stanton, John. 2003a. "EPA Eyes the Elimination of Some Criminal Field Offices." *Congress Daily* (July 7): 1.

———. 2003b. "Environmentalists Worry About EPA Enforcement Shuffle." *Congress Daily* (July 11): 3.

Starek, Roscoe B., III. 1995. "Consumer Protection in the Age of Borderless Markets and the Information Revolution." Remarks before the Conference on Transborder Consumer Regulation and Enforcement, University House, Balmain Crescent, Australian National University, Canberra, July 7.

———. 1997. "The Consumer Protection Pyramid: Education, Self-Regulation, and Law Enforcement." Remarks before the Korea Consumer Festival '97, Seoul, December 2.

Starobin, Paul. 1988. "FCC and Congress Clash over Proper Roles." *Congressional Quarterly Weekly Report* 46, no. 9 (February 27): 479–484.

———. 1989a. "FCC's Patrick Moves to Appease Lawmakers." *Congressional*

Quarterly Weekly Report 47, no. 57 (February 4): 229.

———. 1989b. "Baby Bells Lobby for Chance to Offer New Services." *Congressional Quarterly Weekly Report* 47, no. 87 (February 25): 380–383.

Steorts, Nancy Harvey. 1983. "Protecting Consumers the Reagan Way." *U.S. News and World Report* 95, no. 6 (August 8): 50–51.

Stewart, Richard B. 1975. "The Reformation of American Administrative Law." *Harvard Law Review* 88, no. 8 (June): 1667–1813.

Stigler, George J. 1968. *The Organization of Industry.* Homewood, Ill.: Irwin.

———. 1971. "The Theory of Economic Regulation." *Bell Journal of Economics and Management Science* 2, no. 1 (Spring): 3–21.

Stillman, Richard J. 1996. *The American Bureaucracy: The Core of Modern Government.* 2nd ed. Chicago: Nelson-Hall.

Stockman, David. 1986. *The Triumph of Politics: How the Reagan Revolution Failed.* New York: Harper and Row.

Stokey, Edith, and Richard Zeckhauser. 1978. *A Primer for Policy Analysis.* New York: Norton.

Stoll, Neal R., and Shepard Goldfein. 2002. "Antitrust Trade and Practice: Did the FTC Take a Cruise?" *New York Law Journal* (October 15): 3.

Stone, Deborah A. 1988. *Policy Paradox and Political Reason.* Glenview, Ill.: Scott, Foresman.

Stone, Judith Lee. 1995. "Automobile Safety Regulation." In *Regulation and Consumer Protection,* 2nd ed., eds. Kenneth J. Meier and E. Thomas Garman. Houston: DAME.

Stone, Peter H. 2001. "Block Those Regs!" *National Journal* 33, no. 7 (February 17): 484–487.

Stone, Peter H., and Louis Jacobson. 1999. "From the K Street Corridor." *National Journal* 31, no. 14 (April 3): 899.

Sullivan, E. Thomas. 1986. "The Antitrust Division as a Regulatory Agency: An Enforcement Policy in Transition." *Washington University Law Quarterly* 64, no. 4 (1986): 260–275.

Swallow, Wendy. 1981. "Consumer Product Agency Is Battling for Its Independence and Its Life." *National Journal* 13, no. 26 (June 27): 1163–1165.

Taxpayers for Common Sense. 2005. "Cost Analysis of the Energy Policy Act of 2005." Washington, D.C.

Taylor, Andrew. 1994a. "Interstate Branching Boosted by Panel Vote, Dodd Shift." *Congressional Quarterly Weekly Report* 52, no. 5 (February 5): 230–231.

———. 1994b. "Bill on Interstate Branching Sails Through Senate Panel." *Congressional Quarterly Weekly Report* 52, no. 8 (February 26): 461–462.

———. 1995a. "Once Again, House Panel Bids to Revamp Glass-Steagall." *Congressional Quarterly Weekly Report* 53, no. 17 (April 29): 1161–1165.

———. 1995b. "Committee Approves Narrow Glass-Steagall Rewrite." *Congressional Quarterly Weekly Report* 53, no. 19 (May 13): 1308–1309.

———. 1995c. "Glass-Steagall Bill to Be Paired with Regulatory Relief." *Congressional Quarterly Weekly Report* 53, no. 24 (June 17): 1721–1723.

———. 1995d. "Thrifts Could Be Transformed As Insurance Crisis Looms." *Congressional Quarterly Weekly Report* 53, no. 31 (August 5): 2342–2344.

———. 1995e. "Bankers' Opposition Stalls Glass-Steagall Rewrite." *Congressional Quarterly Weekly Report* 53, no. 41 (October 21): 3193.

———. 1996a. "Glass-Steagall Rewrite Stalls As Industry Foes Do Battle." *Congressional Quarterly Weekly Report* 54, no. 9 (March 2): 539–542.

———. 1996b. "Banking Panel's Leach Pushes to Get Overhaul to Floor."

Congressional Quarterly Weekly Report 54, no. 21 (May 25): 1455.

———. 1996c. "Glass-Steagall Repeal Measure Sparks Raucous Markup." *Congressional Quarterly Weekly Report* 54, no. 23 (June 8): 1582–1583.

———. 1997a. "Banks in No Hurry for Rewrite of Financial Service Laws." *Congressional Quarterly Weekly Report* 55, no. 16 (April 19): 898–900.

———. 1997b. "Under Treasury Plan, Congress to Decide Tough Issues." *Congressional Quarterly Weekly Report* 55, no. 21 (May 24): 1190.

Thompson, Frank J., and Michael J. Scicchitano. 1987. "State Implementation and Federal Enforcement Priorities: Safety Versus Health in OSHA and the States." *Administration and Society* 19 (May): 95–124.

Thurber, James A. 1991. *Divided Democracy: Cooperation and Conflict Between the President and Congress.* Washington, D.C.: Congressional Quarterly.

Timney, Mary. 2004. *Power for the People: Protecting States' Energy Policy Interests in an Era of Deregulation.* Armonk, N.Y.: Sharpe.

Tolchin, Susan J. 1979. "Presidential Power and the Politics of RARG." *Regulation* 3 (July–August): 44–49.

Tolchin, Susan J., and Martin Tolchin. 1983. *Dismantling America: The Rush to Deregulate.* Boston: Houghton Mifflin.

Tollison, Robert D. 1991. "Regulation and Interest Groups." In *Regulation: Economic Theory and History,* ed. Jack High. Ann Arbor: University of Michigan Press.

Trescott, Paul B. 1963. *Financing American Enterprise.* New York: Harper and Row.

Tugwell, Franklin. 1988. *The Energy Crisis and the American Political Economy.* Stanford: Stanford University Press.

Tunstall, Jeremy. 1986. *Communications Deregulation: The Unleashing of America's Communications Industry.* Oxford: Basil Blackwell.

Tussing, Arlon R., and Bob Tippee. 1995. *The Natural Gas Industry: Evolution, Structure, and Economics,* 2nd ed. Tulsa, Okla.: Pennwell.

Uslaner, Eric M. 1989. *Shale Barrel Politics.* Stanford: Stanford University Press.

Van Horn, Carl E., ed. 1992. *The State of the States.* 2nd ed. Washington, D.C.: Congressional Quarterly.

Van Koevering, Thomas, and Nancy Sell. 1986. *Energy: A Conceptual Approach.* Englewood Cliffs, N.J.: Prentice Hall.

Van Natta, Don, Jr. 2002. "Executive Order Followed Energy Industry Recommendation." *New York Times* (April 4): A18.

Varney, Christine. A. 1996. "Advertising and Unfair Competition: FTC Enforcement." Remarks before the American Legal Institute–American Bar Association Eleventh Annual Advanced Course on Product Distribution and Marketing, Snowbird, Utah, January 17.

Victor, Kirk. 1989. "OSHA's Turnabout." *National Journal* 21, no. 47 (November 25): 2889–2892.

———. 1991. "Quayle's Quiet Coup." *National Journal* 23, no. 27 (July 6): 1676–1680.

———. 1992. "Tale of the Red Tape." *National Journal* 24, no. 12 (March 21): 684–687.

———. 1995a. "Sitting Duck." *National Journal* 27, no. 31 (August 5): 1999–2003.

———. 1995b. "Point Man." *National Journal* 27, nos. 33–34 (August 19): 2092–2097.

———. 1996. "Media Monsters." *National Journal* 28, no. 10 (March 2): 480–484.

———. 1997a. "Reach Out and Crush Someone." *National Journal* 29, no. 23 (June

7): 1132–1133.

———. 1997b. "Sending Mixed Signals on Cable TV." *National Journal* 29, no. 40 (October 4): 1962–1963.

———. 1997c. "All Is Not Quiet on the Telecom Front." *National Journal* 29, no. 46 (November 15): 2311–2312.

———. 1998. "Static for the New FCC Chairman." *National Journal* 30, no. 9 (February 28): 460.

———. 1999. "Ringing Endorsements." *National Journal* 31, no. 26 (June 26): 1880–1884.

Vietor, Richard H. K. 1994. *Contrived Competition Regulation and Deregulation in America.* Cambridge: Belknap Press of Harvard University Press.

Vig, Norman J., and Michael E. Kraft. 1984. "Environmental Policy from the Seventies to the Eighties." In *Environmental Policy in the 1980s,* eds. Norman J. Vig and Michael E. Kraft. Washington, D.C.: Congressional Quarterly.

Viscusi, W. Kip. 1982. "Health and Safety." *Regulation* 6 (January–February): 34–37.

———. 1983. *Risk by Choice.* Cambridge: Harvard University Press.

———. 1985. "Cotton Dust Regulation: An OSHA Success Story?" *Journal of Policy Analysis and Management* 4, no. 3: 325–343.

———. 1986. "Reforming OSHA Regulation of Workplace Risks." In *Regulatory Reform: What Actually Happened,* eds. Leonard W. Weiss and Michael W. Klass. Boston: Little, Brown.

———. 1992. *Fatal Tradeoffs: Public and Private Responsibilities for Risk.* New York: Oxford University Press.

Viscusi, W. Kip, John M. Vernon, and Joseph E. Harrington Jr. 1995. *Economics of Regulation and Antitrust.* 2nd ed. Cambridge: MIT Press.

Vogel, David. 1978. "Why Businessmen Distrust Their State: The Political Consciousness of American Corporate Executives." *British Journal of Political Science* 8, no. 1: 45–78.

———. 1989. *Fluctuating Fortunes: The Political Power of Business in America.* New York: Basic.

Walker, Martin. 1996. *The President We Deserve. Bill Clinton: His Rise, Falls, and Comebacks.* New York: Crown.

Wallerstein, Immanuel. 1976. *The Modern World System: Capitalist Agriculture and the Origins of the European World-Economy in the Sixteenth Century.* New York: Academic Press.

Walton, Thomas F., and James Langenfeld. 1989. "Regulatory Reform Under Reagan: The Right Way and the Wrong Way." In *Regulation and the Reagan Era: Politics, Bureaucracy, and the Public Interest,* eds. Roger E. Meiners and Bruce Yandle. New York: Holmes and Meier.

Waterman, Richard. 1989. *Presidential Influence and the Administrative State.* Knoxville: University of Tennessee Press.

Waterman, Richard, Amelia A. Rouse, and Robert L. Wright. 2004. *Bureaucrats, Politics, and the Environment.* Pittsburgh: University of Pittsburgh Press.

Waxman, Henry. 1992. "The Environmental Pollution President." *New York Times* (April 29): A24.

Weaver, Suzanne. 1977. *Decision to Prosecute: Organization and Public Policy in the Antitrust Division.* Cambridge: MIT Press.

Weber, Edward. 1998. *Pluralism by the Rules: Conflict and Cooperation in Environmental Regulation.* Washington, D.C.: Georgetown University Press.

Weidenbaum, Murray L. 1981. *Business, Government, and the Public.* 2nd ed.

Englewood Cliffs, N.J.: Prentice-Hall.

———. 1997. "Regulatory Process Reform." *Regulation* 20 (January–February): 20.

Weingast, Barry R. 1984. "The Congressional-Bureaucratic System: A Principal Agent Perspective (with Applications to the SEC)." *Public Choice* 44: 147–191.

Weingast, Barry R., and Mark J. Moran. 1982. "The Myth of the Runaway Bureaucracy: The Case of the FTC." *Regulation* 6 (May–June): 22–28.

———. 1983. "Bureaucratic Discretion or Congressional Control? Regulatory Policymaking by the Federal Trade Commission." *Journal of Political Economy* 91: 765–800.

Weisman, Jonathan. 1996a. "Senate Approves Nevada Dump, but Opponents See Victory." *Congressional Quarterly Weekly Report* 54, no. 31 (August 3): 2185.

———. 1996b. "Republicans Battle Unions on Hill and on Airwaves." *Congressional Quarterly Weekly Report* 54, no. 32 (August 10): 2250–2252.

———. 1996c. "True Impact of GOP Congress Reaches Well Beyond Bills." *Congressional Quarterly Weekly Report* 54, no. 36 (September 7): 2515–2520.

———. 1996d. "January Resuscitation Likely for Interim Yucca Site Bill." *Congressional Quarterly Weekly Report* 54, no. 39 (September 28): 2751.

———. 1996e. "Drive to Open Power Industry to Competition Gains Steam." *Congressional Quarterly Weekly Report* 54, no. 41 (October 12): 2911–2917.

———. 1996f. "Chances for Quick Action on Deregulation Fading." *Congressional Quarterly Weekly Report* 54, no. 47 (November 23): 3307–3308.

Weiss, Laura B. 1981. "Reagan, Congress Planning Regulatory Machine Repair." *Congressional Quarterly Weekly Report* 39, no. 10 (March 7): 401–414.

Weiss, Leonard W. 1979. "The Structure-Conduct-Performance Paradigm and Antitrust." *University of Pennsylvania Law Review* 127, no. 4 (April): 1104–1140.

Wellborn, David M. 1977. *Governance of Federal Regulatory Agencies.* Knoxville: University of Tennessee Press.

Wells, Jim, James Cooksey, and Nancy Crothers. 2005. *National Energy Policy: Inventory of Major Federal Energy Programs and Status of Policy Recommendations.* Washington, D.C.: Government Accountability Office.

Wells, Robert Marshall. 1995a. "GOP Planning to Topple Wall of Rules Around Workplace." *Congressional Quarterly Weekly Report* 53, no. 19 (May 13): 1328–1330.

———. 1995b. "Labor, HHS Panel Takes Aim at Clinton Initiatives." *Congressional Quarterly Weekly Report* 53, no. 28 (July 15): 2070–2075.

Wenner, Lettie. 1997. "Environmental Policy in the Courts." In *Environmental Policy in the 1990s.* 3rd ed., eds. Norman Vig and Michael Kraft. Washington, D.C.: Congressional Quarterly.

West, Robert. 1974. *Banking Reform and the Federal Reserve.* Ithaca: Cornell University Press.

———. 1977. *Banking Reform and the Federal Reserve.* Ithaca: Cornell University Press.

West, William. 1985. *Administrative Rulemaking: Politics and Process.* Westport: Greenwood.

———. 1995. *Controlling the Bureaucracy: Institutional Constraints in Theory and Practice.* Armonk, N.Y.: Sharpe.

White, Eugene. 1983. *The Regulation and Reform of the American Banking System.* Princeton: Princeton University Press.

Whittle, Richard. 1983. "Administration Seeks Banking Law Revisions."

Congressional Quarterly Weekly Report 41, no. 29 (July 23): 1523.

Wildavsky, Ben. 1996. "Carrying On." *National Journal* 28, no. 18 (May 4): 991–994.

Wilke, John R. 2003. "Ardent Reaganite Plays a New Tune As Head of the FTC." *Wall Street Journal* (April 4): 1.

Williams, Stephen F. 1985. *The Natural Gas Revolution of 1985*. Washington, D.C.: American Enterprise Institute.

Williamson, Oliver E. 1975. *Markets and Hierarchies: Analysis and Antitrust Implications*. New York: Free Press.

———. 1985. *The Economic Institutions of Capitalism: Firms, Markets, Relational Contracting*. New York: Free Press.

Wilson, Graham K. 1985. *The Politics of Safety and Health: Occupational Safety and Health in the United States and Britain*. Oxford: Oxford University Press.

———. 1990. *Business and Politics*. Chatham, N.J.: Chatham House.

Wilson, James Q. 1973. *Political Organizations*. New York: Basic.

———. 1980. *The Politics of Regulation*. New York: Basic.

———. 1984. "The Politics of Regulation." In *The Political Economy: Readings in the Politics and Economics of American Public Policy,* eds. Thomas Ferguson and Joel Rogers. Armonk, N.Y.: Sharpe.

———. 1989. *Bureaucracy: What Government Agencies Do and Why They Do It*. New York: Basic.

Wilson, Woodrow. 1887. "The Study of Administration." *Political Science Quarterly* 2: 197–222.

Wines, Michael. 1981. "They're Still Telling OSHA Horror Stories, but the 'Victims' Are New." *National Journal* 13, no. 45 (November 7): 1985.

———. 1983a. "Scandals at EPA May Have Done in Reagan's Move to Ease Cancer Controls." *National Journal* 15, no. 25 (June 18): 1264–1269.

———. 1983b. "Auchter's Record at OSHA Leaves Labor Outraged, Business Satisfied." *National Journal* 15, no. 40 (October 1): 2008–2013.

Winslow, Walter T. 1985. "Organization and Operation of the Federal Trade Commission." *Antitrust Law Journal* 54, no. 1: 117–121.

Wisenberg, Dinah. 1990. "Looser Leash Likely for 'Baby Bells.'" *Congressional Quarterly Weekly Report* 48, no. 21 (May 26): 1652.

Wittman, Donald A. 1995. *The Myth of Democratic Failure: Why Political Institutions Are Efficient*. Chicago: University of Chicago Press.

Wolak, Frank. 2005. "Lessons from the California Electricity Crisis." In *Electricity Deregulation: Choices and Challenges,* eds. James Griffin and Steven Puller. Chicago: University of Chicago Press.

Wood, B. Dan. 1988. "Principals, Bureaucrats, and Responsiveness in Clean Air Enforcement." *American Political Science Review* 82: 213–234.

———. 1992. "Modeling Federal Implementation As a System: The Clean Air Case." *American Journal of Political Science* 36: 40–67.

Wood, B. Dan, and James Anderson. 1993. "The Politics of Antitrust Regulation." *American Journal of Political Science* 31: 1–39.

Wood, B. Dan, and Richard W. Waterman. 1991. "The Dynamics of Political Control of the Bureaucracy." *American Political Science Review* 85: 801–828.

———. 1993. "The Dynamics of Political Bureaucratic Adaptation." *American Journal of Political Science* 37: 497–528.

Woolley, John. 1993. "Conflict Among Regulators and the Hypothesis of Congressional Dominance." *Journal of Politics* 55, no. 1: 92–114.

Worsham, Jeff. 1997. *Other People's Money: Policy Change, Congress, and Bank Regulation*. Boulder: Westview.

Worsham, Jeff, Marc Allen Eisner, and Evan J. Ringquist. 1997. "Assessing the Assumptions: A Critical Analysis of Agency Theory." *Administration and Society* 28 (February): 419–440.

Yaeger, Mary. 1981. *Competition and Regulation: The Development of Oligopoly in the Meat Packing Industry.* Greenwich, Conn.: JAI.

Yandle, Bruce. 1989. *The Political Limits of Environmental Regulation.* Westport: Quorum.

Yates, Douglas. 1982. *Bureaucratic Democracy: The Search for Democracy and Efficiency in American Government.* Cambridge: Harvard University Press.

Yergin, Daniel. 1991. *The Prize: The Epic Quest for Oil, Money, and Power.* New York: Simon and Schuster.

Young, James H. 1989. *Pure Food: Securing the Federal Food and Drug Act of 1906.* Princeton: Princeton University Press.

Index

Administrative Procedure Act, 41
AFL-CIO: and Ballinger bill defeat, 209; and OSHA standards, 204, 206
Agencies. *See* Regulatory agencies; *specific agency*
Agency theory. *See* Principal-agent theory
Agricultural Adjustment Administration, 36
Agricultural sector: and antitrust legislation, 10; government regulation of, 12; and ICC rate making, 9
Air pollution regulations: and acid rain, 154; and air quality standards, 182; cap-and-trade approach to, 186–187, 188; and Clear Skies initiative, 186–187; deterioration standard in, 11; and New Source Review standard, 187–188; and technological advancement, 15. *See also* Clean Air Act (AAC)
American Bankers Association, 97, 103, 109
American Bar Association's Antitrust Section, 67, 88
American Petroleum Institute (API), 267
American Public Gas Association, 275
American Telephone and Telegraph. *See* AT&T
American Textile Manufacturers v.

Donovan, 201–202
America's Community Bankers, 98
Antitrust agencies: authority limits of, 69–70; budgets, OMB and, 68; congressional oversight of, 69; and international antitrust enforcement, 80; merger and competition issues in, 81–82; policy subsystem actors in, 67; professionalization in, 88
Antitrust Division, Department of Justice: activism of, 74, 78; budget and expenditures, 61, 62, 64–65, 84–85; business community and, 79; civil proceedings in, 62–64; competition advocacy in, 76; Decree Project of, 76; grand jury system in, 64; horizontal bias in, 74, 75, 76, 77; internal efficiency enhancement in, 79; Microsoft investigation of, 82–83, 86–87; and per se offenses, 62, 64; premerger screening task of, 64; and presidential power of appointment, 68; and price theory application, 76; price-fixing cases in, 78; proactive posture of, 62; and "reinventing government" initiative, 79; reorganization and rule reversal in, 76, 78; structure of, 61, 63*fig*
Antitrust Division, Economic Policy Office (EPO), 71, 76; expansion and professionalization of, 72

Antitrust Improvement Act, 72
Antitrust regulation, 58–61; activism in, 85–86; bureaucratic politics perspective on, 75; and business associations, 67; Chicago school of economics and, 71, 73; competition advocacy of, 75; congressional roles in, 66–69; dual authority in, 61; economic doctrines and rationale in, 57, 59–60, 71–74, 75, 76; enforcement in, 66–70, 78, 85–86, 88–89; global economy and, 78; horizontal restraints in, 76, 81; industrial economy and, 35; international enforcement of, 79–81, 82; legislation, 5, 10, 58–61, 77; and market preservation, 4–5, 7–8, 35; mergers and, 58, 72, 74, 75, 76, 77, 81, 84–85; and monopoly power, 57–58; multiple regulators in, 35; partisan battles in, 88; policy subsystem of, 66–70; political dimensions of, 35, 57; power of appointment in, 68; presidential influence over, 66–68; and price discounts/price-fixing, 58, 81; professional codes of ethics in, 75; and monopoly power, 57–58, 35; reform and reversal in, 74–75; rule modifications in, 75; salience of, 60–61, 67; and Sherman Act violations, 57; stakeholders in, 67; statutory imprecision in, 58–59; structure-conduct-performance (SCP) framework in, 59–60, 71, 73; vertical restrictions on, 72, 81. See also Antitrust Division; Federal Trade Commission (FTC)
Arctic National Wildlife Refuge (ANWR), proposals for drilling in, 284, 291
AT&T: aggressive acquisition tactics of, 120; antitrust violations of, 122, 133; breakup of, 133; deregulation of, 14–15; and local market entry, 136; merger activity of, 140, 141; monopoly of, 121, 122
Atomic Energy Commission (AEC), 270; dismantling of, 274
Auchter, Thorne, 205–206
Automobile pollution, and air quality regulations, 154

Banking Act of 1933. See Glass-Steagall

Banking Act
Banking system, 95–100; capital and reserve requirements in, 93; commercial banks in, 96–97; control of, 94; court rulings on, 110; credit unions in, 98–99; and credit union share drafts, 102; duality of, 93, 96, 102; and expansion into new markets, 101–106, 108–112; FDIC insurance of, 97; and Glass-Steagall restrictions, 100, 101, 102, 106–108; industrial loan companies in, 115; and insurance and securities sales, 108, 109; interest-bearing checking in, 104; interstate branching in, 104–105, 107–108; licensing/certification requirements in, 12; mutual savings banks in, 102; nonbank competition with, 101–102; and nonbank-bank loophole, 104–105; and privacy issues, 112, 113–114; regulatory agencies responsible for, 96; reserve banks in, 94; trade associations of, 97; and transaction costs, 7; universal capital requirements for, 106; wholesale financial institutions (woofies) in, 112–113. See also Financial regulation; Savings and loan associations
Barnett Bank v. Nelson, 109
Bell System: antitrust suit against, 121; AT&T's competition with, 141; and "Baby Bells," 122, 133, 135, 141; and broadband market, 142–145; interconnection agreement for, 136; and long-distance service, 133, 135, 138, 140; mergers, 140–141; monopoly of, 121; regulation, 124; and rulings on entry, equipment, and rate-setting, 121–122; technological revolution and, 132; vertical integration strategy in, 119–120, 121. See also Telephony
Bilateral negotiated environmental agreements, 161
Bingham, Eula, 204
Binghaman, Anne K., 78
Bituminous Coal Operators Association (BCOA), 265
Broadcasting regulation: and barriers to entry, 137; licensing in, 125; public

service mission in, 122; roots of, 122–123; Telecommunications Act's provisions for, 136–137

Brokerage firms, bank-like operations of, 102–103

Bureaucratic politics theory, 19–22, 28; applied to Clinton presidency, 184; and antitrust politics, 70, 73; and bureaucrats' self-interest, 20; central theme in, 19; and 1970s' environmental movement, 175; typology of personalities in, 20–21. *See also* Regulatory bureaucracy

Bureaucratic professionalization, and policy complexity, 313–314

Bureau of Consumer Protection (BCP): budget, 247, 251; rule making in, 225

Bureau of Economics, 64, 72–73, 74, 75; gatekeeper function of, 241–242; and regulatory obstruction, 243

Bush, George H. W., administration: antienvironmentalist appointments of, 179; consumer protection policy of, 245–247; energy regulatory policy of, 283–288; environmental policy of, 172–173, 178–180; financial regulatory policy in, 107; and greenhouse gas emissions, 54–55; level of regulatory activity in, 48; New Paradigm of, 47; Quale Council, 44–45; subsystems perspective on, 180

Bush, George W., administration: antitrust policy of, 77, 84–87; and clean air policy, 154, 184–185, 186–189; consumer protection policy of, 251–252; energy policy of, 290–294; environmental policy of, 53, 54–55, 184–189; and EPA enforcement reforms, 185–186; and OSHA policy, 211–218; partnerships and voluntary initiatives of, 16, 161, 215; producer-dominated subsystem in, 290–294; and REGO initiatives, 54; and regulatory review process, 53–54

Business associations: and antitrust enforcement, 67; and consumer regulation, 233–234

Business sector: and compliance costs, 199–200; and devolution of OSHA

regulations, 206; and ergonomics standards, 208, 210, 213; and *The New OSHA* reinvention plan, 209–210; self-inspection in, 206; and small business regulation guidance, 50–51

California's electric utility deregulation experiment, 296–299; catastrophic results of, 297; and divesture of utility monopolies, 297; key elements of, 297; and recovery of "stranded costs," 297

Capture theory, 9–10

Carter administration: antitrust policy of, 71–74, 75; energy policy of, 276–280; environmental policy of, 170, 173; FTC and, 236; gas policy of, 279; and 1979 oil embargo, 276; nuclear policy of, 279–280; OSHA relations with, 199–200, 204–205; regulatory budget of, 44; regulatory reforms of, 40–41; and Three Mile Island accident, 276, 280

Celler-Kefauver Act, 58

Certification requirements, 12, 14

Cheney, Dick, 53, 184, 290–291

Chicago school of economics, antitrust policy influence of, 71, 73

Civil Aeronautics Act, 36

Clayton Antitrust Act, 35, 57–58, 140

Clean Air Act (CAA), 152–155, 181; attempts to revise, 186–187; ethanol requirement in, 289; New Source Review requirements of, 291; 1977 amendments to, 11; reauthorization of, 154, 179

Clean Air Interstate Rule (CAIR), 188

Clean Air Mercury Rule (CAMR), 188–189

Clean Water Act (CWA), 181; amendments to, 177; and civil suits against polluters, 174; goal of zero polluted discharge in, 155; Nixon's veto of, 173; tools for implementing, 155

Climate Partners initiative, 55

Clinton administration, 45–52; antitrust regulation policy of, 77–83; consumer protection policy of, 247–250; energy policy of, 288–289; environmental policy of, 180–184, 187, 188;

and financial regulation/deregulation, 109, 114; FTC relationship with, 78–79; and OSHA regulation, 207–211; principle-agent perspective on, 184; and public-private partnerships, 16, 161; regulatory record of, 48–49; reinventing government (REGO) initiative of, 45, 46, 47, 79; and Republican "Contract with America," 49–50; and Republican-led Congress's environmental agenda, 181–182; subsystems perspective on, 184; and superfund cleanups, 158

Coal: characteristics and distribution of, 259–260; extraction of, 260, 266

Coal industry: clean coal technology in, 287; Energy Policy Act and, 287, 292–293; environmental standards for, 275; and mining/strip mining regulation, 149, 279; and organized labor, 266; and producer trade associations/subsidies, 265; safety concerns in, 260; and subsystem equilibrium, 265–266

Code authorities, 36

Command and control regulations, 13

Commerce Department, and business self-regulation, 35

Communications Act, 119, 122, 123, 124, 125, 134

Community Reinvestment Act, 111

Competitive coalitions, policymaking in, 24

Competitive Equality Banking Act, 106

Complexity: defined, 29; and dominant coalition politics, 30; and elected officials' exercise of control, 29–30; of regulations, 55, 313–314

Comprehensive Environmental Response, Compensation, and Liability Act (CERCLA), 157, 162; amendments to, 177

Congress: agency monitoring of, 26; antitrust regulation and, 66–69, 78; and broadband issues, 142–145; and consumer protection regulation, 69, 74, 76, 222, 232, 234, 244; and dominant coalition politics, 23; and energy policy, 272, 276; energy-related legislation of, 275, 284–285; environmental legislation of, 153, 154, 156–157, 162, 170–171, 173, 177, 181–182; and EPA structure, 163; ergonomics rule and, 213; financial deregulation and, 103–104; ICC rate setting and, 34; mine safety legislation of, 265; natural gas legislation of, 268–269; and new rule review provisions, 51–52; oil industry regulation of, 267; OSHA funding and oversight, 195, 200; and policy salience/complexity, 29; principal-oriented actions of, 177; and radioactive waste disposal, 283; and REGO ("reinventing government") initiative, 47–48; and regulatory reform, 41; and telecommunications regulation, 120, 121, 122, 132–133, 134

Congressional Budget Office (CBO), and significant bills, 50

Congressional Review Act, 210, 213

Conservative think tanks, environmental regulation role of, 169–170

Consumer information provision, as regulatory tool, 13

Consumer Product Safety Act (CPSA), 228, 229, 231, 233

Consumer Product Safety Commission (CPSC), 37, 54, 228–233; budget, 228, 229*fig*, 243, 247, 253; Congress and, 234, 239–240, 245; and corrective remedies, 233–234; court challenges to, 235; creation, background and politics of, 238–239; directorates' role in, 229; economic impact determination in, 231; enforcement duty and options of, 231, 232–233; and intervenor funding, 232; and justification for new standards, 231–232; major consumer protection statutes enforced by, 224*fig;* mandate and jurisdiction, 228; offeror system and, 232, 239, 240, 244; penalties, 233; presidential relations with, 234; reauthorization of, 239, 240–241, 243, 244, 246; reporting requirements of, 246; risk assessment of, 231; rule making, 231, 244, 246–247; scientific analysis in, 231; state and local cooperation with, 229; strategic goals of,

250; structure and size of, 228–229, 230*fig;* violations (2004), 232–233

Consumer protection agencies: and agency capture, 233; business ties with, 233–234; congressional oversight of, 235; and expanded standing in the courts, 235

Consumer protection regulation, 6–7, 35, 108, 221–255; and automobile safety, 221–222; bureaucracy in, 254–255; and caps on civil penalties, 253; complexity and salience of, 222–224; corporate promotion of, 221; corrective actions/recalls in, 253–254; and deceptive marketing practices, 249, 251–252; and elected officials, 224; enforcement record of, 250; and fair labeling, 222, 223; and information scarcity/asymmetry, 6–7; and Nader's Raiders, 222, 225–226; of 1970s, 236–241; offeror process in, 38; and potential for significant harm, 222–223; product standards in, 222; and professional interest associations, 233; of Progressive Era, 221; and the public interest, 221; and public-private partnerships, 250; and resource constraints, 247; rule making in, 233; standard-setting process in, 38; subsystem politics in, 233–235, 245, 253, 254; and transaction costs, 7; venues for interest group influence in, 233; and voluntary standards, 232, 236–238, 239–240, 244–245, 246–247, 250. *See also* Bureau of Consumer Protection (BCP); Consumer Product Safety Commission (CPSC); Federal Trade Commission (FTC)

Continental T.V. v. GTE Sylvania, 71–72, 77–78

Contract with America: critics of, 52; legislation of, 49–52; and regulatory agency control and accountability, 52; and Republic Party platform, 49–50

Coping agencies: defined, 21; principal control in, 27–28

Corn, Morton, 203

Council on Wage and Price Stability (COWPS), 40

Court system, federal: and antitrust agency authority, 69; and antitrust violations, 58; and citizens rights to sue, 172; and economic analysis, 71–72, 77–78; environmental protection decisions of, 172, 174; FCC rulings of, 122; and financial deregulation, 110–111; financial subsystem battles in, 103; and *illegal per se* violations, 58, 72; and OSHA health regulations, 200–202, 206; and partisan differences, 172; and private property rights infringement, 173; and rule of reason, 58–59, 72; and telecommunications regulation, 133, 134; telemarketing rulings of, 252

Craft agencies, defined, 21

Credit unions, regulatory overview of, 98–99

Currency Act of 1863, 92–93

Democratic Party platform, environmental advocacy in, 46

Department of Commerce, and broadcasting regulation, 122

Department of Energy (DOE): creation and functions of, 276; dismantling of, 289; and energy conservation, 283; limited authority of, 276–277; and nuclear waste disposal, 149; organizational structure of, 277, 278*fig;* and product quality standards, 12; Reagan's attempts to abolish, 281; and subsidies, 13

Department of Justice: and AT&T investigation, 120; Environment and Natural Resources Division of, 166; major antitrust statutes enforced by, 59*fig. See also* Antitrust Division

Department of Labor: ergonomics policy of, 214; and OSHA regulations, 199

Depository Institutions Deregulation and Monetary Control Act (DIDMCA), 103

Deregulation: as appropriate policy tool, 15–16; of natural monopolies, 14–15; and negative externalities, 15. *See also specific policy agency, area*

Dingell, John, 104, 105, 106–107, 132,

244, 285–285; and broadband service expansion, 142–145
Do Not Call Implementation Act, 252
Dole, Bob, 50
Dominant coalition politics: and complexity of policy issues, 30; policy production in, 23; and protection of agency autonomy, 175

Economic regulations, versus new social regulations, 3
Economics: and antitrust decisionmaking models, 59–60; and antitrust regulation, 71
Eisenhower administration, and oil import quotas, 268
Elected officials: bureaucrats' information advantage over, 19–20; complexity and salience impacts on, 29–30; core-periphery voting patterns of, 10, 11; interest group alliances with, 22; policy change limitations on, 314; and principal-agent relationship, 25; and regulation rewards, 8; self-interest motivation of, 20; and social regulation, 37
Electric utilities: and block pricing, 280; and deregulation, 294–299; economic-technical-political changes in, 294–295; and exempt wholesale generators (EWGs), 295, 296; FERC authority in, 293, 295; as government-sanctioned monopoly, 294, 296; hydroelectric projects of, 285, 287; and independent power production, 280–281; and net metering, 293; and nondiscriminatory access to transmission grids, 296; PURPA requirements for, 293, 295; and regulatory formats, 271–272; tax breaks for, 285; and utility holding companies, 271; and wholesale competition, 295–296. See also California's electric utility deregulation experiment
Electricity: as natural monopoly, 270; production and transmission of, 263–264; as public versus private provision, 263–264
Emergency Planning and Community Right-to-Know Act (EPCRTKA),

158
Endangered Species Act, 149, 179
Energy: renewable sources of, 264, 274; and comparative US consumption, 259, 260, 261. See also specific energy source
Energy policy, 257–300; activity areas in, 257; administrative strategy in, 275; appliance efficiency standard in, 275; conservation in, 267, 277–279, 280, 284; corporate average fuel economy (CAFÉ) standards in, 275, 277, 284, 286; demand-side focus of, 276; depletion allowances in, 267; and dominant coalition subsystem politics, 258, 273; and federal subsidies (1970–2004), 282fig; and fossil fuel development on public lands, 291; Gulf War impact on, 286; import quotas in, 268; and interstate sale of power, 272; legislation, 284–285, 286–288, 292–294; low salience of, 257–258; and oil embargo (1973–1974), 273; and pipeline construction, 268, 284–285, 286; and policy subsystem reorganization, 276; politics of, 257; and pollution standards, 260; price and entry tools in, 273, 274–275; producer group domination in, 273, 274, 276, 277; reasons for variations in, 265; and regional/state political economies, 260; safety standards in, 260; and self-regulation, 266; state and local, 268, 271, 279; subsystems politics in, 285, 288; supply-side focus on, 274, 292; synthetic fuels program in, 281–282; and tax policy, 267. See also specific energy source, administration
Energy Policy Act, 286–288, 292–294; budgetary analysis of, 292; coal technology and import provisions in, 287; conservation and renewable energy sources in, 292; and electric utilities, 287–288; and fossil fuels, 292–293; goals and provisions of, 286–287; and nuclear power liability, 293; and US dependence on foreign oil, 287
Energy Policy and Conservation Act

(EPCA), standards of, 275
Energy Research and Development Administration (ERDA), 274; merger of, 276
Environmental impact statement, as regulatory tool, 160
Environmental Protection Agency (EPA), 37, 51, 154, 162–168, 292; advocacy stance of, 166; budget, 163, 164*fig*, 176, 177, 179; CERCLA requirements for, 162; congressional environment for, 171–172; creation of, 162; devolution of policy authority in, 176; enforcement stance reforms in, 185–186; environmental advocates appointed to, 173–174; and federal court decisions, 172; and global warming, 182; and hazardous waste disposal, 156–157, 158; and internalized production costs, 6; and intra-agency coordination, 162, 163–164; Office of Enforcement and Compliance Assurance, 185–186; organizational structure of, 163; oversight, 171; pesticide regulation of, 158–160; as procedural organization, 21; professional schisms in, 165–166; as public health agency, 312–313; and Reagan deregulation strategies, 176–177; regional offices of, 167–168; and regulatory negotiation ("reg-neg") and regulatory reinvention at, 183; Republican-controlled oversight of, 181; "Smart Enforcement" plan, 185–186; staff education and recruitment in, 164–166; and state governments, 167, 183–184; statutory obligations of, 162, 164; strategic goals (2003–2008), 163*fig*; traditional enforcement in, 186; and voluntary compliance audits, 186; voluntary environmental program of, 161
Environmental regulation, 149–189; agency autonomy in, 180; command and control, 178; criticism of, 154; economic incentives in, 178–179; economic and technological changes and, 178–179; environmental impact statements in, 152; evolution of, 173–189; executive-legislative inter-

actions in, 170–172; and interinstitutional conflict, 170; and ISO 14001 standards, 161; legislation, reauthorization, and revision of, 161–162; and party positions/party affiliation, 171–172, 175; principal-agent approach to, 177–178, 179, 189; product prohibitions in, 11–12; public interest and market failure as justifications for, 150; public support for, 171, 174, 177, 178; regional political economy approach to, 77; and reinventing government initiative, 183; restructuring of, 186–189; salience and complexity of, 150–151; and statutory activity of 1970s, 174; technical production standards in, 13–14. *See also* Environmental Protection Agency (EPA); Pollution regulation; *specific administration*
Environmental regulatory subsystem, 168–173, 178; advocacy coalitions in, 168–170, 174, 175; bureaucratic politics in, 175; contentious partisanship in, 158; economic rationality coalition in, 169–170, 174, 175; environmental quality coalitions in, 168–169; presidential support in, 170; strategies of Republican-led Congress in, 181–182
Experience goods, and information scarcity, 6
Externalities, defined, 6

Fair Credit Reporting Act, 114
Farm economy, USDA regulations for, 36
Federal Advisory Committee Act (FACA), 128
Federal Communications Act, 36
Federal Communications Commission (FCC), 36; advisory committees of, 128–129; Bell System and, 121–122, 141; broadcasting licensing of, 123, 136; budgetary growth of, 125, 126*fig*; congressional mandate and oversight of, 131, 132–133, 134; creation of, 119; and deregulation via rule making, 134; and economic deregulation, 132–133; investigative

function in, 131; merger standard of, 140; oversight and enforcement responsibilities in, 125; policy bureaus of, 125; policy subsystem of, 131–133; policymaking, 129–131; presidency and, 132, 134; price-cap initiative of, 133; and public interest standards, 141; rule change and rule making in, 128, 129–130; staff offices of, 126–128; and state-level utility commissions, 123, 125–126; structure and functions of, 124–129; and technological change, 131–132, 146; Telecommunications Act and, 137, 138; universal service mission of, 131; and wireless communications, 125

Federal Deposit Insurance Corporation (FDIC), 36, 94, 100–101, 106, 115; bailout, 107; governance and principal regulatory role of, 97

Federal Energy Regulatory Commission (FERC), 276, 285; and California's deregulation experiment, 298–299; and interstate regulation, 271, 272

Federal environmental statutes, 153*fig.* *See also* Environmental regulation

Federal Financial Institutions Examination Council (FFIEC), 99

Federal Home Loan Bank Board (FHLBB), 95, 102, 103; activities of, 98; dismantling of, 106. *See also* Office of Thrift Supervision (OTS)

Federal Home Loan Mortgage Corporation, 98

Federal Insecticide, Fungicide, and Rodenticide Act (FIFRA): purpose and strategies of, 158–159; reform of, 159–160

Federal Power Commission (FPC), 271, 272; gas price regulation of, 267–268, 275; merger of, 276

Federal Register: OSHA rule making published in, 197, 213; and reasons for rule denial, 231

Federal Reserve ("the Fed"): and bank failures, 100–101; Board of Governors, 96–97; budget, 94; and deregulation, 102, 110–111; and economic stability, 94; Great Depression and, 94; and money market funds, 101–102; obligations and activities of, 96; organizational structure and oversight of, 94; regulatory responsibilities of, 97; source of authority in, 95

Federal Reserve Act, 93–94, 96

Federal Reserve Board of Governors, 94

Federal Savings and Loan Insurance Corporation (FSLIC), 36, 95, 98, 104; dismantling of, 106

Federal Trade Commission (FTC): activism of, 73, 236–238, 246, 248; adjudicative activities of, 225; and advertising aimed at children, 237; advertising substantiation concept in, 236; antifraud prosecutions of, 249, 251; antitrust statutes enforced by, 59*fig*; authority and enforcement responsibilities of, 58; budget, 64–65, 74, 77, 84, 225, 237–238, 241, 251; business relations with, 234; case sources and prosecution of, 65–66; competition advocacy of, 75; Congress and, 69, 74, 76; and consumer complaints and redress, 248–249, 251–252; cost-benefit analysis in, 238; creation of, 35; dependence on the courts, 70; and disclosure requirements, 236–237; economic doctrine and analysis in, 64, 66, 71–74, 241–242, 247, 249; enforcement and prosecutions of, 64, 74, 75; Fairness Doctrine and, 236, 238; and interest group mobilization, 237; and international antitrust/consumer protection, 80, 248; and Internet transactions, 248, 252; intervenor funding of, 248; legislation, 223*fig*; 224*fig*, 226–227; mandate and activities of, 225, 227–228; mergers and, 58; 1970s' activities and environment of, 236–238; and occupational self-regulation, 237; organizational features of, 225–226; presidential relations with, 234; professionalization of, 226, 247; and Reagan-Bush presidencies, 241–247; regulatory reform program of, 249; reinvention and new orientation in, 79; reorganization of, 72–73,

74–77, 236; reporting requirements of, 246; rule-making proceedings of, 236–237, 238, 248; and self-regulation, 248; structure of, 64–65, 65*fig*; and telemarketing sales, 249; and unfair/deceptive practices, 242–243, 247. *See* also Bureau of Consumer Protection (BCP)

Federal Trade Commission Act (FTCA), 35, 58, 65, 236, 238, 242

Federal Trade Commission Improvements Act, 73–74, 235, 241

Federal Water Pollution Control Act. *See* Clean Water Act (CWA)

Financial Institutions and the Nation's Economy. See FINE study reform recommendations

Financial Modernization Act, 106

Financial regulation: Congress and, 103–104, 106–116; coordination of activities in, 99; courts' umpire role in, 103; creation of government-backed currency in, 93; and deregulation, 92, 100–116; and deregulation via regulation, 110; and disintermediation, 116; *FINE* study reform recommendations for, 100–101; and Garn—St. Germain deregulation compromise, 103–104; and mergers, 109, 110; and money market funds, 101–102; New Deal, 94–95, 100, 101, 102, 106–108, 115, 116; origin and evolution of, 92–100; and presidential agenda setting, 103; public scrutiny of, 100; and regulator-led deregulation, 103, 104–105, 107, 110; and Republican takeover of Congress, 108–109; salience of, 91–92; and separation of financial intermediaries, 94–95, 100, 106, 108–110; subsystem competition in, 99–103; supervisory uniformity in, 99; technological and policy change impacts on, 101; trade associations and, 97. *See also specific financial intermediary*

Financial Services Act, provisions and impacts of, 111–113, 114

Financial Services Committee, 114

FINE study reform recommendations, 100–101

Food and Drug Administration (FDA), 6–7

Food Quality Protection Act (FQPA), 160

Ford administration, 40; and consumer protection agencies, 239–240; energy crisis response of, 275–276; and FTC reorganization, 236; and OSHA regulations, 203–204

Gall, Mary Sheila, 54, 253

Garn, Jake, 103–104, 105

General Electric, and consumer hazard reporting, 253

Glass-Steagall Banking Act: and bank expansion, 94–95, 110–111; dismantling of, 111; and financial deregulation, 101–105; mandate and reforms of, 36; regulator-backed redefinition of, 106–108

Global environmental problems, 177

Gore, Al, 134, 135; energy policy and, 288; environmental advocacy of, 46; and regulatory review process, 53; and reinventing government initiative, 47, 183, 184; and telecommunications regulation, 134, 135

Gorsuch-Burford, Anne, 176–177

Government Accountability Office (GAO), 290–291

Government Performance and Results Act, 47–48

Gramm, Phil, 111–112

Green Lights (voluntary environmental program), 161

Greenspan, Alan, 108

Hartford Fire Insurance v California, 80

Hart-Scott-Rodino Antitrust Improvements Act, 58

Hazardous air pollutants, and cap-and-trade programs, 188–189

Hazardous and Solid Waste Amendments (HSWA), 156

Hazardous waste regulation, 156–158; cleanup costs in, 157–158; Congress and, 156–157; manifest tracking system for, 156; and superfund legislation, 157–158; tools, 156, 158

Hoover, Herbert, 122

Hunt Commission, 100

Independent Bankers Association of America (IBAA), 97, 103, 105
Independent Insurance Agents of America (IIAA), 109
Independent regulatory commissions (IRCs): adjudication process in, 34; organizational form and powers of, 34; potential for capture and rigidity in, 38; rule-making process in, 34. *See also specific agency*
Industrial coalitions, and environmental policy, 169
Industrial relations regulation, 36
Industrial Union Department v. American Petroleum Institute, 201
Industrial Union Department v. Hodgson, 202
Industry profitability, and regulatory capture, 9–10
Information scarcity, as justification for regulation, 13
Insurance industry, banking system and, 10, 109
Interest groups: and agency decision-making, 26–27; antienvironmental/grassroots, 169–170; by-product theory of, 192; and competitive coalition politics, 24; and public policy formation, 22; and subsystems theory, 22–24
Interior Department: and business self-regulation, 35; Oil and Gas Division of, 266
Internal Revenue Service (IRS), 21
International Antitrust Enforcement Assistance Act, 80
Internet, 138; merger plans for, 141; Voice-over-Internet Protocol (VoIP) in, 145–146
Interstate Commerce Commission (ICC): capture of, 9; creation and mandate of, 34; interstate trucking regulation of, 36; and railroad regulation, 34; rate setting, 34, 35; supervisory role of, 120

Job Creation and Wage Enhancement Act, 49

Johnson, Lyndon, 238
Johnston, J. Bennett, 284, 286, 287, 289
Joint Committee on Atomic Energy (JCAE), 270

Kirkpatrick, Miles, 68, 71, 75, 236
Kyoto Protocol, 54; Republican opposition to, 182–183

Labor unions: and industrial relations regulation, 36; support for OSHA in, 204–205, 206, 207, 214
Leach, Jim, 108–110, 111–112, 115
Legislators. *See* Elected officials
Legislation. *See* Congress; *specific policy area*
Liability conditions, as regulatory tool, 13–14, 157
Licensing requirements, 12, 14; as regulatory tool, 160
Low Level Waste Policy Act, 280

Mann-Elkins Act, 120
Market competition: and cost internalization, 6; and firms as price takers, 5; and information scarcity or asymmetry, 6–7; of monopolies, 5, 8; and public goods, 5–6; and transactions costs, 7
Market failure: as rationale for environmental regulation, 150; sources of, 5, 57
McCain, John, 137–138, 140, 141, 142
Mergers. *See specific policy agency, area*
Methyl tertiary butyl ether (MTBE) manufacturers, liability protection for, 291–292
Metzenbaum, Howard, 77
Miller, James C., III, 74–75, 242–243
Money market funds (MMFs): characteristics of, 101; and reserve requirements, 102
Monopolies: and antitrust regulations, 35, 37–38, 39; regulated, 5; rents, 5, 8, 39. *See also* Natural monopolies
Motor Carrier Act, 36
Municipal Wastewater Treatment Grant program (MWTGP), 155, 156
Munn v. Illinois, 4
Muris, Timothy, 251–252

Nader, Ralph, 37, 38, 221, 222; FTC report of, 225–226; Study Group, antitrust report of, 67
National Association of Broadcasters (NABA), 122
National Bank Act of 1863, 93, 110
National Commission of Product Safety, 238
National Credit Union Association (NCUA), 99; and deregulation debate, 102, 103
National Energy Policy Development Group (NEPDG): key regulatory targets of, 291; secretive deliberations of, 289–290
National Energy Program (NEP I), 277
National Energy Security Act, 284
National Environmental Performance Partnership System (NEPPS), 183–184
National Environmental Policy Act (NEPA), 152, 173
National Highway Traffic Safety Administration, product quality standards of, 12
National Institute for Occupational Safety and Health (NIOSH), 203, 209; chemical exposure standards of, 206; OSHA's relations with, 196, 203; research function of, 194
National Labor Relations Board, 36
National Performance Review, 209
National Pollutant Discharge Elimination System (NPDES), 155
National Recovery Administration (NRA), 36; and oil industry's cartel arrangements, 268
Natural gas: characteristics of, 261; extraction and distribution technology for, 261, 262; importation of, 269; local regulation of, 268; as natural monopoly, 268; and pipeline monopolies, 268, 269; policy subsystem, 268–269; and universal service guarantee, 268
Natural Gas Policy Act, 279
Natural monopolies: broadcasting as, 122–123; defined, 5; creation of, 5; deregulation of, 14–15; rail transportation industry as, 34; telephone service as, 121

New Deal regulations, 35–36; of oil and natural gas, 268–269. *See also* Glass-Steagall Banking Act
New Source Review (NSR) standard, 187–188
Nixon presidency, 38; and banking regulation, 100; clean water act veto of, 173; consumer protection approach of, 236, 238–239; energy crisis response of, 274–275; environment policy of, 173; FTC appointments of, 68; and OSHA regulation, 202–203; Project Independence of, 274; and regulatory reform, 40
North American Electric Reliability Council, 272–273
North American Free Trade Agreement (NAFTA), 80
Nuclear industry: and Clinton budget cuts, 288; Energy Policy Act and, 287, 293; iron triangle subsystem of, 269–270; legislation on, 280; licensing of, 283, 286; Next Generation Nuclear Plant Project of, 293; as public enterprise, 270; and radioactive waste disposal, 263, 280, 285
Nuclear power: and breeder reactor technology, 279–280; civilian, 270; production and fuel cycle of, 262–263
Nuclear Regulatory Commission (NRC), 149, 274, 285; and environmental legislation revision, 162; and licensing of nuclear power plants, 283

Occupational health regulations: asbestos standard in, 201; compliance costs of, 192, 197; design and risk assessment of, 196–197; economic and scientific complexities in, 192–194, 201–202; efforts to weaken, 206; and inspections during Reagan and Carter administrations, 205–206
Occupational Safety and Health Act (OSH Act), 193, 194, 197, 198, 201, 202, 204, 207–208; attempts to amend, 203, 208–209; general duty clause of, 191, 209, 214–215
Occupational Safety and Health

Administration (OSHA), 37, 38, 51, 191–220; activism of, 219; adoption of private-sector standards in, 202; Alliance Program of, 217–218; autonomy, legislative restrictions on, 200; budget and resources, 194*fig*, 205, 207, 211–212; business opposition to, 199, 203, 206; cancer policy of, 204, 206; chemical exposure standards of, 206; compliance assistance of, 209, 212; congressional exemptions/restrictions on, 200, 219; and "cooperative regulator" goal, 206, 212, 213; cost-benefit analysis in, 201–202, 208, 219; creation and early activism of, 191, 202–203; critics of, 192, 202; and decentralization through devolution, 219; elimination of rules in, 212–213; enforcement and penalties in, 198, 199, 202, 203, 205, 207, 209, 214–215, 218; and ergonomics standards and guidelines of, 54, 208, 210–211, 213–215; and funding priorities, 211–212; and "general duty clause" litigation, 214–215; "New Federalism" impacts on, 203; inspections, 203, 205–206, 207, 212, 216; *The New OSHA* blueprint for reinventing, 209–210; organizational structure of, 192–195; organized labor's support for, 204–205, 206, 207, 214; partnerships and voluntarism in, 206, 209–210, 212, 213–216; policy salience and complexity levels in, 192–194, 199; policy subsystem, 199–202; political environment of, 202–218, 219–220; and presidential agendas and tools, 199–200, 218; principal-agent perspective on, 218–219; professional socialization and bias in, 195–196, 197; professional staffing problems at, 203, 206; as professionalized bureaucracy, 219; REGO and, 210, 212–213, 215; and regulation by effect over substance, 204; and regulation reviews, 199–200; and regulatory revocations, 204–205, 206; Republican opposition to empowering, 208; rule making, 197, 199, 202, 208, 210; and standard deletion project, 204; and standard feasibility, 201; standard-setting process in, 197; and state-subsidized plans, 198, 219; violations and penalties of, 198, 204, 207, 209, 212; and voluntarism, 206, 212, 215; and workplace injury and fatality rates, 218. *See also* OSHA Strategic Partnership Program (OSPP)

Occupational Safety and Health Review Commission (OSHRC), 194

Occupational safety regulations, 192; industry's role in development of, 196; as primary OSHA focus, 203–204

Office of Coal and the Bureau of Mines, 265

Office of Information and Regulatory Affairs (OIRA), 50; and cost-benefit analysis requirement, 44, 45; and regulatory review, 46–47, 53–54

Office of Management and Budget (OMB), 31, 42, 175, 234; and antitrust agency budgets, 68; OSHA relations with, 195; and regulation reviews, 199; significant regulation tracking requirement for, 52. *See also* Office of Information and Regulatory Affairs (OIRA)

Office of the Comptroller of the Currency (OCC), 107; creation and responsibilities of, 93, 96; and commercial endeavors by banks, 108, 109; and deregulation, 110; and non-bank-bank loophole, 104–105

Office of Thrift Supervision (OTS), 100–101, 106, 107; organization and tasks of, 98

Oil sector, 288–289; conservation measures in, 274; environmental protection standards for, 275; and gas price deregulation, 274–275, 281; and government policy, 266; policy subsystem of, 266; and price controls/deregulation, 274, 279; and production controls, 266; Strategic Petroleum Reserve of, 275; US dependence on imports of, 261, 274, 283, 287; World War I policy context of, 266–267. *See also* Petroleum

Omnibus Appropriations Act, 52

OSHA Strategic Partnership Program (OSPP), 210; benefits of membership in, 216; defined, 216; labor participation in, 216; and repetitive motion injuries, 216–217

Paperwork Reduction Act, 41; reauthorization of, 50
Patrick, Dennis, 132
Performance standards, as regulatory tool, 160
Pertschuk, M., 236, 237
Pesticide regulation, 158–160; benefit-risk analysis in, 158; criticism of, 162; strategies for, 159; testing and registration requirements in, 159–160
Petroleum: as "common pool" resource, 266; consumption of, 260, 261; characteristics and distribution of, 260–261; extraction technology, 260–261; foreign sources of, 268; resources, 267–268. See also Oil sector
Pitofsky, Robert, 78–79, 247
Poison Prevention Packaging Act, 233–234
Pollution laws, voluntary compliance with, 176
Pollution regulation: and air quality, 152–155, 174; and "best available/best practicable" equipment mandate, 153, 155; Congress and, 153, 154, 159; and evidence of improved quality, 178; indemnification and compensation provisions in, 159; liability conditions in, 157; and marketable emission permits, 154–155; and national ambient air quality standards (NAAQS), 153–154; and National Priorities List sites, 157, 158; and nonpoint water pollution, 155–156; of pesticides, 158–160; and "polluter pays" principle, 157; PSD regulations, 154; standards, 153; state, federal support for, 176; states' role in, 153–154, 155–156, 167; statuary basis for, 149–150, 151–160; and superfund creation, 157; tools and strategies for, 155, 157, 159, 160–162; and toxic elements in water, 156; and types of pollution (residuals), 150; and water quality, 155–156
Powell, Michael, 142–143
Presidency: and consumer protection agencies, 234–235; and environmental regulations, 170; and FCC policy change, 129; and OSHA regulations, 199–200. See also specific administration
President's Task Force on Regulatory Relief, creation of, 42–43
Price controls, as regulation tool, 12
Principal-agent theory, 24–27, 189; and agent discretion, 26–27; and antitrust politics, 70, 73; applicability, and salience/complexity levels, 30; applications of, 177, 184; and bureaucratic professionalization, 28; and congressional-bureaucratic relations, 27; information asymmetry and uncertainty in, 25–26; and interest group involvement, 26
Product quality standards, as regulatory tool, 12
Production agencies: defined, 21; and principal-agent controls, 27
Progressive Era, federal regulations of, 33–35
Prohibitions, as regulatory tool, 11–12
Project XL, 183, 184
Property rights: as regulatory tool, 13–14; and transaction costs, 7
Proxmire, William, 106, 107
Public goods: environmental quality as, 150; nonexcludability and nonrivalry characteristics of, 5–6; telephone service as, 123
Public interest concept, 4
Public policy, defining, 2
Public Utility Holding Company Act (PUHCA), 268, 271, 285, 287; electric utilities and, 287; repeal of, 293–294
Public Utility Regulatory Policy Act (PURPA), 268, 277; conservation mandate of, 280–281; and IPPs, 293, 294, 295; requirements of, 280–281
Pure Food and Drug Act, 35

Quantity regulations, 12

Quayle, Dan, 44, 179

Radio Act, 122
Railroad regulation, 9
Reagan administration: antiregulation stance of, 175–178; antitrust policy of, 68, 74–77; Congress and, 156–157; consumer protection in, 241–245; environmental policy in, 155, 159, 170, 172–173; level of regulatory activity in, 48; market discipline energy policy of, 281–283; nuclear power support of, 282–283; OSHA policy of, 200, 206–207, 219; principle-agent perspective on, 177; regulation agenda and goals in, 42; and regulatory reform, 43–44; subsystems perspective on, 178; telecommunications policy of, 132–133
Regulation Review Committee, 199
Regulation(s): and barriers to entry, 8, 37; and cartel maintenance theory, 8–9; and competition among regional political economies, 10–11; complexity of, 313–314; and consumption of public goods, 5–6; corporate, 36; cost-benefit analysis of, 40 41, 42, 43, 44, 45; debates and criticism, 1, 8, 37; defining, 2–3; and deregulation, 15; and economic recovery/stability, 36; Great Depression and, 35–36; for industry protection, 9–10; and internalization of production costs, 6; and market failure, 4–5, 7; and monopoly power, 35; New Deal, 36–37; rate-setting in, 12; and "regulatory burden," 33; and regulatory review and analysis, 40–41, 43, 199–200; rule-making process in, 38, 40–41, 43, 49; significant, defined, 46. *See also* Social regulation; *specific regulatory area, institution*
Regulatory agencies: administrative leadership of, 31–32; and agency capture, 9–10, 37–38, 39; annual policy meetings of, 46–47; budgets, 54; and budget-maximizing hypothesis, 20; and bureaucratic discretion, 38; citizens' right to sue, 38; coalition politics in, 23–24; Contract with

America impact on, 52; economic cost and benefit analysis in, 8–9, 39–40; economists and policy analysts in, 42; internal review requirements for, 43; mission, redefining, 313; monitoring and oversight of, 26–28; personnel positions and types in, 20–22; policy monopolies of, 23; program and policy goals in, 21; public-private partnerships of, 54, 55; and Reagan regulatory strategy, 43–44; for social regulation, 38; strategic plan requirement for, 47, 53; types, and bureaucrats' behavior, 21–22; and voluntary initiatives, 54, 55; and World War I mobilization, 35
Regulatory Analysis and Review Group (RARG), 40–41; and OSHA regulations, 200
Regulatory bureaucracy, 19–22; executives and managers in, 22; hierarchy of goals in, 21; primary factors affecting behavior in, 21–22; professionalization of, 28
Regulatory commissions, life stages of, 9
Regulatory decisionmaking, 16–17; administrative leadership's role in, 31–32; and coalition building, 26; economic focus in, 41; interest group access to, 26–27; and principal-agent relationships, 25; and subsystems politics, 23–24, 32
Regulatory Flexibility Act, 41, 49; amendment of, 51–52
Regulatory policy: and agency discretion, 41; Chicago school of economics' influence on, 60; and disequilibrium in policy interactions, 28–29; early history and politics of, 33–37; and interest mobilization, 192–193; principal-agent explanation for, 30–31, 32; and salience-complexity interactions, 29–31
Regulatory policy change: bureaucratic politics perspective on, 19–22; nonsystem actors' promotion of, 313; and policy monopoly, 28; principal-agent perspective on, 24–27; subsystems perspective/impact on, 22–24, 315

Regulatory reform: and agency discretion, 41; and budget constraints, 42, 43; and deregulation, 41–42; and economic stagflation of 1970s, 39; interagency quality-of-life review process in, 40; market-based, 42; of 1970s, overview of, 39–42; and regulatory impact analysis, 43. *See also specific agency, policy area*

Regulatory theory: and capture theory, 9–10; comparisons of, 27–28; and 1970s regulatory activities, 174–175. *See also* Bureaucratic politics theory; Principal-agent theory; Subsystem theory

Regulatory tools: appropriateness of, 14; cap-and-trade, 162; in command and control approach, 160; common, 11–14; economic analysis as, 43; for environmental regulation, 155, 159, 160–162; information provision as, 158; overlapping uses of, 14; technological and social impacts on, 14–15

Reich, Robert, 207–208

Reno, Janet, 80, 83

Resolution Trust Corporation, creation of, 106

Robinson-Patman Act, 58

Roosevelt administration, economic stabilization initiatives of, 36

Rural Electrification Administration (REA), creation and stance of, 272

Safety and Health Improvement and Regulatory Reform Act (Ballenger bill), 208–209

Salience: defined, 29; and elected officials' exercise of control, 29–30; of regulations, 55. *See also specific policy agency, area*

Savings and loan associations: ATM services of, 102; crisis and bailout, 105–106; and deposit insurance, 98; and deregulation, 104; distinguished from banks, 97; failures, and presidential involvement, 108–109; inflation and disintermediation problems of, 101; investment and, 104; mergers of, 104, 113; reform recommendations for, 101; regulation and oversight of, 36, 98; and Regulation Q,

97, 103; and trade associations, 98

Scanlon, Terrance, 244–245

Scannell, Gerald F., 207

Securities and Exchange Commission (SEC), creation and mandate of, 36

Sensenbrenner, James, 143–144

Sherman Antitrust Act, 34–35, 57, 58, 72, 122

Small Business Administration, 51

Small Business Regulatory Enforcement Fairness Act, 50–51

Small businesses: and regulatory flexibility analysis, 50–51; and rules involving internal revenue laws, 51

Social regulation: agencies, 37; complexity in, 38–39; and cost-benefit analysis, 39–40; and financial barriers to entry, 39; and New Left activism and public advocacy, 37–38; and 1970s stagflation, 39; rule-making and standard-setting process in, 38; state government implementation of, 50

St. Germain, Fernand, 104, 105, 106–107

State of New York v. Microsoft, 82

State public utility commissions, telecommunications regulation of, 123

States: delegation of regulatory authority to, 206; workplace health and safety enforcement of, 198

Steiger, Janet, 77, 245–246

Subsystems politics: and antitrust politics, 70–71, 73; impact of crises on, 313; and regulatory policy change, 22–24, 315; and resistance to political control, 314–315. *See also specific organization, sector*

Subsystem theory: interest group politics and decisionmaking in, 22–23; variants of, 23–24

Sununu, John, 283

Supreme Court: antitrust regulation and, 35, 72; and appliance efficiency standards, 282; and FCC authority, 141

Tauzin, W. J. "Billy," 114–115, 137, 138; and broadband service expansion, 142–145

Telecommunications Act, 135–139, 146–147; congressional disagreement on, 137–138; implementation of, 137; and industry-specific mergers, 138–139

Telecommunications regulation, 119–147; and broadband service, 142–145; and concentration of ownership debate, 139–140; congressional "Splawn Study" conclusions on, 121; deregulation and, 134–135, 137–139; dominant coalition politics in, 138; enterprise management versus market management of, 123; executive branch and, 132, 141; Fairness Doctrine and, 132; firewalls in, 135; and linkage between carriers, 135; of media market, 139; mergers in, 138–139; principal-agent perspective on, 132; and rate-setting, 124; and regulatory-authored deregulation, 145; salience of, 124, 125*fig*; and state and local barriers to entry, 136; and technological change, 124; universal service theme in, 120. *See also* Federal Communications Commission (FCC)

Telecommunications sector: jurisdiction and oversight of, 134; subsystem politics in, 137–145; and turf wars among Baby Bells, 135; universal service obligation in, 134–135; Voice-over-Internet Protocol (VoIP) in, 145–146. *See also* AT&T; Bell System; Broadcasting regulation; Telephony

Telecommunications technology: policymaking impact of, 132–133; and regulation changes, 124

Telemarketing and Consumer Fraud and Abuse Act, 249

Telephony: and common carrier definition, 120; congressional role in, 131–132; courts' role in, 133; as federal-state joint enterprise, 123; historical overview of, 119–122; as natural monopoly, 123; as public good, 123; rate-of-return pricing in, 132; sources of conflict in, 133; state-level, 124; value-of-service pricing

in, 123. *See also* AT&T; Bell System

Television and radio regulation, 122–123; mergers in, 138, 139; and technological change, 132

Tennessee Valley Authority (TVA), 271–272

Toxic chemicals: industrial regulation of, 203; and workplace health regulations, 192

Transportation Act, 35

Truman, Harry S., 269

Unfunded Mandates Reform Act, 50

United Mine Workers (UMW), 265

United States Postal Service (USPS), and ergonomic risk reduction, 216–217

United States v. AT&T, 122

United States v. Microsoft, 78, 82–83

United States v. Western Electric Company, 121

Uranium Mill Tailings Reduction Act, 280

US Department of Agriculture (USDA), 35, 36

US League of Savings Institutions (USLSI), 98, 103

Voluntary programs: lack of labor participation in, 218; and OSHA's Alliance Program, 217–218; OSPP partnerships with, 216–217

Waxman, Henry, 244

Weinberger, Caspar, 68, 72, 236

Western Electric: Bell's acquisition of, 120; as monopoly, 121. *See also* Telephony

Wheeler-Lea Act, 58

Willis-Graham Act, 121

Wilson, Woodrow, 267

Workplace regulation: benefits of, 192; business sector's objections to, 192–193; cost internalization and, 6; early doctrine and common law on, 191, 192; risk reflected in wage differentials in, 191, 192; and technical production, 13–14. *See also* Occupational safety regulations

About the Book

WHAT IS REGULATION? Why do governments regulate, and how does regulatory change take place? Exploring these and other questions, the second edition of *Contemporary Regulatory Policy* demystifies the field of regulatory politics.

Eisner, Worsham, and Ringquist have completely updated their examination of the regulatory process in seven major areas: antitrust, banking and securities, telecommunications, environmental protection, occupational safety and health, consumer products, and energy. They also address the extent to which presidential partisanship, ideological shifts in Congress, and other forces—both within and external to government bureaucracy—influence regulation. Recognizing that no single theory can sufficiently explain regulatory politics, the authors offer students a comprehensive set of tools for navigating recent policy transitions and considering the future direction of US regulation.

Marc Allen Eisner is Henry Merritt Wriston Chair of Public Policy in the Government Department at Wesleyan University. His publications include *Antitrust and the Triumph of Economics* and *Regulatory Politics in Transition*. **Jeff Worsham** is professor of political science at West Virginia University and author of *Other People's Money: Policy Change, Congress, and Bank Regulation*. **Evan J. Ringquist** is professor of public and environmental affairs at Indiana University. His publications include *Environmental Protection at the State Level*.